NETWORK SECURITY ESSENTIALS:

APPLICATIONS AND STANDARDS

FIFTH EDITION

William Stallings

International Editions contributions by

B. R. Chandavarkar
National Institute of Technology Karnataka, Surathkal

D1334205

PEARSON

Boston   Columbus   Indianapolis   New York   San Francisco   Upper Saddle River
Amsterdam   Cape Town   Dubai   London   Madrid   Milan   Munich   Paris   Montréal   Toronto
Delhi   Mexico City   São Paulo   Sydney   Hong Kong   Seoul   Singapore   Taipei   Tokyo

Editorial Director, ECS: Marcia Horton
Executive Editor: Tracy Johnson
Associate Editor: Carole Snyder
Director of Marketing: Christy Lesko
Marketing Manager: Yez Alayan
Director of Production: Erin Gregg
Managing Editor: Scott Disanno
Associate Managing Editor: Robert Engelhardt
Production Manager: Pat Brown
Publisher, International Edition: Angshuman Chakraborty
Publishing Administrator and Business Analyst,
  International Edition: Shokhi Shah Khandelwal
Senior Print and Media Editor, International Edition: Anuprova
  Dey Chowdhuri
Acquisitions Editor, International Edition: Shivangi Ramachandran

Publishing Administrator, International Edition: Hema Mehta
Project Editor, International Edition: Daniel Luiz
Art Director: Jayne Conte
Cover Designer: Jodi Notowitz
Permissions Supervisor: Michael Joyce
Permissions Administrator: Jenell Forschler
Director, Image Asset Services: Annie Atherton
Manager, Visual Research: Karen Sanatar
Cover Art: Andrea Danti/Shutterstock
Media Project Manager: Renata Butera
Full-Service Project Management: Shiny Rajesh/
  Integra Software Services Pvt. Ltd.
Composition: Integra Software Services Pvt. Ltd.
Cover Printer: Courier/Westford

Pearson Education Limited
Edinburgh Gate
Harlow
Essex CM20 2JE
England

and Associated Companies throughout the world

Visit us on the World Wide Web at:
www.pearsoninternationaleditions.com

© Pearson Education Limited 2014

The rights of William Stallings to be identified as the author of this work have been asserted by him in accordance with the Copyright, Designs and Patents Act 1988.

Authorized adaptation from the United States edition, entitled Network Security Essentials: Applications and Standards, 5th Edition, ISBN 978-0-133-37043-0, by William Stallings, published by Pearson Education © 2014.

ISBN 10: 0-273-79336-5
ISBN 13: 978-027-379336-6

British Library Cataloguing-in-Publication Data
A catalogue record for this book is available from the British Library

10 9 8 7 6 5 4 3 2 1
14 13

Typeset in Times Ten LT Std Roman by Shiny Rajesh/Integra Software Services Pvt. Ltd.

Printed and bound by Courier Westford in The United States of America

The publisher's policy is to use paper manufactured from sustainable forests.

*For Tricia never
dull never boring
the smartest
and bravest
person I know*

CONTENTS

Online Resources 9

Preface 11

About the Author 17

Chapter 1   Introduction 19

  1.1   Computer Security Concepts 22
  1.2   The OSI Security Architecture 26
  1.3   Security Attacks 27
  1.4   Security Services 29
  1.5   Security Mechanisms 33
  1.6   A Model for Network Security 34
  1.7   Standards 37
  1.8   Outline of This Book 37
  1.9   Recommended Reading 38
  1.10   Internet and Web Resources 38
  1.11   Key Terms, Review Questions, and Problems 39

PART ONE CRYPTOGRAPHY 41

Chapter 2   Symmetric Encryption and Message Confidentiality 41

  2.1   Symmetric Encryption Principles 43
  2.2   Symmetric Block Encryption Algorithms 48
  2.3   Random and Pseudorandom Numbers 54
  2.4   Stream Ciphers and RC4 59
  2.5   Cipher Block Modes of Operation 64
  2.6   Recommended Reading 69
  2.7   Key Terms, Review Questions, and Problems 70

Chapter 3   Public-Key Cryptography and Message Authentication 75

  3.1   Approaches to Message Authentication 77
  3.2   Secure Hash Functions 81
  3.3   Message Authentication Codes 88
  3.4   Public-Key Cryptography Principles 94
  3.5   Public-Key Cryptography Algorithms 97
  3.6   Digital Signatures 105
  3.7   Recommended Reading 106
  3.8   Key Terms, Review Questions, and Problems 106

PART TWO NETWORK SECURITY APPLICATIONS 113

Chapter 4   Key Distribution and User Authentication 113

  4.1   Symmetric Key Distribution Using Symmetric Encryption 114
  4.2   Kerberos 116
  4.3   Key Distribution Using Asymmetric Encryption 129

4.4   X.509 Certificates 131
4.5   Public-Key Infrastructure 139
4.6   Federated Identity Management 141
4.7   Recommended Reading 147
4.8   Key Terms, Review Questions, and Problems 148

Chapter 5   Network Access Control and Cloud Security 153

5.1   Network Access Control 154
5.2   Extensible Authentication Protocol 157
5.3   IEEE 802.1X Port-Based Network Access Control 161
5.4   Cloud Computing 163
5.5   Cloud Security Risks and Countermeasures 170
5.6   Data Protection in the Cloud 172
5.7   Cloud Security as a Service 175
5.8   Recommended Reading 178
5.9   Key Terms, Review Questions, and Problems 179

Chapter 6   Transport-Level Security 180

6.1   Web Security Considerations 181
6.2   Secure Sockets Layer (SSL) 183
6.3   Transport Layer Security (TLS) 197
6.4   HTTPS 201
6.5   Secure Shell (SSH) 202
6.6   Recommended Reading 213
6.7   Key Terms, Review Questions, and Problems 214

Chapter 7   Wireless Network Security 216

7.1   Wireless Security 217
7.2   Mobile Device Security 220
7.3   IEEE 802.11 Wireless LAN Overview 224
7.4   IEEE 802.11i Wireless LAN Security 230
7.5   Recommended Reading 244
7.6   Key Terms, Review Questions, and Problems 245

Chapter 8   Electronic Mail Security 248

8.1   Pretty Good Privacy (PGP) 249
8.2   S/MIME 257
8.3   DomainKeys Identified Mail (DKIM) 273
8.4   Recommended Reading 280
8.5   Key Terms, Review Questions, and Problems 280

Chapter 9   IP Security 282

9.1   IP Security Overview 284
9.2   IP Security Policy 288
9.3   Encapsulating Security Payload 294
9.4   Combining Security Associations 301
9.5   Internet Key Exchange 305
9.6   Cryptographic Suites 313
9.7   Recommended Reading 315
9.8   Key Terms, Review Questions, and Problems 315

PART THREE SYSTEM SECURITY 317

Chapter 10 Malicious Software 317

10.1   Types of Malicious Software (Malware) 318
10.2   Propagation—Infected Content—Viruses 321
10.3   Propagation—Vulnerability Exploit—Worms 326
10.4   Propagation—Social Engineering—SPAM E-mail, Trojans 331
10.5   Payload—System Corruption 333
10.6   Payload—Attack Agent—Zombie, Bots 334
10.7   Payload—Information Theft—Keyloggers, Phishing, Spyware 336
10.8   Payload—Stealthing—Backdoors, Rootkits 337
10.9   Countermeasures 339
10.10 Distributed Denial of Service Attacks 345
10.11 Recommended Reading 350
10.12 Key Terms, Review Questions, and Problems 351

Chapter 11 Intruders 354

11.1   Intruders 356
11.2   Intrusion Detection 360
11.3   Password Management 375
11.4   Recommended Reading 386
11.5   Key Terms, Review Questions, and Problems 387

Chapter 12 Firewalls 391

12.1   The Need for Firewalls 392
12.2   Firewall Characteristics 393
12.3   Types of Firewalls 395
12.4   Firewall Basing 401
12.5   Firewall Location and Configurations 404
12.6   Recommended Reading 409
12.7   Key Terms, Review Questions, and Problems 409

APPENDICES 395

Appendix A   Some Aspects of Number Theory 413

A.1   Prime and Relatively Prime Numbers 414
A.2   Modular Arithmetic 416

Appendix B   Projects for Teaching Network Security 418

B.1   Research Projects 419
B.2   Hacking Project 420
B.3   Programming Projects 420
B.4   Laboratory Exercises 421
B.5   Practical Security Assessments 421
B.6   Firewall Projects 421
B.7   Case Studies 422
B.8   Writing Assignments 422
B.9   Reading/Report Assignments 422

References 423

Credits 430

Index 434

ONLINE CHAPTERS AND APPENDICES[1]

Chapter 13 Network Management Security

  13.1 Basic Concepts of SNMP
  13.2 SNMPv1 Community Facility
  13.3 SNMPv3
  13.4 Recommended Reading
  13.5 Key Terms, Review Questions, and Problems

Chapter 14 Legal and Ethical Issues

  14.1 Cybercrime and Computer Crime
  14.2 Intellectual Property
  14.3 Privacy
  14.4 Ethical Issues
  14.5 Recommended Reading
  14.6 Key Terms, Review Questions, and Problems

Chapter 15 SHA-3

  15.1 Evaluation Criteria for SHA-3
  15.2 The SHA-3 Algorithm
  15.3 Recommended Reading
  15.4 Key Terms and Review Questions

Appendix C   **Standards and Standards-Setting Organizations**

Appendix D   **TCP/IP and OSI**

Appendix E   **Pseudorandom Number Generation**

Appendix F   **Kerberos Encryption Techniques**

Appendix G   **Data Compression Using ZIP**

  G.1 Compression Algorithm
  G.2 Decompression Algorithm

Appendix H   **More on PGP**

  H.1 True Random Numbers
  H.2 Pseudorandom Numbers
  H.3 Cryptographic Keys and Key Rings
  H.4 Public-Key Management

Appendix I   **The International Reference Alphabet**

Appendix J   **The Base-Rate Fallacy**

Appendix K   **Radix-64 Conversion**

Glossary

List of acronyms

---

[1]Online chapters, appendices, and other documents are Premium Content, available via the access card at the front of this book

ONLINE RESOURCES

Site	Location	Description
Companion Web site	WilliamStallings.com/NetworkSecurity/	*Student Resources* link: Useful links and documents for students. *Instructor Resources* link: Useful links and documents for instructors.
Premium Content	Click on *Premium Content* link at Companion Web site or at pearsoninternational editions.com/stallings and enter the student access code found on the card in the front of the book.	Online chapters, appendices, and other documents that supplement the book.
Instructor Resource Center (IRC)	Click on *Pearson Resources for Instructors* link at Companion Web site or on *Instructor Resource* link at pearsoninternational editions.com/stallings.	Solutions manual, projects manual, slides, and other useful documents.
Computer Science Student Resource Site	ComputerScienceStudent.com	Useful links and documents for computer science students.

PREFACE

"There is the book, Inspector. I leave it with you, and you cannot doubt that it contains a full explanation."

—*The Adventure of the Lion's Mane,* Sir Arthur Conan Doyle

In this age of universal electronic connectivity, of viruses and hackers, of electronic eavesdropping and electronic fraud, there is indeed no time at which security does not matter. Two trends have come together to make the topic of this book of vital interest. First, the explosive growth in computer systems and their interconnections via networks has increased the dependence of both organizations and individuals on the information stored and communicated using these systems. This, in turn, has led to a heightened awareness of the need to protect data and resources from disclosure, to guarantee the authenticity of data and messages, and to protect systems from network-based attacks. Second, the disciplines of cryptography and network security have matured, leading to the development of practical, readily available applications to enforce network security.

OBJECTIVES

It is the purpose of this book to provide a practical survey of network security applications and standards. The emphasis is on applications that are widely used on the Internet and for corporate networks, and on standards (especially Internet standards) that have been widely deployed.

WHAT'S NEW IN THE FIFTH EDITION

In the four years since the fourth edition of this book was published, the field has seen continued innovations and improvements. In this new edition, I try to capture these changes while maintaining a broad and comprehensive coverage of the entire field. To begin this process of revision, the fourth edition of this book was extensively reviewed by a number of professors who teach the subject and by professionals working in the field. The result is that, in many places, the narrative has been clarified and tightened, and illustrations have been improved.

Beyond these refinements to improve pedagogy and user-friendliness, there have been substantive changes throughout the book. Roughly the same chapter organization has been retained, but much of the material has been revised and new material has been added. The most noteworthy changes are as follows:

- **Network access control:** A new chapter provides coverage of network access control, including a general overview plus discussions of the Extensible Authentication Protocol and IEEE 802.1X.

- **Cloud security:** A new section covers the security issues relating to the exciting new area of cloud computing.

- **SHA-3:** An online chapter covers the new cryptographic hash standard, SHA-3, which was adopted in 2012.
- **Mobile device security:** Mobile device security has become an essential aspect of enterprise network security. A new section covers this important topic.
- **Malicious software:** This chapter provides a different focus from that of the fourth edition. Increasingly we see back door/rootkit type malware installed by social engineering attacks, rather than more classic virus/worm direct infection. And phishing is even more prominent than ever. These trends are reflected in the coverage.
- **Sample syllabus:** The text contains more material than can be conveniently covered in one semester. Accordingly, instructors are provided with several sample syllabi that guide the use of the text within limited time (e.g., 16 weeks or 12 weeks). These samples are based on real-world experience by professors with the first edition.
- **Learning objectives:** Each chapter now begins with a list of learning objectives.

SUPPORT OF ACM/IEEE COMPUTER SCIENCE CURRICULA 2013

The book is intended for both academic and professional audiences. As a textbook, it is intended as a one-semester undergraduate course in cryptography and network security for computer science, computer engineering, and electrical engineering majors. The changes to this edition are intended to provide support of the current draft version of the ACM/IEEE Computer Science Curricula 2013 (CS2013). CS2013 adds Information Assurance and Security (IAS) to the curriculum recommendation as one of the Knowledge Areas in the Computer Science Body of Knowledge. The document states that IAS is now part of the curriculum recommendation because of the critical role of IAS in computer science education. CS2013 divides all course work into three categories: Core-Tier 1 (all topics should be included in the curriculum), Core-Tier-2 (all or almost all topics should be included), and elective (desirable to provide breadth and depth). In the IAS area, CS2013 recommends topics in Fundamental Concepts and Network Security in Tier 1 and Tier 2, and Cryptography topics as elective. This text covers virtually all of the topics listed by CS2013 in these three categories.

The book also serves as a basic reference volume and is suitable for self-study.

PLAN OF THE TEXT

The book is organized in three parts:

- **Part One. Cryptography:** A concise survey of the cryptographic algorithms and protocols underlying network security applications, including encryption, hash functions, message authentication, and digital signatures.
- **Part Two. Network Security Applications:** Covers important network security tools and applications, including key distribution, Kerberos, X.509v3 certificates, Extensible Authentication Protocol, S/MIME, IP Security, SSL/TLS, IEEE 802.11i WiFi security, and cloud security.
- **Part Three. System Security:** Looks at system-level security issues, including the threat of and countermeasures for malicious software and intruders, and the use of firewalls.

The book includes a number of pedagogic features, including the use of numerous figures and tables to clarify the discussions. Each chapter includes a list of key words, review questions, homework problems, and suggestions for further reading. The book also includes an extensive glossary, a list of frequently used acronyms, and a list of references. In addition, a test bank is available to instructors.

INSTRUCTOR SUPPORT MATERIALS

The major goal of this text is to make it as effective a teaching tool for this exciting and fast-moving subject as possible. This goal is reflected both in the structure of the book and in the supporting material. The following supplementary materials that will aid the instructor accompany the text:

* **Solutions manual:** Solutions to all end-of-chapter Review Questions and Problems.
* **Projects manual:** Suggested project assignments for all of the project categories listed below.
* **PowerPoint slides:** A set of slides covering all chapters, suitable for use in lecturing.
* **PDF files:** Reproductions of all figures and tables from the book.
* **Test bank:** A chapter-by-chapter set of questions with a separate file of answers.
* **Sample syllabi:** The text contains more material than can be conveniently covered in one semester. Accordingly, instructors are provided with several sample syllabi that guide the use of the text within limited time. These samples are based on real-world experience by professors who used the fourth edition.

All of these support materials are available at the **Instructor Resource Center (IRC)** for this textbook, which can be reached through the Publisher's Web site www. pearsoninternationaleditions.com/stallings or by clicking on the link labeled *Pearson Resources for Instructors* at this book's Companion Web site at WilliamStallings.com/NetworkSecurity. To gain access to the IRC, please contact your local Pearson sales representative via pearsoninternationaleditions.com/educator/replocator/requestSalesRep.page or call Pearson Faculty Services at 1-800-526-0485.

The **Companion Web site**, at WilliamStallings.com/NetworkSecurity (click on *Instructor Resources* link), includes the following:

* Links to Web sites for other courses being taught using this book
* Sign-up information for an Internet mailing list for instructors using this book to exchange information, suggestions, and questions with each other and with the author

PROJECTS AND OTHER STUDENT EXERCISES

For many instructors, an important component of a network security course is a project or set of projects by which the student gets hands-on experience to reinforce concepts from the text. This book provides an unparalleled degree of support, including a projects component in the course. The IRC includes not only guidance on how to assign and structure the projects but also a set of project assignments that covers a broad range of topics from the text:

* **Hacking project:** This exercise is designed to illuminate the key issues in intrusion detection and prevention.

- **Lab exercises:** A series of projects that involve programming and experimenting with concepts from the book.

- **Research projects:** A series of research assignments that instruct the student to research a particular topic on the Internet and write a report.

- **Programming projects:** A series of programming projects that cover a broad range of topics and that can be implemented in any suitable language on any platform.

- **Practical security assessments:** A set of exercises to examine current infrastructure and practices of an existing organization.

- **Firewall projects:** A portable network firewall visualization simulator is provided, together with exercises for teaching the fundamentals of firewalls.

- **Case studies:** A set of real-world case studies, including learning objectives, case description, and a series of case discussion questions.

- **Writing assignments:** A set of suggested writing assignments, organized by chapter.

- **Reading/report assignments:** A list of papers in the literature—one for each chapter— that can be assigned for the student to read and then write a short report.

This diverse set of projects and other student exercises enables the instructor to use the book as one component in a rich and varied learning experience and to tailor a course plan to meet the specific needs of the instructor and students. See Appendix B in this book for details.

ONLINE DOCUMENTS FOR STUDENTS

For this new edition, a tremendous amount of original supporting material for students has been made available online, at two Web locations. The **Companion Web site**, at WilliamStallings.com/NetworkSecurity (click on *Student Resources* link), includes a list of relevant links organized by chapter and an errata sheet for the book.

Purchasing this textbook new also grants the reader six months of access to the **Premium Content site**, which includes the following materials:

- **Online chapters:** To limit the size and cost of the book, three chapters of the book are provided in PDF format. This includes a chapter on SHA-3, a chapter on SNMP security, and one on legal and ethical issues. The chapters are listed in this book's table of contents.

- **Online appendices:** There are numerous interesting topics that support material found in the text but whose inclusion is not warranted in the printed text. A number of online appendices cover these topics for the interested student. The appendices are listed in this book's table of contents.

- **Homework problems and solutions:** To aid the student in understanding the material, a separate set of homework problems with solutions are available. These enable the students to test their understanding of the text.

- **Key papers:** A number of papers from the professional literature, many hard to find, are provided for further reading.

- **Supporting documents:** A variety of other useful documents are referenced in the text and provided online.

To access the Premium Content site, click on the *Premium Content* link at the Companion Web site or at pearsoninternationaleditions.com/stallings and enter the student access code found on the card in the front of the book.

RELATIONSHIP TO CRYPTOGRAPHY AND NETWORK SECURITY

This book is adapted from *Cryptography and Network Security, Sixth Edition* (CNS6e). CNS6e provides a substantial treatment of cryptography, key management, and user authentication, including detailed analysis of algorithms and a significant mathematical component, all of which covers nearly 500 pages. *Network Security Essentials: Applications and Standards, Fifth Edition* (NSE5e), provides instead a concise overview of these topics in Chapters 2 through 4. NSE5e includes all of the remaining material of CNS6e. NSE5e also covers SNMP security, which is not covered in CNS6e. Thus, NSE5e is intended for college courses and professional readers whose interest is primarily in the application of network security and who do not need or desire to delve deeply into cryptographic theory and principles.

ACKNOWLEDGMENTS

This new edition has benefited from review by a number of people who gave generously of their time and expertise. The following people reviewed all or a large part of the manuscript: Nirdosh Bhatnagar (Santa Clara University), Douglas P. Twitchell (Illinois State University), Yoohwan Kim(University of Nevada, Las Vegas), Steven Tate (University of North Carolina at Greensboro), Kemal Akkaya (Southern Illinois University), Bulent Yener (Rensselaer Polytechnic Institute), Ellen Gethner (University of Colorado, Denver), Stefan A. Robila (Montclair State University), and Albert Levi (Sabanci University, Istanbul, Turkey).

Thanks also to the people who provided detailed technical reviews of one or more chapters: Kashif Aftab, Alan Cantrell, Rajiv Dasmohapatra, Edip Demirbilek, Dan Dieterle, Gerardo Iglesias Galvan, Michel Garcia, David Gueguen, Anasuya Threse Innocent, Dennis Kavanagh, Duncan Keir, Robert Knox, Bo Lin, Kousik Nandy, Nickolay Olshevsky, Massimiliano Sembiante, Oscar So, and Varun Tewari.

Nikhil Bhargava (IIT Delhi) developed the set of online homework problems and solutions. Professor Sreekanth Malladi of Dakota State University developed the hacking exercises. Sanjay Rao and Ruben Torres of Purdue developed the laboratory exercises that appear in the IRC.

The following people contributed project assignments that appear in the instructor's supplement: Henning Schulzrinne (Columbia University), Cetin Kaya Koc (Oregon State University), and David Balenson (Trusted Information Systems and George Washington University). Kim McLaughlin developed the test bank.

Finally, I thank the many people responsible for the publication of the book, all of whom did their usual excellent job. This includes the staff at Pearson, particularly my editor

Tracy Johnson, associate editor Carole Snyder, production supervisor Robert Engelhardt, and production project manager Pat Brown. I also thank Shiny Rajesh and the production staff at Integra for another excellent and rapid job. Thanks also to the marketing and sales staffs at Pearson, without whose efforts this book would not be in front of you.

With all this assistance, little remains for which I can take full credit. However, I am proud to say that, with no help whatsoever, I selected all of the quotations.

The publishers wish to thank Hrishikesh B. Acharya of Indraprastha Institute of Information Technology Delhi for reviewing the content of the International Edition.

ABOUT THE AUTHOR

Dr. William Stallings has authored 17 titles, and counting revised editions, over 40 books on computer security, computer networking, and computer architecture. His writings have appeared in numerous publications, including the *Proceedings of the IEEE, ACM Computing Reviews* and *Cryptologia*.

He has 11 times received the award for the best Computer Science textbook of the year from the Text and Academic Authors Association.

In over 30 years in the field, he has been a technical contributor, technical manager, and an executive with several high-technology firms. He has designed and implemented both TCP/IP-based and OSI-based protocol suites on a variety of computers and operating systems, ranging from microcomputers to mainframes. As a consultant, he has advised government agencies, computer and software vendors, and major users on the design, selection, and use of networking software and products.

He created and maintains the *Computer Science Student Resource Site* at ComputerScienceStudent.com. This site provides documents and links on a variety of subjects of general interest to computer science students (and professionals). He is a member of the editorial board of *Cryptologia*, a scholarly journal devoted to all aspects of cryptology.

Dr. Stallings holds a Ph.D. from MIT in Computer Science and a B.S. from Notre Dame in electrical engineering.

CHAPTER 1

INTRODUCTION

1.1 Computer Security Concepts

    A Definition of Computer Security
    Examples
    The Challenges of Computer Security

1.2 The OSI Security Architecture

1.3 Security Attacks

    Passive Attacks
    Active Attacks

1.4 Security Services

    Authentication
    Access Control
    Data Confidentiality
    Data Integrity
    Nonrepudiation
    Availability Service

1.5 Security Mechanisms

1.6 A Model for Network Security

1.7 Standards

1.8 Outline of This Book

1.9 Recommended Reading

1.10 Internet and Web Resources

    Web Sites for This Book
    Computer Science Student Resource Site
    Other Web Sites

1.11 Key Terms, Review Questions, and Problems

The combination of space, time, and strength that must be considered as the basic elements of this theory of defense makes this a fairly complicated matter. Consequently, it is not easy to find a fixed point of departure.

— On War, Carl Von Clausewitz

The art of war teaches us to rely not on the likelihood of the enemy's not coming, but on our own readiness to receive him; not on the chance of his not attacking, but rather on the fact that we have made our position unassailable.

— The Art of War, Sun Tzu

LEARNING OBJECTIVES

After studying this chapter, you should be able to:

◆ Describe the key security requirements of confidentiality, integrity, and availability.

◆ Discuss the types of security threats and attacks that must be dealt with and give examples of the types of threats and attacks that apply to different categories of computer and network assets.

◆ Summarize the functional requirements for computer security.

◆ Describe the X.800 security architecture for OSI.

The requirements of **information security** within an organization have undergone two major changes in the last several decades. Before the widespread use of data processing equipment, the security of information felt to be valuable to an organization was provided primarily by physical and administrative means. An example of the former is the use of rugged filing cabinets with a combination lock for storing sensitive documents. An example of the latter is personnel screening procedures used during the hiring process.

With the introduction of the computer, the need for automated tools for protecting files and other information stored on the computer became evident. This is especially the case for a shared system, such as a time-sharing system, and the need is even more acute for systems that can be accessed over a public telephone network, data network, or the Internet. The generic name for the collection of tools designed to protect data and to thwart hackers is **computer security**.

The second major change that affected security is the introduction of distributed systems and the use of networks and communications facilities for carrying data between terminal user and computer and between computer and computer. Network security measures are needed to protect data during their transmission. In fact, the term **network security** is somewhat misleading, because virtually all business, government, and academic organizations interconnect their data processing equipment with a collection of interconnected networks.

Such a collection is often referred to as an internet,[1] and the term **internet security** is used.

There are no clear boundaries between these two forms of security. For example, a computer virus may be introduced into a system physically when it arrives on a flash drive or an optical disk and is subsequently loaded onto a computer. Viruses may also arrive over an internet. In either case, once the virus is resident on a computer system, internal computer security tools are needed to detect and recover from the virus.

This book focuses on internet security, which consists of measures to deter, prevent, detect, and correct security violations that involve the transmission of information. That is a broad statement that covers a host of possibilities. To give you a feel for the areas covered in this book, consider the following examples of security violations:

1. User A transmits a file to user B. The file contains sensitive information (e.g., payroll records) that is to be protected from disclosure. User C, who is not authorized to read the file, is able to monitor the transmission and capture a copy of the file during its transmission.

2. A network manager, D, transmits a message to a computer, E, under its management. The message instructs computer E to update an authorization file to include the identities of a number of new users who are to be given access to that computer. User F intercepts the message, alters its contents to add or delete entries, and then forwards the message to E, which accepts the message as coming from manager D and updates its authorization file accordingly.

3. Rather than intercept a message, user F constructs its own message with the desired entries and transmits that message to E as if it had come from manager D. Computer E accepts the message as coming from manager D and updates its authorization file accordingly.

4. An employee is fired without warning. The personnel manager sends a message to a server system to invalidate the employee's account. When the invalidation is accomplished, the server is to post a notice to the employee's file as confirmation of the action. The employee is able to intercept the message and delay it long enough to make a final access to the server to retrieve sensitive information. The message is then forwarded, the action taken, and the confirmation posted. The employee's action may go unnoticed for some considerable time.

5. A message is sent from a customer to a stockbroker with instructions for various transactions. Subsequently, the investments lose value and the customer denies sending the message.

Although this list by no means exhausts the possible types of security violations, it illustrates the range of concerns of network security.

---

[1]We use the term *internet* with a lowercase "i" to refer to any interconnected collection of network. A corporate intranet is an example of an internet. The Internet with a capital "I" may be one of the facilities used by an organization to construct its internet.

This chapter provides a general overview of the subject matter that structures the material in the remainder of the book. We begin with a general discussion of network security services and mechanisms and of the types of attacks they are designed for. Then we develop a general overall model within which the security services and mechanisms can be viewed.

1.1   COMPUTER SECURITY CONCEPTS

A Definition of Computer Security

The NIST *Computer Security Handbook* [NIST95] defines the term *computer security* as

> **Computer Security:** The protection afforded to an automated information system in order to attain the applicable objectives of preserving the integrity, availability, and confidentiality of information system resources (includes hardware, software, firmware, information/data, and telecommunications).

This definition introduces three key objectives that are at the heart of computer security.

- **Confidentiality:** This term covers two related concepts:

    Data[2] confidentiality: Assures that private or confidential information is not made available or disclosed to unauthorized individuals.

    Privacy: Assures that individuals control or influence what information related to them may be collected and stored and by whom and to whom that information may be disclosed.

- **Integrity:** This term covers two related concepts:

    Data integrity: Assures that information and programs are changed only in a specified and authorized manner.

    System integrity: Assures that a system performs its intended function in an unimpaired manner, free from deliberate or inadvertent unauthorized manipulation of the system.

- **Availability:** Assures that systems work promptly and service is not denied to authorized users.

These three concepts form what is often referred to as the **CIA triad**. The three concepts embody the fundamental security objectives for both data and for information and computing services. For example, the NIST *Standards for Security*

---

[2]RFC 4949 defines *information* as "facts and ideas, which can be represented (encoded) as various forms of data," and *data* as "information in a specific physical representation, usually a sequence of symbols that have meaning; especially a representation of information that can be processed or produced by a computer." Security literature typically does not make much of a distinction, nor does this book.

Categorization of Federal Information and Information Systems (FIPS 199) lists confidentiality, integrity, and availability as the three security objectives for information and for information systems. FIPS 199 provides a useful characterization of these three objectives in terms of requirements and the definition of a loss of security in each category.

- **Confidentiality:** Preserving authorized restrictions on information access and disclosure, including means for protecting personal privacy and proprietary information. A loss of confidentiality is the unauthorized disclosure of information.

- **Integrity:** Guarding against improper information modification or destruction, including ensuring information nonrepudiation and authenticity. A loss of integrity is the unauthorized modification or destruction of information.

- **Availability:** Ensuring timely and reliable access to and use of information. A loss of availability is the disruption of access to or use of information or an information system.

Although the use of the CIA triad to define security objectives is well established, some in the security field feel that additional concepts are needed to present a complete picture. Two of the most commonly mentioned are

- **Authenticity:** The property of being genuine and being able to be verified and trusted; confidence in the validity of a transmission, a message, or message originator. This means verifying that users are who they say they are and that each input arriving at the system came from a trusted source.

- **Accountability:** The security goal that generates the requirement for actions of an entity to be traced uniquely to that entity. This supports nonrepudiation, deterrence, fault isolation, intrusion detection and prevention, and after-action recovery and legal action. Because truly secure systems are not yet an achievable goal, we must be able to trace a security breach to a responsible party. Systems must keep records of their activities to permit later forensic analysis to trace security breaches or to aid in transaction disputes.

Examples

We now provide some examples of applications that illustrate the requirements just enumerated.[3] For these examples, we use three levels of impact on organizations or individuals should there be a breach of security (i.e., a loss of confidentiality, integrity, or availability). These levels are defined in FIPS 199:

- **Low:** The loss could be expected to have a limited adverse effect on organizational operations, organizational assets, or individuals. A limited adverse effect means that, for example, the loss of confidentiality, integrity, or availability might (i) cause a degradation in mission capability to an extent and duration that the organization is able to perform its primary functions, but

---

[3]These examples are taken from a security policy document published by the Information Technology Security and Privacy Office at Purdue University.

the effectiveness of the functions is noticeably reduced; (ii) result in minor damage to organizational assets; (iii) result in minor financial loss; or (iv) result in minor harm to individuals.

- **Moderate:** The loss could be expected to have a serious adverse effect on organizational operations, organizational assets, or individuals. A serious adverse effect means that, for example, the loss might (i) cause a significant degradation in mission capability to an extent and duration that the organization is able to perform its primary functions, but the effectiveness of the functions is significantly reduced; (ii) result in significant damage to organizational assets; (iii) result in significant financial loss; or (iv) result in significant harm to individuals that does not involve loss of life or serious, life-threatening injuries.
- **High:** The loss could be expected to have a severe or catastrophic adverse effect on organizational operations, organizational assets, or individuals. A severe or catastrophic adverse effect means that, for example, the loss might (i) cause a severe degradation in or loss of mission capability to an extent and duration that the organization is not able to perform one or more of its primary functions; (ii) result in major damage to organizational assets; (iii) result in major financial loss; or (iv) result in severe or catastrophic harm to individuals involving loss of life or serious, life-threatening injuries.

CONFIDENTIALITY Student grade information is an asset whose confidentiality is considered to be highly important by students. In the United States, the release of such information is regulated by the Family Educational Rights and Privacy Act (FERPA). Grade information should only be available to students, their parents, and employees that require the information to do their job. Student enrollment information may have a moderate confidentiality rating. While still covered by FERPA, this information is seen by more people on a daily basis, is less likely to be targeted than grade information, and results in less damage if disclosed. Directory information (such as lists of students, faculty, or departmental lists) may be assigned a low confidentiality rating or indeed no rating. This information is typically freely available to the public and published on a school's Web site.

INTEGRITY Several aspects of integrity are illustrated by the example of a hospital patient's allergy information stored in a database. The doctor should be able to trust that the information is correct and current. Now suppose that an employee (e.g., a nurse) who is authorized to view and update this information deliberately falsifies the data to cause harm to the hospital. The database needs to be restored to a trusted basis quickly, and it should be possible to trace the error back to the person responsible. Patient allergy information is an example of an asset with a high requirement for integrity. Inaccurate information could result in serious harm or death to a patient and expose the hospital to massive liability.

An example of an asset that may be assigned a moderate level of integrity requirement is a Web site that offers a forum to registered users to discuss some specific topic. Either a registered user or a hacker could falsify some entries or deface the Web site. If the forum exists only for the enjoyment of the users, brings in little or no advertising revenue, and is not used for something important such as research, then potential damage is not severe. The Web master may experience some data, financial, and time loss.

An example of a low-integrity requirement is an anonymous online poll. Many Web sites, such as news organizations, offer these polls to their users with very few safeguards. However, the inaccuracy and unscientific nature of such polls are well understood.

AVAILABILITY The more critical a component or service, the higher is the level of availability required. Consider a system that provides authentication services for critical systems, applications, and devices. An interruption of service results in the inability for customers to access computing resources and for the staff to access the resources they need to perform critical tasks. The loss of the service translates into a large financial loss due to lost employee productivity and potential customer loss.

An example of an asset that typically would be rated as having a moderate availability requirement is a public Web site for a university; the Web site provides information for current and prospective students and donors. Such a site is not a critical component of the university's information system, but its unavailability will cause some embarrassment.

An online telephone directory lookup application would be classified as a low-availability requirement. Although the temporary loss of the application may be an annoyance, there are other ways to access the information, such as a hardcopy directory or the operator.

The Challenges of Computer Security

Computer and network security is both fascinating and complex. Some of the reasons include:

1. Security is not as simple as it might first appear to the novice. The requirements seem to be straightforward; indeed, most of the major requirements for security services can be given self-explanatory, one-word labels: confidentiality, authentication, nonrepudiation, and integrity. But the mechanisms used to meet those requirements can be quite complex, and understanding them may involve rather subtle reasoning.

2. In developing a particular security mechanism or algorithm, one must always consider potential attacks on those security features. In many cases, successful attacks are designed by looking at the problem in a completely different way, therefore exploiting an unexpected weakness in the mechanism.

3. Because of point 2, the procedures used to provide particular services are often counterintuitive. Typically, a security mechanism is complex, and it is not obvious from the statement of a particular requirement that such elaborate measures are needed. It is only when the various aspects of the threat are considered that elaborate security mechanisms make sense.

4. Having designed various security mechanisms, it is necessary to decide where to use them. This is true both in terms of physical placement (e.g., at what points in a network are certain security mechanisms needed) and in a logical sense

[e.g., at what layer or layers of an architecture such as TCP/IP (Transmission Control Protocol/Internet Protocol) should mechanisms be placed].

5. Security mechanisms typically involve more than a particular algorithm or protocol. They also require that participants be in possession of some secret information (e.g., an encryption key), which raises questions about the creation, distribution, and protection of that secret information. There also may be a reliance on communications protocols whose behavior may complicate the task of developing the security mechanism. For example, if the proper functioning of the security mechanism requires setting time limits on the transit time of a message from sender to receiver, then any protocol or network that introduces variable, unpredictable delays may render such time limits meaningless.

6. Computer and network security is essentially a battle of wits between a perpetrator who tries to find holes and the designer or administrator who tries to close them. The great advantage that the attacker has is that he or she need only find a single weakness, while the designer must find and eliminate all weaknesses to achieve perfect security.

7. There is a natural tendency on the part of users and system managers to perceive little benefit from security investment until a security failure occurs.

8. Security requires regular, even constant, monitoring, and this is difficult in today's short-term, overloaded environment.

9. Security is still too often an afterthought to be incorporated into a system after the design is complete rather than being an integral part of the design process.

10. Many users (and even security administrators) view strong security as an impediment to efficient and user-friendly operation of an information system or use of information.

The difficulties just enumerated will be encountered in numerous ways as we examine the various security threats and mechanisms throughout this book.

1.2 THE OSI SECURITY ARCHITECTURE

To assess effectively the security needs of an organization and to evaluate and choose various security products and policies, the manager responsible for computer and network security needs some systematic way of defining the requirements for security and characterizing the approaches to satisfying those requirements. This is difficult enough in a centralized data processing environment; with the use of local and wide area networks, the problems are compounded.

ITU-T[4] Recommendation X.800, *Security Architecture for OSI*, defines such a systematic approach.[5] The OSI security architecture is useful to managers as a way

---

[4]The International Telecommunication Union (ITU) Telecommunication Standardization Sector (ITU-T) is a United Nations-sponsored agency that develops standards, called Recommendations, relating to telecommunications and to open systems interconnection (OSI).

[5]The OSI security architecture was developed in the context of the OSI protocol architecture, which is described in Appendix D. However, for our purposes in this chapter, an understanding of the OSI protocol architecture is not required.

Table 1.1   Threats and Attacks (RFC 4949)

Threat A potential for violation of security, which exists when there is a circumstance, capability, action, or event that could breach security and cause harm. That is, a threat is a possible danger that might exploit a vulnerability.
Attack An assault on system security that derives from an intelligent threat. That is, an intelligent act that is a deliberate attempt (especially in the sense of a method or technique) to evade security services and violate the security policy of a system.

of organizing the task of providing security. Furthermore, because this architecture was developed as an international standard, computer and communications vendors have developed security features for their products and services that relate to this structured definition of services and mechanisms.

For our purposes, the OSI security architecture provides a useful, if abstract, overview of many of the concepts that this book deals with. The OSI security architecture focuses on security attacks, mechanisms, and services. These can be defined briefly as

- **Security attack:** Any action that compromises the security of information owned by an organization.
- **Security mechanism:** A process (or a device incorporating such a process) that is designed to detect, prevent, or recover from a security attack.
- **Security service:** A processing or communication service that enhances the security of the data processing systems and the information transfers of an organization. The services are intended to counter security attacks, and they make use of one or more security mechanisms to provide the service.

In the literature, the terms *threat* and *attack* are commonly used to mean more or less the same thing. Table 1.1 provides definitions taken from RFC 4949, *Internet Security Glossary*.

1.3   SECURITY ATTACKS

A useful means of classifying security attacks, used both in X.800 and RFC 4949, is in terms of *passive attacks* and *active attacks*. A passive attack attempts to learn or make use of information from the system but does not affect system resources. An active attack attempts to alter system resources or affect their operation.

Passive Attacks

Passive attacks (Figure 1.1a) are in the nature of eavesdropping on, or monitoring of, transmissions. The goal of the opponent is to obtain information that is being transmitted. Two types of passive attacks are the release of message contents and traffic analysis.

Figure 1.1   Security Attacks

The **release of message contents** is easily understood. A telephone conversation, an electronic mail message, and a transferred file may contain sensitive or confidential information. We would like to prevent an opponent from learning the contents of these transmissions.

A second type of passive attack, **traffic analysis**, is subtler. Suppose that we had a way of masking the contents of messages or other information traffic so that opponents, even if they captured the message, could not extract the information from the message. The common technique for masking contents is encryption. If we had encryption protection in place, an opponent still might be able to observe the pattern of these messages. The opponent could determine the location and identity of communicating hosts and could observe the frequency and length of messages being exchanged. This information might be useful in guessing the nature of the communication that was taking place.

Passive attacks are very difficult to detect, because they do not involve any alteration of the data. Typically, the message traffic is sent and received in an apparently normal fashion, and neither the sender nor the receiver is aware that a third party has read the messages or observed the traffic pattern. However, it is feasible to prevent the success of these attacks, usually by means of encryption. Thus, the emphasis in dealing with passive attacks is on prevention rather than detection.

Active Attacks

Active attacks (Figure 1.1b) involve some modification of the data stream or the creation of a false stream and can be subdivided into four categories: masquerade, replay, modification of messages, and denial of service.

A **masquerade** takes place when one entity pretends to be a different entity (path 2 of Figure 1.1b is active). A masquerade attack usually includes one of the other forms of active attack. For example, authentication sequences can be captured and replayed after a valid authentication sequence has taken place, thus enabling an authorized entity with few privileges to obtain extra privileges by impersonating an entity that has those privileges.

Replay involves the passive capture of a data unit and its subsequent retransmission to produce an unauthorized effect (paths 1, 2, and 3 active).

Modification of messages simply means that some portion of a legitimate message is altered, or that messages are delayed or reordered, to produce an unauthorized effect (paths 1 and 2 active). For example, a message meaning "Allow John Smith to read confidential file `accounts`" is modified to mean "Allow Fred Brown to read confidential file `accounts`."

The **denial of service** prevents or inhibits the normal use or management of communications facilities (path 3 active). This attack may have a specific target; for example, an entity may suppress all messages directed to a particular destination (e.g., the security audit service). Another form of service denial is the disruption of an entire network—either by disabling the network or by overloading it with messages so as to degrade performance.

Active attacks present the opposite characteristics of passive attacks. Whereas passive attacks are difficult to detect, measures are available to prevent their success. On the other hand, it is quite difficult to prevent active attacks absolutely because of the wide variety of potential physical, software, and network vulnerabilities. Instead, the goal is to detect active attacks and to recover from any disruption or delays caused by them. If the detection has a deterrent effect, it also may contribute to prevention.

1.4 SECURITY SERVICES

X.800 defines a security service as a service that is provided by a protocol layer of communicating open systems and that ensures adequate security of the systems or of data transfers. Perhaps a clearer definition is found in RFC 4949, which provides the following definition: A processing or communication service that is provided by

Table 1.2 Security Services (X.800)

AUTHENTICATION	DATA INTEGRITY
The assurance that the communicating entity is the one that it claims to be.	The assurance that data received are exactly as sent by an authorized entity (i.e., contain no modification, insertion, deletion, or replay).
Peer Entity Authentication Used in association with a logical connection to provide confidence in the identity of the entities connected.	**Connection Integrity with Recovery** Provides for the integrity of all user data on a connection and detects any modification, insertion, deletion, or replay of any data within an entire data sequence, with recovery attempted.
Data-Origin Authentication In a connectionless transfer, provides assurance that the source of received data is as claimed.	**Connection Integrity without Recovery** As above, but provides only detection without recovery.
ACCESS CONTROL	**Selective-Field Connection Integrity** Provides for the integrity of selected fields within the user data of a data block transferred over a connection and takes the form of determination of whether the selected fields have been modified, inserted, deleted, or replayed.
The prevention of unauthorized use of a resource (i.e., this service controls who can have access to a resource, under what conditions access can occur, and what those accessing the resource are allowed to do).	
DATA CONFIDENTIALITY	**Connectionless Integrity** Provides for the integrity of a single connectionless data block and may take the form of detection of data modification. Additionally, a limited form of replay detection may be provided.
The protection of data from unauthorized disclosure.	
Connection Confidentiality The protection of all user data on a connection.	**Selective-Field Connectionless Integrity** Provides for the integrity of selected fields within a single connectionless data block; takes the form of determination of whether the selected fields have been modified.
Connectionless Confidentiality The protection of all user data in a single data block.	
Selective-Field Confidentiality The confidentiality of selected fields within the user data on a connection or in a single data block.	**NONREPUDIATION**
	Provides protection against denial by one of the entities involved in a communication of having participated in all or part of the communication.
Traffic-Flow Confidentiality The protection of the information that might be derived from observation of traffic flows.	**Nonrepudiation, Origin** Proof that the message was sent by the specified party.
	Nonrepudiation, Destination Proof that the message was received by the specified party.

a system to give a specific kind of protection to system resources; security services implement security policies and are implemented by security mechanisms.

X.800 divides these services into five categories and fourteen specific services (Table 1.2). We look at each category in turn.[6]

---

[6]There is no universal agreement about many of the terms used in the security literature. For example, the term *integrity* is sometimes used to refer to all aspects of information security. The term *authentication* is sometimes used to refer both to verification of identity and to the various functions listed under integrity in this chapter. Our usage here agrees with both X.800 and RFC 4949.

Authentication

The **authentication** service is concerned with assuring that a communication is authentic. In the case of a single message, such as a warning or alarm signal, the function of the authentication service is to assure the recipient that the message is from the source that it claims to be from. In the case of an ongoing interaction, such as the connection of a terminal to a host, two aspects are involved. First, at the time of connection initiation, the service assures that the two entities are authentic (i.e., that each is the entity that it claims to be). Second, the service must assure that the connection is not interfered with in such a way that a third party can masquerade as one of the two legitimate parties for the purposes of unauthorized transmission or reception.

Two specific authentication services are defined in X.800:

- **Peer entity authentication:** Provides for the corroboration of the identity of a peer entity in an association. Two entities are considered peers if they implement the same protocol in different systems (e.g., two TCP modules in two communicating systems). Peer entity authentication is provided for use at the establishment of or during the data transfer phase of a connection. It attempts to provide confidence that an entity is not performing either a masquerade or an unauthorized replay of a previous connection.

- **Data origin authentication:** Provides for the corroboration of the source of a data unit. It does not provide protection against the duplication or modification of data units. This type of service supports applications like electronic mail, where there are no prior interactions between the communicating entities.

Access Control

In the context of network security, **access control** is the ability to limit and control the access to host systems and applications via communications links. To achieve this, each entity trying to gain access must first be identified, or authenticated, so that access rights can be tailored to the individual.

Data Confidentiality

Confidentiality is the protection of transmitted data from passive attacks. With respect to the content of a data transmission, several levels of protection can be identified. The broadest service protects all user data transmitted between two users over a period of time. For example, when a TCP connection is set up between two systems, this broad protection prevents the release of any user data transmitted over the TCP connection. Narrower forms of this service can also be defined, including the protection of a single message or even specific fields within a message. These refinements are less useful than the broad approach and may even be more complex and expensive to implement.

The other aspect of confidentiality is the protection of traffic flow from analysis. This requires that an attacker not be able to observe the source and destination, frequency, length, or other characteristics of the traffic on a communications facility.

Data Integrity

As with confidentiality, **integrity** can apply to a stream of messages, a single message, or selected fields within a message. Again, the most useful and straightforward approach is total stream protection.

A connection-oriented integrity service deals with a stream of messages and assures that messages are received as sent with no duplication, insertion, modification, reordering, or replays. The destruction of data is also covered under this service. Thus, the connection-oriented integrity service addresses both message stream modification and denial of service. On the other hand, a connectionless integrity service deals with individual messages without regard to any larger context and generally provides protection against message modification only.

We can make a distinction between service with and without recovery. Because the integrity service relates to active attacks, we are concerned with detection rather than prevention. If a violation of integrity is detected, then the service may simply report this violation, and some other portion of software or human intervention is required to recover from the violation. Alternatively, there are mechanisms available to recover from the loss of integrity of data, as we will review subsequently. The incorporation of automated recovery mechanisms is typically the more attractive alternative.

Nonrepudiation

Nonrepudiation prevents either sender or receiver from denying a transmitted message. Thus, when a message is sent, the receiver can prove that the alleged sender in fact sent the message. Similarly, when a message is received, the sender can prove that the alleged receiver in fact received the message.

Availability Service

Both X.800 and RFC 4949 define **availability** to be the property of a system or a system resource being accessible and usable upon demand by an authorized system entity, according to performance specifications for the system (i.e., a system is available if it provides services according to the system design whenever users request them). A variety of attacks can result in the loss of or reduction in availability. Some of these attacks are amenable to automated countermeasures, such as authentication and encryption, whereas others require some sort of physical action to prevent or recover from loss of availability of elements of a distributed system.

X.800 treats availability as a property to be associated with various security services. However, it makes sense to call out specifically an availability service. An availability service is one that protects a system to ensure its availability. This service addresses the security concerns raised by denial-of-service attacks. It depends on proper management and control of system resources and thus depends on access control service and other security services.

1.5   SECURITY MECHANISMS

Table 1.3 lists the security mechanisms defined in X.800. The mechanisms are divided into those that are implemented in a specific protocol layer, such as TCP or an application-layer protocol, and those that are not specific to any particular protocol layer or security service. These mechanisms will be covered in the appropriate places in the book, so we do not elaborate now except to comment on the definition of encipherment. X.800 distinguishes between reversible

Table 1.3   Security Mechanisms (X.800)

SPECIFIC SECURITY MECHANISMS	PERVASIVE SECURITY MECHANISMS
May be incorporated into the appropriate protocol layer in order to provide some of the OSI security services.	Mechanisms that are not specific to any particular OSI security service or protocol layer.
Encipherment The use of mathematical algorithms to transform data into a form that is not readily intelligible. The transformation and subsequent recovery of the data depend on an algorithm and zero or more encryption keys.	**Trusted Functionality** That which is perceived to be correct with respect to some criteria (e.g., as established by a security policy).
Digital Signature Data appended to, or a cryptographic transformation of, a data unit that allows a recipient of the data unit to prove the source and integrity of the data unit and protect against forgery (e.g., by the recipient).	**Security Label** The marking bound to a resource (which may be a data unit) that names or designates the security attributes of that resource.
Access Control A variety of mechanisms that enforce access rights to resources.	**Event Detection** Detection of security-relevant events.
Data Integrity A variety of mechanisms used to assure the integrity of a data unit or stream of data units.	**Security Audit Trail** Data collected and potentially used to facilitate a security audit, which is an independent review and examination of system records and activities.
Authentication Exchange A mechanism intended to ensure the identity of an entity by means of information exchange.	**Security Recovery** Deals with requests from mechanisms, such as event handling and management functions, and takes recovery actions.
Traffic Padding The insertion of bits into gaps in a data stream to frustrate traffic analysis attempts.	
Routing Control Enables selection of particular physically secure routes for certain data and allows routing changes, especially when a breach of security is suspected.	
Notarization The use of a trusted third party to assure certain properties of a data exchange.	

Table 1.4   Relationship between Security Services and Mechanisms

Service	Encipherment	Digital signature	Access control	Data integrity	Authentication exchange	Traffic padding	Routing control	Notarization
Peer entity authentication	Y	Y			Y			
Data origin authentication	Y	Y						
Access control			Y					
Confidentiality	Y						Y	
Traffic flow confidentiality	Y					Y	Y	
Data integrity	Y	Y		Y				
Nonrepudiation		Y		Y				Y
Availability				Y	Y			

encipherment mechanisms and irreversible encipherment mechanisms. A reversible encipherment mechanism is simply an encryption algorithm that allows data to be encrypted and subsequently decrypted. Irreversible encipherment mechanisms include hash algorithms and message authentication codes, which are used in digital signature and message authentication applications.

Table 1.4, based on one in X.800, indicates the relationship between security services and security mechanisms.

1.6   A MODEL FOR NETWORK SECURITY

A model for much of what we will be discussing is captured, in very general terms, in Figure 1.2. A message is to be transferred from one party to another across some sort of Internet service. The two parties, who are the *principals* in this transaction, must cooperate for the exchange to take place. A logical information channel is established by defining a route through the Internet from source to destination and by the cooperative use of communication protocols (e.g., TCP/IP) by the two principals.

Security aspects come into play when it is necessary or desirable to protect the information transmission from an opponent who may present a threat to confidentiality, authenticity, and so on. All of the techniques for providing security have two components:

1. A security-related transformation on the information to be sent. Examples include the encryption of the message, which scrambles the message so that it

Figure 1.2   Model for Network Security

is unreadable by the opponent, and the addition of a code based on the contents of the message, which can be used to verify the identity of the sender.

2. Some secret information shared by the two principals and, it is hoped, unknown to the opponent. An example is an encryption key used in conjunction with the transformation to scramble the message before transmission and unscramble it on reception.[7]

A trusted third party may be needed to achieve secure transmission. For example, a third party may be responsible for distributing the secret information to the two principals while keeping it from any opponent. Or a third party may be needed to arbitrate disputes between the two principals concerning the authenticity of a message transmission.

This general model shows that there are four basic tasks in designing a particular security service:

1. Design an algorithm for performing the security-related transformation. The algorithm should be such that an opponent cannot defeat its purpose.

2. Generate the secret information to be used with the algorithm.

3. Develop methods for the distribution and sharing of the secret information.

4. Specify a protocol to be used by the two principals that make use of the security algorithm and the secret information to achieve a particular security service.

Parts One and Two of this book concentrate on the types of security mechanisms and services that fit into the model shown in Figure 1.2. However, there are

---

[7]Chapter 3 discusses a form of encryption, known as asymmetric encryption, in which only one of the two principals needs to have the secret information.

other security-related situations of interest that do not neatly fit this model but are considered in this book. A general model of these other situations is illustrated by Figure 1.3, which reflects a concern for protecting an information system from unwanted access. Most readers are familiar with the concerns caused by the existence of hackers who attempt to penetrate systems that can be accessed over a network. The hacker can be someone who, with no malign intent, simply gets satisfaction from breaking and entering a computer system. The intruder can be a disgruntled employee who wishes to do damage or a criminal who seeks to exploit computer assets for financial gain (e.g., obtaining credit card numbers or performing illegal money transfers).

Another type of unwanted access is the placement in a computer system of logic that exploits vulnerabilities in the system and that can affect application programs as well as utility programs, such as editors and compilers. Programs can present two kinds of threats:

1. **Information access threats:** Intercept or modify data on behalf of users who should not have access to that data.

2. **Service threats:** Exploit service flaws in computers to inhibit use by legitimate users.

Viruses and worms are two examples of software attacks. Such attacks can be introduced into a system by means of a disk that contains the unwanted logic concealed in otherwise useful software. They also can be inserted into a system across a network; this latter mechanism is of more concern in network security.

The **security mechanisms** needed to cope with unwanted access fall into two broad categories (see Figure 1.3). The first category might be termed a gatekeeper function. It includes password-based login procedures that are designed to deny access to all but authorized users and screening logic that is designed to detect and reject worms, viruses, and other similar attacks. Once either an unwanted user or unwanted software gains access, the second line of defense consists of a variety of internal controls that monitor activity and analyze stored information in an attempt to detect the presence of unwanted intruders. These issues are explored in Part Three.

Figure 1.3 Network Access Security Model

1.7 STANDARDS

Many of the security techniques and applications described in this book have been specified as standards. Additionally, standards have been developed to cover management practices and the overall architecture of security mechanisms and services. Throughout this book, we describe the most important standards in use or being developed for various aspects of cryptography and network security. Various organizations have been involved in the development or promotion of these standards. The most important (in the current context) of these organizations are as follows.

- **National Institute of Standards and Technology:** NIST is a U.S. federal agency that deals with measurement science, standards, and technology related to U.S. government use and to the promotion of U.S. private-sector innovation. Despite its national scope, NIST **Federal Information Processing Standards (FIPS)** and **Special Publications (SP)** have a worldwide impact.
- **Internet Society:** ISOC is a professional membership society with worldwide organizational and individual membership. It provides leadership in addressing issues that confront the future of the Internet and is the organization home for the groups responsible for Internet infrastructure standards, including the Internet Engineering Task Force (IETF) and the Internet Architecture Board (IAB). These organizations develop Internet standards and related specifications, all of which are published as **Requests for Comments (RFCs)**.

A more detailed discussion of these organizations is contained in Appendix C.

1.8 OUTLINE OF THIS BOOK

This chapter serves as an introduction to the entire book. The remainder of the book is organized into three parts.

Part One: Provides a concise survey of the cryptographic algorithms and protocols underlying network security applications, including encryption, hash functions, and digital signatures.

Part Two: Examines the use of cryptographic algorithms and security protocols to provide security over networks and the Internet. Topics covered include key management, user authentication, network access control, cloud security, transport-level security, wireless network security, e-mail security, and IP security.

Part Three: Deals with security facilities designed to protect a computer system from security threats, including intruders, viruses, and worms. This part also looks at firewall technology.

In addition, two online chapters cover network management security and legal and ethical issues.

1.9 RECOMMENDED READING

[STAL12] provides a broad introduction to computer security. [SCHN00] is valuable reading for any practitioner in the field of computer or network security: It discusses the limitations of technology (and cryptography in particular) in providing security and the need to consider the hardware, the software implementation, the networks, and the people involved in providing and attacking security.

It is useful to read some of the classic tutorial papers on computer security; these provide a historical perspective from which to appreciate current work and thinking.[8] The papers to read are [WARE79], [BROW72], [SALT75], [SHAN77], and [SUMM84]. Two more recent, short treatments of computer security are [ANDR04] and [LAMP04]. [NIST95] is an exhaustive (290 pages) treatment of the subject. Another good treatment is [NRC91]. Also useful is [FRAS97].

ANDR04   Andrews, M., and Whittaker, J. "Computer Security." *IEEE Security and Privacy*, September/October 2004.

BROW72   Browne, P. "Computer Security—A Survey." *ACM SIGMIS Database*, Fall 1972.

FRAS97   Fraser, B. *Site Security Handbook.* RFC 2196, September 1997.

LAMP04   Lampson, B. "Computer Security in the Real World." *Computer*, June 2004.

NIST95   National Institute of Standards and Technology. *An Introduction to Computer Security: The NIST Handbook.* Special Publication 800–12. October 1995.

NRC91   National Research Council. *Computers at Risk: Safe Computing in the Information Age.* Washington, D.C.: National Academy Press, 1991.

SALT75   Saltzer, J., and Schroeder, M. "The Protection of Information in Computer Systems." *Proceedings of the IEEE*, September 1975.

SCHN00   Schneier, B. *Secrets and Lies: Digital Security in a Networked World.* New York: Wiley 2000.

SHAN77   Shanker, K. "The Total Computer Security Problem: An Overview." *Computer*, June 1977.

STAL12   Stallings, W., and Brown, L. *Computer Security, Second Edition.* Upper Saddle River, NJ: Prentice Hall, 2012.

SUMM84   Summers, R. "An Overview of Computer Security." *IBM Systems Journal*, Vol. 23, No. 4, 1984.

WARE79   Ware, W., ed. *Security Controls for Computer Systems.* RAND Report 609–1. October 1979.

1.10 INTERNET AND WEB RESOURCES

There are a number of resources available on the Internet and the Web to support this book and to help one keep up with developments in this field.

---

[8]These classic papers are available in the Premium Content Web site for this book.

Web Sites for This Book

Three Web sites provide additional resources for students and instructors.

There is a **Companion Website** for this book at WilliamStallings.com/NetworkSecurity. For students, this Web site includes a list of relevant links, organized by chapter, and an errata list for the book. For instructors, this Web site provides links to course pages by professors teaching from this book.

There is also an access-controlled **Premium Content Website** that provides a wealth of supporting material, including additional online chapters, additional online appendices, a set of homework problems with solutions, copies of a number of key papers in this field, and a number of other supporting documents. See the card at the front of this book for access information.

Finally, additional material for instructors, including a solutions manual and a projects manual, PowerPoint slides, and copies of all figures and tables, is available at the **Instructor Resource Center (IRC)** for this book. See Preface for details and access information.

Computer Science Student Resource Site

I also maintain the **Computer Science Student Resource Site**, at ComputerScienceStudent.com. The purpose of this site is to provide documents, information, and links for computer science students and professionals. Links and documents are organized into six categories:

- **Math:** Includes a basic math refresher, a queuing analysis primer, a number system primer, and links to numerous math sites.
- **How-to:** Advice and guidance for solving homework problems, writing technical reports, and preparing technical presentations.
- **Research resources:** Links to important collections of papers, technical reports, and bibliographies.
- **Computer science careers:** Useful links and documents for those considering a career in computer science.
- **Miscellaneous:** A variety of other interesting documents and links.
- **Humor and other diversions:** You have to take your mind off your work once in a while.

Other Web Sites

Numerous Web sites provide information related to the topics of this book. The Companion Web site provides links to these sites, organized by chapter. In addition, there are a number of forums dealing with cryptography available on the Internet. Links to these forums are provided at the Companion Web site.

1.11 KEY TERMS, REVIEW QUESTIONS, AND PROBLEMS

Key Terms

access control	denial of service	passive attack
active attack	encryption	replay
authentication	integrity	security attacks
authenticity	intruder	security mechanisms
availability	masquerade	security services
data confidentiality	nonrepudiation	traffic analysis
data integrity	OSI security architecture	

Review Questions

1.1   What are the three key objectives of computer security?

1.2   What is the difference between passive and active security threats?

1.3   What is the difference between security threats and attacks?

1.4   Why are passive attacks difficult to detect and active attacks difficult to prevent?

1.5   Identify the different security attacks prevented by the security mechanisms defined in X.800.

Problems

1.1   Consider an automated teller machine (ATM) in which users provide a personal identification number (PIN) and a card for account access. Give examples of confidentiality, integrity, and availability requirements associated with the system. In each case, indicate the degree of importance of the requirement.

1.2   Repeat Problem 1.1 for a system that provides authentication services for critical systems, applications, and devices.

1.3   Consider a desktop publishing system used to produce documents for various organizations.
      a.   Give an example of a type of publication for which confidentiality of the stored data is the most important requirement.
      b.   Give an example of a type of publication in which data integrity is the most important requirement.
      c.   Give an example in which system availability is the most important requirement.

1.4   For each of the following assets, assign a low, moderate, or high impact level for the loss of confidentiality, availability, and integrity, respectively. Justify your answers.
      a.   An organization managing public information on its Web server.
      b.   A law-enforcement organization managing extremely sensitive investigative information.
      c.   A financial organization managing routine administrative information (not privacy-related information).
      d.   An information system used for large acquisitions in a contracting organization that contains both sensitive, presolicitation phase contract information and routine administrative information. Assess the impact for the two data sets separately and the information system as a whole.
      e.   A power plant contains a SCADA (supervisory control and data acquisition) system controlling the distribution of electric power for a large military installation. The SCADA system contains both real-time sensor data and routine administrative information. Assess the impact for the two data sets separately and the information system as a whole.

1.5   Draw a matrix similar to Table 1.4 that shows the relationship between security attacks and mechanisms.

1.6   Draw a matrix similar to Table 1.4 that shows the relationship between security mechanisms and services.

1.7   Read all of the classic papers cited in Section 1.9. Compose a 500-1000 word paper (or 8 to 12 slide PowerPoint presentation) that summarizes the key concepts that emerge from these papers, emphasizing concepts that are common to most or all of the papers.

CHAPTER 2

SYMMETRIC ENCRYPTION AND MESSAGE CONFIDENTIALITY

2.1 Symmetric Encryption Principles

> Cryptography
> Cryptanalysis
> Feistel Cipher Structure

2.2 Symmetric Block Encryption Algorithms

> Data Encryption Standard
> Triple DES
> Advanced Encryption Standard

2.3 Random and Pseudorandom Numbers

> The Use of Random Numbers
> TRNGs, PRNGs, and PRFs
> Algorithm Design

2.4 Stream Ciphers and RC4

> Stream Cipher Structure
> The RC4 Algorithm

2.5 Cipher Block Modes of Operation

> Electronic Codebook Mode
> Cipher Block Chaining Mode
> Cipher Feedback Mode
> Counter Mode

2.6 Recommended Reading

2.7 Key Terms, Review Questions, and Problems

"I have solved other ciphers of an abstruseness ten thousand times greater. Circum-stances, and a certain bias of mind, have led me to take interest in such riddles, and it may well be doubted whether human ingenuity can construct an enigma of the kind which human ingenuity may not, by proper application, resolve."

— *The Gold Bug*, Edgar Allen Poe

Amongst the tribes of Central Australia every man, woman, and child has a secret or sacred name which is bestowed by the older men upon him or her soon after birth, and which is known to none but the fully initiated members of the group. This secret name is never mentioned except upon the most solemn occasions; to utter it in the hearing of men of another group would be a most serious breach of tribal custom. When mentioned at all, the name is spoken only in a whisper, and not until the most elaborate precautions have been taken that it shall be heard by no one but members of the group. The native thinks that a stranger knowing his secret name would have special power to work him ill by means of magic.

— *The Golden Bough*, Sir James George Frazer

LEARNING OBJECTIVES

After studying this chapter, you should be able to:

◆ Present an overview of the main concepts of symmetric cryptography.

◆ Explain the difference between cryptanalysis and brute-force attack.

◆ Summarize the functionality of DES.

◆ Present an overview of AES.

◆ Explain the concepts of randomness and unpredictability with respect to random numbers.

◆ Understand the differences among true random number generators, pseu-dorandom number generators, and pseudorandom functions.

◆ Present an overview of stream ciphers and RC4.

◆ Compare and contrast ECB, CBC, CFB, and counter modes of operation.

Symmetric encryption, also referred to as conventional encryption, secret-key, or single-key encryption, was the only type of encryption in use prior to the develop-ment of public-key encryption in the late 1970s.[1] It remains by far the most widely used of the two types of encryption.

---

[1]Public-key encryption was first described in the open literature in 1976; the National Security Agency (NSA) claims to have discovered it some years earlier.

This chapter begins with a look at a general model for the symmetric encryption process; this will enable us to understand the context within which the algorithms are used. Then we look at three important block encryption algorithms: DES, triple DES, and AES. This is followed by a discussion of random and pseudorandom number generation. Next, the chapter introduces symmetric stream encryption and describes the widely used stream cipher RC4. Finally, we look at the important topic of block cipher modes of operation.

2.1 SYMMETRIC ENCRYPTION PRINCIPLES

A **symmetric encryption** scheme has five ingredients (Figure 2.1):

- **Plaintext:** This is the original message or data that is fed into the algorithm as input.
- **Encryption algorithm:** The **encryption** algorithm performs various substitutions and transformations on the plaintext.
- **Secret key:** The secret key is also input to the algorithm. The exact substitutions and transformations performed by the algorithm depend on the key.
- **Ciphertext:** This is the scrambled message produced as output. It depends on the plaintext and the secret key. For a given message, two different keys will produce two different ciphertexts.
- **Decryption algorithm:** This is essentially the encryption algorithm run in reverse. It takes the ciphertext and the same secret key and produces the original plaintext.

There are two requirements for secure use of symmetric encryption:

1. We need a strong encryption algorithm. At a minimum, we would like the algorithm to be such that an opponent who knows the algorithm and has access to one or more ciphertexts would be unable to decipher the ciphertext or figure out the key. This requirement is usually stated in a stronger form: The opponent should be unable to decrypt ciphertext or discover the key even

Figure 2.1 Simplified Model of Symmetric Encryption

if he or she is in possession of a number of ciphertexts together with the plaintext that produced each ciphertext.

2. Sender and receiver must have obtained copies of the secret key in a secure fashion and must keep the key secure. If someone can discover the key and knows the algorithm, all communication using this key is readable.

It is important to note that the security of symmetric encryption depends on the secrecy of the key, not the secrecy of the algorithm. That is, it is assumed that it is impractical to decrypt a message on the basis of the ciphertext *plus* knowledge of the encryption/decryption algorithm. In other words, we do not need to keep the algorithm secret; we need to keep only the key secret.

This feature of symmetric encryption is what makes it feasible for widespread use. The fact that the algorithm need not be kept secret means that manufacturers can and have developed low-cost chip implementations of data encryption algorithms. These chips are widely available and incorporated into a number of products. With the use of symmetric encryption, the principal security problem is maintaining the secrecy of the key.

Cryptography

Cryptographic systems are generically classified along three independent dimensions:

1. **The type of operations used for transforming plaintext to ciphertext.** All encryption algorithms are based on two general principles: substitution, in which each element in the plaintext (bit, letter, group of bits or letters) is mapped into another element, and transposition, in which elements in the plaintext are rearranged. The fundamental requirement is that no information be lost (i.e., that all operations be reversible). Most systems, referred to as product systems, involve multiple stages of substitutions and transpositions.

2. **The number of keys used.** If both sender and receiver use the same key, the system is referred to as symmetric, single-key, secret-key, or conventional encryption. If the sender and receiver each use a different key, the system is referred to as asymmetric, two-key, or public-key encryption.

3. **The way in which the plaintext is processed.** A **block cipher** processes the input one block of elements at a time, producing an output block for each input block. A **stream cipher** processes the input elements continuously, producing output one element at a time, as it goes along.

Cryptanalysis

The process of attempting to discover the plaintext or key is known as **cryptanalysis**. The strategy used by the cryptanalyst depends on the nature of the encryption scheme and the information available to the cryptanalyst.

Table 2.1 summarizes the various types of cryptanalytic attacks based on the amount of information known to the cryptanalyst. The most difficult problem is presented when all that is available is the *ciphertext only*. In some cases, not even the encryption algorithm is known, but in general, we can assume that the opponent

Table 2.1   Types of Attacks on Encrypted Messages

Type of Attack	Known to Cryptanalyst
Ciphertext only	• Encryption algorithm • Ciphertext to be decoded
Known plaintext	• Encryption algorithm • Ciphertext to be decoded • One or more plaintext–ciphertext pairs formed with the secret key
Chosen plaintext	• Encryption algorithm • Ciphertext to be decoded • Plaintext message chosen by cryptanalyst, together with its corresponding ciphertext generated with the secret key
Chosen ciphertext	• Encryption algorithm • Ciphertext to be decoded • Purported ciphertext chosen by cryptanalyst, together with its corresponding decrypted plaintext generated with the secret key
Chosen text	• Encryption algorithm • Ciphertext to be decoded • Plaintext message chosen by cryptanalyst, together with its corresponding ciphertext generated with the secret key • Purported ciphertext chosen by cryptanalyst, together with its corresponding decrypted plaintext generated with the secret key

does know the algorithm used for encryption. One possible attack under these circumstances is the brute-force approach of trying all possible keys. If the key space is very large, this becomes impractical. Thus, the opponent must rely on an analysis of the ciphertext itself, generally applying various statistical tests to it. To use this approach, the opponent must have some general idea of the type of plaintext that is concealed, such as English or French text, an EXE file, a Java source listing, an accounting file, and so on.

The ciphertext-only attack is the easiest to defend against because the opponent has the least amount of information to work with. In many cases, however, the analyst has more information. The analyst may be able to capture one or more plaintext messages as well as their encryptions. Or the analyst may know that certain plaintext patterns will appear in a message. For example, a file that is encoded in the Postscript format always begins with the same pattern, or there may be a standardized header or banner to an electronic funds transfer message, and so on. All of these are examples of *known plaintext*. With this knowledge, the analyst may be able to deduce the key on the basis of the way in which the known plaintext is transformed.

Closely related to the known-plaintext attack is what might be referred to as a probable-word attack. If the opponent is working with the encryption of some general prose message, he or she may have little knowledge of what is in the message. However, if the opponent is after some very specific information, then parts of the message may be known. For example, if an entire accounting file is being transmitted, the opponent may know the placement of certain key words in the header of the file. As another example, the source code for a program developed by a corporation might include a copyright statement in some standardized position.

If the analyst is able somehow to get the source system to insert into the system a message chosen by the analyst, then a *chosen-plaintext* attack is possible. In general, if the analyst is able to choose the messages to encrypt, the analyst may deliberately pick patterns that can be expected to reveal the structure of the key.

Table 2.1 lists two other types of attack: chosen ciphertext and chosen text. These are less commonly employed as cryptanalytic techniques but are nevertheless possible avenues of attack.

Only relatively weak algorithms fail to withstand a ciphertext-only attack. Generally, an encryption algorithm is designed to withstand a known-plaintext attack.

An encryption scheme is **computationally secure** if the ciphertext generated by the scheme meets one or both of the following criteria:

- The cost of breaking the cipher exceeds the value of the encrypted information.
- The time required to break the cipher exceeds the useful lifetime of the information.

Unfortunately, it is very difficult to estimate the amount of effort required to cryptanalyze ciphertext successfully. However, assuming there are no inherent mathematical weaknesses in the algorithm, then a brute-force approach is indicated. A **brute-force attack** involves trying every possible key until an intelligible translation of the ciphertext into plaintext is obtained. On average, half of all possible keys must be tried to achieve success. That is, if there are x different keys, on average an attacker would discover the actual key after $x/2$ tries. It is important to note that there is more to a brute-force attack than simply running through all possible keys. Unless known plaintext is provided, the analyst must be able to recognize plaintext as plaintext. If the message is just plaintext in English, then the result pops out easily, although the task of recognizing English would have to be automated. If the text message has been compressed before encryption, then recognition is more difficult. And if the message is some more general type of data, such as a numerical file, and this has been compressed, the problem becomes even more difficult to automate. Thus, to supplement the brute-force approach, some degree of knowledge about the expected plaintext is needed, and some means of automatically distinguishing plaintext from garble is also needed.

Feistel Cipher Structure

Many symmetric block encryption algorithms, including DES, have a structure first described by Horst Feistel of IBM in 1973 [FEIS73] and shown in Figure 2.2. The inputs to the encryption algorithm are a plaintext block of length $2w$ bits and a key K. The plaintext block is divided into two halves, LE_0 and RE_0. The two halves of the data pass through n rounds of processing and then combine to produce the ciphertext block. Each round i has as inputs LE_{i-1} and RE_{i-1} derived from the previous round, as well as a subkey K_i derived from the overall K. In general, the subkeys K_i are different from K and from each other and are generated from the key by a subkey generation algorithm. In Figure 2.2, 16 rounds are used, although any

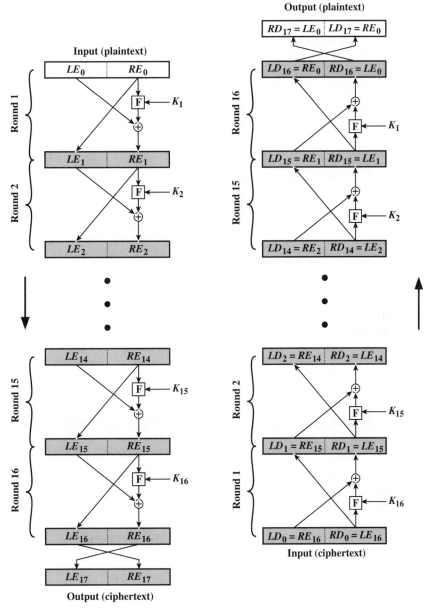

Figure 2.2 Feistel Encryption and Decryption (16 rounds)

number of rounds could be implemented. The right-hand side of Figure 2.2 shows the decryption process.

All rounds have the same structure. A substitution is performed on the left half of the data. This is done by applying a *round function* F to the right half of the data and then taking the exclusive-OR (XOR) of the output of that function and the left half of the data. The round function has the same general structure for each round but is parameterized by the round subkey K_i. Following this substitution, a permutation is performed that consists of the interchange of the two halves of the data.

The **Feistel structure** is a particular example of the more general structure used by all symmetric block ciphers. In general, a symmetric block cipher consists of a sequence of rounds, with each round performing substitutions and permutations conditioned by a secret key value. The exact realization of a symmetric block cipher depends on the choice of the following parameters and design features.

- **Block size:** Larger block sizes mean greater security (all other things being equal) but reduced encryption/decryption speed. A block size of 128 bits is a reasonable trade-off and is nearly universal among recent block cipher designs.
- **Key size:** Larger key size means greater security but may decrease encryption/decryption speed. The most common key length in modern algorithms is 128 bits.
- **Number of rounds:** The essence of a symmetric block cipher is that a single round offers inadequate security but that multiple rounds offer increasing security. A typical size is from 10 to 16 rounds.
- **Subkey generation algorithm:** Greater complexity in this algorithm should lead to greater difficulty of cryptanalysis.
- **Round function:** Again, greater complexity generally means greater resistance to cryptanalysis.

There are two other considerations in the design of a symmetric block cipher:

- **Fast software encryption/decryption:** In many cases, encryption is embedded in applications or utility functions in such a way as to preclude a hardware implementation. Accordingly, the speed of execution of the algorithm becomes a concern.
- **Ease of analysis:** Although we would like to make our algorithm as difficult as possible to cryptanalyze, there is great benefit in making the algorithm easy to analyze. That is, if the algorithm can be concisely and clearly explained, it is easier to analyze that algorithm for cryptanalytic vulnerabilities and therefore develop a higher level of assurance as to its strength. DES, for example, does not have an easily analyzed functionality.

Decryption with a symmetric block cipher is essentially the same as the encryption process. The rule is as follows: Use the ciphertext as input to the algorithm, but use the subkeys K_i in reverse order. That is, use K_n in the first round, K_{n-1} in the second round, and so on until K_1 is used in the last round. This is a nice feature, because it means we need not implement two different algorithms—one for encryption and one for decryption.

2.2 SYMMETRIC BLOCK ENCRYPTION ALGORITHMS

The most commonly used symmetric encryption algorithms are block ciphers. A **block cipher** processes the plaintext input in fixed-sized blocks and produces a block of ciphertext of equal size for each plaintext block. This section focuses on the three most important symmetric block ciphers: the Data Encryption Standard (DES), triple DES (3DES), and the Advanced Encryption Standard (AES).

Data Encryption Standard

The most widely used encryption scheme is based on the **Data Encryption Standard (DES)** issued in 1977, as Federal Information Processing Standard 46 (FIPS 46) by the National Bureau of Standards, now known as the National Institute of Standards and Technology (NIST). The algorithm itself is referred to as the Data Encryption Algorithm (DEA).[2]

DESCRIPTION OF THE ALGORITHM The plaintext is 64 bits in length and the key is 56 bits in length; longer plaintext amounts are processed in 64-bit blocks. The DES structure is a minor variation of the Feistel network shown in Figure 2.2. There are 16 rounds of processing. From the original 56-bit key, 16 subkeys are generated, one of which is used for each round.

The process of decryption with DES is essentially the same as the encryption process. The rule is as follows: Use the ciphertext as input to the DES algorithm, but use the subkeys K_i in reverse order. That is, use K_{16} on the first iteration, K_{15} on the second iteration, and so on until K_1 is used on the 16th and last iteration.

THE STRENGTH OF DES Concerns about the strength of DES fall into two categories: concerns about the algorithm itself and concerns about the use of a 56-bit key. The first concern refers to the possibility that cryptanalysis is possible by exploiting the characteristics of the DES algorithm. Over the years, there have been numerous attempts to find and exploit weaknesses in the algorithm, making DES the most-studied encryption algorithm in existence. Despite numerous approaches, no one has so far succeeded in discovering a fatal weakness in DES.[3]

A more serious concern is key length. With a key length of 56 bits, there are 2^{56} possible keys, which is approximately 7.2×10^{16} keys. Thus, on the face of it, a brute-force attack appears impractical. Assuming that on average half the key space has to be searched, a single machine performing one DES encryption per microsecond would take more than a thousand years to break the cipher.

However, the assumption of one encryption per microsecond is overly conservative. DES finally and definitively proved insecure in July 1998, when the Electronic Frontier Foundation (EFF) announced that it had broken a DES encryption using a special-purpose "DES cracker" machine that was built for less than $250,000. The attack took less than three days. The EFF has published a detailed description of the machine, enabling others to build their own cracker [EFF98]. And, of course, hardware prices will continue to drop as speeds increase, making DES virtually worthless.

With current technology, it is not even necessary to use special, purpose-built hardware. Rather, the speed of commercial, off-the-shelf processors threaten the

---

[2]The terminology is a bit confusing. Until recently, the terms *DES* and *DEA* could be used interchangeably. However, the most recent edition of the DES document includes a specification of the DEA described here plus the triple DEA (3DES) described subsequently. Both DEA and 3DES are part of the Data Encryption Standard. Furthermore, until the recent adoption of the official term *3DES*, the triple DEA algorithm was typically referred to as *triple DES* and written as 3DES. For the sake of convenience, we will use 3DES.

[3]At least, no one has publicly acknowledged such a discovery.

Table 2.2 Average Time Required for Exhaustive Key Search

Key Size (bits)	Cipher	Number of Alternative Keys	Time Required at 10^9 Decryptions/s	Time Required at 10^{13} Decryptions/s
56	DES	$2^{56} \approx 7.2 \times 10^{16}$	2^{55} ns = 1.125 years	1 hour
128	AES	$2^{128} \approx 3.4 \times 10^{38}$	2^{127} ns = 5.3×10^{21} years	5.3×10^{17} years
168	Triple DES	$2^{168} \approx 3.7 \times 10^{50}$	2^{167} ns = 5.8×10^{33} years	5.8×10^{29} years
192	AES	$2^{192} \approx 6.3 \times 10^{57}$	2^{191} ns = 9.8×10^{40} years	9.8×10^{36} years
256	AES	$2^{256} \approx 1.2 \times 10^{77}$	2^{255} ns = 1.8×10^{60} years	1.8×10^{56} years

security of DES. A paper from Seagate Technology [SEAG08] suggests that a rate of one billion (10^9) key combinations per second is reasonable for today's multicore computers. Recent offerings confirm this. Both Intel and AMD now offer hardware-based instructions to accelerate the use of AES. Tests run on a contemporary multicore Intel machine resulted in an encryption rate of about half a billion [BASU12]. Another recent analysis suggests that with contemporary supercomputer technology, a rate of 10^{13} encryptions/s is reasonable [AROR12].

Considering these results, Table 2.2 shows how much time is required for a brute-force attack for various key sizes. As can be seen, a single PC can break DES in about a year; if multiple PCs work in parallel, the time is drastically shortened. And today's supercomputers should be able to find a key in about an hour. Key sizes of 128 bits or greater are effectively unbreakable using simply a brute-force approach. Even if we managed to speed up the attacking system by a factor of 1 trillion (10^{12}), it would still take over 100,000 years to break a code using a 128-bit key.

Fortunately, there are a number of alternatives to DES, the most important of which are triple DES and AES, discussed in the remainder of this section.

Triple DES

Triple DES (3DES) was first standardized for use in financial applications in ANSI standard X9.17 in 1985. 3DES was incorporated as part of the Data Encryption Standard in 1999 with the publication of FIPS 46-3.

3DES uses three keys and three executions of the DES algorithm. The function follows an encrypt-decrypt-encrypt (EDE) sequence (Figure 2.3a):

$$C = \mathrm{E}(K_3, \mathrm{D}(K_2, \mathrm{E}(K_1, P)))$$

where

$$C = \text{ciphertext}$$
$$P = \text{plaintext}$$
$$\mathrm{E}[K, X] = \text{encryption of } X \text{ using key } K$$
$$\mathrm{D}[K, Y] = \text{decryption of } Y \text{ using key } K$$

Decryption is simply the same operation with the keys reversed (Figure 2.3b):

$$P = \mathrm{D}(K_1, \mathrm{E}(K_2, \mathrm{D}(K_3, C)))$$

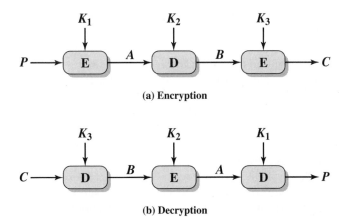

(a) Encryption

(b) Decryption

Figure 2.3   Triple DES

There is no cryptographic significance to the use of decryption for the second stage of 3DES encryption. Its only advantage is that it allows users of 3DES to decrypt data encrypted by users of the older single DES:

$$C = E(K_1, D(K_1, E(K_1, P))) = E[K, P]$$

With three distinct keys, 3DES has an effective key length of 168 bits. FIPS 46-3 also allows for the use of two keys, with $K_1 = K_3$; this provides for a key length of 112 bits. FIPS 46-3 includes the following guidelines for 3DES.

- 3DES is the FIPS-approved symmetric encryption algorithm of choice.
- The original DES, which uses a single 56-bit key, is permitted under the standard for legacy systems only. New procurements should support 3DES.
- Government organizations with legacy DES systems are encouraged to transition to 3DES.
- It is anticipated that 3DES and the Advanced Encryption Standard (AES) will coexist as FIPS-approved algorithms, allowing for a gradual transition to AES.

It is easy to see that 3DES is a formidable algorithm. Because the underlying cryptographic algorithm is DEA, 3DES can claim the same resistance to cryptanalysis based on the algorithm as is claimed for DEA. Furthermore, with a 168-bit key length, brute-force attacks are effectively impossible.

Ultimately, AES is intended to replace 3DES, but this process will take a number of years. NIST anticipates that 3DES will remain an approved algorithm (for U.S. government use) for the foreseeable future.

Advanced Encryption Standard

3DES has two attractions that assure its widespread use over the next few years. First, with its 168-bit key length, it overcomes the vulnerability to brute-force attack of DEA. Second, the underlying encryption algorithm in 3DES is the same as in DEA. This algorithm has been subjected to more scrutiny than any other encryption algorithm over a longer period of time, and no effective cryptanalytic attack based on the algorithm rather than brute force has been found. Accordingly, there is a high level of confidence that 3DES is very resistant to cryptanalysis. If security were the only consideration, then 3DES would be an appropriate choice for a standardized encryption algorithm for decades to come.

The principal drawback of 3DES is that the algorithm is relatively sluggish in software. The original DEA was designed for mid-1970s hardware implementation and does not produce efficient software code. 3DES, which has three times as many rounds as DEA, is correspondingly slower. A secondary drawback is that both DEA and 3DES use a 64-bit block size. For reasons of both efficiency and security, a larger block size is desirable.

Because of these drawbacks, 3DES is not a reasonable candidate for long-term use. As a replacement, NIST in 1997 issued a call for proposals for a new **Advanced Encryption Standard (AES)**, which should have a security strength equal to or better than 3DES and significantly improved efficiency. In addition to these general requirements, NIST specified that AES must be a symmetric block cipher with a block length of 128 bits and support for key lengths of 128, 192, and 256 bits. Evaluation criteria included security, computational efficiency, memory requirements, hardware and software suitability, and flexibility.

In a first round of evaluation, 15 proposed algorithms were accepted. A second round narrowed the field to five algorithms. NIST completed its evaluation process and published a final standard (FIPS PUB 197) in November of 2001. NIST selected Rijndael as the proposed AES algorithm. The two researchers who developed and submitted Rijndael for the AES are both cryptographers from Belgium: Dr. Joan Daemen and Dr. Vincent Rijmen.

OVERVIEW OF THE ALGORITHM AES uses a block length of 128 bits and a key length that can be 128, 192, or 256 bits. In the description of this section, we assume a key length of 128 bits, which is likely to be the one most commonly implemented.

The input to the encryption and decryption algorithms is a single 128-bit block. In FIPS PUB 197, this block is depicted as a square matrix of bytes. This block is copied into the **State** array, which is modified at each stage of encryption or decryption. After the final stage, **State** is copied to an output matrix. Similarly, the 128-bit key is depicted as a square matrix of bytes. This key is then expanded into an array of key schedule words: Each word is four bytes and the total key schedule is 44 words for the 128-bit key. The ordering of bytes within a matrix is by column. So, for example, the first four bytes of a 128-bit plaintext input to the encryption cipher occupy the first column of the **in** matrix, the second four bytes occupy the second column, and so on. Similarly, the first four bytes of the expanded key, which form a word, occupy the first column of the **w** matrix.

The following comments give some insight into AES.

1. One noteworthy feature of this structure is that it is not a Feistel structure. Recall that in the classic Feistel structure, half of the data block is used to modify the other half of the data block, and then the halves are swapped. AES does not use a Feistel structure but processes the entire data block in parallel during each round using substitutions and permutation.

2. The key that is provided as input is expanded into an array of forty-four 32-bit words, $\mathbf{w}[i]$. Four distinct words (128 bits) serve as a round key for each round.

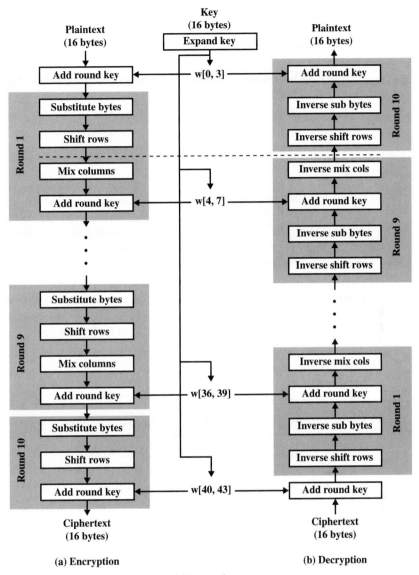

Figure 2.4 AES Encryption and Decryption

3. Four different stages are used, one of permutation and three of substitution (Figure 2.4):
   - **Substitute bytes:** Uses a table, referred to as an S-box,[4] to perform a byte-by-byte substitution of the block.
   - **Shift rows:** A simple permutation that is performed row by row.
   - **Mix columns:** A substitution that alters each byte in a column as a function of all of the bytes in the column.

---

[4]The term *S-box*, or substitution box, is commonly used in the description of symmetric ciphers to refer to a table used for a table-lookup type of substitution mechanism.

  • **Add round key:** A simple bitwise XOR of the current block with a portion of the expanded key.

4. The structure is quite simple. For both encryption and decryption, the cipher begins with an Add Round Key stage, followed by nine rounds that each includes all four stages, followed by a tenth round of three stages. Figure 2.5 depicts the structure of a full encryption round.

5. Only the Add Round Key stage makes use of the key. For this reason, the cipher begins and ends with an Add Round Key stage. Any other stage, applied at the beginning or end, is reversible without knowledge of the key and so would add no security.

6. The Add Round Key stage by itself would not be formidable. The other three stages together scramble the bits, but by themselves, they would provide no security because they do not use the key. We can view the cipher as alternating operations of XOR encryption (Add Round Key) of a block, followed by scrambling of the block (the other three stages), followed by XOR encryption, and so on. This scheme is both efficient and highly secure.

7. Each stage is easily reversible. For the Substitute Byte, Shift Row, and Mix Columns stages, an inverse function is used in the decryption algorithm. For the Add Round Key stage, the inverse is achieved by XORing the same round key to the block, using the result that $A \oplus B \oplus B = A$.

8. As with most block ciphers, the decryption algorithm makes use of the expanded key in reverse order. However, the decryption algorithm is not identical to the encryption algorithm. This is a consequence of the particular structure of AES.

9. Once it is established that all four stages are reversible, it is easy to verify that decryption does recover the plaintext. Figure 2.4 lays out encryption and decryption going in opposite vertical directions. At each horizontal point (e.g., the dashed line in the figure), **State** is the same for both encryption and decryption.

10. The final round of both encryption and decryption consists of only three stages. Again, this is a consequence of the particular structure of AES and is required to make the cipher reversible.

2.3 RANDOM AND PSEUDORANDOM NUMBERS

Random numbers play an important role in the use of encryption for various network security applications. We provide an overview in this section. The topic is examined in more detail in Appendix E.

The Use of Random Numbers

A number of network security algorithms based on cryptography make use of random numbers. For example,

  • Generation of keys for the RSA public-key encryption algorithm (described in Chapter 3) and other public-key algorithms.

State

SubBytes

State

ShiftRows

State

MixColumns

State

AddRoundKey

State

Figure 2.5 AES Encryption Round

55

- Generation of a stream key for symmetric stream cipher (discussed in the following section).
- Generation of a symmetric key for use as a temporary **session key**. This function is used in a number of networking applications, such as Transport Layer Security (Chapter 5), Wi-Fi (Chapter 6), e-mail security (Chapter 7), and IP security (Chapter 8).
- In a number of key distribution scenarios, such as Kerberos (Chapter 4), random numbers are used for handshaking to prevent replay attacks.

These applications give rise to two distinct and not necessarily compatible requirements for a sequence of random numbers: randomness and unpredictability.

RANDOMNESS Traditionally, the concern in the generation of a sequence of allegedly random numbers has been that the sequence of numbers be random in some well-defined statistical sense. The following criteria are used to validate that a sequence of numbers is random.

- **Uniform distribution:** The distribution of bits in the sequence should be uniform; that is, the frequency of occurrence of ones and zeros should be approximately the same.
- **Independence:** No one subsequence in the sequence can be inferred from the others.

Although there are well-defined tests for determining that a sequence of numbers matches a particular distribution, such as the uniform distribution, there is no such test to "prove" independence. Rather, a number of tests can be applied to demonstrate if a sequence does not exhibit independence. The general strategy is to apply a number of such tests until the confidence that independence exists is sufficiently strong.

In the context of our discussion, the use of a sequence of numbers that appear statistically random often occurs in the design of algorithms related to cryptography. For example, a fundamental requirement of the RSA public-key encryption scheme discussed in Chapter 3 is the ability to generate prime numbers. In general, it is difficult to determine if a given large number N is prime. A brute-force approach would be to divide N by every odd integer less than $\sqrt{N}$. If N is on the order, say, of 10^{150} (a not uncommon occurrence in public-key cryptography), such a brute-force approach is beyond the reach of human analysts and their computers. However, a number of effective algorithms exist that test the primality of a number by using a sequence of randomly chosen integers as input to relatively simple computations. If the sequence is sufficiently long (but far, far less than $\sqrt{10^{150}}$), the primality of a number can be determined with near certainty. This type of approach, known as randomization, crops up frequently in the design of algorithms. In essence, if a problem is too hard or time-consuming to solve exactly, a simpler, shorter approach based on randomization is used to provide an answer with any desired level of confidence.

UNPREDICTABILITY In applications such as reciprocal authentication and session key generation, the requirement is not so much that the sequence of numbers be statistically random but that the successive members of the sequence are unpredictable. With "true" random sequences, each number is statistically independent of other numbers in the sequence and therefore unpredictable. However, as is discussed shortly, true random numbers are not always used; rather, sequences of numbers that appear to be random are generated by some algorithm. In this latter case, care must be taken that an opponent not be able to predict future elements of the sequence on the basis of earlier elements.

TRNGs, PRNGs, and PRFs

Cryptographic applications typically make use of algorithmic techniques for random number generation. These algorithms are deterministic and therefore produce sequences of numbers that are not statistically random. However, if the algorithm is good, the resulting sequences will pass many reasonable tests of randomness. Such numbers are referred to as **pseudorandom numbers**.

You may be somewhat uneasy about the concept of using numbers generated by a deterministic algorithm as if they were random numbers. Despite what might be called philosophical objections to such a practice, it generally works. That is, under most circumstances, pseudorandom numbers will perform as well as if they were random for a given use. The phrase "as well as" is unfortunately subjective, but the use of pseudorandom numbers is widely accepted. The same principle applies in statistical application, in which a statistician takes a sample of a population and assumes that the results will be approximately the same as if the whole population were measured.

Figure 2.6 contrasts a **true random number generator (TRNG)** with two forms of pseudorandom number generators. A TRNG takes as input a source that is effectively random; the source is often referred to as an **entropy source**. In essence, the entropy source is drawn from the physical environment of the computer and could include things such as keystroke timing patterns, disk electrical activity, mouse movements, and instantaneous values of the system clock. The source, or combination of sources, serves as input to an algorithm that produces random binary output. The TRNG may simply involve conversion of an analog source to a binary output. The TRNG may involve additional processing to overcome any bias in the source.

In contrast, a PRNG takes as input a fixed value, called the **seed**, and produces a sequence of output bits using a deterministic algorithm. Typically, as shown in Figure 2.6, there is some feedback path by which some of the results of the algorithm are fed back as input as additional output bits are produced. The important thing to note is that the output bit stream is determined solely by the input value or values, so that an adversary who knows the algorithm and the seed can reproduce the entire bit stream.

Figure 2.6 shows two different forms of PRNGs, based on application.

- **Pseudorandom number generator:** An algorithm that is used to produce an open-ended sequence of bits is referred to as a PRNG. A common application

TRNG = true random number generator
PRNG = pseudorandom number generator
PRF = pseudorandom function

Figure 2.6 Random and Pseudorandom Number Generators

for an open-ended sequence of bits is as input to a symmetric stream cipher, as discussed in the following section.

- **Pseudorandom function (PRF):** A PRF is used to produce a pseudorandom string of bits of some fixed length. Examples are symmetric encryption keys and nonces. Typically, the PRF takes as input a seed plus some context specific values, such as a user ID or an application ID. A number of examples of PRFs will be seen throughout this book.

Other than the number of bits produced, there is no difference between a PRNG and a PRF. The same algorithms can be used in both applications. Both require a seed and both must exhibit randomness and unpredictability. Furthermore, a PRNG application may also employ context-specific input.

Algorithm Design

Cryptographic PRNGs have been the subject of much research over the years, and a wide variety of algorithms have been developed. These fall roughly into two categories:

- **Purpose-built algorithms:** These are algorithms designed specifically and solely for the purpose of generating pseudorandom bit streams. Some of these algorithms are used for a variety of PRNG applications; several of these are described in the next section. Others are designed specifically for use in a stream cipher. The most important example of the latter is RC4, described in the next section.

- **Algorithms based on existing cryptographic algorithms:** Cryptographic algorithms have the effect of randomizing input. Indeed, this is a requirement of such algorithms. For example, if a symmetric block cipher produced ciphertext that had certain regular patterns in it, it would aid in the process of cryptanalysis. Thus, cryptographic algorithms can serve as the core of PRNGs. Three broad categories of cryptographic algorithms are commonly used to create PRNGs:

  —**Symmetric block ciphers**

  —**Asymmetric ciphers**

  —**Hash functions and message authentication codes**

Any of these approaches can yield a cryptographically strong PRNG. A purpose-built algorithm may be provided by an operating system for general use. For applications that already use certain cryptographic algorithms for encryption or authentication, it makes sense to re-use the same code for the PRNG. Thus, all of these approaches are in common use.

2.4   STREAM CIPHERS AND RC4

A *block cipher* processes the input one block of elements at a time, producing an output block for each input block. A *stream cipher* processes the input elements continuously, producing output one element at a time as it goes along. Although block ciphers are far more common, there are certain applications in which a stream cipher is more appropriate. Examples are given subsequently in this book. In this section, we look at perhaps the most popular symmetric stream cipher, RC4. We begin with an overview of stream cipher structure, and then examine RC4.

Stream Cipher Structure

A typical stream cipher encrypts plaintext one byte at a time, although a stream cipher may be designed to operate on one bit at a time or on units larger than a byte at a time. Figure 2.7 is a representative diagram of stream cipher structure. In this structure, a key is input to a pseudorandom bit generator that produces a stream of 8-bit numbers that are apparently random. The pseudorandom stream is unpredictable without knowledge of the input key and has an apparently random character. The output of the generator, called a **keystream**, is combined one byte at a time with the plaintext stream using the bitwise exclusive-OR (XOR) operation. For example, if the next byte generated by the generator is 01101100 and the next plaintext byte is 11001100, then the resulting ciphertext byte is

$$
\begin{array}{ll}
\ 11001100 & \text{plaintext} \\
\oplus\ \underline{01101100} & \text{key stream} \\
\ 10100000 & \text{ciphertext}
\end{array}
$$

Figure 2.7 Stream Cipher Diagram

Decryption requires the use of the same pseudorandom sequence:

$$
\begin{array}{ll}
 10100000 & \text{ciphertext} \\
\oplus\ \underline{01101100} & \text{key stream} \\
 11001100 & \text{plaintext}
\end{array}
$$

[KUMA97] lists the following important design considerations for a stream cipher.

1. The encryption sequence should have a large period. A pseudorandom number generator uses a function that produces a deterministic stream of bits that eventually repeats. The longer the period of repeat, the more difficult it will be to do cryptanalysis.

2. The keystream should approximate the properties of a true random number stream as close as possible. For example, there should be an approximately equal number of 1s and 0s. If the keystream is treated as a stream of bytes, then all of the 256 possible byte values should appear approximately equally often. The more random-appearing the keystream is, the more randomized the ciphertext is, making cryptanalysis more difficult.

3. Note from Figure 2.7 that the output of the pseudorandom number generator is conditioned on the value of the input key. To guard against brute-force attacks, the key needs to be sufficiently long. The same considerations as apply for block ciphers are valid here. Thus, with current technology, a key length of at least 128 bits is desirable.

With a properly designed pseudorandom number generator, a stream cipher can be as secure as block cipher of comparable key length. A potential advantage of a stream cipher is that stream ciphers that do not use block ciphers as a building block are typically faster and use far less code than do block ciphers. The example in this chapter, RC4, can be implemented in just a few lines of code. In recent years, this advantage has diminished with the introduction of AES, which is quite efficient in software. Furthermore, hardware acceleration techniques are now available for AES. For example, the Intel AES Instruction Set has machine instructions for one round of encryption and decryption and key generation. Using the hardware instructions results in speedups of about an order of magnitude compared to pure software implementations [XU10].

One advantage of a block cipher is that you can reuse keys. In contrast, if two plaintexts are encrypted with the same key using a stream cipher, then cryptanalysis is often quite simple [DAWS96]. If the two ciphertext streams are XORed together, the result is the XOR of the original plaintexts. If the plaintexts are text strings, credit card numbers, or other byte streams with known properties, then cryptanalysis may be successful.

For applications that require encryption/decryption of a stream of data (such as over a data-communications channel or a browser/Web link), a stream cipher might be the better alternative. For applications that deal with blocks of data (such as file transfer, e-mail, and database), block ciphers may be more appropriate. However, either type of cipher can be used in virtually any application.

The RC4 Algorithm

RC4 is a stream cipher designed in 1987 by Ron Rivest for RSA Security. It is a variable key-size stream cipher with byte-oriented operations. The algorithm is based on the use of a random permutation. Analysis shows that the period of the cipher is overwhelmingly likely to be greater than 10100 [ROBS95a]. Eight to sixteen machine operations are required per output byte, and the cipher can be expected to run very quickly in software. RC4 is used in the Secure Sockets Layer/Transport Layer Security (SSL/TLS) standards that have been defined for communication between Web browsers and servers. It is also used in the Wired Equivalent Privacy (WEP) protocol and the newer WiFi Protected Access (WPA) protocol that are part of the IEEE 802.11 wireless LAN standard. RC4 was kept as a trade secret by RSA Security. In September 1994, the RC4 algorithm was anonymously posted on the Internet on the Cypherpunks anonymous remailers list.

The RC4 algorithm is remarkably simple and quite easy to explain. A variable-length key of from 1 to 256 bytes (8 to 2048 bits) is used to initialize a 256-byte state vector S, with elements $S[0], S[1], \ldots, S[255]$. At all times, S contains a permutation of all 8-bit numbers from 0 through 255. For encryption and decryption, a byte k (see Figure 2.7) is generated from S by selecting one of the 255 entries in a systematic fashion. As each value of k is generated, the entries in S are once again permuted.

INITIALIZATION OF S To begin, the entries of S are set equal to the values from 0 through 255 in ascending order; that is, $S[0] = 0, S[1] = 1, \ldots, S[255] = 255$. A temporary vector, T, is also created. If the length of the key K is 256 bytes, then K is transferred to T. Otherwise, for a key of length *keylen* bytes, the first *keylen* elements of T are copied from K, and then K is repeated as many times as necessary to fill out T. These preliminary operations can be summarized as:

```
/* Initialization */
for i = 0 to 255 do
S[i] = i;
T[i] = K[i mod keylen];
```

Next we use T to produce the initial permutation of S. This involves starting with S[0] and going through to S[255] and, for each S[i], swapping S[i] with another byte in S according to a scheme dictated by T[i]:

```
/* Initial Permutation of S */
j = 0;
for i = 0 to 255 do
    j = (j + S[i] + T[i]) mod 256;
    Swap (S[i], S[j]);
```

Because the only operation on S is a swap, the only effect is a permutation. S still contains all the numbers from 0 through 255.

STREAM GENERATION Once the S vector is initialized, the input key is no longer used. Stream generation involves cycling through all the elements of S[i] and, for each S[i], swapping S[i] with another byte in S according to a scheme dictated by the current configuration of S. After S[255] is reached, the process continues, starting over again at S[0]:

```
/* Stream Generation */
i, j = 0;
while (true)
    i = (i + 1) mod 256;
    j = (j + S[i]) mod 256;
    Swap (S[i], S[j]);
    t = (S[i] + S[j]) mod 256;
    k = S[t];
```

To encrypt, XOR the value k with the next byte of plaintext. To decrypt, XOR the value k with the next byte of ciphertext.

Figure 2.8 illustrates the RC4 logic.

STRENGTH OF RC4 A number of papers have been published analyzing methods of attacking RC4 (e.g., [KNUD98], [FLUH00], [MANT01]). None of these approaches is practical against RC4 with a reasonable key length, such as 128 bits. A more serious problem is reported in [FLUH01]. The authors demonstrate that the WEP protocol, intended to provide confidentiality on 802.11 wireless LAN

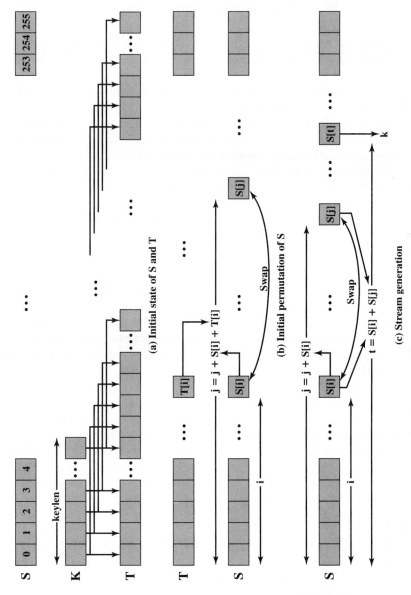

Figure 2.8   RC4

63

networks, is vulnerable to a particular attack approach. In essence, the problem is not with RC4 itself but the way in which keys are generated for use as input to RC4. This particular problem does not appear to be relevant to other applications using RC4 and can be remedied in WEP by changing the way in which keys are generated. This problem points out the difficulty in designing a secure system that involves both cryptographic functions and protocols that make use of them.

2.5 CIPHER BLOCK MODES OF OPERATION

A symmetric block cipher processes one block of data at a time. In the case of DES and 3DES, the block length is $b = 64$ bits; for AES, the block length is $b = 128$ bits. For longer amounts of plaintext, it is necessary to break the plaintext into b-bit blocks (padding the last block if necessary). To apply a block cipher in a variety of applications, five **modes of operation** have been defined by NIST (Special Publication 800-38A). The five modes are intended to cover virtually all of the possible applications of encryption for which a block cipher could be used. These modes are intended for use with any symmetric block cipher, including triple DES and AES. The most important modes are described briefly in the remainder of this section.

Electronic Codebook Mode

The simplest way to proceed is using what is known as **electronic codebook (ECB) mode**, in which plaintext is handled b bits at a time and each block of plaintext is encrypted using the same key. The term *codebook* is used because, for a given key, there is a unique ciphertext for every b-bit block of plaintext. Therefore, one can imagine a gigantic codebook in which there is an entry for every possible b-bit plaintext pattern showing its corresponding ciphertext.

With ECB, if the same b-bit block of plaintext appears more than once in the message, it always produces the same ciphertext. Because of this, for lengthy messages, the ECB mode may not be secure. If the message is highly structured, it may be possible for a cryptanalyst to exploit these regularities. For example, if it is known that the message always starts out with certain predefined fields, then the cryptanalyst may have a number of known plaintext–ciphertext pairs to work with. If the message has repetitive elements with a period of repetition a multiple of b bits, then these elements can be identified by the analyst. This may help in the analysis or may provide an opportunity for substituting or rearranging blocks.

To overcome the security deficiencies of ECB, we would like a technique in which the same plaintext block, if repeated, produces different ciphertext blocks.

Cipher Block Chaining Mode

In the **cipher block chaining (CBC) mode** (Figure 2.9), the input to the encryption algorithm is the XOR of the current plaintext block and the preceding ciphertext block; the same key is used for each block. In effect, we have chained together the processing of the sequence of plaintext blocks. The input to the encryption function

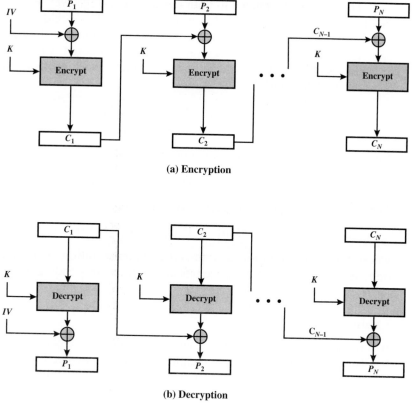

(a) Encryption

(b) Decryption

Figure 2.9   Cipher Block Chaining (CBC) Mode

for each plaintext block bears no fixed relationship to the plaintext block. Therefore, repeating patterns of b bits are not exposed.

For decryption, each cipher block is passed through the decryption algorithm. The result is XORed with the preceding ciphertext block to produce the plaintext block. To see that this works, we can write

$$C_j = \mathrm{E}(K, [C_{j-1} \oplus P_j])$$

where $\mathrm{E}[K, X]$ is the encryption of plaintext X using key K, and $\oplus$ is the exclusive-OR operation. Then

$$\mathrm{D}(K, C_j) = \mathrm{D}(K, \mathrm{E}(K, [C_{j-1} \oplus P_j]))$$
$$\mathrm{D}(K, C_j) = C_{j-1} \oplus P_j$$
$$C_{j-1} \oplus \mathrm{D}(K, C_j) = C_{j-1} \oplus C_{j-1} \oplus P_j = P_j$$

which verifies Figure 2.9b.

To produce the first block of ciphertext, an initialization vector (IV) is XORed with the first block of plaintext. On decryption, the IV is XORed with the output of the decryption algorithm to recover the first block of plaintext.

The IV must be known to both the sender and receiver. For maximum security, the IV should be protected as well as the key. This could be done by sending the IV using ECB encryption. One reason for protecting the IV is as follows: If an opponent is able to fool the receiver into using a different value for IV, then the opponent is able to invert selected bits in the first block of plaintext. To see this, consider the following:

$$C_1 = E(K, [IV \oplus P_1])$$
$$P_1 = IV \oplus D(K, C_1)$$

Now use the notation that $X[j]$ denotes the jth bit of the b-bit quantity X. Then

$$P_1[i] = IV[i] \oplus D(K, C_1)[i]$$

Then, using the properties of XOR, we can state

$$P_1[i]' = IV[i]' \oplus D(K, C_1)[i]$$

where the prime notation denotes bit complementation. This means that if an opponent can predictably change bits in IV, the corresponding bits of the received value of P_1 can be changed.

Cipher Feedback Mode

It is possible to convert any block cipher into a stream cipher by using the **cipher feedback (CFB) mode**. A stream cipher eliminates the need to pad a message to be an integral number of blocks. It also can operate in real time. Thus, if a character stream is being transmitted, each character can be encrypted and transmitted immediately using a character-oriented stream cipher.

One desirable property of a stream cipher is that the ciphertext be of the same length as the plaintext. Thus, if 8-bit characters are being transmitted, each character should be encrypted using 8 bits. If more than 8 bits are used, transmission capacity is wasted.

Figure 2.10 depicts the CFB scheme. In the figure, it is assumed that the unit of transmission is s bits; a common value is $s = 8$. As with CBC, the units of plaintext are chained together, so that the ciphertext of any plaintext unit is a function of all the preceding plaintext.

First, consider encryption. The input to the encryption function is a b-bit shift register that is initially set to some initialization vector (IV). The leftmost (most significant) s bits of the output of the encryption function are XORed with the first unit of plaintext P_1 to produce the first unit of ciphertext C_1, which is then transmitted. In addition, the contents of the shift register are shifted left by s bits, and C_1 is placed in the rightmost (least significant) s bits of the shift register. This process continues until all plaintext units have been encrypted.

For decryption, the same scheme is used, except that the received ciphertext unit is XORed with the output of the encryption function to produce the plaintext unit. Note that it is the *encryption* function that is used, not the decryption function. This is easily explained. Let $S_s(X)$ be defined as the most significant s bits of X. Then

$$C_1 = P_1 \oplus S_s[E(K, IV)]$$

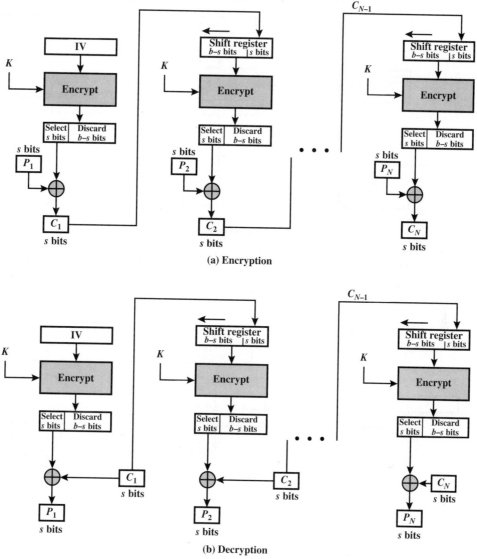

Figure 2.10 *s*-bit Cipher Feedback (CFB) Mode

Therefore,

$$P_1 = C_1 \oplus S_s[E(K, \text{IV})]$$

The same reasoning holds for subsequent steps in the process.

Counter Mode

Although interest in the **counter mode (CTR)** has increased recently, with applications to ATM (asynchronous transfer mode) network security and IPSec (IP security), this mode was proposed early on (e.g., [DIFF79]).

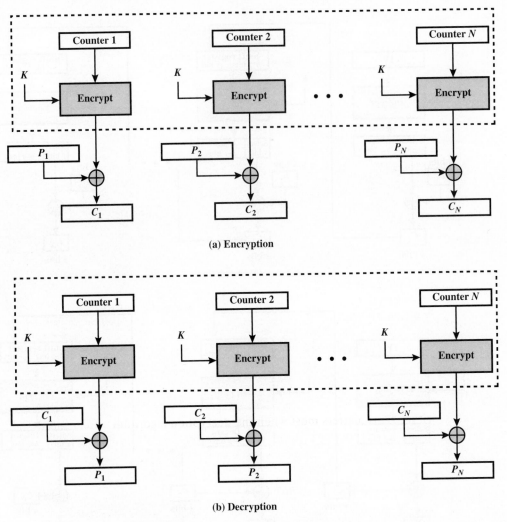

Figure 2.11   Counter (CTR) Mode

Figure 2.11 depicts the CTR mode. A counter equal to the plaintext block size is used. The only requirement stated in SP 800-38A is that the counter value must be different for each plaintext block that is encrypted. Typically, the counter is initialized to some value and then incremented by 1 for each subsequent block (modulo 2^b, where b is the block size). For encryption, the counter is encrypted and then XORed with the plaintext block to produce the ciphertext block; there is no chaining. For decryption, the same sequence of counter values is used, with each encrypted counter XORed with a ciphertext block to recover the corresponding plaintext block.

[LIPM00] lists the following advantages of CTR mode.

- **Hardware efficiency:** Unlike the chaining modes, encryption (or decryption) in CTR mode can be done in parallel on multiple blocks of plaintext or ciphertext. For the chaining modes, the algorithm must complete the computation on one block before beginning on the next block. This limits the maximum throughput of the algorithm to the reciprocal of the time for one execution of block encryption or decryption. In CTR mode, the throughput is only limited by the amount of parallelism that is achieved.

- **Software efficiency:** Similarly, because of the opportunities for parallel execution in CTR mode, processors that support parallel features (such as aggressive pipelining, multiple instruction dispatch per clock cycle, a large number of registers, and SIMD instructions) can be effectively utilized.

- **Preprocessing:** The execution of the underlying encryption algorithm does not depend on input of the plaintext or ciphertext. Therefore, if sufficient memory is available and security is maintained, preprocessing can be used to prepare the output of the encryption boxes that feed into the XOR functions in Figure 2.11. When the plaintext or ciphertext input is presented, then the only computation is a series of XORs. Such a strategy greatly enhances throughput.

- **Random access:** The ith block of plaintext or ciphertext can be processed in random-access fashion. With the chaining modes, block C_i cannot be computed until the $i-1$ prior block are computed. There may be applications in which a ciphertext is stored, and it is desired to decrypt just one block; for such applications, the random access feature is attractive.

- **Provable security:** It can be shown that CTR is at least as secure as the other modes discussed in this section.

- **Simplicity:** Unlike ECB and CBC modes, CTR mode requires only the implementation of the encryption algorithm and not the decryption algorithm. This matters most when the decryption algorithm differs substantially from the encryption algorithm, as it does for AES. In addition, the decryption key scheduling need not be implemented.

2.6 RECOMMENDED READING

The topics in this chapter are covered in greater detail in [STAL13]. For coverage of cryptographic algorithms, [SCHN96] is an essential reference work; it contains descriptions of virtually every cryptographic algorithm and protocol published up to the time of the writing of the book. Another worthwhile and detailed survey is [MENE97]. A more in-depth treatment, with rigorous mathematical discussion, is [STIN06].

MENE97 Menezes, A.; van Oorschot, P.; and Vanstone, S. *Handbook of Applied Cryptography.* Boca Raton, FL: CRC Press, 1997.

SCHN96 Schneier, B. *Applied Cryptography.* New York: Wiley, 1996.

STAL13 Stallings, W. *Cryptography and Network Security: Principles and Practice, Sixth Edition.* Upper Saddle River, NJ: Prentice Hall, 2013.

STIN06 Stinson, D. *Cryptography: Theory and Practice.* Boca Raton, FL: Chapman&Hall/ CRC Press, 2006.

2.7 KEY TERMS, REVIEW QUESTIONS, AND PROBLEMS

Key Terms

Advanced Encryption Standard (AES)	Cryptography	keystream
block cipher	Data Encryption Standard (DES)	link encryption
brute-force attack	decryption	plaintext
cipher block chaining (CBC) mode	electronic codebook (ECB) mode	session key
cipher feedback (CFB) mode	encryption	stream cipher
ciphertext	end-to-end encryption	subkey
counter mode (CTR)	Feistel cipher	symmetric encryption
cryptanalysis	key distribution	triple DES (3DES)

Review Questions

2.1 What is symmetric encryption? What are the two requirements for secure use of symmetric encryption?

2.2 What is cryptanalysis? Summarize the various types of cryptanalytic attacks on encrypted messages.

2.3 List the parameters of a symmetric block cipher for greater security.

2.4 What is a block cipher? Name the important symmetric block ciphers.

2.5 Describe the data encryption algorithm for 64-bit length plaintext and 56-bit length key.

2.6 Describe the encryption and decryption of triple DES.

2.7 What are the advantages and disadvantages of triple DES?

2.8 List the important design criteria for a stream cipher.

Problems

2.1 This problem uses a real-world example of a symmetric cipher, from an old U.S. Special Forces manual (public domain). The document, filename *SpecialForces.pdf*, is available at this book's Web site.

    a. Using the two keys (memory words) *cryptographic* and *network security*, encrypt the following message:

> Be at the third pillar from the left outside the lyceum theatre tonight at seven. If you are distrustful bring two friends.

> Make reasonable assumptions about how to treat redundant letters and excess letters in the memory words and how to treat spaces and punctuation. Indicate what your assumptions are. *Note:* The message is from the Sherlock Holmes novel *The Sign of Four*.

    b. Decrypt the ciphertext. Show your work.

    c. Comment on when it would be appropriate to use this technique and what its advantages are.

2.2 Consider a very simple symmetric block encryption algorithm in which 64-bits blocks of plaintext are encrypted using a 128-bit key. Encryption is defined as

$$C = (P \oplus K_1) \boxplus K_0$$

where C = ciphertext, K = secret key, K_0 = leftmost 64 bits of K, K_1 = rightmost 64 bits of K, $\oplus$ = bitwise exclusive OR, and $\boxplus$ is addition mod 2^{64}.

    a. Show the decryption equation. That is, show the equation for P as a function of C, K_0, and K_1.

    b. Suppose an adversary has access to two sets of plaintexts and their corresponding ciphertexts and wishes to determine K. We have the two equations:

$$C = (P \oplus K_1) \boxplus K_0; \ C' = (P' \oplus K_1) \boxplus K_0$$

First, derive an equation in one unknown (e.g., K_0). Is it possible to proceed further to solve for K_0?

2.3   Perhaps the simplest "serious" symmetric block encryption algorithm is the Tiny Encryption Algorithm (TEA). TEA operates on 64-bit blocks of plaintext using a 128-bit key. The plaintext is divided into two 32-bit blocks (L_0, R_0), and the key is divided into four 32-bit blocks (K_0, K_1, K_2, K_3). Encryption involves repeated application of a pair of rounds, defined as follows for rounds i and $i+1$:

$$L_i = R_{i-1}$$
$$R_i = L_{i-1} \boxplus F(R_{i-1}, K_0, K_1, \delta_i)$$
$$L_{i+1} = R_i$$
$$R_{i+1} = L_i \boxplus F(R_i, K_2, K_3, \delta_{i+1})$$

where F is defined as

$$F(M, K_j, K_k, \delta_i) = ((M \ll 4) \boxplus K_j) \oplus ((M \gg 5) \boxplus K_k) \oplus (M \boxplus \delta_i)$$

and where the logical shift of x by y bits is denoted by $x \ll y$, the logical right shift of x by y bits is denoted by $x \gg y$, and δ_i is a sequence of predetermined constants.

    a. Comment on the significance and benefit of using the sequence of constants.

    b. Illustrate the operation of TEA using a block diagram or flow chart type of depiction.

    c. If only one pair of rounds is used, then the ciphertext consists of the 64-bit block (L_2, R_2). For this case, express the decryption algorithm in terms of equations.

    d. Repeat part (c) using an illustration similar to that used for part (b).

2.4   Show that Feistel decryption is the inverse of Feistel encryption.

2.5   Consider a Feistel cipher composed of 14 rounds with block length 128 bits and key length 128 bits. Suppose that, for a given k, the key scheduling algorithm determines values for the first seven round keys, $k_1, k_2, \ldots, k_8$, and then sets

$$k_8 = k_7, k_9 = k_6, k_{10} = k_5, \ldots, k_{14} = k_1$$

Suppose you have a ciphertext c. Explain how, with access to an encryption oracle, you can decrypt c and determine m using just a single oracle query. This shows that such a cipher is vulnerable to a chosen plaintext attack. (An encryption oracle can be thought of as a device that, when given a plaintext, returns the corresponding ciphertext. The internal details of the device are not known to you, and you cannot break open the device. You can only gain information from the oracle by making queries to it and observing its responses.)

2.6   For any block cipher, the fact that it is a nonlinear function is crucial to its security. To see this, suppose that we have a linear block cipher EL that encrypts 128-bit blocks of plaintext into 128-bit blocks of ciphertext. Let $EL(k, m)$ denote the encryption of a 128-bit message m under a key k (the actual bit length of k is irrelevant). Thus,

$$EL(k, [m_1 \oplus m_2]) = EL(k, m_1) \oplus EL(k, m_2) \text{ for all 128-bit patterns } m_1, m_2$$

Describe how, with 128 chosen ciphertexts, an adversary can decrypt any ciphertext without knowledge of the secret key k. (A "chosen ciphertext" means that an adversary has the ability to choose a ciphertext and then obtain its decryption. Here, you have 128 plaintext–ciphertext pairs to work with, and you have the ability to choose the value of the ciphertexts.)

2.7 Suppose you have a true random bit generator where each bit in the generated stream has the same probability of being a 0 or 1 as any other bit in the stream and that the bits are not correlated; that is, the bits are generated from identical independent distribution. However, the bit stream is biased. The probability of a 1 is $0.5 - \delta$ and the probability of a 0 is $0.5 + \delta$ where $0 < \delta < 0.5$. A simple deskewing algorithm is as follows: Examine the bit stream as a sequence of nonoverlapping pairs. Discard all 00 and 11 pairs. Replace each 01 pair with 0 and each 10 pair with 1.
   a. What is the probability of occurrence of each pair in the original sequence?
   b. What is the probability of occurrence of 0 and 1 in the modified sequence?
   c. What is the expected number of input bits to produce x output bits?
   d. Suppose that the algorithm uses overlapping successive bit pairs instead of nonoverlapping successive bit pairs. That is, the first output bit is based on input bits 1 and 2, the second output bit is based on input bits 2 and 3, and so on. What can you say about the output bit stream?

2.8 Another approach to deskewing is to consider the bit stream as a sequence of nonoverlapping groups of n bits each and output the parity of each group. That is, if a group contains an odd number of ones, the output is 1; otherwise the output is 0.
   a. Express this operation in terms of a basic Boolean function.
   b. Assume, as in the Problem 2.7, that the probability of a 1 is $0.5 - \delta$. If each group consists of 2 bits, what is the probability of an output of 1?
   c. If each group consists of 3 bits, what is the probability of an output of 1?
   d. Generalize the result to find the probability of an output of 1 for input groups of n bits.

2.9 What RC4 key value will leave S unchanged during initialization? That is, after the initial permutation of S, the entries of S will be equal to the values from 0 through 255 in ascending order.

2.10 RC4 has a secret internal state which is a permutation of all the possible values of the vector **S** and the two indices i and j.
   a. Using a straightforward scheme to store the internal state, how many bits are used?
   b. Suppose we think of it from the point of view of how much information is represented by the state. In that case, we need to determine how many different states there are, then take the log to the base 2 to find out how many bits of information this represents. Using this approach, how many bits would be needed to represent the state?

2.11 Alice and Bob agree to communicate privately via e-mail using a scheme based on RC4, but they want to avoid using a new secret key for each transmission. Alice and Bob privately agree on a 128-bit key k. To encrypt a message m consisting of a string of bits, the following procedure is used.
   1. Choose a random 80-bit value v
   2. Generate the ciphertext $c = RC4(v \| k) \oplus m$
   3. Send the bit string $(v \| c)$
   a. Suppose Alice uses this procedure to send a message m to Bob. Describe how Bob can recover the message m from $(v \| c)$ using k.
   b. If an adversary observes several values $(v_1 \| c_1), (v_2 \| c_2), \ldots$ transmitted between Alice and Bob, how can he or she determine when the same key stream has been used to encrypt two messages?

2.12 With the ECB mode, if there is an error in a block of the transmitted ciphertext, only the corresponding plaintext block is affected. However, in the CBC mode, this error propagates. For example, an error in the transmitted C_1 (Figure 2.9) obviously corrupts P_1 and P_2.
   a. Are any blocks beyond P_2 affected?
   b. Suppose that there is a bit error in the source version of P_1. Through how many ciphertext blocks is this error propagated? What is the effect at the receiver?

2.13 Is it possible to perform encryption operations in parallel on multiple blocks of plaintext in CBC mode? How about decryption?

2.14 Suppose an error occurs in a block of ciphertext on transmission using CBC. What effect is produced on the recovered plaintext blocks?

2.15 CBC-Pad is a block cipher mode of operation used in the RC5 block cipher, but it could be used in any block cipher. CBC-Pad handles plaintext of any length. The ciphertext is longer than the plaintext by at most the size of a single block. Padding is used to assure that the plaintext input is a multiple of the block length. It is assumed that the original plaintext is an integer number of bytes. This plaintext is padded at the end by from 1 to bb bytes, where bb equals the block size in bytes. The pad bytes are all the same and set to a byte that represents the number of bytes of padding. For example, if there are 8 bytes of padding, each byte has the bit pattern **00001000**. Why not allow zero bytes of padding? That is, if the original plaintext is an integer multiple of the block size, why not refrain from padding?

2.16 Padding may not always be appropriate. For example, one might wish to store the encrypted data in the same memory buffer that originally contained the plaintext. In that case, the ciphertext must be the same length as the original plaintext. A mode for that purpose is the ciphertext stealing (CTS) mode. Figure 2.12a shows an implementation of this mode.

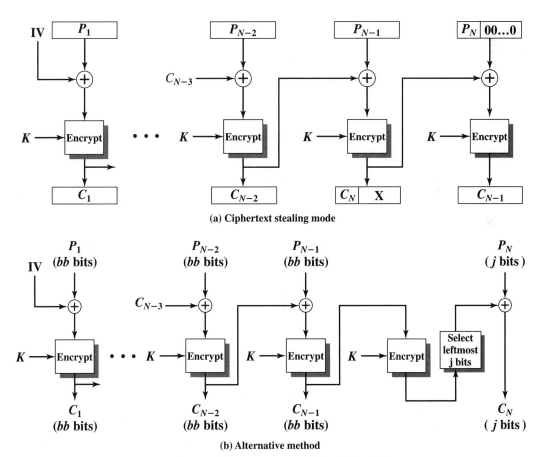

(a) Ciphertext stealing mode

(b) Alternative method

Figure 2.12 Block Cipher Modes for Plaintext not a Multiple of Block Size

      a. Explain how it works.

      b. Describe how to decrypt C_{n-1} and C_n.

2.17 Figure 2.12b shows an alternative to CTS for producing ciphertext of equal length to the plaintext when the plaintext is not an integer multiple of the block size.

      a. Explain the algorithm.

      b. Explain why CTS is preferable to this approach illustrated in Figure 2.12b.

2.18 If a bit error occurs in the transmission of a ciphertext character in 8-bit CFB mode, how far does the error propagate?

CHAPTER 3

PUBLIC-KEY CRYPTOGRAPHY AND MESSAGE AUTHENTICATION

3.1 Approaches to Message Authentication

Authentication Using Conventional Encryption
Message Authentication without Message Encryption

3.2 Secure Hash Functions

Hash Function Requirements
Security of Hash Functions
Simple Hash Functions
The SHA Secure Hash Function
SHA-3

3.3 Message Authentication Codes

HMAC
MACs Based on Block Ciphers

3.4 Public-Key Cryptography Principles

Public-Key Encryption Structure
Applications for Public-Key Cryptosystems
Requirements for Public-Key Cryptography

3.5 Public-Key Cryptography Algorithms

The RSA Public-Key Encryption Algorithm
Diffie–Hellman Key Exchange
Other Public-Key Cryptography Algorithms

3.6 Digital Signatures

3.7 Recommended Reading

3.8 Key Terms, Review Questions, and Problems

Every Egyptian received two names, which were known respectively as the true name and the good name, or the great name and the little name; and while the good or little name was made public, the true or great name appears to have been carefully concealed.

— *The Golden Bough*, Sir James George Frazer

To guard against the baneful influence exerted by strangers is therefore an elementary dictate of savage prudence. Hence before strangers are allowed to enter a district, or at least before they are permitted to mingle freely with the inhabitants, certain ceremonies are often performed by the natives of the country for the purpose of disarming the strangers of their magical powers, or of disinfecting, so to speak, the tainted atmosphere by which they are supposed to be surrounded.

— *The Golden Bough*, Sir James George Frazer

LEARNING OBJECTIVES

After studying this chapter, you should be able to:

◆ Define the term *message authentication code*.

◆ List and explain the requirements for a message authentication code.

◆ Explain why a hash function used for message authentication needs to be secured.

◆ Understand the differences among preimage resistant, second preimage resistant, and collision resistant properties.

◆ Understand the operation of SHA-512.

◆ Present an overview of HMAC.

◆ Present an overview of the basic principles of public-key cryptosystems.

◆ Explain the two distinct uses of public-key cryptosystems.

◆ Present an overview of the RSA algorithm.

◆ Define Diffie–Hellman key exchange.

◆ Understand the man-in-the-middle attack.

In addition to message confidentiality, message authentication is an important network security function. This chapter examines three aspects of message authentication. First, we look at the use of message authentication codes and hash functions to provide message authentication. Then we look at public-key encryption principles and two specific public-key algorithms. These algorithms are useful in the exchange of conventional encryption keys. Then we look at the use of public-key encryption to produce digital signatures, which provides an enhanced form of message authentication.

3.1 APPROACHES TO MESSAGE AUTHENTICATION

Encryption protects against passive attack (eavesdropping). A different requirement is to protect against active attack (falsification of data and transactions). Protection against such attacks is known as message authentication.

A message, file, document, or other collection of data is said to be authentic when it is genuine and comes from its alleged source. Message authentication is a procedure that allows communicating parties to verify that received messages are authentic.[1] The two important aspects are to verify that the contents of the message have not been altered and that the source is authentic. We may also wish to verify a message's timeliness (it has not been artificially delayed and replayed) and sequence relative to other messages flowing between two parties. All of these concerns come under the category of data integrity as described in Chapter 1.

Authentication Using Conventional Encryption

It would seem possible to perform authentication simply by the use of symmetric encryption. If we assume that only the sender and receiver share a key (which is as it should be), then only the genuine sender would be able to encrypt a message successfully for the other participant, provided the receiver can recognize a valid message. Furthermore, if the message includes an error-detection code and a sequence number, the receiver is assured that no alterations have been made and that sequencing is proper. If the message also includes a timestamp, the receiver is assured that the message has not been delayed beyond that normally expected for network transit.

In fact, symmetric encryption alone is not a suitable tool for data authentication. To give one simple example, in the ECB mode of encryption, if an attacker reorders the blocks of ciphertext, then each block will still decrypt successfully. However, the reordering may alter the meaning of the overall data sequence. Although sequence numbers may be used at some level (e.g., each IP packet), it is typically not the case that a separate sequence number will be associated with each b-bit block of plaintext. Thus, block reordering is a threat.

Message Authentication without Message Encryption

In this section, we examine several approaches to message authentication that do not rely on encryption. In all of these approaches, an authentication tag is generated and appended to each message for transmission. The message itself is not encrypted and can be read at the destination independent of the authentication function at the destination.

Because the approaches discussed in this section do not encrypt the message, message confidentiality is not provided. As was mentioned, message encryption by itself does not provide a secure form of authentication. However, it is possible to combine authentication and confidentiality in a single algorithm by encrypting a

---

[1]For simplicity, for the remainder of this chapter, we refer to *message authentication*. By this we mean both authentication of transmitted messages and of stored data (*data authentication*).

message plus its authentication tag. Typically, however, message authentication is provided as a separate function from message encryption. [DAVI89] suggests three situations in which message authentication without confidentiality is preferable:

1. There are a number of applications in which the same message is broadcast to a number of destinations. Two examples are notification to users that the network is now unavailable and an alarm signal in a control center. It is cheaper and more reliable to have only one destination responsible for monitoring authenticity. Thus, the message must be broadcast in plaintext with an associated message authentication tag. The responsible system performs authentication. If a violation occurs, the other destination systems are alerted by a general alarm.

2. Another possible scenario is an exchange in which one side has a heavy load and cannot afford the time to decrypt all incoming messages. Authentication is carried out on a selective basis with messages being chosen at random for checking.

3. Authentication of a computer program in plaintext is an attractive service. The computer program can be executed without having to decrypt it every time, which would be wasteful of processor resources. However, if a message authentication tag were attached to the program, it could be checked whenever assurance is required of the integrity of the program.

Thus, there is a place for both authentication and encryption in meeting security requirements.

MESSAGE AUTHENTICATION CODE   One authentication technique involves the use of a secret key to generate a small block of data, known as a **message authentication code (MAC)**, that is appended to the message. This technique assumes that two communicating parties, say A and B, share a common secret key K_{AB}. When A has a message to send to B, it calculates the message authentication code as a function of the message and the key: $MAC_M = F(K_{AB}, M)$. The message plus code are transmitted to the intended recipient. The recipient performs the same calculation on the received message, using the same secret key, to generate a new message authentication code. The received code is compared to the calculated code (Figure 3.1). If we assume that only the receiver and the sender know the identity of the secret key, and if the received code matches the calculated code, then the following statements apply:

1. The receiver is assured that the message has not been altered. If an attacker alters the message but does not alter the code, then the receiver's calculation of the code will differ from the received code. Because the attacker is assumed not to know the secret key, the attacker cannot alter the code to correspond to the alterations in the message.

2. The receiver is assured that the message is from the alleged sender. Because no one else knows the secret key, no one else could prepare a message with a proper code.

3. If the message includes a sequence number (such as is used with HDLC and TCP), then the receiver can be assured of the proper sequence, because an attacker cannot successfully alter the sequence number.

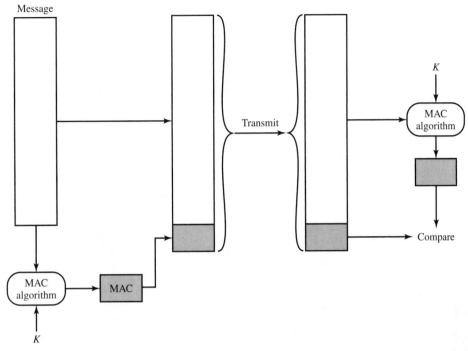

Figure 3.1 Message Authentication Using a Message Authentication Code

A number of algorithms could be used to generate the code. The NIST specification, FIPS PUB 113, recommends the use of DES. DES is used to generate an encrypted version of the message, and the last number of bits of ciphertext are used as the code. A 16- or 32-bit code is typical.

The process just described is similar to encryption. One difference is that the authentication algorithm need not be reversible, as it must for decryption. Because of the mathematical properties of the authentication function, it is less vulnerable to being broken than encryption.

ONE-WAY HASH FUNCTION An alternative to the message authentication code is the **one-way hash function**. As with the message authentication code, a hash function accepts a variable-size message M as input and produces a fixed-size message digest $H(M)$ as output. Unlike the MAC, a hash function does not take a secret key as input. To authenticate a message, the message digest is sent with the message in such a way that the message digest is authentic.

Figure 3.2 illustrates three ways in which the message can be authenticated. The message digest can be encrypted using conventional encryption (part a); if it is assumed that only the sender and receiver share the encryption key, then authenticity is assured. The message digest can be encrypted using public-key encryption (part b); this is explained in Section 3.5. The public-key approach has two advantages: (1) It provides a digital signature as well as message authentication. (2) It does not require the distribution of keys to communicating parties.

Figure 3.2 Message Authentication Using a One-Way Hash Function

These two approaches also have an advantage over approaches that encrypt the entire message in that less computation is required. Nevertheless, there has been interest in developing a technique that avoids encryption altogether. Several reasons for this interest are pointed out in [TSUD92]:

- Encryption software is quite slow. Even though the amount of data to be encrypted per message is small, there may be a steady stream of messages into and out of a system.

- Encryption hardware costs are nonnegligible. Low-cost chip implementations of DES are available, but the cost adds up if all nodes in a network must have this capability.

- Encryption hardware is optimized toward large data sizes. For small blocks of data, a high proportion of the time is spent in initialization/invocation overhead.

- An encryption algorithm may be protected by a patent.

Figure 3.2c shows a technique that uses a hash function but no encryption for message authentication. This technique assumes that two communicating parties, say A and B, share a common secret value S_{AB}. When A has a message to send to B, it calculates the hash function over the concatenation of the secret value and the message: $MD_M = H(S_{AB} \| M)$.[2] It then sends $[M \| MD_M]$ to B. Because B possesses S_{AB}, it can recompute $H(S_{AB} \| M)$ and verify MD_M. Because the secret value itself is not sent, it is not possible for an attacker to modify an intercepted message. As long as the secret value remains secret, it is also not possible for an attacker to generate a false message.

A variation on the third technique, called HMAC, is the one adopted for IP security (described in Chapter 9); it also has been specified for SNMPv3 (Chapter 13).

3.2 SECURE HASH FUNCTIONS

The one-way hash function, or **secure hash function**, is important not only in message authentication but in digital signatures. In this section, we begin with a discussion of requirements for a secure hash function. Then we look at the most important hash function, SHA.

Hash Function Requirements

The purpose of a hash function is to produce a "fingerprint" of a file, message, or other block of data. To be useful for message authentication, a hash function H must have the following properties:

1. H can be applied to a block of data of any size.
2. H produces a fixed-length output.
3. $H(x)$ is relatively easy to compute for any given x, making both hardware and software implementations practical.
4. For any given code h, it is computationally infeasible to find x such that $H(x) = h$. A hash function with this property is referred to as **one-way** or **preimage resistant**.[3]

---

[2] $\|$ denotes concatenation.
[3] For $f(x) = y$, x is said to be a preimage of y. Unless f is one-to-one, there may be multiple preimage values for a given y.

5. For any given block x, it is computationally infeasible to find $y \neq x$ with $H(y) = H(x)$. A hash function with this property is referred to as **second preimage resistant**. This is sometimes referred to as **weak collision resistant**.

6. It is computationally infeasible to find any pair (x, y) such that $H(x) = H(y)$. A hash function with this property is referred to as **collision resistant**. This is sometimes referred to as **strong collision resistant**.

The first three properties are requirements for the practical application of a hash function to message authentication. The fourth property, preimage resistant, is the "one-way" property: It is easy to generate a code given a message, but virtually impossible to generate a message given a code. This property is important if the authentication technique involves the use of a secret value (Figure 3.2c). The secret value itself is not sent; however, if the hash function is not one way, an attacker can easily discover the secret value: If the attacker can observe or intercept a transmission, the attacker obtains the message M and the hash code $C = H(S_{AB} \| M)$. The attacker then inverts the hash function to obtain $S_{AB} \| M = H^{-1}(C)$. Because the attacker now has both M and $S_{AB} \| M$, it is a trivial matter to recover S_{AB}.

The second preimage resistant property guarantees that it is impossible to find an alternative message with the same hash value as a given message. This prevents forgery when an encrypted hash code is used (Figures 3.2a and b). If this property were not true, an attacker would be capable of the following sequence: First, observe or intercept a message plus its encrypted hash code; second, generate an unencrypted hash code from the message; third, generate an alternate message with the same hash code.

A hash function that satisfies the first five properties in the preceding list is referred to as a weak hash function. If the sixth property is also satisfied, then it is referred to as a strong hash function. The sixth property, collision resistant, protects against a sophisticated class of attack known as the birthday attack. Details of this attack are beyond the scope of this book. The attack reduces the strength of an m-bit hash function from 2^m to $2^{m/2}$. See [STAL13] for details.

In addition to providing authentication, a message digest also provides data integrity. It performs the same function as a frame check sequence: If any bits in the message are accidentally altered in transit, the message digest will be in error.

Security of Hash Functions

As with symmetric encryption, there are two approaches to attacking a secure hash function: cryptanalysis and brute-force attack. As with symmetric encryption algorithms, cryptanalysis of a hash function involves exploiting logical weaknesses in the algorithm.

The strength of a hash function against brute-force attacks depends solely on the length of the hash code produced by the algorithm. For a hash code of length n, the level of effort required is proportional to the following:

Preimage resistant	2^n
Second preimage resistant	2^n
Collision resistant	$2^{n/2}$

If collision resistance is required (and this is desirable for a general-purpose secure hash code), then the value $2^{n/2}$ determines the strength of the hash code against brute-force attacks. Van Oorschot and Wiener [VANO94] presented a design for a $10 million collision search machine for MD5, which has a 128-bit hash length, that could find a collision in 24 days. Thus, a 128-bit code may be viewed as inadequate. The next step up, if a hash code is treated as a sequence of 32 bits, is a 160-bit hash length. With a hash length of 160 bits, the same search machine would require over four thousand years to find a collision. With today's technology, the time would be much shorter, so that 160 bits now appears suspect.

Simple Hash Functions

All hash functions operate using the following general principles. The input (message, file, etc.) is viewed as a sequence of n-bit blocks. The input is processed one block at a time in an iterative fashion to produce an n-bit hash function.

One of the simplest hash functions is the bit-by-bit exclusive-OR (XOR) of every block. This can be expressed as

$$C_i = b_{i1} \oplus b_{i2} \oplus \cdots \oplus b_{im}$$

where

$C_i = i$th bit of the hash code, $1 \le i \le n$

$m = $ number of n-bit blocks in the input

$b_{ij} = i$th bit in jth block

$\oplus = $ XOR operation

Figure 3.3 illustrates this operation; it produces a simple parity for each bit position and is known as a longitudinal redundancy check. It is reasonably effective for random data as a data integrity check. Each n-bit hash value is equally likely. Thus, the probability that a data error will result in an unchanged hash value is 2^{-n}. With more predictably formatted data, the function is less effective. For example, in most normal text files, the high-order bit of each octet is always zero. So if a 128-bit hash value is used, instead of an effectiveness of 2^{-128}, the hash function on this type of data has an effectiveness of 2^{-112}.

	bit 1	bit 2	$\bullet \bullet \bullet$	bit n
Block 1	b_{11}	b_{21}		b_{n1}
Block 2	b_{12}	b_{22}		b_{n2}
	$\bullet$	$\bullet$	$\bullet$	$\bullet$
Block m	b_{1m}	b_{2m}		b_{nm}
Hash code	C_1	C_2		C_n

Figure 3.3 Simple Hash Function Using Bitwise XOR

A simple way to improve matters is to perform a 1-bit circular shift, or rotation, on the hash value after each block is processed. The procedure can be summarized as

1. Initially set the n-bit hash value to zero.
2. Process each successive n-bit block of data:
   a. Rotate the current hash value to the left by one bit.
   b. XOR the block into the hash value.

This has the effect of "randomizing" the input more completely and overcoming any regularities that appear in the input.

Although the second procedure provides a good measure of data integrity, it is virtually useless for data security when an encrypted hash code is used with a plaintext message, as in Figures 3.2a and b. Given a message, it is an easy matter to produce a new message that yields that hash code: Simply prepare the desired alternate message and then append an n-bit block that forces the combined new message plus block to yield the desired hash code.

Although a simple XOR or rotated XOR (RXOR) is insufficient if only the hash code is encrypted, you may still feel that such a simple function could be useful when the message as well as the hash code are encrypted. But one must be careful. A technique originally proposed by the National Bureau of Standards used the simple XOR applied to 64-bit blocks of the message and then an encryption of the entire message using the cipher block chaining (CBC) mode. We can define the scheme as follows: Given a message consisting of a sequence of 64-bit blocks X_1, $X_2, \ldots, X_N$, define the hash code C as the block-by-block XOR or all blocks and append the hash code as the final block:

$$C = X_{N+1} = X_1 \oplus X_2 \oplus \cdots \oplus X_N$$

Next, encrypt the entire message plus hash code using CBC mode to produce the encrypted message $Y_1, Y_2, \ldots, Y_{N+1}$. [JUEN85] points out several ways in which the ciphertext of this message can be manipulated in such a way that it is not detectable by the hash code. For example, by the definition of CBC (Figure 2.9), we have

$$X_1 = IV \oplus D(K, Y_1)$$
$$X_i = Y_{i-1} \oplus D(K, Y_i)$$
$$X_{N+1} = Y_N \oplus D(K, Y_{N+1})$$

But X_{N+1} is the hash code:

$$X_{N+1} = X_1 \oplus X_2 \oplus \cdots \oplus X_N$$
$$= [IV \oplus D(K, Y_1)] \oplus [Y_1 \oplus D(K, Y_2)] \oplus \cdots \oplus [Y_{N-1} \oplus D(K, Y_N)]$$

Because the terms in the preceding equation can be XORed in any order, it follows that the hash code would not change if the ciphertext blocks were permuted.

The SHA Secure Hash Function

In recent years, the most widely used hash function has been the Secure Hash Algorithm (SHA). Indeed, because virtually every other widely used hash function had been found to have substantial cryptanalytic weaknesses, SHA was more or less the last remaining standardized hash algorithm by 2005. SHA was developed

Table 3.1 Comparison of SHA Parameters

	SHA-1	**SHA-224**	**SHA-256**	**SHA-384**	**SHA-512**
Message Digest Size	160	224	256	384	512
Message Size	$< 2^{64}$	$< 2^{64}$	$< 2^{64}$	$< 2^{128}$	$< 2^{128}$
Block Size	512	512	512	1024	1024
Word Size	32	32	32	64	64
Number of Steps	80	64	64	80	80

Note: All sizes are measured in bits.

by the National Institute of Standards and Technology (NIST) and published as a federal information processing standard (FIPS 180) in 1993. When weaknesses were discovered in SHA (now known as SHA-0), a revised version was issued as FIPS 180-1 in 1995 and is referred to as **SHA-1**. The actual standards document is entitled "Secure Hash Standard." SHA is based on the hash function MD4, and its design closely models MD4.

SHA-1 produces a hash value of 160 bits. In 2002, NIST produced a revised version of the standard, FIPS 180-2, that defined three new versions of SHA with hash value lengths of 256, 384, and 512 bits known as SHA-256, SHA-384, and SHA-512, respectively. Collectively, these hash algorithms are known as **SHA-2**. These new versions have the same underlying structure and use the same types of modular arithmetic and logical binary operations as SHA-1. A revised document was issued as FIP PUB 180-3 in 2008, which added a 224-bit version (Table 3.1). SHA-1 and SHA-2 are also specified in RFC 6234, which essentially duplicates the material in FIPS 180-3 but adds a C code implementation.

In 2005, NIST announced the intention to phase out approval of SHA-1 and move to a reliance on SHA-2 by 2010. Shortly thereafter, a research team described an attack in which two separate messages could be found that deliver the same SHA-1 hash using 2^{69} operations, far fewer than the 2^{80} operations previously thought needed to find a collision with an SHA-1 hash [WANG05]. This result should hasten the transition to SHA-2.

In this section, we provide a description of SHA-512. The other versions are quite similar.

The algorithm takes as input a message with a maximum length of less than 2^{128} bits and produces as output a 512-bit message digest. The input is processed in 1024-bit blocks. Figure 3.4 depicts the overall processing of a message to produce a digest. The processing consists of the following steps.

Step 1 Append padding bits: The message is padded so that its length is congruent to 896 modulo 1024 [length $\equiv$ 896 (mod 1024)]. Padding is always added, even if the message is already of the desired length. Thus, the number of padding bits is in the range of 1 to 1024. The padding consists of a single 1 bit followed by the necessary number of 0 bits.

Step 2 Append length: A block of 128 bits is appended to the message. This block is treated as an unsigned 128-bit integer (most significant byte first) and contains the length of the original message (before the padding).

Figure 3.4 Message Digest Generation Using SHA-512

The outcome of the first two steps yields a message that is an integer multiple of 1024 bits in length. In Figure 3.4, the expanded message is represented as the sequence of 1024-bit blocks $M_1, M_2, \ldots, M_N$, so that the total length of the expanded message is $N \times 1024$ bits.

Step 3 **Initialize hash buffer:** A 512-bit buffer is used to hold intermediate and final results of the hash function. The buffer can be represented as eight 64-bit registers (a, b, c, d, e, f, g, h). These registers are initialized to the following 64-bit integers (hexadecimal values):

$$a = \text{6A09E667F3BCC908} \qquad e = \text{510E527FADE682D1}$$
$$b = \text{BB67AE8584CAA73B} \qquad f = \text{9B05688C2B3E6C1F}$$
$$c = \text{3C6EF372FE94F82B} \qquad g = \text{1F83D9ABFB41BD6B}$$
$$d = \text{A54FF53A5F1D36F1} \qquad h = \text{5BE0CD19137E2179}$$

These values are stored in big-endian format, which is the most significant byte of a word in the low-address (leftmost) byte position. These words were obtained by taking the first sixty-four bits of the fractional parts of the square roots of the first eight prime numbers.

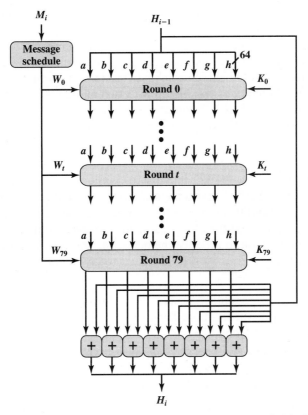

Figure 3.5   SHA-512 Processing of a Single 1024-Bit Block

Step 4 Process message in 1024-bit (128-word) blocks: The heart of the algorithm
is a module that consists of 80 rounds; this module is labeled F in Figure 3.4.
The logic is illustrated in Figure 3.5.

Each round takes as input the 512-bit buffer value **abcdefgh** and
updates the contents of the buffer. At input to the first round, the buffer has
the value of the intermediate hash value, H_{i-1}. Each round t makes use of
a 64-bit value W_t derived from the current 1024-bit block being processed
(M_i). Each round also makes use of an additive constant K_t, where $0 \le t \le 79$
indicates one of the 80 rounds. These words represent the first 64 bits of the
fractional parts of the cube roots of the first 80 prime numbers. The constants provide a "randomized" set of 64-bit patterns, which should eliminate
any regularities in the input data.

The output of the 80th round is added to the input to the first round
(H_{i-1}) to produce H_i. The addition is done independently for each of the
eight words in the buffer with each of the corresponding words in H_{i-1}, using
addition modulo 2^{64}.

Step 5 Output: After all N 1024-bit blocks have been processed, the output from
the Nth stage is the 512-bit message digest.

The SHA-512 algorithm has the property that every bit of the hash code is a function of every bit of the input. The complex repetition of the basic function F produces results that are well mixed; that is, it is unlikely that two messages chosen at random, even if they exhibit similar regularities, will have the same hash code. Unless there is some hidden weakness in SHA-512, which has not so far been published, the difficulty of coming up with two messages having the same message digest is on the order of 2^{256} operations, while the difficulty of finding a message with a given digest is on the order of 2^{512} operations.

SHA-3

SHA-2, particularly the 512-bit version, would appear to provide unassailable security. However, SHA-2 shares the same structure and mathematical operations as its predecessors, and this is a cause for concern. Because it would take years to find a suitable replacement for SHA-2, should it become vulnerable, NIST announced in 2007 a competition to produce the next-generation NIST hash function, which is to be called SHA-3. Following are the basic requirements that must be satisfied by any candidate for SHA-3:

1. It must be possible to replace SHA-2 with SHA-3 in any application by a simple drop-in substitution. Therefore, SHA-3 must support hash value lengths of 224, 256, 384, and 512 bits.

2. SHA-3 must preserve the online nature of SHA-2. That is, the algorithm must process comparatively small blocks (512 or 1024 bits) at a time instead of requiring that the entire message be buffered in memory before processing it.

In 2012, NIST selected a winning submission and formally published SHA-3. A detailed presentation of SHA-3 is provided in Chapter 15.

3.3 MESSAGE AUTHENTICATION CODES

HMAC

In recent years, there has been increased interest in developing a MAC derived from a cryptographic hash code, such as SHA-1. The motivations for this interest are as follows:

- Cryptographic hash functions generally execute faster in software than conventional encryption algorithms such as DES.
- Library code for cryptographic hash functions is widely available.

A hash function such as SHA-1 was not designed for use as a MAC and cannot be used directly for that purpose because it does not rely on a secret key. There have been a number of proposals for the incorporation of a secret key into an existing hash algorithm. The approach that has received the most support is HMAC [BELL96a, BELL96b]. HMAC has been issued as RFC 2104, has been chosen as the mandatory-to-implement MAC for IP Security, and is used in other Internet protocols, such as Transport Layer Security (TLS) and Secure Electronic Transaction (SET).

HMAC DESIGN OBJECTIVES RFC 2104 lists the following design objectives for HMAC.

- To use, without modifications, available hash functions. In particular, hash functions that perform well in software, and for which code is freely and widely available
- To allow for easy replaceability of the embedded hash function in case faster or more secure hash functions are found or required
- To preserve the original performance of the hash function without incurring a significant degradation
- To use and handle keys in a simple way
- To have a well-understood cryptographic analysis of the strength of the authentication mechanism based on reasonable assumptions on the embedded hash function

The first two objectives are important to the acceptability of HMAC. HMAC treats the hash function as a "black box." This has two benefits. First, an existing implementation of a hash function can be used as a module in implementing HMAC. In this way, the bulk of the HMAC code is prepackaged and ready to use without modification. Second, if it is ever desired to replace a given hash function in an HMAC implementation, all that is required is to remove the existing hash function module and drop in the new module. This could be done if a faster hash function were desired. More important, if the security of the embedded hash function were compromised, the security of HMAC could be retained simply by replacing the embedded hash function with a more secure one.

The last design objective in the preceding list is, in fact, the main advantage of HMAC over other proposed hash-based schemes. HMAC can be proven secure provided that the embedded hash function has some reasonable cryptographic strengths. We return to this point later in this section, but first we examine the structure of HMAC.

HMAC ALGORITHM Figure 3.6 illustrates the overall operation of HMAC. The following terms are defined:

H = embedded hash function (e.g., SHA-1)

M = message input to HMAC (including the padding specified in the embedded hash function)

Y_i = ith block of M, $0 \le i \le (L - 1)$

L = number of blocks in M

b = number of bits in a block

n = length of hash code produced by embedded hash function

K = secret key; if key length is greater than b, the key is input to the hash function to produce an n-bit key; recommended length is $> n$

K^+ = K padded with zeros on the left so that the result is b bits in length

ipad = 00110110 (36 in hexadecimal) repeated $b/8$ times

opad = 01011100 (5C in hexadecimal) repeated $b/8$ times

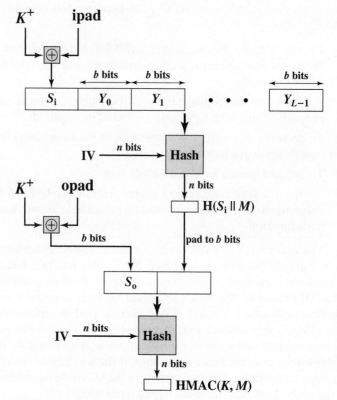

Figure 3.6 HMAC Structure

Then HMAC can be expressed as

$$\text{HMAC}(K, M) = \text{H}[(K^+ \oplus \text{opad}) \,\|\, \text{H}[(K^+ \oplus \text{ipad}) \,\|\, M]]$$

In words, HMAC is defined as follows:

1. Append zeros to the left end of K to create a b-bit string K^+ (e.g., if K is of length 160 bits and $b = 512$, then K will be appended with 44 zero bytes).
2. XOR (bitwise exclusive-OR) K^+ with ipad to produce the b-bit block S_i.
3. Append M to S_i.
4. Apply H to the stream generated in step 3.
5. XOR K^+ with opad to produce the b-bit block S_o.
6. Append the hash result from step 4 to S_o.
7. Apply H to the stream generated in step 6 and output the result.

Note that the XOR with ipad results in flipping one-half of the bits of K. Similarly, the XOR with opad results in flipping one-half of the bits of K, but a different set of bits. In effect, by passing S_i and S_o through the hash algorithm, we have pseudorandomly generated two keys from K.

HMAC should execute in approximately the same time as the embedded hash function for long messages. HMAC adds three executions of the basic hash function (for S_i, S_o, and the block produced from the inner hash).

MACs Based on Block Ciphers

In this section, we look at several MACs based on the use of a block cipher.

CIPHER-BASED MESSAGE AUTHENTICATION CODE (CMAC) The Cipher-based Message Authentication Code mode of operation is for use with AES and triple DES. It is specified in NIST Special Publication 800-38B.

First, let us consider the operation of CMAC when the message is an integer multiple n of the cipher block length b. For AES, $b = 128$, and for triple DES, $b = 64$. The message is divided into n blocks $(M_1, M_2, \ldots, M_n)$. The algorithm makes use of a k-bit encryption key K and an n-bit key, K_1. For AES, the key size k is 128, 192, or 256 bits; for triple DES, the key size is 112 or 168 bits. CMAC is calculated as follows (Figure 3.7).

$$C_1 = E(K, M_1)$$
$$C_2 = E(K, [M_2 \oplus C_1])$$
$$C_3 = E(K, [M_3 \oplus C_2])$$
$$\cdot$$
$$\cdot$$
$$\cdot$$
$$C_n = E(K, [M_N \oplus C_{n-1} \oplus K_1])$$
$$T = \text{MSB}_{Tlen}(C_n)$$

where

$\quad T \qquad$ = message authentication code, also referred to as the tag
$\quad Tlen \quad$ = bit length of T
$\quad \text{MSB}_s(X)$ = the s leftmost bits of the bit string X

If the message is not an integer multiple of the cipher block length, then the final block is padded to the right (least significant bits) with a 1 and as many 0s as necessary so that the final block is also of length b. The CMAC operation then proceeds as before, except that a different n-bit key K_2 is used instead of K_1.

To generate the two n-bit keys, the block cipher is applied to the block that consists entirely of 0 bits. The first subkey is derived from the resulting ciphertext by a left shift of one bit and, conditionally, by XORing a constant that depends on the block size. The second subkey is derived in the same manner from the first subkey.

COUNTER WITH CIPHER BLOCK CHAINING-MESSAGE AUTHENTICATION CODE The Counter with Cipher Block Chaining-Message Authentication Code (CCM) mode of operation, defined in NIST SP 800-38C, is referred to as an **authenticated encryption** mode. "Authenticated encryption" is a term used to describe encryption systems that simultaneously protect confidentiality and authenticity (integrity) of communications. Many applications and protocols require both forms of security, but until recently the two services have been designed separately.

(a) Message length is integer multiple of block size

(b) Message length is not integer multiple of block size

Figure 3.7   Cipher-Based Message Authentication Code

The key algorithmic ingredients of CCM are the AES encryption algorithm (Section 2.2), the CTR mode of operation (Section 2.5), and the CMAC authentication algorithm. A single key K is used for both encryption and MAC algorithms. The input to the CCM encryption process consists of three elements.

1. Data that will be both authenticated and encrypted. This is the plaintext message P of data block.

2. Associated data A that will be authenticated but not encrypted. An example is a protocol header that must be transmitted in the clear for proper protocol operation but which needs to be authenticated.

3. A nonce N that is assigned to the payload and the associated data. This is a unique value that is different for every instance during the lifetime of a protocol association and is intended to prevent replay attacks and certain other types of attacks.

Figure 3.8 illustrates the operation of CCM. For authentication, the input includes the nonce, the associated data, and the plaintext. This input is formatted as a sequence of blocks B_0 through B_r. The first block contains the nonce plus some formatting bits that indicate the lengths of the N, A, and P elements. This is followed by zero or more blocks that contain A, followed by zero of more blocks that contain P. The resulting sequence of blocks serves as input to the CMAC algorithm,

(a) Authentication

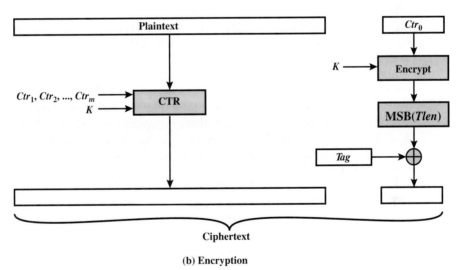

(b) Encryption

Figure 3.8   Counter with Cipher Block Chaining-Message Authentication Code

which produces a MAC value with length *Tlen*, which is less than or equal to the block length (Figure 3.8a).

For encryption, a sequence of counters is generated that must be independent of the nonce. The authentication tag is encrypted in CTR mode using the single counter *Ctr₀*. The *Tlen* most significant bits of the output are XORed with the tag to produce an encrypted tag. The remaining counters are used for the CTR mode encryption of the plaintext (Figure 2.11). The encrypted plaintext is concatenated with the encrypted tag to form the ciphertext output (Figure 3.8b).

3.4 PUBLIC-KEY CRYPTOGRAPHY PRINCIPLES

Of equal importance to conventional encryption is **public-key encryption**, which finds use in message authentication and key distribution. This section looks first at the basic concept of public-key encryption and takes a preliminary look at key distribution issues. Section 3.5 examines the two most important public-key algorithms: RSA and Diffie–Hellman. Section 3.6 introduces digital signatures.

Public–Key Encryption Structure

Public-key encryption, first publicly proposed by Diffie and Hellman in 1976 [DIFF76], is the first truly revolutionary advance in encryption in literally thousands of years. Public-key algorithms are based on mathematical functions rather than on simple operations on bit patterns, such as are used in symmetric encryption algorithms. More important, public-key cryptography is asymmetric, involving the use of two separate keys—in contrast to the symmetric conventional encryption, which uses only one key. The use of two keys has profound consequences in the areas of confidentiality, key distribution, and authentication.

Before proceeding, we should first mention several common misconceptions concerning public-key encryption. One is that public-key encryption is more secure from cryptanalysis than conventional encryption. In fact, the security of any encryption scheme depends on (1) the length of the key and (2) the computational work involved in breaking a cipher. There is nothing in principle about either conventional or public-key encryption that makes one superior to another from the point of view of resisting cryptanalysis. A second misconception is that public-key encryption is a general-purpose technique that has made conventional encryption obsolete. On the contrary, because of the computational overhead of current public-key encryption schemes, there seems no foreseeable likelihood that conventional encryption will be abandoned. Finally, there is a feeling that key distribution is trivial when using public-key encryption, compared to the rather cumbersome handshaking involved with key distribution centers for conventional encryption. In fact, some form of protocol is needed, often involving a central agent, and the procedures involved are no simpler or any more efficient than those required for conventional encryption.

A public-key encryption scheme has six ingredients (Figure 3.9a).

- **Plaintext:** This is the readable message or data that is fed into the algorithm as input.

- **Encryption algorithm:** The encryption algorithm performs various transformations on the plaintext.

- **Public and private key:** This is a pair of keys that have been selected so that if one is used for encryption, the other is used for decryption. The exact transformations performed by the encryption algorithm depend on the public or private key that is provided as input.

- **Ciphertext:** This is the scrambled message produced as output. It depends on the plaintext and the key. For a given message, two different keys will produce two different ciphertexts.

Figure 3.9   Public-Key Cryptography

- **Decryption algorithm:** This algorithm accepts the ciphertext and the matching key and produces the original plaintext.

As the names suggest, the public key of the pair is made public for others to use, while the private key is known only to its owner. A general-purpose public-key cryptographic algorithm relies on one key for encryption and a different but related key for decryption.

The essential steps are the following:

1. Each user generates a pair of keys to be used for the encryption and decryption of messages.

2. Each user places one of the two keys in a public register or other accessible file. This is the public key. The companion key is kept private. As Figure 3.9a suggests, each user maintains a collection of public keys obtained from others.

3. If Bob wishes to send a private message to Alice, Bob encrypts the message using Alice's public key.

4. When Alice receives the message, she decrypts it using her private key. No other recipient can decrypt the message because only Alice knows Alice's private key.

With this approach, all participants have access to public keys, and private keys are generated locally by each participant and therefore need never be distributed. As long as a user protects his or her private key, incoming communication is secure. At any time, a user can change the private key and publish the companion public key to replace the old public key.

The key used in conventional encryption is typically referred to as a **secret key**. The two keys used for public-key encryption are referred to as the **public key** and the **private key**. Invariably, the private key is kept secret, but it is referred to as a private key rather than a secret key to avoid confusion with conventional encryption.

Applications for Public-Key Cryptosystems

Before proceeding, we need to clarify one aspect of public-key cryptosystems that is otherwise likely to lead to confusion. Public-key systems are characterized by the use of a cryptographic type of algorithm with two keys, one held private and one available publicly. Depending on the application, the sender uses either the sender's private key, the receiver's public key, or both to perform some type of cryptographic function. In broad terms, we can classify the use of public-key cryptosystems into three categories:

- **Encryption/decryption:** The sender encrypts a message with the recipient's public key.

- **Digital signature:** The sender "signs" a message with its private key. Signing is achieved by a cryptographic algorithm applied to the message or to a small block of data that is a function of the message.

- **Key exchange:** Two sides cooperate to exchange a session key. Several different approaches are possible, involving the private key(s) of one or both parties.

Some algorithms are suitable for all three applications, whereas others can be used only for one or two of these applications. Table 3.2 indicates the applications supported by the algorithms discussed in this chapter: RSA and Diffie–Hellman. This table also includes the Digital Signature Standard (DSS) and elliptic-curve cryptography, also mentioned later in this chapter.

Table 3.2 Applications for Public-Key Cryptosystems

Algorithm	Encryption/Decryption	Digital Signature	Key Exchange
RSA	Yes	Yes	Yes
Diffie–Hellman	No	No	Yes
DSS	No	Yes	No
Elliptic curve	Yes	Yes	Yes

Requirements for Public-Key Cryptography

The cryptosystem illustrated in Figure 3.9 depends on a cryptographic algorithm based on two related keys. Diffie and Hellman postulated this system without demonstrating that such algorithms exist. However, they did lay out the conditions that such algorithms must fulfill [DIFF76]:

1. It is computationally easy for a party B to generate a pair (public key PU_b, private key PR_b).

2. It is computationally easy for a sender A, knowing the public key and the message to be encrypted, M, to generate the corresponding ciphertext:

$$C = E(PU_b, M)$$

3. It is computationally easy for the receiver B to decrypt the resulting ciphertext using the private key to recover the original message:

$$M = D(PR_b, C) = D[PR_b, E(PU_b, M)]$$

4. It is computationally infeasible for an opponent, knowing the public key, PU_b, to determine the private key, PR_b.

5. It is computationally infeasible for an opponent, knowing the public key, PU_b, and a ciphertext, C, to recover the original message, M.

We can add a sixth requirement that, although useful, is not necessary for all public-key applications.

1. Either of the two related keys can be used for encryption, with the other used for decryption.

$$M = D[PU_b, E(PR_b, M)] = D[PR_b, E(PU_b, M)]$$

3.5 PUBLIC-KEY CRYPTOGRAPHY ALGORITHMS

The two most widely used public-key algorithms are RSA and Diffie–Hellman. We look at both of these in this section and then briefly introduce two other algorithms.[4]

---

[4]This section uses some elementary concepts from number theory. For a review, see Appendix A.

The RSA Public-Key Encryption Algorithm

One of the first public-key schemes was developed in 1977 by Ron Rivest, Adi Shamir, and Len Adleman at MIT and first published in 1978 [RIVE78]. The RSA scheme has since that time reigned supreme as the most widely accepted and implemented approach to public-key encryption. **RSA** is a block cipher in which the plaintext and ciphertext are integers between 0 and $n - 1$ for some n.

Encryption and decryption are of the following form period for some plaintext block M and ciphertext block C:

$$C = M^e \bmod n$$
$$M = C^d \bmod n = (M^e)^d \bmod n = M^{ed} \bmod n$$

Both sender and receiver must know the values of n and e, and only the receiver knows the value of d. This is a public-key encryption algorithm with a public key of $KU = \{e, n\}$ and a private key of $KR = \{d, n\}$. For this algorithm to be satisfactory for public-key encryption, the following requirements must be met.

1. It is possible to find values of e, d, n such that $M^{ed} \bmod n = M$ for all $M < n$.

2. It is relatively easy to calculate M^e and C^d for all values of $M < n$.

3. It is infeasible to determine d given e and n.

The first two requirements are easily met. The third requirement can be met for large values of e and n.

Figure 3.10 summarizes the RSA algorithm. Begin by selecting two prime numbers p and q and calculating their product n, which is the modulus for encryption and decryption. Next, we need the quantity $\phi(n)$, referred to as the Euler totient of n, which is the number of positive integers less than n and relatively prime to n. Then select an integer e that is relatively prime to $\phi(n)$ [i.e., the greatest common divisor of e and $\phi(n)$ is 1]. Finally, calculate d as the multiplicative inverse of e, modulo $\phi(n)$. It can be shown that d and e have the desired properties.

Suppose that user A has published its public key and that user B wishes to send the message M to A. Then B calculates $C = M^e \ (\bmod \ n)$ and transmits C. On receipt of this ciphertext, user A decrypts by calculating $M = C^d \ (\bmod \ n)$.

An example, from [SING99], is shown in Figure 3.11. For this example, the keys were generated as follows:

1. Select two prime numbers, $p = 17$ and $q = 11$.

2. Calculate $n = pq = 17 \times 11 = 187$.

3. Calculate $\phi(n) = (p - 1)(q - 1) = 16 \times 10 = 160$.

4. Select e such that e is relatively prime to $\phi(n) = 160$ and less than $\phi(n)$; we choose $e = 7$.

5. Determine d such that $de \bmod 160 = 1$ and $d < 160$. The correct value is $d = 23$, because $23 \times 7 = 161 = (1 \times 160) + 1$.

The resulting keys are public key $PU = \{7, 187\}$ and private key $PR = \{23, 187\}$. The example shows the use of these keys for a plaintext input of $M = 88$.

Figure 3.10   The RSA Algorithm

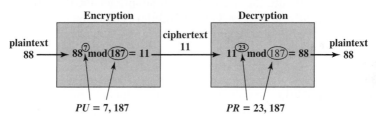

Figure 3.11   Example of RSA Algorithm

For encryption, we need to calculate $C = 88^7 \bmod 187$. Exploiting the properties of modular arithmetic, we can do this as follows:

$88^7 \bmod 187 = [(88^4 \bmod 187) \times (88^2 \bmod 187) \times (88^1 \bmod 187)] \bmod 187$

$88^1 \bmod 187 = 88$

$88^2 \bmod 187 = 7744 \bmod 187 \ = 77$

$88^4 \bmod 187 = 59{,}969{,}536 \bmod 187 \ = 132$

$88^7 \bmod 187 = (88 \times 77 \times 132) \bmod 187 = 894{,}432 \bmod 187 = 11$

For decryption, we calculate $M = 11^{23} \bmod 187$:

$$11^{23} \bmod 187 = [(11^1 \bmod 187) \times (11^2 \bmod 187) \times (11^4 \bmod 187) \times$$
$$(11^8 \bmod 187) \times (11^8 \bmod 187)] \bmod 187$$

$$11^1 \bmod 187 = 11$$

$$11^2 \bmod 187 = 121$$

$$11^4 \bmod 187 = 14{,}641 \bmod 187 = 55$$

$$11^8 \bmod 187 = 214{,}358{,}881 \bmod 187 = 33$$

$$11^{23} \bmod 187 = (11 \times 121 \times 55 \times 33 \times 33) \bmod 187$$
$$= 79{,}720{,}245 \bmod 187 = 88$$

There are two possible approaches to defeating the RSA algorithm. The first is the brute-force approach: Try all possible private keys. Thus, the larger the number of bits in e and d, the more secure is the algorithm. However, because the calculations involved (both in key generation and in encryption/decryption) are complex, the larger the size of the key, the slower the system will run.

Most discussions of the cryptanalysis of RSA have focused on the task of factoring n into its two prime factors. For a large n with large prime factors, factoring is a hard problem, but not as hard as it used to be. A striking illustration of this occurred in 1977; the three inventors of RSA challenged *Scientific American* readers to decode a cipher they printed in Martin Gardner's "Mathematical Games" column [GARD77]. They offered a $100 reward for the return of a plaintext sentence, an event they predicted might not occur for some 40 quadrillion years. In April of 1994, a group working over the Internet and using over 1600 computers claimed the prize after only eight months of work [LEUT94]. This challenge used a public-key size (length of n) of 129 decimal digits (approximately 428 bits). This result does not invalidate the use of RSA; it simply means that larger key sizes must be used. Currently, a 1024-bit key size (about 300 decimal digits) is considered strong enough for virtually all applications.

Diffie–Hellman Key Exchange

The first published public-key algorithm appeared in the seminal paper by Diffie and Hellman that defined public-key cryptography [DIFF76] and is generally referred to as the **Diffie–Hellman key exchange**. A number of commercial products employ this key exchange technique.

The purpose of the algorithm is to enable two users to exchange a secret key securely that then can be used for subsequent encryption of messages. The algorithm itself is limited to the exchange of the keys.

The Diffie–Hellman algorithm depends for its effectiveness on the difficulty of computing discrete logarithms. Briefly, we can define the discrete logarithm in the following way. First, we define a primitive root of a prime number p as one whose powers generate all the integers from 1 to $p - 1$. That is, if a is a primitive root of the prime number p, then the numbers

$$a \bmod p, a^2 \bmod p, \ldots, a^{p-1} \bmod p$$

are distinct and consist of the integers from 1 through $p - 1$ in some permutation.

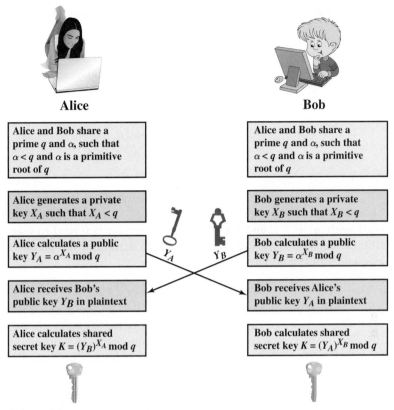

Figure 3.12 The Diffie–Hellman Key Exchange

For any integer b less than p and a primitive root a of prime number p, one can find a unique exponent i such that

$$b = a^i \bmod p \quad 0 \le i \le (p - 1)$$

The exponent i is referred to as the discrete logarithm, or index, of b for the base a, mod p. We denote this value as $\mathrm{dlog}_{a,p}(b)$.[5]

THE ALGORITHM With this background, we can define the Diffie–Hellman key exchange, which is summarized in Figure 3.12. For this scheme, there are two publicly known numbers: a prime number q and an integer α that is a primitive root of q. Suppose the users A and B wish to exchange a key. User A selects a random integer $X_A < q$ and computes $Y_A = \alpha^{X_A} \bmod q$. Similarly, user B independently selects a random integer $X_B < q$ and computes $Y_B = \alpha^{X_B} \bmod q$. Each side keeps the X value private and makes the Y value available publicly to the other side. User A computes

---

[5]Many texts refer to the discrete logarithm as the *index*. There is no generally agreed notation for this concept, much less an agreed name.

the key as $K = (Y_B)^{X_A} \bmod q$ and user B computes the key as $K = (Y_A)^{X_B} \bmod q$. These two calculations produce identical results:

$$
\begin{aligned}
K &= (Y_B)^{X_A} \bmod q \\
&= (\alpha^{X_B} \bmod q)^{X_A} \bmod q \\
&= (\alpha^{X_B})^{X_A} \bmod q \\
&= \alpha^{X_B X_A} \bmod q \\
&= (\alpha^{X_A})^{X_B} \bmod q \\
&= (\alpha^{X_A} \bmod q)^{X_B} \bmod q \\
&= (Y_A)^{X_B} \bmod q
\end{aligned}
$$

The result is that the two sides have exchanged a secret value. Furthermore, because X_A and X_B are private, an adversary only has the following ingredients to work with: q, α, Y_A, and Y_B. Thus, the adversary is forced to take a discrete logarithm to determine the key. For example, to determine the private key of user B, an adversary must compute

$$X_B = \text{dlog}_{\alpha,q}(Y_B)$$

The adversary can then calculate the key K in the same manner as user B does.

The security of the Diffie–Hellman key exchange lies in the fact that, while it is relatively easy to calculate exponentials modulo a prime, it is very difficult to calculate discrete logarithms. For large primes, the latter task is considered infeasible.

Here is an example. Key exchange is based on the use of the prime number $q = 353$ and a primitive root of 353, in this case $\alpha = 3$. A and B select secret keys $X_A = 97$ and $X_B = 233$, respectively. Each computes its public key:

A computes $Y_A = 3^{97} \bmod 353 = 40$.

B computes $Y_B = 3^{233} \bmod 353 = 248$.

After they exchange public keys, each can compute the common secret key:

A computes $K = (Y_B)^{X_A} \bmod 353 = 248^{97} \bmod 353 = 160$.

B computes $K = (Y_A)^{X_B} \bmod 353 = 40^{233} \bmod 353 = 160$.

We assume an attacker would have available the following information:

$$q = 353; \quad a = 3; \quad Y_A = 40; \quad Y_B = 248$$

In this simple example, it would be possible to determine the secret key 160 by brute force. In particular, an attacker E can determine the common key by discovering a solution to the equation $3^a \bmod 353 = 40$ or the equation $3^b \bmod 353 = 248$. The brute-force approach is to calculate powers of 3 modulo 353, stopping when the result equals either 40 or 248. The desired answer is reached with the exponent value of 97, which provides $3^{97} \bmod 353 = 40$.

With larger numbers, the problem becomes impractical.

KEY EXCHANGE PROTOCOLS Figure 3.12 shows a simple protocol that makes use of the Diffie–Hellman calculation. Suppose that user A wishes to set up a connection with user B and use a secret key to encrypt messages on that connection. User A can generate a one-time private key X_A, calculate Y_A, and send that to user B. User B responds by generating a private value X_B, calculating Y_B, and sending Y_B to user A. Both users can now calculate the key. The necessary public values q and α would need to be known ahead of time. Alternatively, user A could pick values for q and include those in the first message.

As an example of another use of the Diffie–Hellman algorithm, suppose that a group of users (e.g., all users on a LAN) each generate a long-lasting private value X_A and calculate a public value Y_A. These public values, together with global public values for q and α, are stored in some central directory. At any time, user B can access user A's public value, calculate a secret key, and use that to send an encrypted message to user A. If the central directory is trusted, then this form of communication provides both confidentiality and a degree of authentication. Because only A and B can determine the key, no other user can read the message (confidentiality). Recipient A knows that only user B could have created a message using this key (authentication). However, the technique does not protect against replay attacks.

MAN-IN-THE-MIDDLE ATTACK The protocol depicted in Figure 3.12 is insecure against a man-in-the-middle attack. Suppose Alice and Bob wish to exchange keys, and Darth is the adversary. The attack proceeds as follows (Figure 3.13):

1. Darth prepares for the attack by generating two random private keys X_{D1} and X_{D2}, and then computing the corresponding public keys Y_{D1} and Y_{D2}.
2. Alice transmits Y_A to Bob.
3. Darth intercepts Y_A and transmits Y_{D1} to Bob. Darth also calculates $K2 = (Y_A)^{X_{D2}} \bmod q$.
4. Bob receives Y_{D1} and calculates $K1 = (Y_{D1})^{X_B} \bmod q$.
5. Bob transmits Y_B to Alice.
6. Darth intercepts Y_B and transmits Y_{D2} to Alice. Darth calculates $K1 = (Y_B)^{X_{D1}} \bmod q$.
7. Alice receives Y_{D2} and calculates $K2 = (Y_{D2})^{X_A} \bmod q$.

At this point, Bob and Alice think that they share a secret key. Instead Bob and Darth share secret key $K1$, and Alice and Darth share secret key $K2$. All future communication between Bob and Alice is compromised in the following way:

1. Alice sends an encrypted message M: $E(K2, M)$.
2. Darth intercepts the encrypted message and decrypts it to recover M.
3. Darth sends Bob $E(K1, M)$ or $E(K1, M')$, where M' is any message. In the first case, Darth simply wants to eavesdrop on the communication without altering it. In the second case, Darth wants to modify the message going to Bob.

The key exchange protocol is vulnerable to such an attack because it does not authenticate the participants. This vulnerability can be overcome with the use of digital signatures and public-key certificates; these topics are explored later in this chapter and in Chapter 4.

Figure 3.13 Man-in-the-Middle Attack

Other Public-Key Cryptography Algorithms

Two other public-key algorithms have found commercial acceptance: DSS and elliptic-curve cryptography.

DIGITAL SIGNATURE STANDARD The National Institute of Standards and Technology (NIST) has published Federal Information Processing Standard FIPS PUB 186, known as the **Digital Signature Standard (DSS)**. The DSS makes use of the SHA-1 and presents a new digital signature technique, the Digital Signature Algorithm (DSA). The DSS was originally proposed in 1991 and revised in 1993 in response to public feedback concerning the security of the scheme. There was a further minor revision in 1996. The DSS uses an algorithm that is designed to provide only the digital signature function. Unlike RSA, it cannot be used for encryption or key exchange.

ELLIPTIC-CURVE CRYPTOGRAPHY The vast majority of the products and standards that use public-key cryptography for encryption and digital signatures use RSA.

The bit length for secure RSA use has increased over recent years, and this has put a heavier processing load on applications using RSA. This burden has ramifications, especially for electronic commerce sites that conduct large numbers of secure transactions. Recently, a competing system has begun to challenge RSA: **elliptic curve cryptography (ECC)**. Already, ECC is showing up in standardization efforts, including the IEEE P1363 Standard for Public-Key Cryptography.

The principal attraction of ECC compared to RSA is that it appears to offer equal security for a far smaller bit size, thereby reducing processing overhead. On the other hand, although the theory of ECC has been around for some time, it is only recently that products have begun to appear and that there has been sustained cryptanalytic interest in probing for weaknesses. Thus, the confidence level in ECC is not yet as high as that in RSA.

ECC is fundamentally more difficult to explain than either RSA or Diffie–Hellman, and a full mathematical description is beyond the scope of this book. The technique is based on the use of a mathematical construct known as the elliptic curve.

3.6 DIGITAL SIGNATURES

Public-key encryption can be used in another way, as illustrated in Figure 3.9b. Suppose that Bob wants to send a message to Alice, and although it is not important that the message be kept secret, he wants Alice to be certain that the message is indeed from him. In this case, Bob uses his own private key to encrypt the message. When Alice receives the ciphertext, she finds that she can decrypt it with Bob's public key, thus proving that the message must have been encrypted by Bob. No one else has Bob's private key, and therefore no one else could have created a ciphertext that could be decrypted with Bob's public key. Therefore, the entire encrypted message serves as a **digital signature**. In addition, it is impossible to alter the message without access to Bob's private key, so the message is authenticated both in terms of source and in terms of data integrity.

In the preceding scheme, the entire message is encrypted. Although validating both author and contents, this requires a great deal of storage. Each document must be kept in plaintext to be used for practical purposes. A copy also must be stored in ciphertext so that the origin and contents can be verified in case of a dispute. A more efficient way of achieving the same results is to encrypt a small block of bits that is a function of the document. Such a block, called an authenticator, must have the property that it is infeasible to change the document without changing the authenticator. If the authenticator is encrypted with the sender's private key, it serves as a signature that verifies origin, content, and sequencing. A secure hash code such as SHA-1 can serve this function. Figure 3.2b illustrates this scenario.

It is important to emphasize that the encryption process just described does not provide confidentiality. That is, the message being sent is safe from alteration but not safe from eavesdropping. This is obvious in the case of a signature based on a portion of the message, because the rest of the message is transmitted in the clear. Even in the case of complete encryption, there is no protection of confidentiality because any observer can decrypt the message by using the sender's public key.

3.7 RECOMMENDED READING

Solid treatments of hash functions and message authentication codes are found in [STIN06] and [MENE97].

The recommended treatments of encryption provided in Chapter 2 cover public-key as well as conventional encryption. [DIFF88] describes in detail the several attempts to devise secure two-key cryptoalgorithms and the gradual evolution of a variety of protocols based on them.

DIFF88 Diffie, W. "The First Ten Years of Public-Key Cryptography." *Proceedings of the IEEE,* May 1988.

MENE97 Menezes, A.; Oorschot, P.; and Vanstone, S. *Handbook of Applied Cryptography.* Boca Raton, FL: CRC Press, 1997.

STIN06 Stinson, D. *Cryptography: Theory and Practice.* Boca Raton, FL: Chapman & Hall/ CRC Press, 2006.

3.8 KEY TERMS, REVIEW QUESTIONS, AND PROBLEMS

Key Terms

authenticated encryption	key exchange	public-key certificate
Diffie–Hellman key exchange	MD5	public-key encryption
digital signature	message authentication	RSA
Digital Signature Standard (DSS)	message authentication code (MAC)	secret key
elliptic-curve cryptography (ECC)	message digest	secure hash function
HMAC	one-way hash function	SHA-1
	private key	strong collision resistant
	public key	weak collision resistant

Review Questions

3.1   What is message authentication? How is the authenticity of a message decided?

3.2   What is a message authentication code?

3.3   What is a one-way hash function? How is it different from message authentication code?

3.4   List the properties of a strong hash function.

3.5   Compare SHA-1 and SHA-2 with respect to SHA parameters.

3.6   Lists the design objectives for HMAC.

3.7   Differentiate between public-key cryptosystem and symmetric encryption algorithm.

3.8   List the public-key cryptography algorithm used in digital signatures, encryption/ decryption, and key exchange.

3.9   In what way is the Diffie–Hellman key exchange algorithm insecure against a man-in-the-middle attack?

Problems

3.1 Consider a 32-bit hash function defined as the concatenation of two 16-bit functions: XOR and RXOR, which are defined in Section 3.2 as "two simple hash functions."

    a. Will this checksum detect all errors caused by an odd number of error bits? Explain.

    b. Will this checksum detect all errors caused by an even number of error bits? If not, characterize the error patterns that will cause the checksum to fail.

    c. Comment on the effectiveness of this function for use as a hash function for authentication.

3.2 Suppose $H(m)$ is a collision-resistant hash function that maps a message of arbitrary bit length into an n-bit hash value. Is it true that, for all messages x, x' with $x \neq x'$, we have $H(x) \neq H(x')$? Explain your answer.

3.3 State the value of the padding field in SHA-512 if the length of the message is

    a. 4987 bits

    b. 4199 bits

    c. 1227 bits

3.4 State the value of the length field in SHA-512 if the length of the message is

    a. 3967 bits

    b. 3968 bits

    c. 3969 bits

3.5 **a.** Consider the following hash function. Messages are in the form of a sequence of decimal numbers, $M = (a_1, a_2, \ldots, a_t)$. The hash value h is calculated as $\left(\sum_{i=1}^{t} a_i \right) \bmod n$, for some predefined value n. Does this hash function satisfy any of the requirements for a hash function listed in Section 3.2? Explain your answer.

    b. Repeat part (a) for the hash function $h = \left(\sum_{i=1}^{t} (a_i)^2 \right) \bmod n$.

    c. Calculate the hash function of part (b) for $M = (237, 632, 913, 423, 349)$ and $n = 757$.

3.6 This problem introduces a hash function similar in spirit to SHA that operates on letters instead of binary data. It is called the *toy tetragraph hash* (tth).[6] Given a message consisting of a sequence of letters, tth produces a hash value consisting of four letters. First, tth divides the message into blocks of 16 letters, ignoring spaces, punctuation, and capitalization. If the message length is not divisible by 16, it is padded out with nulls. A four-number running total is maintained that starts out with the value $(0, 0, 0, 0)$; this is input to the compression function for processing the first block. The compression function consists of two rounds. **Round 1:** Get the next block of text and arrange it as a row-wise 4 block of text and covert it to numbers (A = 0, B = 1, etc.). For example, for the block ABCDEFGHIJKLMNOP, we have

A	B	C	D
E	F	G	H
I	J	K	L
M	N	O	P

0	1	2	3
4	5	6	7
8	9	10	11
12	13	14	15

Then, add each column mod 26 and add the result to the running total, mod 26. In this example, the running total is $(24, 2, 6, 10)$. **Round 2:** Using the matrix from round 1,

---

[6]I thank William K. Mason of the magazine staff of *The Cryptogram* for providing this example.

rotate the first row left by 1, second row left by 2, third row left by 3, and reverse the order of the fourth row. In our example:

B	C	D	A
G	H	E	F
L	I	J	K
P	O	N	M

1	2	3	0
6	7	4	5
11	8	9	10
15	14	13	12

Now, add each column mod 26 and add the result to the running total. The new running total is (5, 7, 9, 11). This running total is now the input into the first round of the compression function for the next block of text. After the final block is processed, convert the final running total to letters. For example, if the message is ABCDE FGHIJKLMNOP, then the hash is FHJL.

a. Draw figures comparable to Figures 3.4 and 3.5 to depict the overall tth logic and the compression function logic.

b. Calculate the hash function for the 48-letter message "I leave twenty million dollars to my friendly cousin Bill."

c. To demonstrate the weakness of tth, find a 48-letter block that produces the same hash as that just derived. *Hint:* Use lots of A's.

3.7 It is possible to use a hash function to construct a block cipher with a structure similar to DES. Because a hash function is one way and a block cipher must be reversible (to decrypt), how is it possible?

3.8 Now consider the opposite problem: Use an encryption algorithm to construct a one-way hash function. Consider using RSA with a known key. Then process a message consisting of a sequence of blocks as follows: Encrypt the first block, XOR the result with the second block and encrypt again, and so on. Show that this scheme is not secure by solving the following problem. Given a two-block message B1, B2, and its hash, we have

$$RSAH(B1, B2) = RSA(RSA(B1) \oplus B2)$$

Given an arbitrary block C1, choose C2 so that RSAH(C1, C2) = RSAH(B1, B2). Thus, the hash function does not satisfy weak collision resistance.

3.9 One of the most widely used MACs, referred to as the Data Authentication Algorithm, is based on DES. The algorithm is both a FIPS publication (FIPS PUB 113) and an ANSI standard (X9.17). The algorithm can be defined as using the cipher block chaining (CBC) mode of operation of DES with an initialization vector of zero (Figure 2.9). The data (e.g., message, record, file, or program) to be authenticated is grouped into contiguous 64-bit blocks: $P_1, P_2, \ldots, P_N$. If necessary, the final block is padded on the right with 0s to form a full 64-bit block. The MAC consists of either the entire ciphertext block C_N or the leftmost M bits of the block with $16 \leq M \leq 64$. Show that the same result can be produced using the cipher feedback mode.

3.10 In this problem, we will compare the security services that are provided by digital signatures (DS) and message authentication codes (MAC). We assume that Oscar is able to observe all messages sent from Alice to Bob and vice versa. Oscar has no knowledge of any keys but the public one in case of DS. State whether and how (i) DS and (ii) MAC protect against each attack. The value auth(x) is computed with a DS or a MAC algorithm, respectively.

a. (Message integrity) Alice sends a message x = "Transfer $1000 to Mark" in the clear and also sends auth(x) to Bob. Oscar intercepts the message and replaces "Mark" with "Oscar." Will Bob detect this?

b. (Replay) Alice sends a message x = "Transfer $1000 to Oscar" in the clear and also sends auth(x) to Bob. Oscar observes the message and signature and sends them 100 times to Bob. Will Bob detect this?

    c. (Sender Authentication with cheating third party) Oscar claims that he sent some message x with a valid `auth(x)` to Bob, but Alice claims the same. Can Bob clear the question in either case?

    d. (Authentication with Bob cheating) Bob claims that he received a message x with a valid signature `auth(x)` from Alice (e.g., "Transfer $1000 from Alice to Bob") but Alice claims she has never sent it. Can Alice clear this question in either case?

3.11 Figure 3.14 shows an alternative means of implementing HMAC.

    a. Describe the operation of this implementation.

    b. What potential benefit does this implementation have over that shown in Figure 3.6?

3.12 In this problem, we demonstrate that for CMAC, a variant that XORs the second key after applying the final encryption doesn't work. Let us consider this for the case of the message being an integer multiple of the block size. Then the variant can be expressed as $VMAC(K, M) = CBC(K, M) \oplus K_1$. Now suppose an adversary is able to ask for the MACs of three messages: the message $\mathbf{0} = 0^n$, where n is the cipher block size; the message $\mathbf{1} = 1^n$; and the message $\mathbf{1} \| \mathbf{0}$. As a result of these three queries, the adversary gets $T_0 = CBC(K, \mathbf{0}) \oplus K_1$; $T_1 = CBC(K, \mathbf{1}) \oplus K_1$ and $T_2 = CBC(K, [CBC(K, \mathbf{1})]) \oplus K_1$. Show that the adversary can compute the correct MAC for the (unqueried) message $\mathbf{0} \| (T_0 \oplus T_1)$.

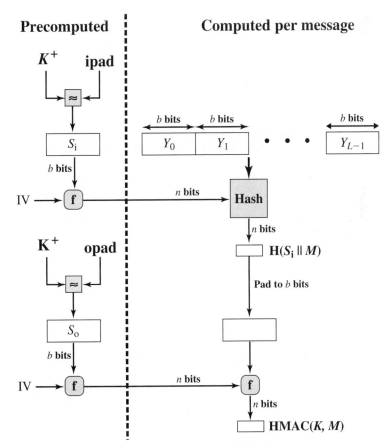

Figure 3.14 Efficient Implementation of HMAC

3.13 Prior to the discovery of any specific public-key schemes, such as RSA, an existence proof was developed whose purpose was to demonstrate that public-key encryption is possible in theory. Consider the functions $f_1(x_1) = z_1$; $f_2(x_2, y_2) = z_2$; $f_3(x_3, y_3) = z_3$, where all values are integers with $1 \leq x_i, y_i, z_i \leq N$. Function f_1 can be represented by a vector M1 of length N in which the kth entry is the value of $f_1(k)$. Similarly, f_2 and f_3 can be represented by $N \times N$ matrices M2 and M3. The intent is to represent the encryption/decryption process by table lookups for tables with very large values of N. Such tables would be impractically huge but in principle could be constructed. The scheme works as follows: Construct M1 with a random permutation of all integers between 1 and N; that is, each integer appears exactly once in M1. Construct M2 so that each row contains a random permutation of the first N integers. Finally, fill in M3 to satisfy the condition:

$$f_3(f_2(f_1(k), p), k) = p \quad \text{for all } k, p \text{ with } 1 \leq k, p \leq N$$

In words,

1. M1 takes an input k and produces an output x.
2. M2 takes inputs x and p giving output z.
3. M3 takes inputs z and k and produces p.

The three tables, once constructed, are made public.

a. It should be clear that it is possible to construct M3 to satisfy the preceding condition. As an example, fill in M3 for the following simple case:

M1 =

5
4
2
3
1

M2 =

5	2	3	4	1
4	2	5	1	3
1	3	2	4	5
3	1	4	2	5
2	5	3	4	1

M3 =

Convention: The ith element of M1 corresponds to $k = i$. The ith row of M2 corresponds to $x = i$; the jth column of M2 corresponds to $p = j$. The ith row of M3 corresponds to $z = i$; the jth column of M3 corresponds to $k = j$.

b. Describe the use of this set of tables to perform encryption and decryption between two users.

c. Argue that this is a secure scheme.

3.14 Perform encryption and decryption using the RSA algorithm (Figure 3.10) for the following:
a. $p = 3; q = 11, e = 7; M = 2$
b. $p = 5; q = 11, e = 3; M = 5$
c. $p = 7; q = 11, e = 17; M = 2$
d. $p = 11; q = 13, e = 11; M = 3$
e. $p = 17; q = 11, e = 7; M = 88$

Hint: Decryption is not as hard as you think; use some finesse.

3.15 In a public-key system using RSA, you intercept the ciphertext $C = 16$ sent to a user whose public key is $e = 6, n = 40$. What is the plaintext M?

3.16 In an RSA system, the public key of a given user is $e = 7, n = 137$. What is the private key of this user?

3.17 Suppose we have a set of blocks encoded with the RSA algorithm and we don't have the private key. Assume $n = pq$, e is the public key. Suppose also someone tells us they know one of the plaintext blocks has a common factor with n. Does this help us in any way?

3.18 Show how RSA can be represented by matrices M1, M2, and M3 of Problem 3.4.

3.19 Consider the following scheme.
1. Pick an odd number, E.
2. Pick two prime numbers, P and Q, where $(P - 1)(Q - 1) - 1$ is evenly divisible by E.
3. Multiply P and Q to get N.
4. Calculate $D = \dfrac{(P - 1)(Q - 1)(E - 1) + 1}{E}$.

Is this scheme equivalent to RSA? Show why or why not.

3.20 Suppose Bob uses the RSA cryptosystem with a very large modulus n for which the factorization cannot be found in a reasonable amount of time. Suppose Alice sends a message to Bob by representing each alphabetic character as an integer between 0 and 25 (A → 0, ..., Z → 25), and then encrypting each number separately using RSA with large e and large n. Is this method secure? If not, describe the most efficient attack against this encryption method.

3.21 Consider a Diffie–Hellman scheme with a common prime $q = 353$ and a primitive root $\alpha = 3$.
a. If user A has public key $Y_A = 40$, what is A's private key X_A?
b. If user B has public key $Y_B = 248$, what is the shared secret key K?

CHAPTER 4

KEY DISTRIBUTION AND USER AUTHENTICATION

4.1 Symmetric Key Distribution Using Symmetric Encryption

4.2 Kerberos

Kerberos Version 4
Kerberos Version 5

4.3 Key Distribution Using Asymmetric Encryption

Public-Key Certificates
Public-Key Distribution of Secret Keys

4.4 X.509 Certificates

Certificates
X.509 Version 3

4.5 Public-Key Infrastructure

PKIX Management Functions
PKIX Management Protocols

4.6 Federated Identity Management

Identity Management
Identity Federation

4.7 Recommended Reading

4.8 Key Terms, Review Questions, and Problems

No Singhalese, whether man or woman, would venture out of the house without a bunch of keys in his hand, for without such a talisman he would fear that some devil might take advantage of his weak state to slip into his body.

— *The Golden Bough*, Sir James George Frazer

LEARNING OBJECTIVES

After studying this chapter, you should be able to:

◆ Understand the issues involved in the use of symmetric encryption to distribute symmetric keys.

◆ Give a presentation on Kerberos.

◆ Explain the differences between versions 4 and 5 of Kerberos.

◆ Understand the issues involved in the use of asymmetric encryption to distribute symmetric keys.

◆ List and explain the elements in an X.509 certificate.

◆ Present an overview of public-key infrastructure concepts.

◆ Understand the need for a federated identity management system.

This chapter covers two important related concepts. First is the complex topic of cryptographic key distribution, involving cryptographic, protocol, and management considerations. This chapter gives the reader a feel for the issues involved and provides a broad survey of the various aspects of key management and distribution.

This chapter also examines some of the authentication functions that have been developed to support network-based user authentication. The chapter includes a detail discussion of one of the earliest and also one of the most widely used key distribution and user authentication services: Kerberos. Next, the chapter looks at key distribution schemes that rely on asymmetric encryption. This is followed by a discussion of X.509 certificates and public-key infrastructure. Finally, the concept of federated identity management is introduced.

4.1 SYMMETRIC KEY DISTRIBUTION USING SYMMETRIC ENCRYPTION

For symmetric encryption to work, the two parties to an exchange must share the same key, and that key must be protected from access by others. Furthermore, frequent key changes are usually desirable to limit the amount of data compromised if an attacker learns the key. Therefore, the strength of any cryptographic system rests with the "key distribution technique," a term that refers to the means of delivering a key to two parties that wish to exchange data, without allowing others to see the key. Key distribution can be achieved in a number of ways. For two parties A and B, there are the following options:

1. A key could be selected by A and physically delivered to B.
2. A third party could select the key and physically deliver it to A and B.
3. If A and B have previously and recently used a key, one party could transmit the new key to the other, using the old key to encrypt the new key.
4. If A and B each have an encrypted connection to a third party C, C could deliver a key on the encrypted links to A and B.

Options 1 and 2 call for manual delivery of a key. For link encryption, this is a reasonable requirement, because each link encryption device is only going to be exchanging data with its partner on the other end of the link. However, for end-to-end encryption over a network, manual delivery is awkward. In a distributed system, any given host or terminal may need to engage in exchanges with many other hosts and terminals over time. Thus, each device needs a number of keys supplied dynamically. The problem is especially difficult in a wide-area distributed system.

Option 3 is a possibility for either link encryption or end-to-end encryption, but if an attacker ever succeeds in gaining access to one key, then all subsequent keys are revealed. Even if frequent changes are made to the link encryption keys, these should be done manually. To provide keys for end-to-end encryption, option 4 is preferable.

For **option 4**, two kinds of keys are used:

- **Session key:** When two end systems (hosts, terminals, etc.) wish to communicate, they establish a logical connection (e.g., virtual circuit). For the duration of that logical connection, called a session, all user data are encrypted with a one-time session key. At the conclusion of the session the session key is destroyed.

- **Permanent key:** A permanent key is a key used between entities for the purpose of distributing session keys.

A necessary element of option 4 is a **key distribution center (KDC)**. The KDC determines which systems are allowed to communicate with each other. When permission is granted for two systems to establish a connection, the key distribution center provides a one-time session key for that connection.

In general terms, the operation of a KDC proceeds as follows:

1. When host A wishes to set up a connection to host B, it transmits a connection-request packet to the KDC. The communication between A and the KDC is encrypted using a master key shared only by A and the KDC.
2. If the KDC approves the connection request, it generates a unique one-time session key. It encrypts the session key using the permanent key it shares with A and delivers the encrypted session key to A. Similarly, it encrypts the session key using the permanent key it shares with B and delivers the encrypted session key to B.
3. A and B can now set up a logical connection and exchange messages and data, all encrypted using the temporary session key.

The automated key distribution approach provides the flexibility and dynamic characteristics needed to allow a number of users to access a number of servers and for the servers to exchange data with each other. The most widely used application that implements this approach is Kerberos, described in the next section.

4.2 KERBEROS

Kerberos is a key distribution and user authentication service developed at MIT. The problem that Kerberos addresses is this: Assume an open distributed environment in which users at workstations wish to access services on servers distributed throughout the network. We would like for servers to be able to restrict access to authorized users and to be able to authenticate requests for service. In this environment, a workstation cannot be trusted to identify its users correctly to network services. In particular, the following three threats exist:

1. A user may gain access to a particular workstation and pretend to be another user operating from that workstation.

2. A user may alter the network address of a workstation so that the requests sent from the altered workstation appear to come from the impersonated workstation.

3. A user may eavesdrop on exchanges and use a replay attack to gain entrance to a server or to disrupt operations.

In any of these cases, an unauthorized user may be able to gain access to services and data that he or she is not authorized to access. Rather than building elaborate authentication protocols at each server, Kerberos provides a centralized authentication server whose function is to authenticate users to servers and servers to users. Kerberos relies exclusively on symmetric encryption, making no use of public-key encryption.

Two versions of Kerberos are in use. Version 4 [MILL88, STEI88] implementations still exist, although this version is being phased out. Version 5 [KOHL94] corrects some of the security deficiencies of version 4 and has been issued as a proposed Internet Standard (RFC 4120).

Because of the complexity of Kerberos, it is best to start with a description of version 4. This enables us to see the essence of the Kerberos strategy without considering some of the details required to handle subtle security threats. Then, we examine version 5.

Kerberos Version 4

Version 4 of Kerberos makes use of DES, in a rather elaborate protocol, to provide the authentication service. Viewing the protocol as a whole, it is difficult to see the need for the many elements contained therein. Therefore, we adopt a strategy used by Bill Bryant [BRYA88] and build up to the full protocol by looking first at several hypothetical dialogues. Each successive dialogue adds additional complexity to counter security vulnerabilities revealed in the preceding dialogue.

After examining the protocol, we look at some other aspects of version 4.

A SIMPLE AUTHENTICATION DIALOGUE In an unprotected network environment, any client can apply to any server for service. The obvious security risk is that of impersonation. An opponent can pretend to be another client and obtain unauthorized privileges on server machines. To counter this threat, servers must be able to confirm the identities of clients who request service. Each server can be required to undertake this task for each client/server interaction, but in an open environment, this places a substantial burden on each server.

An alternative is to use an **authentication server (AS)** that knows the passwords of all users and stores these in a centralized database. In addition, the AS shares a unique secret key with each server. These keys have been distributed physically or in some other secure manner. Consider the following hypothetical dialogue:[1]

$$\textbf{(1)} \; C \rightarrow AS: \quad ID_C \| P_C \| ID_V$$
$$\textbf{(2)} \; AS \rightarrow C: \quad Ticket$$
$$\textbf{(3)} \; C \rightarrow V: \quad ID_C \| Ticket$$
$$Ticket = E(K_v, [ID_C \| AD_C \| ID_V])$$

where

$$
\begin{aligned}
C &= \text{client} \\
AS &= \text{authentication server} \\
V &= \text{server} \\
ID_C &= \text{identifier of user on C} \\
ID_V &= \text{identifier of V} \\
P_C &= \text{password of user on C} \\
AD_C &= \text{network address of C} \\
K_v &= \text{secret encryption key shared by AS and V}
\end{aligned}
$$

In this scenario, the user logs on to a workstation and requests access to server V. The client module C in the user's workstation requests the user's password and then sends a message to the AS that includes the user's ID, the server's ID, and the user's password. The AS checks its database to see if the user has supplied the proper password for this user ID and whether this user is permitted access to server V. If both tests are passed, the AS accepts the user as authentic and must now convince the server that this user is authentic. To do so, the AS creates a **ticket** that contains the user's ID and network address and the server's ID. This ticket is encrypted using the secret key shared by the AS and this server. This ticket is then sent back to C. Because the ticket is encrypted, it cannot be altered by C or by an opponent.

With this ticket, C can now apply to V for service. C sends a message to V containing C's ID and the ticket. V decrypts the ticket and verifies that the user ID in the ticket is the same as the unencrypted user ID in the message. If these two match, the server considers the user authenticated and grants the requested service.

---

[1]The portion to the left of the colon indicates the sender and receiver, the portion to the right indicates the contents of the message, and the symbol ∥ indicates concatenation.

Each of the ingredients of message (3) is significant. The ticket is encrypted to prevent alteration or forgery. The server's ID (ID_V) is included in the ticket so that the server can verify that it has decrypted the ticket properly. ID_C is included in the ticket to indicate that this ticket has been issued on behalf of C. Finally, AD_C serves to counter the following threat. An opponent could capture the ticket transmitted in message (2), then use the name ID_C, and transmit a message of form (3) from another workstation. The server would receive a valid ticket that matches the user ID and grant access to the user on that other workstation. To prevent this attack, the AS includes in the ticket the network address from which the original request came. Now the ticket is valid only if it is transmitted from the same workstation that initially requested the ticket.

A More Secure Authentication Dialogue   Although the foregoing scenario solves some of the problems of authentication in an open network environment, problems remain. Two in particular stand out. First, we would like to minimize the number of times that a user has to enter a password. Suppose each ticket can be used only once. If user C logs on to a workstation in the morning and wishes to check his or her mail at a mail server, C must supply a password to get a ticket for the mail server. If C wishes to check the mail several times during the day, each attempt requires reentering the password. We can improve matters by saying that tickets are reusable. For a single logon session, the workstation can store the mail-server ticket after it is received and use it on behalf of the user for multiple accesses to the mail server.

However, under this scheme, it remains the case that a user would need a new ticket for every different service. If a user wished to access a print server, a mail server, a file server, and so on, the first instance of each access would require a new ticket and hence require the user to enter the password.

The second problem is that the earlier scenario involved a plaintext transmission of the password [message (1)]. An eavesdropper could capture the password and use any service accessible to the victim.

To solve these additional problems, we introduce a scheme for avoiding plaintext passwords and a new server, known as the **ticket-granting server (TGS)**. The new (but still hypothetical) scenario is as follows.

Once per user logon session:

(1) C → AS: $ID_C \| ID_{tgs}$
(2) AS → C: $E(K_c, Ticket_{tgs})$

Once per type of service:

(3) C → TGS: $ID_C \| ID_V \| Ticket_{tgs}$
(4) TGS → C: $Ticket_v$

Once per service session:

(5) C → V: $ID_C \| Ticket_v$

$Ticket_{tgs} = E(K_{tgs}, [ID_C \| AD_C \| ID_{tgs} \| TS_1 \| Lifetime_1])$
$Ticket_v = E(K_v, [ID_C \| AD_C \| ID_v \| TS_2 \| Lifetime_2])$

The new service, TGS, issues **tickets** to users who have been authenticated to AS. Thus, the user first requests a ticket-granting ticket (*Ticket$_{tgs}$*) from the AS. The client module in the user workstation saves this ticket. Each time the user requires access to a new service, the client applies to the TGS, using the ticket to authenticate itself. The TGS then grants a ticket for the particular service. The client saves each service-granting ticket and uses it to authenticate its user to a server each time a particular service is requested. Let us look at the details of this scheme:

1. The client requests a ticket-granting ticket on behalf of the user by sending its user's ID to the AS, together with the TGS ID, indicating a request to use the TGS service.

2. The AS responds with a ticket that is encrypted with a key that is derived from the user's password (K_C), which is already stored at the AS. When this response arrives at the client, the client prompts the user for his or her password, generates the key, and attempts to decrypt the incoming message. If the correct password is supplied, the ticket is successfully recovered.

Because only the correct user should know the password, only the correct user can recover the ticket. Thus, we have used the password to obtain credentials from Kerberos without having to transmit the password in plaintext. The ticket itself consists of the ID and network address of the user and the ID of the TGS. This corresponds to the first scenario. The idea is that the client can use this ticket to request multiple service-granting tickets. So the ticket-granting ticket is to be reusable. However, we do not wish an opponent to be able to capture the ticket and use it. Consider the following scenario: An opponent captures the login ticket and waits until the user has logged off his or her workstation. Then the opponent either gains access to that workstation or configures his workstation with the same network address as that of the victim. The opponent would be able to reuse the ticket to spoof the TGS. To counter this, the ticket includes a **timestamp**, indicating the date and time at which the ticket was issued, and a **lifetime**, indicating the length of time for which the ticket is valid (e.g., eight hours). Thus, the client now has a reusable ticket and need not bother the user for a password for each new service request. Finally, note that the ticket-granting ticket is encrypted with a secret key known only to the AS and the TGS. This prevents alteration of the ticket. The ticket is reencrypted with a key based on the user's password. This assures that the ticket can be recovered only by the correct user, providing the authentication.

Now that the client has a ticket-granting ticket, access to any server can be obtained with steps 3 and 4.

3. The client requests a service-granting ticket on behalf of the user. For this purpose, the client transmits a message to the TGS containing the user's ID, the ID of the desired service, and the ticket-granting ticket.

4. The TGS decrypts the incoming ticket using a key shared only by the AS and the TGS (K_{tgs}) and verifies the success of the decryption by the presence of its ID. It checks to make sure that the lifetime has not expired. Then it compares the user ID and network address with the incoming information to authenticate the user. If the user is permitted access to the server V, the TGS issues a ticket to grant access to the requested service.

The service-granting ticket has the same structure as the ticket-granting ticket. Indeed, because the TGS is a server, we would expect that the same elements are needed to authenticate a client to the TGS and to authenticate a client to an application server. Again, the ticket contains a timestamp and lifetime. If the user wants access to the same service at a later time, the client can simply use the previously acquired service-granting ticket and need not bother the user for a password. Note that the ticket is encrypted with a secret key (K_v) known only to the TGS and the server, preventing alteration.

Finally, with a particular service-granting ticket, the client can gain access to the corresponding service with step 5.

5. The client requests access to a service on behalf of the user. For this purpose, the client transmits a message to the server containing the user's ID and the service-granting ticket. The server authenticates by using the contents of the ticket.

This new scenario satisfies the two requirements of only one password query per user session and protection of the user password.

THE VERSION 4 AUTHENTICATION DIALOGUE Although the foregoing scenario enhances security compared to the first attempt, two additional problems remain. The heart of the first problem is the lifetime associated with the ticket-granting ticket. If this lifetime is very short (e.g., minutes), then the user will be repeatedly asked for a password. If the lifetime is long (e.g., hours), then an opponent has a greater opportunity for replay. An opponent could eavesdrop on the network and capture a copy of the ticket-granting ticket and then wait for the legitimate user to log out. Then the opponent could forge the legitimate user's network address and send the message of step (3) to the TGS. This would give the opponent unlimited access to the resources and files available to the legitimate user.

Similarly, if an opponent captures a service-granting ticket and uses it before it expires, the opponent has access to the corresponding service.

Thus, we arrive at an additional requirement. A network service (the TGS or an application service) must be able to prove that the person using a ticket is the same person to whom that ticket was issued.

The second problem is that there may be a requirement for servers to authenticate themselves to users. Without such authentication, an opponent could sabotage the configuration so that messages to a server were directed to another location. The false server then would be in a position to act as a real server, capture any information from the user, and deny the true service to the user.

We examine these problems in turn and refer to Table 4.1, which shows the actual Kerberos protocol. Figure 4.1 provides simplified overview.

Table 4.1 Summary of Kerberos Version 4 Message Exchanges

(1) C → AS $ID_c \| ID_{tgs} \| TS_1$

(2) AS → C $E(K_c, [K_{c,tgs} \| ID_{tgs} \| TS_2 \| Lifetime_2 \| Ticket_{tgs}])$

$Ticket_{tgs} = E(K_{tgs}, [K_{c,tgs} \| ID_C \| AD_C \| ID_{tgs} \| TS_2 \| Lifetime_2])$

(a) Authentication Service Exchange to obtain ticket-granting ticket

Table 4.1 Continued

(3) C → TGS	$ID_v \,\|\, Ticket_{tgs} \,\|\, Authenticator_c$
(4) TGS → C	$E(K_{c,tgs}, [K_{c,v} \,\|\, ID_v \,\|\, TS_4 \,\|\, Ticket_v])$

$$Ticket_{tgs} = E(K_{tgs}, [K_{c,tgs} \,\|\, ID_C \,\|\, AD_C \,\|\, ID_{tgs} \,\|\, TS_2 \,\|\, Lifetime_2])$$

$$Ticket_v = E(K_v, [K_{c,v} \,\|\, ID_C \,\|\, AD_C \,\|\, ID_v \,\|\, TS_4 \,\|\, Lifetime_4])$$

$$Authenticator_c = E(K_{c,tgs}, [ID_C \,\|\, AD_C \,\|\, TS_3])$$

(b) Ticket-Granting Service Exchange to obtain service-granting ticket

(5) C → V	$Ticket_v \,\|\, Authenticator_c$
(6) V → C	$E(K_{c,v}, [TS_5 + 1])$ (for mutual authentication)

$$Ticket_v = E(K_v, [K_{c,v} \,\|\, ID_C \,\|\, AD_C \,\|\, ID_v \,\|\, TS_4 \,\|\, Lifetime_4])$$

$$Authenticator_c = E(K_{c,v}, [ID_C \,\|\, AD_C \,\|\, TS_5])$$

(c) Client/Server Authentication Exchange to obtain service

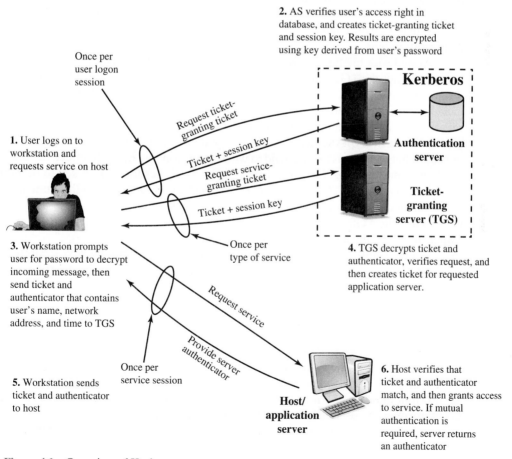

2. AS verifies user's access right in database, and creates ticket-granting ticket and session key. Results are encrypted using key derived from user's password

Once per user logon session

Kerberos

1. User logs on to workstation and requests service on host

Request ticket-granting ticket

Ticket + session key

Request service-granting ticket

Ticket + session key

Authentication server

Ticket-granting server (TGS)

3. Workstation prompts user for password to decrypt incoming message, then send ticket and authenticator that contains user's name, network address, and time to TGS

Once per type of service

4. TGS decrypts ticket and authenticator, verifies request, and then creates ticket for requested application server.

Request service

Provide server authenticator

5. Workstation sends ticket and authenticator to host

Once per service session

Host/ application server

6. Host verifies that ticket and authenticator match, and then grants access to service. If mutual authentication is required, server returns an authenticator

Figure 4.1 Overview of Kerberos

First, consider the problem of captured ticket-granting tickets and the need to determine that the ticket presenter is the same as the client for whom the ticket was issued. The threat is that an opponent will steal the ticket and use it before it expires. To get around this problem, let us have the AS provide both the client and the TGS with a secret piece of information in a secure manner. Then the client can prove its identity to the TGS by revealing the secret information, again in a secure manner. An efficient way of accomplishing this is to use an encryption key as the secure information; this is referred to as a session key in Kerberos.

Table 4.1a shows the technique for distributing the session key. As before, the client sends a message to the AS requesting access to the TGS. The AS responds with a message, encrypted with a key derived from the user's password (K_C), that contains the ticket. The encrypted message also contains a copy of the session key, $K_{C,tgs}$, where the subscripts indicate that this is a session key for C and TGS. Because this session key is inside the message encrypted with K_C, only the user's client can read it. The same session key is included in the ticket, which can be read only by the TGS. Thus, the session key has been securely delivered to both C and the TGS.

Note that several additional pieces of information have been added to this first phase of the dialogue. Message (1) includes a timestamp, so that the AS knows that the message is timely. Message (2) includes several elements of the ticket in a form accessible to C. This enables C to confirm that this ticket is for the TGS and to learn its expiration time.

Armed with the ticket and the session key, C is ready to approach the TGS. As before, C sends the TGS a message that includes the ticket plus the ID of the requested service [message (3) in Table 4.1b]. In addition, C transmits an authenticator, which includes the ID and address of C's user and a timestamp. Unlike the ticket, which is reusable, the authenticator is intended for use only once and has a very short lifetime. The TGS can decrypt the ticket with the key that it shares with the AS. This ticket indicates that user C has been provided with the session key $K_{C,tgs}$. In effect, the ticket says, "Anyone who uses $K_{C,tgs}$ must be C." The TGS uses the session key to decrypt the authenticator. The TGS can then check the name and address from the authenticator with that of the ticket and with the network address of the incoming message. If all match, then the TGS is assured that the sender of the ticket is indeed the ticket's real owner. In effect, the authenticator says, "At time TS_3, I hereby use $K_{C,tgs}$." Note that the ticket does not prove anyone's identity but is a way to distribute keys securely. It is the authenticator that proves the client's identity. Because the authenticator can be used only once and has a short lifetime, the threat of an opponent stealing both the ticket and the authenticator for presentation later is countered.

The reply from the TGS in message (4) follows the form of message (2). The message is encrypted with the session key shared by the TGS and C and includes a session key to be shared between C and the server V, the ID of V, and the timestamp of the ticket. The ticket itself includes the same session key.

C now has a reusable service-granting ticket for V. When C presents this ticket, as shown in message (5), it also sends an authenticator. The server can decrypt the ticket, recover the session key, and decrypt the authenticator.

If mutual authentication is required, the server can reply as shown in message (6) of Table 4.1. The server returns the value of the timestamp from the authenticator, incremented by 1, and encrypted in the session key. C can decrypt this message

Figure 4.2 Kerberos Exchanges

to recover the incremented timestamp. Because the message was encrypted by the session key, C is assured that it could have been created only by V. The contents of the message assure C that this is not a replay of an old reply.

Finally, at the conclusion of this process, the client and server share a secret key. This key can be used to encrypt future messages between the two or to exchange a new random session key for that purpose.

Figure 4.2 illustrates the Kerberos exchanges among the parties. Table 4.2 summarizes the justification for each of the elements in the Kerberos protocol.

KERBEROS REALMS AND MULTIPLE KERBERI A full-service Kerberos environment consisting of a Kerberos server, a number of clients, and a number of application servers requires the following:

1. The Kerberos server must have the user ID and hashed passwords of all participating users in its database. All users are registered with the Kerberos server.

2. The Kerberos server must share a secret key with each server. All servers are registered with the Kerberos server.

Such an environment is referred to as a **Kerberos realm**. The concept of **realm** can be explained as follows. A Kerberos realm is a set of managed nodes that share

Table 4.2 Rationale for the Elements of the Kerberos Version 4 Protocol

Message (1)	Client requests ticket-granting ticket.
ID_C	Tells AS identity of user from this client.
ID_{tgs}	Tells AS that user requests access to TGS.
TS_1	Allows AS to verify that client's clock is synchronized with that of AS.
Message (2)	AS returns ticket-granting ticket.
K_c	Encryption is based on user's password, enabling AS and client to verify password, and protecting contents of message (2).
$K_{c,tgs}$	Copy of session key accessible to client created by AS to permit secure exchange between client and TGS without requiring them to share a permanent key.
ID_{tgs}	Confirms that this ticket is for the TGS.
TS_2	Informs client of time this ticket was issued.
$Lifetime_2$	Informs client of the lifetime of this ticket.
$Ticket_{tgs}$	Ticket to be used by client to access TGS.

(a) Authentication Service Exchange

Message (3)	Client requests service-granting ticket.
ID_V	Tells TGS that user requests access to server V.
$Ticket_{tgs}$	Assures TGS that this user has been authenticated by AS.
$Authenticator_c$	Generated by client to validate ticket.
Message (4)	TGS returns service-granting ticket.
$K_{c,tgs}$	Key shared only by C and TGS protects contents of message (4).
$K_{c,v}$	Copy of session key accessible to client created by TGS to permit secure exchange between client and server without requiring them to share a permanent key.
ID_V	Confirms that this ticket is for server V.
TS_4	Informs client of time this ticket was issued.
$Ticket_V$	Ticket to be used by client to access server V.
$Ticket_{tgs}$	Reusable so that user does not have to reenter password.
K_{tgs}	Ticket is encrypted with key known only to AS and TGS, to prevent tampering.
$K_{c,tgs}$	Copy of session key accessible to TGS used to decrypt authenticator, thereby authenticating ticket.
ID_C	Indicates the rightful owner of this ticket.
AD_C	Prevents use of ticket from workstation other than one that initially requested the ticket.
ID_{tgs}	Assures server that it has decrypted ticket properly.
TS_2	Informs TGS of time this ticket was issued.
$Lifetime_2$	Prevents replay after ticket has expired.
$Authenticator_c$	Assures TGS that the ticket presenter is the same as the client for whom the ticket was issued has very short lifetime to prevent replay.

Table 4.2   Continued

$K_{c,tgs}$	Authenticator is encrypted with key known only to client and TGS, to prevent tampering.
ID_C	Must match ID in ticket to authenticate ticket.
AD_C	Must match address in ticket to authenticate ticket.
TS_3	Informs TGS of time this authenticator was generated.

(b) Ticket-Granting Service Exchange

Message (5)	Client requests service.
$Ticket_V$	Assures server that this user has been authenticated by AS.
$Authenticator_c$	Generated by client to validate ticket.
Message (6)	Optional authentication of server to client.
$K_{c,v}$	Assures C that this message is from V.
$TS_5 + 1$	Assures C that this is not a replay of an old reply.
$Ticket_v$	Reusable so that client does not need to request a new ticket from TGS for each access to the same server.
K_v	Ticket is encrypted with key known only to TGS and server, to prevent tampering.
$K_{c,v}$	Copy of session key accessible to client; used to decrypt authenticator, thereby authenticating ticket.
ID_C	Indicates the rightful owner of this ticket.
AD_C	Prevents use of ticket from workstation other than one that initially requested the ticket.
ID_V	Assures server that it has decrypted ticket properly.
TS_4	Informs server of time this ticket was issued.
$Lifetime_4$	Prevents replay after ticket has expired.
$Authenticator_c$	Assures server that the ticket presenter is the same as the client for whom the ticket was issued; has very short lifetime to prevent replay.
$K_{c,v}$	Authenticator is encrypted with key known only to client and server, to prevent tampering.
ID_C	Must match ID in ticket to authenticate ticket.
AD_c	Must match address in ticket to authenticate ticket.
TS_5	Informs server of time this authenticator was generated.

(c) Client/Server Authentication Exchange

the same Kerberos database. The Kerberos database resides on the Kerberos master computer system, which should be kept in a physically secure room. A read-only copy of the Kerberos database might also reside on other Kerberos computer systems. However, all changes to the database must be made on the master computer system. Changing or accessing the contents of a Kerberos database requires the Kerberos master password. A related concept is that of a **Kerberos principal**, which is a service or user that is known to the Kerberos system. Each Kerberos principal is identified by its principal name. Principal names consist of three parts: a service or user name, an instance name, and a realm name.

Networks of clients and servers under different administrative organizations typically constitute different realms. That is, it generally is not practical or does not conform to administrative policy to have users and servers in one administrative domain registered with a Kerberos server elsewhere. However, users in one realm may need access to servers in other realms, and some servers may be willing to provide service to users from other realms, provided that those users are authenticated.

Kerberos Version 5

Kerberos version 5 is specified in RFC 4120 and provides a number of improvements over version 4 [KOHL94]. To begin, we provide an overview of the changes from version 4 to version 5 and then look at the version 5 protocol.

DIFFERENCES BETWEEN VERSIONS 4 AND 5 Version 5 is intended to address the limitations of version 4 in two areas: environmental shortcomings and technical deficiencies. We briefly summarize the improvements in each area. Kerberos version 4 did not fully address the need to be of general purpose. This led to the following **environmental shortcomings**.

1. **Encryption system dependence:** Version 4 requires the use of DES. Export restriction on DES as well as doubts about the strength of DES were thus of concern. In version 5, ciphertext is tagged with an encryption-type identifier so that any encryption technique may be used. Encryption keys are tagged with a type and a length, allowing the same key to be used in different algorithms and allowing the specification of different variations on a given algorithm.

2. **Internet protocol dependence:** Version 4 requires the use of Internet Protocol (IP) addresses. Other address types, such as the ISO network address, are not accommodated. Version 5 network addresses are tagged with type and length, allowing any network address type to be used.

3. **Message byte ordering:** In version 4, the sender of a message employs a byte ordering of its own choosing and tags the message to indicate least significant byte in lowest address or most significant byte in lowest address. This technique works but does not follow established conventions. In version 5, all message structures are defined using Abstract Syntax Notation One (ASN.1) and Basic Encoding Rules (BER), which provide an unambiguous byte ordering.

4. **Ticket lifetime:** Lifetime values in version 4 are encoded in an 8-bit quantity in units of five minutes. Thus, the maximum lifetime that can be expressed is $2^8 \times 5 = 1280$ minutes (a little over 21 hours). This may be inadequate for some applications (e.g., a long-running simulation that requires valid Kerberos credentials throughout execution). In version 5, tickets include an explicit start time and end time, allowing tickets with arbitrary lifetimes.

5. **Authentication forwarding:** Version 4 does not allow credentials issued to one client to be forwarded to some other host and used by some other client. This capability would enable a client to access a server and have that server access another server on behalf of the client. For example, a client issues a request to a print server that then accesses the client's file from a file server, using the client's credentials for access. Version 5 provides this capability.

6. **Interrealm authentication:** In version 4, interoperability among N realms requires on the order of N^2 Kerberos-to-Kerberos relationships, as described earlier. Version 5 supports a method that requires fewer relationships, as described shortly.

Apart from these environmental limitations, there are **technical deficiencies** in the version 4 protocol itself. Most of these deficiencies were documented in [BELL90], and version 5 attempts to address these. The deficiencies are the following.

1. **Double encryption:** Note in Table 4.1 [messages (2) and (4)] that tickets provided to clients are encrypted twice—once with the secret key of the target server and then again with a secret key known to the client. The second encryption is not necessary and is computationally wasteful.

2. **PCBC encryption:** Encryption in version 4 makes use of a nonstandard mode of DES known as **propagating cipher block chaining (PCBC)**.[2] It has been demonstrated that this mode is vulnerable to an attack involving the interchange of ciphertext blocks [KOHL89]. PCBC was intended to provide an integrity check as part of the encryption operation. Version 5 provides explicit integrity mechanisms, allowing the standard CBC mode to be used for encryption. In particular, a checksum or hash code is attached to the message prior to encryption using CBC.

3. **Session keys:** Each ticket includes a session key that is used by the client to encrypt the authenticator sent to the service associated with that ticket. In addition, the session key subsequently may be used by the client and the server to protect messages passed during that session. However, because the same ticket may be used repeatedly to gain service from a particular server, there is the risk that an opponent will replay messages from an old session to the client or the server. In version 5, it is possible for a client and server to negotiate a subsession key, which is to be used only for that one connection. A new access by the client would result in the use of a new subsession key.

4. **Password attacks:** Both versions are vulnerable to a password attack. The message from the AS to the client includes material encrypted with a key based on the client's password.[3] An opponent can capture this message and attempt to decrypt it by trying various passwords. If the result of a test decryption is of the proper form, then the opponent has discovered the client's password and may subsequently use it to gain authentication credentials from Kerberos. This is the same type of password attack described in Chapter 10, with the same kinds of countermeasures being applicable. Version 5 does provide a mechanism known as preauthentication, which should make password attacks more difficult, but it does not prevent them.

THE VERSION 5 AUTHENTICATION DIALOGUE   Table 4.3 summarizes the basic version 5 dialogue. This is best explained by comparison with version 4 (Table 4.1).

---

[2]This is described in Appendix F.
[3]Appendix F describes the mapping of passwords to encryption keys.

Table 4.3 Summary of Kerberos Version 5 Message Exchanges

---

(1) C → AS $\quad Options \parallel ID_c \parallel Realm_c \parallel ID_{tgs} \parallel Times \parallel Nonce_1$

(2) AS → C $\quad Realm_c \parallel ID_C \parallel Ticket_{tgs} \parallel E(K_c, [K_{c,tgs} \parallel Times \parallel Nonce_1 \parallel Realm_{tgs} \parallel ID_{tgs}])$

$\qquad\qquad Ticket_{tgs} = E(K_{tgs}, [Flags \parallel K_{c,tgs} \parallel Realm_c \parallel ID_C \parallel AD_C \parallel Times])$

(a) Authentication Service Exchange to obtain ticket-granting ticket

---

(3) C → TGS $\quad Options \parallel ID_v \parallel Times \parallel \parallel Nonce_2 \parallel Ticket_{tgs} \parallel Authenticator_c$

(4) TGS → C $\quad Realm_c \parallel ID_C \parallel Ticket_v \parallel E(K_{c,tgs}, [K_{c,v} \parallel Times \parallel Nonce_2 \parallel Realm_v \parallel ID_v])$

$\qquad\qquad Ticket_{tgs} = E(K_{tgs}, [Flags \parallel K_{c,tgs} \parallel Realm_c \parallel ID_C \parallel AD_C \parallel Times])$

$\qquad\qquad Ticket_v = E(K_v, [Flags \parallel K_{c,v} \parallel Realm_c \parallel ID_C \parallel AD_C \parallel Times])$

$\qquad\qquad Authenticator_c = E(K_{c,tgs}, [ID_C \parallel Realm_c \parallel TS_1])$

(b) Ticket-Granting Service Exchange to obtain service-granting ticket

---

(5) C → V $\quad Options \parallel Ticket_v \parallel Authenticator_c$

(6) V → C $\quad E_{K_{c,v}}[TS_2 \parallel Subkey \parallel Seq\#]$

$\qquad\qquad Ticket_v = E(K_v, [Flags \parallel K_{c,v} \parallel Realm_c \parallel ID_C \parallel AD_C \parallel Times])$

$\qquad\qquad Authenticator_c = E(K_{c,v}, [ID_C \parallel Realm_c \parallel TS_2 \parallel Subkey \parallel Seq\#])$

(c) Client/Server Authentication Exchange to obtain service

First, consider the **authentication service exchange**. Message (1) is a client request for a ticket-granting ticket. As before, it includes the ID of the user and the TGS. The following new elements are added:

- **Realm:** Indicates realm of user.
- **Options:** Used to request that certain flags be set in the returned ticket.
- **Times:** Used by the client to request the following time settings in the ticket:

  from: the desired start time for the requested ticket

  till: the requested expiration time for the requested ticket

  rtime: requested renew-till time
- **Nonce:** A random value to be repeated in message (2) to assure that the response is fresh and has not been replayed by an opponent.

Message (2) returns a ticket-granting ticket, identifying information for the client, and a block encrypted using the encryption key based on the user's password. This block includes the session key to be used between the client and the TGS, times specified in message (1), the nonce from message (1), and TGS identifying information. The ticket itself includes the session key, identifying information for the client, the requested time values, and flags that reflect the status of this ticket and the requested options. These flags introduce significant new functionality to version 5. For now, we defer a discussion of these flags and concentrate on the overall structure of the version 5 protocol.

Let us now compare the **ticket-granting service exchange** for versions 4 and 5. We see that message (3) for both versions includes an authenticator, a ticket, and the name of the requested service. In addition, version 5 includes requested times and options for the ticket and a nonce — all with functions similar to those of message (1). The authenticator itself is essentially the same as the one used in version 4.

Message (4) has the same structure as message (2). It returns a ticket plus information needed by the client, with the information encrypted using the session key now shared by the client and the TGS.

Finally, for the **client/server authentication exchange**, several new features appear in version 5. In message (5), the client may request as an option that mutual authentication is required. The authenticator includes several new fields:

- **Subkey:** The client's choice for an encryption key to be used to protect this specific application session. If this field is omitted, the session key from the ticket ($K_{C,V}$) is used.

- **Sequence number:** An optional field that specifies the starting sequence number to be used by the server for messages sent to the client during this session. Messages may be sequence numbered to detect replays.

If mutual authentication is required, the server responds with message (6). This message includes the timestamp from the authenticator. Note that in version 4, the timestamp was incremented by one. This is not necessary in version 5, because the nature of the format of messages is such that it is not possible for an opponent to create message (6) without knowledge of the appropriate encryption keys. The subkey field, if present, overrides the subkey field, if present, in message (5). The optional sequence number field specifies the starting sequence number to be used by the client.

4.3 KEY DISTRIBUTION USING ASYMMETRIC ENCRYPTION

One of the major roles of public-key encryption is to address the problem of key distribution. There are actually two distinct aspects to the use of public-key encryption in this regard.

- The distribution of public keys.
- The use of public-key encryption to distribute secret keys.

We examine each of these areas in turn.

Public-Key Certificates

On the face of it, the point of public-key encryption is that the public key is public. Thus, if there is some broadly accepted public-key algorithm, such as RSA, any participant can send his or her public key to any other participant or broadcast the key to the community at large. Although this approach is convenient, it has a major weakness. Anyone can forge such a public announcement. That is, some user could

Figure 4.3 Public-Key Certificate Use

pretend to be user A and send a public key to another participant or broadcast such a public key. Until such time as user A discovers the forgery and alerts other participants, the forger is able to read all encrypted messages intended for A and can use the forged keys for authentication.

The solution to this problem is the **public-key certificate**. In essence, a certificate consists of a public key plus a user ID of the key owner, with the whole block signed by a trusted third party. Typically, the third party is a certificate authority (CA) that is trusted by the user community, such as a government agency or a financial institution. A user can present his or her public key to the authority in a secure manner and obtain a certificate. The user can then publish the certificate. Anyone needing this user's public key can obtain the certificate and verify that it is valid by way of the attached trusted signature. Figure 4.3 illustrates the process.

One scheme has become universally accepted for formatting public-key certificates: the X.509 standard. X.509 certificates are used in most network security applications, including IP security, secure sockets layer (SSL), and S/MIME—all of which are discussed in subsequent chapters. X.509 is examined in detail in the next section.

Public-Key Distribution of Secret Keys

With conventional encryption, a fundamental requirement for two parties to communicate securely is that they share a secret key. Suppose Bob wants to create a messaging application that will enable him to exchange e-mail securely with anyone who has access to the Internet or to some other network that the two of them share. Suppose Bob wants to do this using conventional encryption. With conventional encryption, Bob and his correspondent, say, Alice, must come up with a way to share a unique secret key that no one else knows. How are they going to do that? If Alice is in the next room from Bob, Bob could generate a key and write it down on a piece of paper or store it on a diskette and hand it to Alice. But if Alice is on the other side of the continent or the world, what can Bob do? He could encrypt this key using conventional encryption and e-mail it to Alice, but this means that Bob and Alice must share a secret key to encrypt this new secret key. Furthermore, Bob and everyone else who uses this new e-mail package faces the same problem with every potential correspondent: Each pair of correspondents must share a unique secret key.

One approach is the use of Diffie–Hellman key exchange. This approach is indeed widely used. However, it suffers the drawback that, in its simplest form, Diffie–Hellman provides no authentication of the two communicating partners.

A powerful alternative is the use of public-key certificates. When Bob wishes to communicate with Alice, Bob can do the following:

1. Prepare a message.
2. Encrypt that message using conventional encryption with a one-time conventional session key.
3. Encrypt the session key using public-key encryption with Alice's public key.
4. Attach the encrypted session key to the message and send it to Alice.

Only Alice is capable of decrypting the session key and therefore of recovering the original message. If Bob obtained Alice's public key by means of Alice's public-key certificate, then Bob is assured that it is a valid key.

4.4 X.509 CERTIFICATES

ITU-T recommendation X.509 is part of the X.500 series of recommendations that define a directory service. The directory is, in effect, a server or distributed set of servers that maintains a database of information about users. The information includes a mapping from user name to network address, as well as other attributes and information about the users.

X.509 defines a framework for the provision of authentication services by the X.500 directory to its users. The directory may serve as a repository of public-key certificates. Each certificate contains the public key of a user and is signed with the private key of a trusted certification authority. In addition, X.509 defines alternative authentication protocols based on the use of public-key certificates.

X.509 is an important standard because the certificate structure and authentication protocols defined in X.509 are used in a variety of contexts. For example, the X.509 certificate format is used in S/MIME (Chapter 8), IP Security (Chapter 9), and SSL/TLS (Chapter 6).

X.509 was initially issued in 1988. The standard was subsequently revised to address some of the security concerns documented in [IANS90] and [MITC90]; a revised recommendation was issued in 1993. A third version was issued in 1995 and revised in 2000.

X.509 is based on the use of public-key cryptography and digital signatures. The standard does not dictate the use of a specific algorithm but recommends

RSA. The digital signature scheme is assumed to require the use of a hash function. Again, the standard does not dictate a specific hash algorithm. The 1988 recommendation included the description of a recommended hash algorithm; this algorithm has since been shown to be insecure and was dropped from the 1993 recommendation. Figure 4.3 illustrates the generation of a public-key certificate.

Certificates

The heart of the X.509 scheme is the public-key certificate associated with each user. These user certificates are assumed to be created by some trusted certification authority (CA) and placed in the directory by the CA or by the user. The directory server itself is not responsible for the creation of public keys or for the certification function; it merely provides an easily accessible location for users to obtain certificates.

Figure 4.4a shows the general format of a certificate, which includes the following elements.

- **Version:** Differentiates among successive versions of the certificate format; the default is version 1. If the Issuer Unique Identifier or Subject Unique Identifier are present, the value must be version 2. If one or more extensions are present, the version must be version 3.

- **Serial number:** An integer value, unique within the issuing CA, that is unambiguously associated with this certificate.

(a) **X.509 certificate**

(b) **Certificate revocation list**

Figure 4.4   X.509 Formats

- **Signature algorithm identifier:** The algorithm used to sign the certificate, together with any associated parameters. Because this information is repeated in the Signature field at the end of the certificate, this field has little, if any, utility.

- **Issuer name:** X.500 name of the CA that created and signed this certificate.

- **Period of validity:** Consists of two dates: the first and last on which the certificate is valid.

- **Subject name:** The name of the user to whom this certificate refers. That is, this certificate certifies the public key of the subject who holds the corresponding private key.

- **Subject's public-key information:** The public key of the subject, plus an identifier of the algorithm for which this key is to be used, together with any associated parameters.

- **Issuer unique identifier:** An optional bit string field used to identify uniquely the issuing CA in the event the X.500 name has been reused for different entities.

- **Subject unique identifier:** An optional bit string field used to identify uniquely the subject in the event the X.500 name has been reused for different entities.

- **Extensions:** A set of one or more extension fields. Extensions were added in version 3 and are discussed later in this section.

- **Signature:** Covers all of the other fields of the certificate; it contains the hash code of the other fields encrypted with the CA's private key. This field includes the signature algorithm identifier.

The unique identifier fields were added in version 2 to handle the possible reuse of subject and/or issuer names over time. These fields are rarely used.

The standard uses the following notation to define a certificate:

$$CA \ll A \gg = CA\ \{V, SN, AI, CA, UCA, A, UA, Ap, T^A\}$$

where

$Y \ll X \gg$ = the certificate of user X issued by certification authority Y

$Y\ \{I\}$ = the signing of I by Y; consists of I with an encrypted hash code appended

V = version of the certificate

SN = serial number of the certificate

AI = identifier of the algorithm used to sign the certificate

CA = name of certificate authority

UCA = optional unique identifier of the CA

A = name of user A

UA = optional unique identifier of the user A

Ap = public key of user A

T^A = period of validity of the certificate

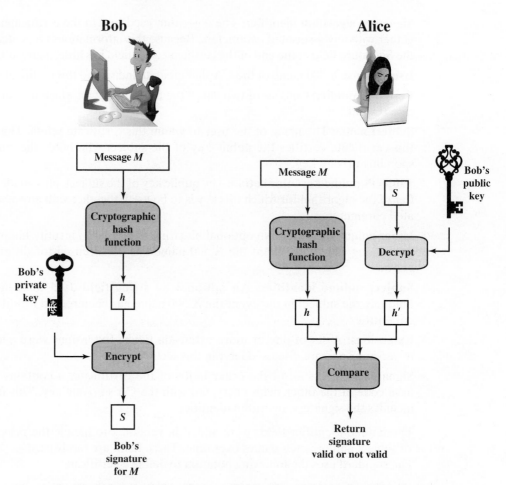

Figure 4.5 Simplified Depiction of Essential Elements of Digital Signature Process

The CA signs the certificate with its private key. If the corresponding public key is known to a user, then that user can verify that a certificate signed by the CA is valid. This is the typical digital signature approach, as illustrated in Figure 4.5.

OBTAINING A USER'S CERTIFICATE User certificates generated by a CA have the following characteristics:

- Any user with access to the public key of the CA can verify the user public key that was certified.

- No party other than the certification authority can modify the certificate without this being detected.

Because certificates are unforgeable, they can be placed in a directory without the need for the directory to make special efforts to protect them.

If all users subscribe to the same CA, then there is a common trust of that CA. All user certificates can be placed in the directory for access by all users. In addition, a user can transmit his or her certificate directly to other users. In either case, once B is in possession of A's certificate, B has confidence that messages it encrypts with A's public key will be secure from eavesdropping and that messages signed with A's private key are unforgeable.

If there is a large community of users, it may not be practical for all users to subscribe to the same CA. Because it is the CA that signs certificates, each participating user must have a copy of the CA's own public key to verify signatures. This public key must be provided to each user in an absolutely secure way (with respect to integrity and authenticity) so that the user has confidence in the associated certificates. Thus, with many users, it may be more practical for there to be a number of CAs, each of which securely provides its public key to some fraction of the users.

Now suppose that A has obtained a certificate from certification authority X_1 and B has obtained a certificate from CA X_2. If A does not securely know the public key of X_2, then B's certificate, issued by X_2, is useless to A. A can read B's certificate, but A cannot verify the signature. However, if the two CAs have securely exchanged their own public keys, the following procedure will enable A to obtain B's public key.

1. A obtains (from the directory) the certificate of X_2 signed by X_1. Because A securely knows X_1's public key, A can obtain X_2's public key from its certificate and verify it by means of X_1's signature on the certificate.

2. A then goes back to the directory and obtains the certificate of B signed by X_2. Because A now has a trusted copy of X_2's public key, A can verify the signature and securely obtain B's public key.

A has used a chain of certificates to obtain B's public key. In the notation of X.509, this chain is expressed as

$$X_1 \ll X_2 \gg X_2 \ll B \gg$$

In the same fashion, B can obtain A's public key with the reverse chain:

$$X_2 \ll X_1 \gg X_1 \ll A \gg$$

This scheme need not be limited to a chain of two certificates. An arbitrarily long path of CAs can be followed to produce a chain. A chain with N elements would be expressed as

$$X_1 \ll X_2 \gg X_2 \ll X_3 \gg \ldots X_N \ll B \gg$$

In this case, each pair of CAs in the chain (X_i, X_{i+1}) must have created certificates for each other.

All of these certificates of CAs by CAs need to appear in the directory, and the user needs to know how they are linked to follow a path to another user's public-key certificate. X.509 suggests that CAs be arranged in a hierarchy so that navigation is straightforward.

Figure 4.6, taken from X.509, is an example of such a hierarchy. The connected circles indicate the hierarchical relationship among the CAs; the associated boxes indicate certificates maintained in the directory for each CA entry. The directory entry for each CA includes two types of certificates:

- **Forward certificates:** Certificates of X generated by other CAs
- **Reverse certificates:** Certificates generated by X that are the certificates of other CAs

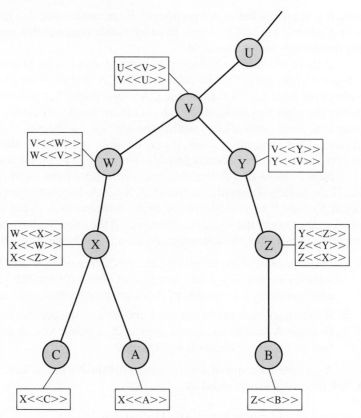

Figure 4.6 X.509 Hierarchy: A Hypothetical Example

In this example, user A can acquire the following certificates from the directory to establish a certification path to B:

$$X \ll W \gg \; W \ll V \gg \; V \ll Y \gg \; Y \ll Z \gg \; Z \ll B \gg$$

When A has obtained these certificates, it can unwrap the certification path in sequence to recover a trusted copy of B's public key. Using this public key, A can send encrypted messages to B. If A wishes to receive encrypted messages back from B or to sign messages sent to B, then B will require A's public key, which can be obtained from the certification path:

$$Z \ll Y \gg \; Y \ll V \gg \; V \ll W \gg \; W \ll X \gg \; X \ll A \gg$$

B can obtain this set of certificates from the directory or A can provide them as part of its initial message to B.

REVOCATION OF CERTIFICATES   Recall from Figure 4.4 that each certificate includes a period of validity, much like a credit card. Typically, a new certificate is issued just before the expiration of the old one. In addition, it may be desirable on occasion to revoke a certificate before it expires for one of the following reasons.

1. The user's private key is assumed to be compromised.

2. The user is no longer certified by this CA. Reasons for this include subject's name has changed, the certificate is superseded, or the certificate was not issued in conformance with the CA's policies.

3. The CA's certificate is assumed to be compromised.

Each CA must maintain a list consisting of all revoked but not expired certificates issued by that CA, including both those issued to users and to other CAs. These lists also should be posted on the directory.

Each certificate revocation list (CRL) posted to the directory is signed by the issuer and includes (Figure 4.4b) the issuer's name, the date the list was created, the date the next CRL is scheduled to be issued, and an entry for each revoked certificate. Each entry consists of the serial number of a certificate and revocation date for that certificate. Because serial numbers are unique within a CA, the serial number is sufficient to identify the certificate.

When a user receives a certificate in a message, the user must determine whether the certificate has been revoked. The user could check the directory each time a certificate is received. To avoid the delays (and possible costs) associated with directory searches, it is likely that the user would maintain a local cache of certificates and lists of revoked certificates.

X.509 Version 3

The X.509 version 2 format does not convey all of the information that recent design and implementation experience has shown to be needed. [FORD95] lists the following requirements not satisfied by version 2:

1. The Subject field is inadequate to convey the identity of a-key owner to a public-key user. X.509 names may be relatively short and lacking in obvious identification details that may be needed by the user.

2. The Subject field is also inadequate for many applications, which typically recognize entities by an Internet e-mail address, a URL, or some other Internet-related identification.

3. There is a need to indicate security policy information. This enables a security application or function, such as IPSec, to relate an X.509 certificate to a given policy.

4. There is a need to limit the damage that can result from a faulty or malicious CA by setting constraints on the applicability of a particular certificate.

5. It is important to be able to identify different keys used by the same owner at different times. This feature supports key life cycle management, in particular the ability to update key pairs for users and CAs on a regular basis or under exceptional circumstances.

Rather than continue to add fields to a fixed format, standards developers felt that a more flexible approach was needed. Thus, version 3 includes a number of optional extensions that may be added to the version 2 format. Each extension consists of an extension identifier, a criticality indicator, and an extension value.

The criticality indicator indicates whether an extension can be safely ignored. If the indicator has a value of TRUE and an implementation does not recognize the extension, it must treat the certificate as invalid.

The certificate extensions fall into three main categories: key and policy information, subject and issuer attributes, and certification path constraints.

KEY AND POLICY INFORMATION These extensions convey additional information about the subject and issuer keys, plus indicators of certificate policy. A certificate policy is a named set of rules that indicates the applicability of a certificate to a particular community and/or class of application with common security requirements. For example, a policy might be applicable to the authentication of electronic data interchange (EDI) transactions for the trading of goods within a given price range.

This area includes the following:

- **Authority key identifier:** Identifies the public key to be used to verify the signature on this certificate or CRL. Enables distinct keys of the same CA to be differentiated. One use of this field is to handle CA key pair updating.

- **Subject key identifier:** Identifies the public key being certified. Useful for subject key pair updating. Also, a subject may have multiple key pairs and, correspondingly, different certificates for different purposes (e.g., digital signature and encryption key agreement).

- **Key usage:** Indicates a restriction imposed as to the purposes for which, and the policies under which, the certified public key may be used. May indicate one or more of the following: digital signature, nonrepudiation, key encryption, data encryption, key agreement, CA signature verification on certificates, and CA signature verification on CRLs.

- **Private-key usage period:** Indicates the period of use of the private key corresponding to the public key. Typically, the private key is used over a different period from the validity of the public key. For example, with digital signature keys, the usage period for the signing private key is typically shorter than that for the verifying public key.

- **Certificate policies:** Certificates may be used in environments where multiple policies apply. This extension lists policies that the certificate is recognized as supporting, together with optional qualifier information.

- **Policy mappings:** Used only in certificates for CAs issued by other CAs. Policy mappings allow an issuing CA to indicate that one or more of that issuer's policies can be considered equivalent to another policy used in the subject CA's domain.

CERTIFICATE SUBJECT AND ISSUER ATTRIBUTES These extensions support alternative names, in alternative formats, for a certificate subject or certificate issuer and can convey additional information about the certificate subject to increase a certificate user's confidence that the certificate subject is a particular person or entity. For example, information such as postal address, position within a corporation, or picture image may be required.

The extension fields in this area include the following:

- **Subject alternative name:** Contains one or more alternative names, using any of a variety of forms. This field is important for supporting certain applications, such as electronic mail, EDI, and IPSec, which may employ their own name forms.
- **Issuer alternative name:** Contains one or more alternative names, using any of a variety of forms.
- **Subject directory attributes:** Conveys any desired X.500 directory attribute values for the subject of this certificate.

CERTIFICATION PATH CONSTRAINTS These extensions allow constraint specifications to be included in certificates issued for CAs by other CAs. The constraints may restrict the types of certificates that can be issued by the subject CA or that may occur subsequently in a certification chain.

The extension fields in this area include the following:

- **Basic constraints:** Indicates if the subject may act as a CA. If so, a certification path length constraint may be specified.
- **Name constraints:** Indicates a name space within which all subject names in subsequent certificates in a certification path must be located.
- **Policy constraints:** Specifies constraints that may require explicit certificate policy identification or inhibit policy mapping for the remainder of the certification path.

4.5 PUBLIC-KEY INFRASTRUCTURE

RFC 4949 (*Internet Security Glossary*) defines public-key infrastructure (PKI) as the set of hardware, software, people, policies, and procedures needed to create, manage, store, distribute, and revoke digital certificates based on asymmetric cryptography. The principal objective for developing a PKI is to enable secure, convenient, and efficient acquisition of public keys. The Internet Engineering Task Force (IETF) Public Key Infrastructure X.509 (PKIX) working group has been the driving force behind setting up a formal (and generic) model based on X.509 that is suitable for deploying a certificate-based architecture on the Internet. This section describes the PKIX model.

Figure 4.7 shows the interrelationship among the key elements of the PKIX model. These elements are

- **End entity:** A generic term used to denote end users, devices (e.g., servers, routers), or any other entity that can be identified in the subject field of a public key certificate. End entities typically consume and/or support PKI-related services.
- **Certification authority (CA):** The issuer of certificates and (usually) certificate revocation lists (CRLs). It may also support a variety of administrative functions, although these are often delegated to one or more registration authorities.

Figure 4.7   PKIX Architectural Model

- **Registration authority (RA):** An optional component that can assume a number of administrative functions from the CA. The RA is often associated with the end entity registration process, but can assist in a number of other areas as well.

- **CRL issuer:** An optional component that a CA can delegate to publish CRLs.

- **Repository:** A generic term used to denote any method for storing certificates and CRLs so that they can be retrieved by end entities.

PKIX Management Functions

PKIX identifies a number of management functions that potentially need to be supported by management protocols. These are indicated in Figure 4.7 and include the following:

- **Registration:** This is the process whereby a user first makes itself known to a CA (directly, or through an RA), prior to that CA issuing a certificate or certificates for that user. Registration begins the process of enrolling in a PKI. Registration usually involves some off-line or online procedure for mutual authentication. Typically, the end entity is issued one or more shared secret keys used for subsequent authentication.

- **Initialization:** Before a client system can operate securely, it is necessary to install key materials that have the appropriate relationship with keys stored elsewhere in the infrastructure. For example, the client needs to be securely initialized with the public key and other assured information of the trusted CA(s) to be used in validating certificate paths.

- **Certification:** This is the process in which a CA issues a certificate for a user's public key and returns that certificate to the user's client system and/or posts that certificate in a repository.

- **Key pair recovery:** Key pairs can be used to support digital signature creation and verification, encryption and decryption, or both. When a key pair is used for encryption/decryption, it is important to provide a mechanism to recover the necessary decryption keys when normal access to the keying material is no longer possible, otherwise it will not be possible to recover the encrypted data. Loss of access to the decryption key can result from forgotten passwords/PINs, corrupted disk drives, damage to hardware tokens, and so on. Key pair recovery allows end entities to restore their encryption/decryption key pair from an authorized key backup facility (typically, the CA that issued the end entity's certificate).

- **Key pair update:** All key pairs need to be updated regularly (i.e., replaced with a new key pair) and new certificates issued. Update is required when the certificate lifetime expires and as a result of certificate revocation.

- **Revocation request:** An authorized person advises a CA of an abnormal situation requiring certificate revocation. Reasons for revocation include private key compromise, change in affiliation, and name change.

- **Cross-certification:** Two CAs exchange information used in establishing a cross-certificate. A cross-certificate is a certificate issued by one CA to another CA that contains a CA signature key used for issuing certificates.

PKIX Management Protocols

The PKIX working group has defined two alternative management protocols between PKIX entities that support the management functions listed in the preceding subsection. RFC 2510 defines the certificate management protocols (CMP). Within CMP, each of the management functions is explicitly identified by specific protocol exchanges. CMP is designed to be a flexible protocol able to accommodate a variety of technical, operational, and business models.

RFC 2797 defines certificate management messages over CMS (CMC), where CMS refers to RFC 2630, cryptographic message syntax. CMC is built on earlier work and is intended to leverage existing implementations. Although all of the PKIX functions are supported, the functions do not all map into specific protocol exchanges.

4.6 FEDERATED IDENTITY MANAGEMENT

Federated identity management is a relatively new concept dealing with the use of a common identity management scheme across multiple enterprises and numerous applications and supporting many thousands, even millions, of users. We begin our overview with a discussion of the concept of identity management and then examine federated identity management.

Identity Management

Identity management is a centralized, automated approach to provide enterprise-wide access to resources by employees and other authorized individuals. The focus of identity management is defining an identity for each user (human or process), associating attributes with the identity, and enforcing a means by which a user can verify identity. The central concept of an identity management system is the use of single sign-on (SSO). SSO enables a user to access all network resources after a single authentication.

[PELT07] lists the following as the principal elements of an identity management system.

- **Authentication:** Confirmation that a user corresponds to the user name provided.
- **Authorization:** Granting access to specific services and/or resources based on the authentication.
- **Accounting:** A process for logging access and authorization.
- **Provisioning:** The enrollment of users in the system.
- **Workflow automation:** Movement of data in a business process.
- **Delegated administration:** The use of role-based access control to grant permissions.
- **Password synchronization:** Creating a process for single sign-on (SSO) or reduced sign-on (RSO). Single sign-on enables a user to access all network resources after a single authentication. RSO may involve multiple sign-ons but requires less user effort than if each resource and service maintained its own authentication facility.
- **Self-service password reset:** Enables the user to modify his or her password.
- **Federation:** A process where authentication and permission will be passed on from one system to another—usually across multiple enterprises, thereby reducing the number of authentications needed by the user.

Note that Kerberos contains a number of elements of an identity management system.

Figure 4.8 [LINN06] illustrates entities and data flows in a generic identity management architecture. A **principal** is an identity holder. Typically, this is a human user that seeks access to resources and services on the network. User devices, agent processes, and server systems may also function as principals. Principals authenticate themselves to an **identity provider**. The identity provider associates authentication information with a principal, as well as attributes and one or more identifiers.

Increasingly, digital identities incorporate attributes other than simply an identifier and authentication information (such as passwords and biometric information). An **attribute service** manages the creation and maintenance of such attributes. For example, a user needs to provide a shipping address each time an order is placed at a new Web merchant, and this information needs to be revised

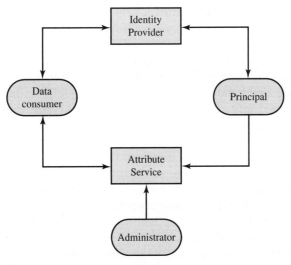

Figure 4.8 Generic Identity Management Architecture

when the user moves. Identity management enables the user to provide this information once, so that it is maintained in a single place and released to data consumers in accordance with authorization and privacy policies. Users may create some of the attributes to be associated with their digital identity, such as address. **Administrators** may also assign attributes to users, such as roles, access permissions, and employee information.

Data consumers are entities that obtain and employ data maintained and provided by identity and attribute providers, which are often used to support authorization decisions and to collect audit information. For example, a database server or file server is a data consumer that needs a client's credentials so as to know what access to provide to that client.

Identity Federation

Identity federation is, in essence, an extension of identity management to multiple security domains. Such domains include autonomous internal business units, external business partners, and other third-party applications and services. The goal is to provide the sharing of digital identities so that a user can be authenticated a single time and then access applications and resources across multiple domains. Because these domains are relatively autonomous or independent, no centralized control is possible. Rather, the cooperating organizations must form a federation based on agreed standards and mutual levels of trust to securely share digital identities.

Federated identity management refers to the agreements, standards, and technologies that enable the portability of identities, identity attributes, and entitlements across multiple enterprises and numerous applications and supports many thousands, even millions, of users. When multiple organizations implement interoperable federated identity schemes, an employee in one organization can use a single sign-on to access services across the federation with trust relationships associated with the identity. For example, an employee may log onto her corporate intranet and be authenticated to perform authorized functions and access authorized services on that intranet. The employee could then access her health benefits from an outside health-care provider without having to reauthenticate.

Beyond SSO, federated identity management provides other capabilities. One is a standardized means of representing attributes. Increasingly, digital identities incorporate attributes other than simply an identifier and authentication information (such as passwords and biometric information). Examples of attributes include account numbers, organizational roles, physical location, and file ownership. A user may have multiple identifiers; for example, each identifier may be associated with a unique role with its own access permissions.

Another key function of federated identity management is identity mapping. Different security domains may represent identities and attributes differently. Furthermore, the amount of information associated with an individual in one domain may be more than is necessary in another domain. The federated identity management protocols map identities and attributes of a user in one domain to the requirements of another domain.

Figure 4.9 illustrates entities and data flows in a generic federated identity management architecture.

The identity provider acquires attribute information through dialogue and protocol exchanges with users and administrators. For example, a user needs to provide a shipping address each time an order is placed at a new Web merchant, and this information needs to be revised when the user moves. Identity management enables the user to provide this information once, so that it is maintained in a single place and released to data consumers in accordance with authorization and privacy policies.

Service providers are entities that obtain and employ data maintained and provided by identity providers, often to support authorization decisions and to collect audit information. For example, a database server or file server is a data consumer that needs a client's credentials so as to know what access to provide to that client. A service provider can be in the same domain as the user and the identity provider. The power of this approach is for federated identity management, in which the service provider is in a different domain (e.g., a vendor or supplier network).

STANDARDS Federated identity management uses a number of standards as the building blocks for secure identity exchange across different domains or heterogeneous systems. In essence, organizations issue some form of security tickets for their users that can be processed by cooperating partners. Identity federation standards are thus concerned with defining these tickets in terms of content and format, providing protocols for exchanging tickets, and performing a number of management tasks. These tasks include configuring systems to perform attribute transfers and identity mapping, and performing logging and auditing functions. The key standards are as follows:

- **The Extensible Markup Language (XML):** A markup language uses sets of embedded tags or labels to characterize text elements within a document so as to indicate their appearance, function, meaning, or context. XML documents

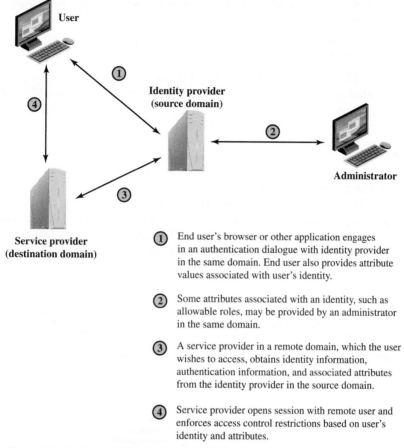

Figure 4.9   Federated Identity Operation

User

Identity provider (source domain)

Administrator

Service provider (destination domain)

① End user's browser or other application engages in an authentication dialogue with identity provider in the same domain. End user also provides attribute values associated with user's identity.

② Some attributes associated with an identity, such as allowable roles, may be provided by an administrator in the same domain.

③ A service provider in a remote domain, which the user wishes to access, obtains identity information, authentication information, and associated attributes from the identity provider in the source domain.

④ Service provider opens session with remote user and enforces access control restrictions based on user's identity and attributes.

appear similar to HTML (Hypertext Markup Language) documents that are visible as Web pages, but provide greater functionality. XML includes strict definitions of the data type of each field, thus supporting database formats and semantics. XML provides encoding rules for commands that are used to transfer and update data objects.

- **The Simple Object Access Protocol (SOAP):** A minimal set of conventions for invoking code using XML over HTTP. It enables applications to request services from one another with XML-based requests and receive responses as data formatted with XML. Thus, XML defines data objects and structures, and SOAP provides a means of exchanging such data objects and performing remote procedure calls related to these objects. See [ROS06] for an informative discussion.

- **WS-Security:** A set of SOAP extensions for implementing message integrity and confidentiality in Web services. To provide for secure exchange of SOAP messages among applications, WS-Security assigns security tokens to each message for use in authentication.

- **Security Assertion Markup Language (SAML):** An XML-based language for the exchange of security information between online business partners. SAML conveys authentication information in the form of assertions about subjects. Assertions are statements about the subject issued by an authoritative entity.

The challenge with federated identity management is to integrate multiple technologies, standards, and services to provide a secure, user-friendly utility. The key, as in most areas of security and networking, is the reliance on a few mature standards widely accepted by industry. Federated identity management seems to have reached this level of maturity.

EXAMPLES To get some feel for the functionality of identity federation, we look at three scenarios, taken from [COMP06]. In the first scenario (Figure 4.10a), Workplace.com contracts with Health.com to provide employee health benefits. An employee uses a Web interface to sign on to Workplace.com and goes through an authentication procedure there. This enables the employee to access authorized services and resources at Workplace.com. When the employee clicks on a

(a) Federation based on account linking

(b) Federation based on roles

(c) Chained Web Services

Figure 4.10 Federated Identity Scenarios

link to access health benefits, her browser is redirected to Health.com. At the same time, the Workplace.com software passes the user's identifier to Health.com in a secure manner. The two organizations are part of a federation that cooperatively exchanges user identifiers. Health.com maintains user identities for every employee at Workplace.com and associates with each identity health-benefits information and access rights. In this example, the linkage between the two companies is based on account information and user participation is browser based.

Figure 4.10b shows a second type of browser-based scheme. PartsSupplier.com is a regular supplier of parts to Workplace.com. In this case, a role-based access control (RBAC) scheme is used for access to information. An engineer of Workplace.com authenticates at the employee portal at Workplace.com and clicks on a link to access information at PartsSupplier.com. Because the user is authenticated in the role of an engineer, he is taken to the technical documentation and troubleshooting portion of PartSupplier.com's Web site without having to sign on. Similarly, an employee in a purchasing role signs on at Workplace.com and is authorized, in that role, to place purchases at PartSupplier.com without having to authenticate to PartSupplier.com. For this scenario, PartSupplier.com does not have identity information for individual employees at Workplace.com. Rather, the linkage between the two federated partners is in terms of roles.

The scenario illustrated in Figure 4.10c can be referred to as document based rather than browser based. In this third example, Workplace.com has a purchasing agreement with PinSupplies.com, and PinSupplies.com has a business relationship with E-Ship.com. An employee of Workplace.com signs on and is authenticated to make purchases. The employee goes to a procurement application that provides a list of Workplace.com's suppliers and the parts that can be ordered. The user clicks on the PinSupplies button and is presented with a purchase order Web page (HTML page). The employee fills out the form and clicks the submit button. The procurement application generates an XML/SOAP document that it inserts into the envelope body of an XML-based message. The procurement application then inserts the user's credentials in the envelope header of the message, together with Workplace.com's organizational identity. The procurement application posts the message to the PinSupplies.com's purchasing Web service. This service authenticates the incoming message and processes the request. The purchasing Web service then sends a SOAP message its shipping partner to fulfill the order. The message includes a PinSupplies.com security token in the envelope header and the list of items to be shipped as well as the end user's shipping information in the envelope body. The shipping Web service authenticates the request and processes the shipment order.

4.7 RECOMMENDED READING

An exhaustive and essential resource on the topics of this chapter is the three-volume NIST SP800-57 [BARK12, BARK05, BARK09]. [FUMY93] is a good survey of key management principles. Another interesting survey, which looks at many key management techniques, is [HEGL06].

A painless way to get a grasp of Kerberos concepts is found in [BRYA88]. One of the best treatments of Kerberos is [KOHL94].

[PERL99] reviews various trust models that can be used in a PKI. [GUTM02] highlights difficulties in PKI use and recommends approaches for an effective PKI.

[SHIM05] provides a brief overview of federated identity management and examines one approach to standardization. [BHAT07] describes an integrated approach to federated identity management coupled with management of access control privileges.

BARK12 Barker, E., et al. *Recommendation for Key Management—Part 1: General.* NIST SP800-57, June 2012.

BARK05 Barker, E., et al. *Recommendation for Key Management—Part 2: Best Practices for Key Management Organization.* NIST SP800-57, August 2005.

BARK09 Barker, E., et al. *Recommendation for Key Management—Part 3: Specific Key Management Guidance.* NIST SP800-57, December 2009.

BHAT07 Bhatti, R.; Bertino, E.; and Ghafoor, A. "An Integrated Approach to Federated Identity and Privilege Management in Open Systems." *Communications of the ACM*, February 2007.

BRYA88 Bryant, W. *Designing an Authentication System: A Dialogue in Four Scenes.* Project Athena document, February 1988. Available at http://web.mit.edu/kerberos/www/dialogue.html.

FUMY93 Fumy, S., and Landrock, P. "Principles of Key Management." *IEEE Journal on Selected Areas in Communications*, June 1993.

GUTM02 Gutmann, P. "PKI: It's Not Dead, Just Resting." *Computer*, August 2002.

HEGL06 Hegland, A., et al. "A Survey of Key Management in Ad Hoc Networks." *IEEE Communications Surveys & Tutorials.* 3rd Quarter, 2006.

KOHL94 Kohl, J.; Neuman, B.; and Ts'o, T. "The Evolution of the Kerberos Authentication Service." in Brazier, F., and Johansen, D. *Distributed Open Systems.* Los Alamitos, CA: IEEE Computer Society Press, 1994. Available at http://web.mit.edu/kerberos/www/papers.html.

PERL99 Perlman, R. "An Overview of PKI Trust Models." *IEEE Network*, November/December 1999.

SHIM05 Shim, S.; Bhalla, G.; and Pendyala, V. "Federated Identity Management." *Computer*, December 2005.

4.8 KEY TERMS, REVIEW QUESTIONS, AND PROBLEMS

Key Terms

authentication	key distribution center (KDC)	public-key certificate
authentication server (AS)	key management	public-key directory
federated identity management	master key	realm
identity management	mutual authentication	replay attack
Kerberos	nonce	ticket
Kerberos realm	one-way authentication	ticket-granting server (TGS)
key distribution	propagating cipher block chaining (PCBC) mode	timestamp
		X.509 certificate

Review Questions

4.1   Explain the operation of a key distribution center.

4.2   What are the advantages of the automated key distribution approach?

4.3   What is Kerberos?

4.4   Identify the security threats that exist in an open distributed network.

4.5   In the context of Kerberos, what is a realm?

4.6   What are the ingredients of a authentication server's ticket? Explain the significance of each.

4.7   List the environmental shortcomings and technical deficiencies of Kerberos version 4.

4.8   Identify the weakness of a public key distribution with a public key algorithm. How can it be fixed?

4.9   What is a X.509 certificate?

4.10 Explain the different fields of the public-key certificate of the X.509 scheme.

4.11 What is public-key infrastructure?

4.12 What are the key elements of the PKIX model?

4.13 Name the PKIX certificate management protocols.

4.14 What is federated identity management?

Problems

4.1   "We are under great pressure, Holmes." Detective Lestrade looked nervous. "We have learned that copies of sensitive government documents are stored in computers of one foreign embassy here in London. Normally these documents exist in electronic form only on a selected few government computers that satisfy the most stringent security requirements. However, sometimes they must be sent through the network connecting all government computers. But all messages in this network are encrypted using a top secret encryption algorithm certified by our best crypto experts. Even the NSA and the KGB are unable to break it. And now these documents have appeared in hands of diplomats of a small, otherwise insignificant, country. And we have no idea how it could happen."

"But you do have some suspicion who did it, do you?" asked Holmes.

"Yes, we did some routine investigation. There is a man who has legal access to one of the government computers and has frequent contacts with diplomats from the embassy. But the computer he has access to is not one of the trusted ones where these documents are normally stored. He is the suspect, but we have no idea how he could obtain copies of the documents. Even if he could obtain a copy of an encrypted document, he couldn't decrypt it."

"Hmm, please describe the communication protocol used on the network." Holmes opened his eyes, thus proving that he had followed Lestrade's talk with an attention that contrasted with his sleepy look.

"Well, the protocol is as follows. Each node N of the network has been assigned a unique secret key K_n. This key is used to secure communication between the node and a trusted server. That is, all the keys are stored also on the server. User A, wishing to send a secret message M to user B, initiates the following protocol:

1. A generates a random number R and sends to the server his name A, destination B, and $E(K_a, R)$.
2. Server responds by sending $E(K_b, R)$ to A.
3. A sends $E(R, M)$ together with $E(K_b, R)$ to B.
4. B knows K_b, thus decrypts $E(K_b, R)$ to get R and will subsequently use R to decrypt $E(R, M)$ to get M.

You see that a random key is generated every time a message has to be sent. I admit the man could intercept messages sent between the top secret trusted nodes, but I see no way he could decrypt them."

"Well, I think you have your man, Lestrade. The protocol isn't secure because the server doesn't authenticate users who send him a request. Apparently designers of the protocol have believed that sending $E(K_x, R)$ implicitly authenticates user X as the sender, as only X (and the server) knows K_x. But you know that $E(K_x, R)$ can be intercepted and later replayed. Once you understand where the hole is, you will be able to obtain enough evidence by monitoring the man's use of the computer he has access to. Most likely he works as follows: After intercepting $E(K_a, R)$ and $E(R, M)$ (see steps 1 and 3 of the protocol), the man, let's denote him as Z, will continue by pretending to be A and..."

Finish the sentence for Holmes.

4.2   There are three typical ways to use nonces as challenges. Suppose N_a is a nonce generated by A, A and B share key K, and f() is a function (such as increment). The three usages are

Usage 1	Usage 2	Usage 3
(1) A → B: N_a	(1) A → B: $E(K, N_a)$	(1) A → B: $E(K, N_a)$
(2) B → A: $E(K, N_a)$	(2) B → A: N_a	(2) B → A: $E(K, f(N_a))$

Describe situations for which each usage is appropriate.

4.3   Show that a random error in one block of ciphertext is propagated to all subsequent blocks of plaintext in PCBC mode (see Figure F.2 in Appendix F).

4.4   Suppose that, in PCBC mode, blocks C_i and C_{i+1} are interchanged during transmission. Show that this affects only the decrypted blocks P_i and P_{i+1} but not subsequent blocks.

4.5   In addition to providing a standard for public-key certificate formats, X.509 specifies an authentication protocol. The original version of X.509 contains a security flaw. The essence of the protocol is

$$A \rightarrow B: \quad A\,\{t_A, r_A, ID_B\}$$
$$B \rightarrow A: \quad B\,\{t_B, r_B, ID_A, r_A\}$$
$$A \rightarrow B: \quad A\,\{r_B\}$$

where t_A and t_B are timestamps, r_A and r_B are nonces, and the notation X {Y} indicates that the message Y is transmitted, encrypted, and signed by X.

The text of X.509 states that checking timestamps t_A and t_B is optional for three-way authentication. But consider the following example: Suppose A and B have used the preceding protocol on some previous occasion, and that opponent C has intercepted the preceding three messages. In addition, suppose that timestamps are not used and are all set to 0. Finally, suppose C wishes to impersonate A to B. C initially sends the first captured message to B:

$$C \rightarrow B: \quad A\,\{0, r_A, ID_B\}$$

B responds, thinking it is talking to A but is actually talking to C:

$$B \rightarrow C: \quad B\,\{0, r'_B, ID_A, r_A\}$$

C meanwhile causes A to initiate authentication with C by some means. As a result, A sends C the following:

$$A \rightarrow C: \quad A\,\{0, r'_A, ID_C\}$$

C responds to A using the same nonce provided to C by B.

$$C \rightarrow A: \quad C\,\{0, r'_B, ID_A, r'_A\}$$

A responds with

$$A \rightarrow C: \quad A\,\{r'_B\}$$

This is exactly what C needs to convince B that it is talking to A, so C now repeats the incoming message back out to B.

$$C \rightarrow B: \quad A \{r'_B\}$$

So B will believe it is talking to A, whereas it is actually talking to C. Suggest a simple solution to this problem that does not involve the use of timestamps.

4.6 Consider a one-way authentication technique based on asymmetric encryption:

$$A \rightarrow B: \quad ID_A$$
$$B \rightarrow A: \quad R_1$$
$$A \rightarrow B: \quad E(PR_a, R_1)$$

a. Explain the protocol.
b. What type of attack is this protocol susceptible to?

4.7 Consider a one-way authentication technique based on asymmetric encryption:

$$A \rightarrow B: \quad ID_A$$
$$B \rightarrow A: \quad E(PU_a, R_2)$$
$$A \rightarrow B: \quad R_2$$

a. Explain the protocol.
b. What type of attack is this protocol susceptible to?

4.8 In Kerberos, how do servers verify the authenticity of the client using the ticket?

4.9 In Kerberos, how does an authentication server protect a ticket from being altered by the client or opponent?

4.10 How is ticket reuse by an opponent prevented in Kerberos?

4.11 What is the purpose of a session key in Kerberos? How is it distributed by the AS?

4.12 The 1988 version of X.509 lists properties that RSA keys must satisfy to be secure, given current knowledge about the difficulty of factoring large numbers. The discussion concludes with a constraint on the public exponent and the modulus n:

> It must be ensured that $e > \log_2(n)$ to prevent attack by taking the eth root mod n to disclose the plaintext.

Although the constraint is correct, the reason given for requiring it is incorrect. What is wrong with the reason given and what is the correct reason?

4.13 Find at least one intermediate certification authority's certificate and one trusted root certification authority's certificate on your computer (e.g., in the browser). Print screenshots of both the general and details tab for each certificate.

4.14 NIST defines the term "cryptoperiod" as the time span during which a specific key is authorized for use or in which the keys for a given system or application may remain in effect. One document on key management uses the following time diagram for a shared secret key.

Originator Usage Period

Recipient Usage Period

Cryptoperiod

Explain the overlap by giving an example application in which the originator's usage period for the shared secret key begins before the recipient's usage period and also ends before the recipient's usage period.

4.15 Consider the following protocol, designed to let A and B decide on a fresh, shared session key K'_{AB}. We assume that they already share a long-term key K_{AB}.

1. $A \rightarrow B$: A, N_A
2. $B \rightarrow A$: $E(K_{AB}, [N_A, K'_{AB}])$
3. $A \rightarrow B$: $E(K'_{AB}, N_A)$

   a. We first try to understand the protocol designer's reasoning:
   - Why would A and B believe after the protocol ran that they share K'_{AB} with the other party?
   - Why would they believe that this shared key is fresh?

   In both cases, you should explain both the reasons of both A and B, so your answer should complete the following sentences.

   A believes that she shares K'_{AB} with B since . . .
   B believes that he shares K'_{AB} with A since . . .
   A believes that K'_{AB} is fresh since . . .
   B believes that K'_{AB} is fresh since . . .

   b. Assume now that A starts a run of this protocol with B. However, the connection is intercepted by the adversary C. Show how C can start a new run of the protocol using reflection, causing A to believe that she has agreed on a fresh key with B (in spite of the fact that she has only been communicating with C). Thus, in particular, the belief in (a) is false.

   c. Propose a modification of the protocol that prevents this attack.

4.16 List the different management functions of the PKIX model.

4.17 Explain the entities and data flows of generic identity management architecture.

4.18 Consider the following protocol:

$$A \rightarrow KDC: \quad ID_A \| ID_B \| N_1$$
$$KDC \rightarrow A: \quad E(K_a, [K_S \| ID_B \| N_1 \| E(K_b, [K_S \| ID_A])])$$
$$A \rightarrow B: \quad E(K_b, [K_S \| ID_A])$$
$$B \rightarrow A: \quad E(K_S, N_2)$$
$$A \rightarrow B: \quad E(K_S, f(N_2))$$

   a. Explain the protocol.
   b. Can you think of a possible attack on this protocol? Explain how it can be done.
   c. Mention a possible technique to get around the attack — not a detailed mechanism, just the basics of the idea.

   Note: The remaining problems deal with a cryptographic product developed by IBM, which is briefly described in a document at this book's Web site in `IBMCrypto.pdf`. *Try these problems after reviewing the document.*

4.19 What is the effect of adding the instruction EMK_i?

$$EMK_i: X \rightarrow E(KMH_i, X) \quad i = 0, 1$$

4.20 Suppose N different systems use the IBM Cryptographic Subsystem with host master keys KMH[i] ($i = 1, 2, \ldots, N$). Devise a method for communicating between systems without requiring the system to either share a common host master key or to divulge their individual host master keys. *Hint*: Each system needs three variants of its host master key.

4.21 The principal objective of the IBM Cryptographic Subsystem is to protect transmissions between a terminal and the processing system. Devise a procedure, perhaps adding instructions, which will allow the processor to generate a session key KS and distribute it to Terminal i and Terminal j without having to store a key-equivalent variable in the host.

CHAPTER 5

NETWORK ACCESS CONTROL AND CLOUD SECURITY

5.1 Network Access Control

Elements of a Network Access Control System
Network Access Enforcement Methods

5.2 Extensible Authentication Protocol

Authentication Methods
EAP Exchanges

5.3 IEEE 802.1X Port-Based Network Access Control

5.4 Cloud Computing

Cloud Computing Elements
Cloud Computing Reference Architecture

5.5 Cloud Security Risks and Countermeasures

5.6 Data Protection in the Cloud

5.7 Cloud Security as a Service

5.8 Recommended Reading

5.9 Key Terms, Review Questions, and Problems

"No ticket! Dear me, Watson, this is really very singular. According to my experience it is not possible to reach the platform of a Metropolitan train without exhibiting one's ticket."

— *The Adventure of the Bruce-Partington Plans,* Sir Arthur Conan Doyle

LEARNING OBJECTIVES

After studying this chapter, you should be able to:

◆ Discuss the principal elements of a network access control system.

◆ Discuss the principal network access enforcement methods.

◆ Present an overview of the Extensible Authentication Protocol.

◆ Understand the operation and role of the IEEE 802.1X Port-Based Network Access Control mechanism.

◆ Present an overview of cloud computing concepts.

◆ Understand the unique security issues related to cloud computing.

This chapter begins our discussion of network security, focusing on two key topics: network access control and cloud security. We begin with an overview of network access control systems, summarizing the principal elements and techniques involved in such a system. Next, we discuss the Extensible Authentication Protocol and IEEE 802.1X, two widely implemented standards that are the foundation of many network access control systems.

The remainder of the chapter deals with cloud security. We begin with an overview of cloud computing, and follow this with a discussion of cloud security issues.

5.1 NETWORK ACCESS CONTROL

Network access control (NAC) is an umbrella term for managing access to a network. NAC authenticates users logging into the network and determines what data they can access and actions they can perform. NAC also examines the health of the user's computer or mobile device (the endpoints).

Elements of a Network Access Control System

NAC systems deal with three categories of components:

- **Access requestor (AR):** The AR is the node that is attempting to access the network and may be any device that is managed by the NAC system, including workstations, servers, printers, cameras, and other IP-enabled devices. ARs are also referred to as **supplicants**, or simply, clients.

- **Policy server:** Based on the AR's posture and an enterprise's defined policy, the policy server determines what access should be granted. The policy server often relies on backend systems, including antivirus, patch management, or a user directory, to help determine the host's condition.

- **Network access server (NAS):** The NAS functions as an access control point for users in remote locations connecting to an enterprise's internal network. Also called a **media gateway**, a **remote access server (RAS)**, or a **policy server**, an NAS may include its own authentication services or rely on a separate authentication service from the policy server.

Figure 5.1 is a generic network access diagram. A variety of different ARs seek access to an enterprise network by applying to some type of NAS. The first step is generally to authenticate the AR. Authentication typically involves some sort of secure protocol and the use of cryptographic keys. Authentication may be performed by the NAS, or the NAS may mediate the authentication process. In the latter case, authentication takes place between the supplicant and an authentication server that is part of the policy server or that is accessed by the policy server.

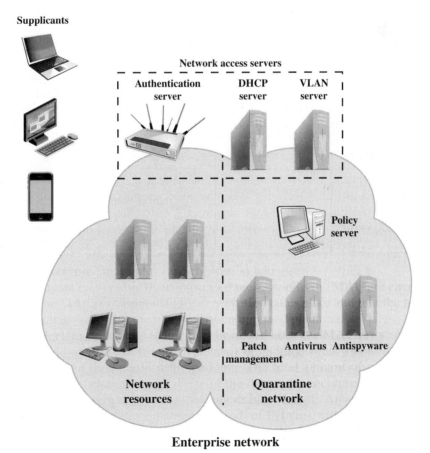

Figure 5.1   Network Access Control Context

The authentication process serves a number of purposes. It verifies a supplicant's claimed identity, which enables the policy server to determine what access privileges, if any, the AR may have. The authentication exchange may result in the establishment of session keys to enable future secure communication between the supplicant and resources on the enterprise network.

Typically, the policy server or a supporting server will perform checks on the AR to determine if it should be permitted interactive remote access connectivity. These checks—sometimes called health, suitability, screening, or assessment checks—require software on the user's system to verify compliance with certain requirements from the organization's secure configuration baseline. For example, the user's antimalware software must be up-to-date, the operating system must be fully patched, and the remote computer must be owned and controlled by the organization. These checks should be performed before granting the AR access to the enterprise network. Based on the results of these checks, the organization can determine whether the remote computer should be permitted to use interactive remote access. If the user has acceptable authorization credentials but the remote computer does not pass the health check, the user and remote computer should be denied network access or have limited access to a quarantine network so that authorized personnel can fix the security deficiencies. Figure 5.1 indicates that the quarantine portion of the enterprise network consists of the policy server and related AR suitability servers. There may also be application servers that do not require the normal security threshold be met.

Once an AR has been authenticated and cleared for a certain level of access to the enterprise network, the NAS can enable the AR to interact with resources in the enterprise network. The NAS may mediate every exchange to enforce a security policy for this AR, or may use other methods to limit the privileges of the AR.

Network Access Enforcement Methods

Enforcement methods are the actions that are applied to ARs to regulate access to the enterprise network. Many vendors support multiple enforcement methods simultaneously, allowing the customer to tailor the configuration by using one or a combination of methods. The following are common NAC enforcement methods.

- **IEEE 802.1X:** This is a link layer protocol that enforces authorization before a port is assigned an IP address. IEEE 802.1X makes use of the Extensible Authentication Protocol for the authentication process. Sections 5.2 and 5.3 cover the Extensible Authentication Protocol and IEEE 802.1X, respectively.

- **Virtual local area networks (VLANs):** In this approach, the enterprise network, consisting of an interconnected set of LANs, is segmented logically into a number of virtual LANs.[1] The NAC system decides to which of the

---

[1] A VLAN is a logical subgroup within a LAN that is created via software rather than manually moving cables in the wiring closet. It combines user stations and network devices into a single unit regardless of the physical LAN segment they are attached to and allows traffic to flow more efficiently within populations of mutual interest. VLANs are implemented in port-switching hubs and LAN switches.

network's VLANs it will direct an AR, based on whether the device needs security remediation, Internet access only, or some level of network access to enterprise resources. VLANs can be created dynamically and VLAN membership, of both enterprise servers and ARs, may overlap. That is, an enterprise server or an AR may belong to more than one VLAN.

- **Firewall:** A firewall provides a form of NAC by allowing or denying network traffic between an enterprise host and an external user. Firewalls are discussed in Chapter 12.

- **DHCP management:** The Dynamic Host Configuration Protocol (DHCP) is an Internet protocol that enables dynamic allocation of IP addresses to hosts. A DHCP server intercepts DHCP requests and assigns IP addresses instead. Thus, NAC enforcement occurs at the IP layer based on subnet and IP assignment. A DCHP server is easy to install and configure, but is subject to various forms of IP spoofing, providing limited security.

There are a number of other enforcement methods available from vendors. The ones in the preceding list are perhaps the most common, and IEEE 802.1X is by far the most commonly implemented solution.

5.2 EXTENSIBLE AUTHENTICATION PROTOCOL

The Extensible Authentication Protocol (EAP), defined in RFC 3748, acts as a framework for network access and authentication protocols. EAP provides a set of protocol messages that can encapsulate various authentication methods to be used between a client and an authentication server. EAP can operate over a variety of network and link level facilities, including point-to-point links, LANs, and other networks, and can accommodate the authentication needs of the various links and networks. Figure 5.2 illustrates the protocol layers that form the context for EAP.

Figure 5.2 EAP Layered Context

Authentication Methods

EAP supports multiple authentication methods. This is what is meant by referring to EAP as *extensible*. EAP provides a generic transport service for the exchange of authentication information between a client system and an authentication server. The basic EAP transport service is extended by using a specific authentication protocol, or method, that is installed in both the EAP client and the authentication server.

Numerous methods have been defined to work over EAP. The following are commonly supported EAP methods:

- **EAP-TLS (EAP Transport Layer Security):** EAP-TLS (RFC 5216) defines how the TLS protocol (described in Chapter 6) can be encapsulated in EAP messages. EAP-TLS uses the handshake protocol in TLS, not its encryption method. Client and server authenticate each other using digital certificates. Client generates a pre-master secret key by encrypting a random number with the server's public key and sends it to the server. Both client and server use the pre-master to generate the same secret key.

- **EAP-TTLS (EAP Tunneled TLS):** EAP-TTLS is like EAP-TLS, except only the server has a certificate to authenticate itself to the client first. As in EAP-TLS, a secure connection (the "tunnel") is established with secret keys, but that connection is used to continue the authentication process by authenticating the client and possibly the server again using any EAP method or legacy method such as PAP (Password Authentication Protocol) and CHAP (Challenge-Handshake Authentication Protocol). EAP-TTLS is defined in RFC 5281.

- **EAP-GPSK (EAP Generalized Pre-Shared Key):** EAP-GPSK, defined in RFC 5433, is an EAP method for mutual authentication and session key derivation using a Pre-Shared Key (PSK). EAP-GPSK specifies an EAP method based on pre-shared keys and employs secret key-based cryptographic algorithms. Hence, this method is efficient in terms of message flows and computational costs, but requires the existence of pre-shared keys between each peer and EAP server. The set up of these pairwise secret keys is part of the peer registration, and thus, must satisfy the system preconditions. It provides a protected communication channel when mutual authentication is successful for both parties to communicate over and is designed for authentication over insecure networks such as IEEE 802.11. EAP-GPSK does not require any public-key cryptography. The EAP method protocol exchange is done in a minimum of four messages.

- **EAP-IKEv2:** It is based on the Internet Key Exchange protocol version 2 (IKEv2), which is described in Chapter 9. It supports mutual authentication and session key establishment using a variety of methods. EAP-TLS is defined in RFC 5106.

EAP Exchanges

Whatever method is used for authentication, the authentication information and authentication protocol information are carried in EAP messages.

Figure 5.3   EAP Protocol Exchanges

RFC 3748 defines the goal of the exchange of EAP messages to be successful authentication. In the context of RFC 3748, *successful authentication* is an exchange of EAP messages, as a result of which the authenticator decides to allow access by the peer, and the peer decides to use this access. The authenticator's decision typically involves both authentication and authorization aspects; the peer may successfully authenticate to the authenticator, but access may be denied by the authenticator due to policy reasons.

Figure 5.3 indicates a typical arrangement in which EAP is used. The following components are involved:

- **EAP peer:** Client computer that is attempting to access a network.
- **EAP authenticator:** An access point or NAS that requires EAP authentication prior to granting access to a network.
- **Authentication server:** A server computer that negotiates the use of a specific EAP method with an EAP peer, validates the EAP peer's credentials, and authorizes access to the network. Typically, the authentication server is a Remote Authentication Dial-In User Service (RADIUS) server.

The authentication server functions as a backend server that can authenticate peers as a service to a number of EAP authenticators. The EAP authenticator then makes the decision of whether to grant access. This is referred to as the **EAP pass-through mode**. Less commonly, the authenticator takes over the role of the EAP server; that is, only two parties are involved in the EAP execution.

As a first step, a lower-level protocol, such as PPP (point-to-point protocol) or IEEE 802.1X, is used to connect to the EAP authenticator. The software entity in the EAP peer that operates at this level is referred to as the **supplicant**. EAP messages containing the appropriate information for a chosen EAP method are then exchanged between the EAP peer and the authentication server.

EAP messages may include the following fields:

- **Code:** Identifies the Type of EAP message. The codes are Request (1), Response (2), Success (3), and Failure (4).
- **Identifier:** Used to match Responses with Requests.
- **Length:** Indicates the length, in octets, of the EAP message, including the Code, Identifier, Length, and Data fields.
- **Data:** Contains information related to authentication. Typically, the Data field consists of a Type subfield, indicating the type of data carried, and a Type-Data field.

The Success and Failure messages do not include a Data field.

The EAP authentication exchange proceeds as follows. After a lower-level exchange that established the need for an EAP exchange, the authenticator sends a Request to the peer to request an identity, and the peer sends a Response with the identity information. This is followed by a sequence of Requests by the authenticator and Responses by the peer for the exchange of authentication information. The information exchanged and the number of Request–Response exchanges needed depend on the authentication method. The conversation continues until either (1) the authenticator determines that it cannot authenticate the peer and transmits an EAP Failure or (2) the authenticator determines that successful authentication has occurred and transmits an EAP Success.

Figure 5.4 gives an example of an EAP exchange. Not shown in the figure is a message or signal sent from the EAP peer to the authenticator using some protocol

Figure 5.4   EAP Message Flow in Pass-Through Mode

other than EAP and requesting an EAP exchange to grant network access. One protocol used for this purpose is IEEE 802.1X, discussed in the next section. The first pair of EAP Request and Response messages is of Type identity, in which the authenticator requests the peer's identity, and the peer returns its claimed identity in the Response message. This Response is passed through the authenticator to the authentication server. Subsequent EAP messages are exchanged between the peer and the authentication server.

Upon receiving the identity Response message from the peer, the server selects an EAP method and sends the first EAP message with a Type field related to an authentication method. If the peer supports and accepts the selected EAP method, it replies with the corresponding Response message of the same type. Otherwise, the peer sends a NAK, and the EAP server either selects another EAP method or aborts the EAP execution with a failure message. The selected EAP method determines the number of Request/Response pairs. During the exchange the appropriate authentication information, including key material, is exchanged. The exchange ends when the server determines that authentication has succeeded or that no further attempt can be made and authentication has failed.

5.3 IEEE 802.1X PORT-BASED NETWORK ACCESS CONTROL

IEEE 802.1X Port-Based Network Access Control was designed to provide access control functions for LANs. Table 5.1 briefly defines key terms used in the IEEE 802.11 standard. The terms *supplicant*, *network access point*, and *authentication server* correspond to the EAP terms *peer*, *authenticator*, and *authentication server*, respectively.

Until the AS authenticates a supplicant (using an authentication protocol), the authenticator only passes control and authentication messages between the supplicant and the AS; the 802.1X control channel is unblocked, but the 802.11 data channel is blocked. Once a supplicant is authenticated and keys are provided, the authenticator can forward data from the supplicant, subject to predefined access control limitations for the supplicant to the network. Under these circumstances, the data channel is unblocked.

As indicated in Figure 5.5, 802.1X uses the concepts of controlled and uncontrolled ports. Ports are logical entities defined within the authenticator and refer to physical network connections. Each logical port is mapped to one of these two types of physical ports. An uncontrolled port allows the exchange of protocol data units (PDUs) between the supplicant and the AS, regardless of the authentication state of the supplicant. A controlled port allows the exchange of PDUs between a supplicant and other systems on the network only if the current state of the supplicant authorizes such an exchange.

The essential element defined in 802.1X is a protocol known as EAPOL (EAP over LAN). EAPOL operates at the network layers and makes use of an IEEE 802 LAN, such as Ethernet or Wi-Fi, at the link level. EAPOL enables a supplicant to communicate with an authenticator and supports the exchange of EAP packets for authentication.

The most common EAPOL packets are listed in Table 5.2. When the supplicant first connects to the LAN, it does not know the MAC address of the

Table 5.1   Terminology Related to IEEE 802.1X

Authenticator An entity at one end of a point-to-point LAN segment that facilities authentication of the entity to the other end of the link.
Authentication exchange The two-party conversation between systems performing an authentication process.
Authentication process The cryptographic operations and supporting data frames that perform the actual authentication.
Authentication server (AS) An entity that provides an authentication service to an authenticator. This service determines, from the credentials provided by supplicant, whether the supplicant is authorized to access the services provided by the system in which the authenticator resides.
Authentication transport The datagram session that actively transfers the authentication exchange between two systems.
Bridge port A port of an IEEE 802.1D or 802.1Q bridge.
Edge port A bridge port attached to a LAN that has no other bridges attached to it.
Network access port A point of attachment of a system to a LAN. It can be a physical port, such as a single LAN MAC attached to a physical LAN segment, or a logical port, for example, an IEEE 802.11 association between a station and an access point.
Port access entity (PAE) The protocol entity associated with a port. It can support the protocol functionality associated with the authenticator, the supplicant, or both.
Supplicant An entity at one end of a point-to-point LAN segment that seeks to be authenticated by an authenticator attached to the other end of that link.

authenticator. Actually it doesn't know whether there is an authenticator present at all. By sending an **EAPOL-Start** packet to a special group-multicast address reserved for IEEE 802.1X authenticators, a supplicant can determine whether an authenticator is present and let it know that the supplicant is ready. In many cases, the authenticator will already be notified that a new device has connected from some hardware notification. For example, a hub knows that a cable is plugged in before the device sends any data. In this case the authenticator may preempt the Start message with its own message. In either case the authenticator sends an EAP-Request Identity message encapsulated in an **EAPOL-EAP** packet. The EAPOL-EAP is the EAPOL frame type used for transporting EAP packets.

The authenticator uses the **EAP-Key** packet to send cryptographic keys to the supplicant once it has decided to admit it to the network. The **EAP-Logoff** packet type indicates that the supplicant wishes to be disconnected from the network.

The EAPOL packet format includes the following fields:

- **Protocol version:** version of EAPOL.
- **Packet type:** indicates start, EAP, key, logoff, etc.

Figure 5.5   802.1X Access Control

Table 5.2   Common EAPOL Frame Types

Frame Type	Definition
EAPOL-EAP	Contains an encapsulated EAP packet.
EAPOL-Start	A supplicant can issue this packet instead of waiting for a challenge from the authenticator.
EAPOL-Logoff	Used to return the state of the port to unauthorized when the supplicant if finished using the network.
EAPOL-Key	Used to exchange cryptographic keying information.

- **Packet body length:** If the packet includes a body, this field indicates the body length.
- **Packet body:** The payload for this EAPOL packet. An example is an EAP packet.

Figure 5.6 shows an example of exchange using EAPOL. In Chapter 7, we examine the use of EAP and EAPOL in the context of IEEE 802.11 wireless LAN security.

5.4 CLOUD COMPUTING

There is an increasingly prominent trend in many organizations to move a substantial portion of or even all information technology (IT) operations to an Internet-connected infrastructure known as enterprise cloud computing. This section provides an overview of cloud computing.

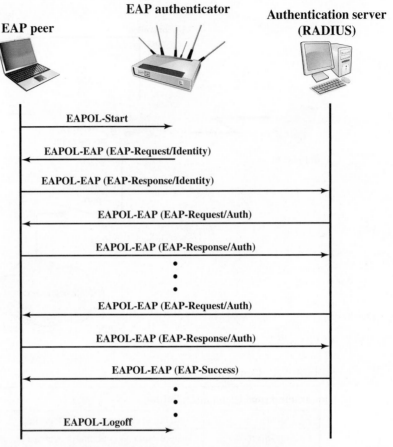

Figure 5.6   Example Timing Diagram for IEEE 802.1X

Cloud Computing Elements

NIST defines cloud computing, in NIST SP-800-145 (*The NIST Definition of Cloud Computing*), as follows:

> **Cloud computing:** A model for enabling ubiquitous, convenient, on-demand network access to a shared pool of configurable computing resources (e.g., networks, servers, storage, applications, and services) that can be rapidly provisioned and released with minimal management effort or service provider interaction. This cloud model promotes availability and is composed of five essential characteristics, three service models, and four deployment models.

The definition refers to various models and characteristics, whose relationship is illustrated in Figure 5.7. The essential characteristics of cloud computing include the following:

- **Broad network access:** Capabilities are available over the network and accessed through standard mechanisms that promote use by heterogeneous thin

Figure 5.7   Cloud Computing Elements

or thick client platforms (e.g., mobile phones, laptops, and PDAs) as well as other traditional or cloud-based software services.

- **Rapid elasticity:** Cloud computing gives you the ability to expand and reduce resources according to your specific service requirement. For example, you may need a large number of server resources for the duration of a specific task. You can then release these resources upon completion of the task.

- **Measured service:** Cloud systems automatically control and optimize resource use by leveraging a metering capability at some level of abstraction appropriate to the type of service (e.g., storage, processing, bandwidth, and active user accounts). Resource usage can be monitored, controlled, and reported, providing transparency for both the provider and consumer of the utilized service.

- **On-demand self-service:** A consumer can unilaterally provision computing capabilities, such as server time and network storage, as needed automatically without requiring human interaction with each service provider. Because the service is on demand, the resources are not permanent parts of your IT infrastructure.

- **Resource pooling:** The provider's computing resources are pooled to serve multiple consumers using a multi-tenant model, with different physical and virtual resources dynamically assigned and reassigned according to consumer demand. There is a degree of location independence in that the customer generally has no control or knowledge of the exact location of the provided resources, but may be able to specify location at a higher level of abstraction (e.g., country, state, or data center). Examples of resources include storage, processing, memory, network bandwidth, and virtual machines. Even private clouds tend to pool resources between different parts of the same organization.

NIST defines three **service models**, which can be viewed as nested service alternatives:

- **Software as a service (SaaS):** The capability provided to the consumer is to use the provider's applications running on a cloud infrastructure. The applications are accessible from various client devices through a thin client interface such as a Web browser. Instead of obtaining desktop and server licenses for software products it uses, an enterprise obtains the same functions from the cloud service. SaaS saves the complexity of software installation, maintenance, upgrades, and patches. Examples of services at this level are Gmail, Google's e-mail service, and Salesforce.com, which helps firms keep track of their customers.

- **Platform as a service (PaaS):** The capability provided to the consumer is to deploy onto the cloud infrastructure consumer-created or acquired applications created using programming languages and tools supported by the provider. PaaS often provides middleware-style services such as database and component services for use by applications. In effect, PaaS is an operating system in the cloud.

- **Infrastructure as a service (IaaS):** The capability provided to the consumer is to provision processing, storage, networks, and other fundamental computing resources where the consumer is able to deploy and run arbitrary software, which can include operating systems and applications. IaaS enables customers to combine basic computing services, such as number crunching and data storage, to build highly adaptable computer systems.

NIST defines four **deployment models**:

- **Public cloud:** The cloud infrastructure is made available to the general public or a large industry group and is owned by an organization selling cloud services. The cloud provider is responsible both for the cloud infrastructure and for the control of data and operations within the cloud.

- **Private cloud:** The cloud infrastructure is operated solely for an organization. It may be managed by the organization or a third party and may exist on premise or off premise. The cloud provider (CP) is responsible only for the infrastructure and not for the control.

- **Community cloud:** The cloud infrastructure is shared by several organizations and supports a specific community that has shared concerns (e.g., mission, security requirements, policy, and compliance considerations). It may be managed by the organizations or a third party and may exist on premise or off premise.

- **Hybrid cloud:** The cloud infrastructure is a composition of two or more clouds (private, community, or public) that remain unique entities but are bound together by standardized or proprietary technology that enables data and application portability (e.g., cloud bursting for load balancing between clouds).

Figure 5.8 illustrates the typical cloud service context. An enterprise maintains workstations within an enterprise LAN or set of LANs, which are connected by a router through a network or the Internet to the cloud service provider. The cloud service provider maintains a massive collection of servers, which it manages with a variety of network management, redundancy, and security tools. In the figure, the cloud infrastructure is shown as a collection of blade servers, which is a common architecture.

Figure 5.8 Cloud Computing Context

Cloud Computing Reference Architecture

NIST SP 500-292 (*NIST Cloud Computing Reference Architecture*) establishes a reference architecture, described as follows:

> The NIST cloud computing reference architecture focuses on the requirements of "what" cloud services provide, not a "how to" design solution and implementation. The reference architecture is intended to facilitate the understanding of the operational intricacies in cloud computing. It does not represent the system architecture of a specific cloud computing system; instead it is a tool for describing, discussing, and developing a system-specific architecture using a common framework of reference.

NIST developed the reference architecture with the following objectives in mind:

- to illustrate and understand the various cloud services in the context of an overall cloud computing conceptual model
- to provide a technical reference for consumers to understand, discuss, categorize, and compare cloud services
- to facilitate the analysis of candidate standards for security, interoperability, and portability and reference implementations

The reference architecture, depicted in Figure 5.9, defines five major actors in terms of the roles and responsibilities:

- **Cloud consumer:** A person or organization that maintains a business relationship with, and uses service from, cloud providers.

Figure 5.9 NIST Cloud Computing Reference Architecture

- **Cloud provider:** A person, organization, or entity responsible for making a service available to interested parties.
- **Cloud auditor:** A party that can conduct independent assessment of cloud services, information system operations, performance, and security of the cloud implementation.
- **Cloud broker:** An entity that manages the use, performance, and delivery of cloud services, and negotiates relationships between CPs and cloud consumers.
- **Cloud carrier:** An intermediary that provides connectivity and transport of cloud services from CPs to cloud consumers.

The roles of the cloud consumer and provider have already been discussed. To summarize, a **cloud provider** can provide one or more of the cloud services to meet IT and business requirements of **cloud consumers**. For each of the three service models (SaaS, PaaS, IaaS), the CP provides the storage and processing facilities needed to support that service model, together with a cloud interface for cloud service consumers. For SaaS, the CP deploys, configures, maintains, and updates the operation of the software applications on a cloud infrastructure so that the services are provisioned at the expected service levels to cloud consumers. The consumers of SaaS can be organizations that provide their members with access to software applications, end users who directly use software applications, or software application administrators who configure applications for end users.

For PaaS, the CP manages the computing infrastructure for the platform and runs the cloud software that provides the components of the platform, such as runtime software execution stack, databases, and other middleware components. Cloud consumers of PaaS can employ the tools and execution resources provided by CPs to develop, test, deploy, and manage the applications hosted in a cloud environment.

For IaaS, the CP acquires the physical computing resources underlying the service, including the servers, networks, storage, and hosting infrastructure. The IaaS cloud consumer in turn uses these computing resources, such as a virtual computer, for their fundamental computing needs.

The **cloud carrier** is a networking facility that provides connectivity and transport of cloud services between cloud consumers and CPs. Typically, a CP will set up service level agreements (SLAs) with a cloud carrier to provide services consistent with the level of SLAs offered to cloud consumers, and may require the cloud carrier to provide dedicated and secure connections between cloud consumers and CPs.

A **cloud broker** is useful when cloud services are too complex for a cloud consumer to easily manage. Three areas of support can be offered by a cloud broker:

- **Service intermediation:** These are value-added services, such as identity management, performance reporting, and enhanced security.
- **Service aggregation:** The broker combines multiple cloud services to meet consumer needs not specifically addressed by a single CP, or to optimize performance or minimize cost.
- **Service arbitrage:** This is similar to service aggregation except that the services being aggregated are not fixed. Service arbitrage means a broker has the flexibility to choose services from multiple agencies. The cloud broker, for example, can use a credit-scoring service to measure and select an agency with the best score.

A **cloud auditor** can evaluate the services provided by a CP in terms of security controls, privacy impact, performance, and so on. The auditor is an independent entity that can assure that the CP conforms to a set of standards.

5.5 CLOUD SECURITY RISKS AND COUNTERMEASURES

In general terms, security controls in cloud computing are similar to the security controls in any IT environment. However, because of the operational models and technologies used to enable cloud service, cloud computing may present risks that are specific to the cloud environment. The essential concept in this regard is that the enterprise loses a substantial amount of control over resources, services, and applications but must maintain accountability for security and privacy policies.

The Cloud Security Alliance [CSA10] lists the following as the top cloud-specific security threats, together with suggested countermeasures:

- **Abuse and nefarious use of cloud computing:** For many CPs, it is relatively easy to register and begin using cloud services, some even offering free limited trial periods. This enables attackers to get inside the cloud to conduct various attacks, such as spamming, malicious code attacks, and denial of service. PaaS providers have traditionally suffered most from this kind of attacks; however, recent evidence shows that hackers have begun to target IaaS vendors as well. The burden is on the CP to protect against such attacks, but cloud service clients must monitor activity with respect to their data and resources to detect any malicious behavior.

  Countermeasures include (1) stricter initial registration and validation processes; (2) enhanced credit card fraud monitoring and coordination; (3) comprehensive introspection of customer network traffic; and (4) monitoring public blacklists for one's own network blocks.

- **Insecure interfaces and APIs:** CPs expose a set of software interfaces or APIs that customers use to manage and interact with cloud services. The security and availability of general cloud services are dependent upon the security of these basic APIs. From authentication and access control to encryption and activity monitoring, these interfaces must be designed to protect against both accidental and malicious attempts to circumvent policy.

  Countermeasures include (1) analyzing the security model of CP interfaces; (2) ensuring that strong authentication and access controls are implemented in concert with encrypted transmission; and (3) understanding the dependency chain associated with the API.

- **Malicious insiders:** Under the cloud computing paradigm, an organization relinquishes direct control over many aspects of security and, in doing so, confers an unprecedented level of trust onto the CP. One grave concern is the risk of malicious insider activity. Cloud architectures necessitate certain roles that are extremely high risk. Examples include CP system administrators and managed security service providers.

  Countermeasures include the following: (1) enforce strict supply chain management and conduct a comprehensive supplier assessment; (2) specify human resource requirements as part of legal contract; (3) require transparency into overall information security and management practices, as well as compliance reporting; and (4) determine security breach notification processes.

- **Shared technology issues:** IaaS vendors deliver their services in a scalable way by sharing infrastructure. Often, the underlying components that make up this infrastructure (CPU caches, GPUs, etc.) were not designed to offer strong isolation properties for a multi-tenant architecture. CPs typically approach this risk by the use of isolated virtual machines for individual clients. This approach is still vulnerable to attack, by both insiders and outsiders, and so can only be a part of an overall security strategy.

  Countermeasures include the following: (1) implement security best practices for installation/configuration; (2) monitor environment for unauthorized changes/activity; (3) promote strong authentication and access control for administrative access and operations; (4) enforce SLAs for patching and vulnerability remediation; and (5) conduct vulnerability scanning and configuration audits.

- **Data loss or leakage:** For many clients, the most devastating impact from a security breach is the loss or leakage of data. We address this issue in the next subsection.

  Countermeasures include the following: (1) implement strong API access control; (2) encrypt and protect integrity of data in transit; (3) analyze data protection at both design and run time; and (4) implement strong key generation, storage and management, and destruction practices.

- **Account or service hijacking:** Account or service hijacking, usually with stolen credentials, remains a top threat. With stolen credentials, attackers can often access critical areas of deployed cloud computing services, allowing them to compromise the confidentiality, integrity, and availability of those services.

  Countermeasures include the following: (1) prohibit the sharing of account credentials between users and services; (2) leverage strong two-factor authentication techniques where possible; (3) employ proactive monitoring to detect unauthorized activity; and (4) understand CP security policies and SLAs.

- **Unknown risk profile:** In using cloud infrastructures, the client necessarily cedes control to the CP on a number of issues that may affect security. Thus the client must pay attention to and clearly define the roles and responsibilities involved for managing risks. For example, employees may deploy applications and data resources at the CP without observing the normal policies and procedures for privacy, security, and oversight.

  Countermeasures include (1) disclosure of applicable logs and data; (2) partial/full disclosure of infrastructure details (e.g., patch levels and firewalls); and (3) monitoring and alerting on necessary information.

Similar lists have been developed by the European Network and Information Security Agency [ENIS09] and NIST [JANS11].

5.6 DATA PROTECTION IN THE CLOUD

As can be seen from the previous section, there are numerous aspects to cloud security and numerous approaches to providing cloud security measures. A further example is seen in the NIST guidelines for cloud security, specified in SP-800-14 and listed in Table 5.3. Thus, the topic of cloud security is well beyond the scope of this chapter. In this section, we focus on one specific element of cloud security.

Table 5.3   NIST Guidelines on Security and Privacy Issues and Recommendations

Governance

Extend organizational practices pertaining to the policies, procedures, and standards used for application development and service provisioning in the cloud, as well as the design, implementation, testing, use, and monitoring of deployed or engaged services.

   Put in place audit mechanisms and tools to ensure organizational practices are followed throughout the system life cycle.

Compliance

Understand the various types of laws and regulations that impose security and privacy obligations on the organization and potentially impact cloud computing initiatives, particularly those involving data location, privacy and security controls, records management, and electronic discovery requirements.

   Review and assess the cloud provider's offerings with respect to the organizational requirements to be met and ensure that the contract terms adequately meet the requirements.

   Ensure that the cloud provider's electronic discovery capabilities and processes do not compromise the privacy or security of data and applications.

Trust

Ensure that service arrangements have sufficient means to allow visibility into the security and privacy controls and processes employed by the cloud provider, and their performance over time.

   Establish clear, exclusive ownership rights over data.

   Institute a risk management program that is flexible enough to adapt to the constantly evolving and shifting risk landscape for the life cycle of the system.

   Continuously monitor the security state of the information system to support ongoing risk management decisions.

Architecture

Understand the underlying technologies that the cloud provider uses to provision services, including the implications that the technical controls involved have on the security and privacy of the system, over the full system life cycle and across all system components.

Identity and access management

Ensure that adequate safeguards are in place to secure authentication, authorization, and other identity and access management functions, and are suitable for the organization.

Software isolation

Understand virtualization and other logical isolation techniques that the cloud provider employs in its multi-tenant software architecture, and assess the risks involved for the organization.

Data protection

Evaluate the suitability of the cloud provider's data management solutions for the organizational data concerned and the ability to control access to data, to secure data while at rest, in transit, and in use, and to sanitize data.

   Take into consideration the risk of collating organizational data with those of other organizations whose threat profiles are high or whose data collectively represent significant concentrated value.

Table 5.3   Continued

Fully understand and weigh the risks involved in cryptographic key management with the facilities available in the cloud environment and the processes established by the cloud provider.

Availability

Understand the contract provisions and procedures for availability, data backup and recovery, and disaster recovery, and ensure that they meet the organization's continuity and contingency planning requirements.

Ensure that during an intermediate or prolonged disruption or a serious disaster, critical operations can be immediately resumed, and that all operations can be eventually reinstituted in a timely and organized manner.

Incident response

Understand the contract provisions and procedures for incident response and ensure that they meet the requirements of the organization.

Ensure that the cloud provider has a transparent response process in place and sufficient mechanisms to share information during and after an incident.

Ensure that the organization can respond to incidents in a coordinated fashion with the cloud provider in accordance with their respective roles and responsibilities for the computing environment.

There are many ways to compromise data. Deletion or alteration of records without a backup of the original content is an obvious example. Unlinking a record from a larger context may render it unrecoverable, as can storage on unreliable media. Loss of an encoding key may result in effective destruction. Finally, unauthorized parties must be prevented from gaining access to sensitive data.

The threat of data compromise increases in the cloud, due to the number of and interactions between risks and challenges that are either unique to the cloud or more dangerous because of the architectural or operational characteristics of the cloud environment.

Database environments used in cloud computing can vary significantly. Some providers support a **multi-instance model**, which provides a unique DBMS running on a virtual machine instance for each cloud subscriber. This gives the subscriber complete control over role definition, user authorization, and other administrative tasks related to security. Other providers support a **multi-tenant model**, which provides a predefined environment for the cloud subscriber that is shared with other tenants, typically through tagging data with a subscriber identifier. Tagging gives the appearance of exclusive use of the instance, but relies on the CP to establish and maintain a sound secure database environment.

Data must be secured while at rest, in transit, and in use, and access to the data must be controlled. The client can employ encryption to protect data in transit, though this involves key management responsibilities for the CP. The client can enforce access control techniques but, again, the CP is involved to some extent depending on the service model used.

For data at rest, the ideal security measure is for the client to encrypt the database and only store encrypted data in the cloud, with the CP having no access to the encryption key. So long as the key remains secure, the CP has no ability to read the data, although corruption and other denial-of-service attacks remain a risk.

A straightforward solution to the security problem in this context is to encrypt the entire database and not provide the encryption/decryption keys to the service provider. This solution by itself is inflexible. The user has little ability to

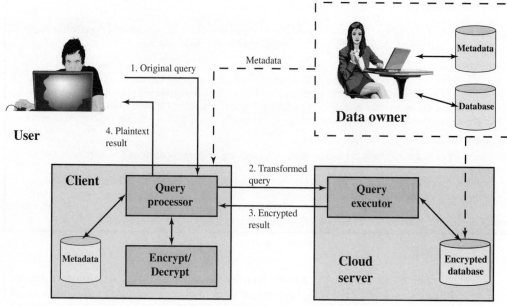

Figure 5.10   An Encryption Scheme for a Cloud-Based Database

access individual data items based on searches or indexing on key parameters, but rather would have to download entire tables from the database, decrypt the tables, and work with the results. To provide more flexibility, it must be possible to work with the database in its encrypted form.

An example of such an approach, depicted in Figure 5.10, is reported in [DAMI05] and [DAMI03]. A similar approach is described in [HACI02]. Four entities are involved:

- **Data owner:** An organization that produces data to be made available for controlled release, either within the organization or to external users.
- **User:** Human entity that presents requests (queries) to the system. The user could be an employee of the organization who is granted access to the database via the server, or a user external to the organization who, after authentication, is granted access.
- **Client:** Frontend that transforms user queries into queries on the encrypted data stored on the server.
- **Server:** An organization that receives the encrypted data from a data owner and makes them available for distribution to clients. The server could in fact be owned by the data owner but, more typically, is a facility owned and maintained by an external provider. For our discussion, the server is a cloud server.

Before continuing this discussion, we need to define some database terms. In relational database parlance, the basic building block is a **relation**, which is a flat table. Rows are referred to as **tuples**, and columns are referred to as **attributes**. A **primary key** is defined to be a portion of a row used to uniquely identify a row in a table; the primary key consists of one or more column names.[2] For example, in an employee table, the employee ID is sufficient to uniquely identify a row in a particular table.

Let us first examine the simplest possible arrangement based on this scenario. Suppose that each individual item in the database is encrypted separately, all using the same encryption key. The encrypted database is stored at the server, but the server does not have the encryption key. Thus, the data are secure at the server. Even if someone were able to hack into the server's system, all he or she would have access to is encrypted data. The client system does have a copy of the encryption key. A user at the client can retrieve a record from the database with the following sequence:

1. The user issues a query for fields from one or more records with a specific value of the primary key.

2. The query processor at the client encrypts the primary key, modifies the query accordingly, and transmits the query to the server.

3. The server processes the query using the encrypted value of the primary key and returns the appropriate record or records.

4. The query processor decrypts the data and returns the results.

This method is certainly straightforward but is quite limited. For example, suppose the Employee table contains a salary attribute and the user wishes to retrieve all records for salaries less than $70K. There is no obvious way to do this, because the attribute value for salary in each record is encrypted. The set of encrypted values does not preserve the ordering of values in the original attribute.

There are a number of ways to extend the functionality of this approach. For example, an unencrypted index value can be associated with a given attribute and the table can be partitioned based on these index values, enabling a user to retrieve a certain portion of the table. The details of such schemes are beyond our scope. See [STAL12] for more detail.

5.7 CLOUD SECURITY AS A SERVICE

The term **security as a service (SecaaS)** has generally meant a package of security services offered by a service provider that offloads much of the security responsibility from an enterprise to the security service provider. Among the services typically provided are authentication, antivirus, antimalware/-spyware, intrusion detection, and security event management. In the context of cloud computing, cloud security as a service, designated SecaaS, is a segment of the SaaS offering of a CP.

The Cloud Security Alliance defines SecaaS as the provision of security applications and services via the cloud either to cloud-based infrastructure and software or from the cloud to the customers' on-premise systems [CSA11b]. The Cloud Security Alliance has identified the following SecaaS categories of service:

- Identity and access management
- Data loss prevention

---

[2]Note that a primary key has nothing to do with cryptographic keys. A primary key in a database is a means of indexing into the database.

- Web security
- E-mail security
- Security assessments
- Intrusion management
- Security information and event management
- Encryption
- Business continuity and disaster recovery
- Network security

In this section, we examine these categories with a focus on security of the cloud-based infrastructure and services (Figure 5.11).

Identity and access management (IAM) includes people, processes, and systems that are used to manage access to enterprise resources by assuring that the identity of an entity is verified, and then granting the correct level of access based on this assured identity. One aspect of identity management is identity provisioning, which has to do with providing access to identified users and subsequently

Figure 5.11 Elements of Cloud Security as a Service

deprovisioning, or deny access, to users when the client enterprise designates such users as no longer having access to enterprise resources in the cloud. Another aspect of identity management is for the cloud to participate in the federated identity management scheme (see Chapter 4) used by the client enterprise. Among other requirements, the cloud service provider (CSP) must be able to exchange identity attributes with the enterprise's chosen identity provider.

The access management portion of IAM involves authentication and access control services. For example, the CSP must be able to authenticate users in a trustworthy manner. The access control requirements in SPI environments include establishing trusted user profile and policy information, using it to control access within the cloud service, and doing this in an auditable way.

Data loss prevention (DLP) is the monitoring, protecting, and verifying the security of data at rest, in motion, and in use. Much of DLP can be implemented by the cloud client, such as discussed in Section 5.6. The CSP can also provide DLP services, such as implementing rules about what functions can be performed on data in various contexts.

Web security is real-time protection offered either on premise through software/appliance installation or via the cloud by proxying or redirecting Web traffic to the CP. This provides an added layer of protection on top of things like antiviruses to prevent malware from entering the enterprise via activities such as Web browsing. In addition to protecting against malware, a cloud-based Web security service might include usage policy enforcement, data backup, traffic control, and Web access control.

A CSP may provide a Web-based e-mail service, for which security measures are needed. **E-mail security** provides control over inbound and outbound e-mail, protecting the organization from phishing, malicious attachments, enforcing corporate polices such as acceptable use and spam prevention. The CSP may also incorporate digital signatures on all e-mail clients and provide optional e-mail encryption.

Security assessments are third-part audits of cloud services. While this service is outside the province of the CSP, the CSP can provide tools and access points to facilitate various assessment activities.

Intrusion management encompasses intrusion detection, prevention, and response. The core of this service is the implementation of intrusion detection systems (IDSs) and intrusion prevention systems (IPSs) at entry points to the cloud and on servers in the cloud. An IDS is a set of automated tools designed to detect unauthorized access to a host system. We discuss this in Chapter 10. An IPS incorporates IDS functionality but also includes mechanisms designed to block traffic from intruders.

Security information and event management (SIEM) aggregates (via push or pull mechanisms) log and event data from virtual and real networks, applications, and systems. This information is then correlated and analyzed to provide real-time reporting and alerting on information/events that may require intervention or other type of response. The CSP typically provides an integrated service that can put together information from a variety of sources both within the cloud and within the client enterprise network.

Encryption is a pervasive service that can be provided for data at rest in the cloud, e-mail traffic, client-specific network management information, and identity information. Encryption services provided by the CSP involve a range of complex issues, including key management, how to implement virtual private network (VPN) services in the cloud, application encryption, and data content access.

Business continuity and disaster recovery comprise measures and mechanisms to ensure operational resiliency in the event of any service interruptions. This is an area where the CSP, because of economies of scale, can offer obvious benefits to a cloud service client [WOOD10]. The CSP can provide backup at multiple locations, with reliable failover and disaster recovery facilities. This service must include a flexible infrastructure, redundancy of functions and hardware, monitored operations, geographically distributed data centers, and network survivability.

Network security consists of security services that allocate access, distribute, monitor, and protect the underlying resource services. Services include perimeter and server firewalls and denial-of-service protection. Many of the other services listed in this section, including intrusion management, identity and access management, data loss protection, and Web security, also contribute to the network security service.

5.8 RECOMMENDED READING

[NERC11] is a useful overview of the elements of an NAC system. [GEER10] is a concise overview of NAC systems.

[HOEP09] is an excellent introduction to EAP. [CHEN05b] provides a good overview of EAP and 802.1X. [CHEN05a] provides more detailed coverage of 802.1X.

[JANS11] is a worthwhile, systematic treatment of cloud security issues. Other useful treatments, providing differing perspectives, are [HASS10], [BALA09], [ANTH10], and [CSA11a].

ANTH10 Anthes, G. "Security in the Cloud." *Communications of the ACM*, November 2010.

BALA09 Balachandra, R.; Ramakrishna, P.; and Rakshit, A. "Cloud Security Issues." *Proceedings, 2009 IEEE International Conference on Services Computing*, 2009.

CHEN05a Chen, J.; Jiang, M.; and Liu, Y. "Wireless LAN Security and IEEE 802.i." *IEEE Wireless Communications*, February 2005.

CHEN05b Chen, J., and Wang, Y. "Extensible Authentication Protocol (EAP) and IEEE 802.1x: Tutorial and Empirical Experience." *IEEE Radio Communications*, December 2005.

CSA11a Cloud Security Alliance. *Security Guidance for Critical Areas of Focus in Cloud Computing V2.1*. CSA Report, 2011.

GEER10 Geer, D. "Whatever Happened to Network-Access-Control Technology?" *Computer*, September 2010.

HASS10 Hassan, T.; Joshi, J.; and Ahn, G. "Security and Privacy Challenges in Cloud Computing Environments." *IEEE Security & Privacy*, November/December 2010.

HOEP09 Hoeper, K., and Chen, L. *Recommendation for EAP Methods Used in Wireless Network Access Authentication*. NIST Special Publication 800-120, September 2009.

JANS11 Jansen, W., and Grance, T. *Guidelines on Security and Privacy in Public Cloud Computing*. NIST Special Publication 800-144, January 2011.

NERC11 North American Electric Reliability Corp. *Guidance for Secure Interactive Remote Access*. July 2011. www.nerc.com

5.9 KEY TERMS, REVIEW QUESTIONS, AND PROBLEMS

Key Terms

access requestor (AR)	EAP-GPSK	network access control
authentication server	EAP-IKEv2	(NAC)
cloud	EAP over LAN (EAPOL)	network access server (NAS)
cloud auditor	EAP method	platform as a service (PaaS)
cloud broker	EAP pass-through mode	policy server
cloud carrier	EAP peer	private cloud
cloud computing	EAP-TLS	public cloud
cloud consumer	EAP-TTLS	remote access server (RAS)
cloud provider	Extensible Authentication	security as a service (SecaaS)
community cloud	Protocol (EAP)	software as a service (SaaS)
Dynamic Host Configuration	firewall	supplicant
Protocol (DHCP)	IEEE 802.1X	virtual local area network
EAP authenticator	media gateway	(VLAN)

Review Questions

5.1 Name the elements of a network access control system.

5.2 What is network access enforcement? Name the different NAC enforcement methods.

5.3 Name the different components of an EAP environment.

5.4 Explain the different fields of an EAP message.

5.5 Explain the different EAPOL frame types.

5.6 What are the essential characteristics of cloud computing?

5.7 Name the cloud computing service and deployment models defined by NIST.

5.8 What are the five major actors of the cloud computing reference architecture?

5.9 What is SecaaS in cloud computing?

Problems

5.1 Investigate the network access control scheme used at your school or place of employment. Draw a diagram and describe the principal components.

5.2 Figure 5.1 suggests that EAP can be described in the context of a four-layer model. Indicate the functions and formats of each of the four layers. You may need to refer to RFC 3748.

5.3 Find and view several YouTube videos that discuss cloud security. Identify the URLs of three videos that you think do a good job communicating the essential issues and approaches for cloud security. If you could only recommend one to fellow students, which would you pick? Why? Summarize your recommendations and justification in a brief paper (250–500 words) or a three- to five-slide PowerPoint presentation.

CHAPTER 6

TRANSPORT-LEVEL SECURITY

6.1 Web Security Considerations

Web Security Threats
Web Traffic Security Approaches

6.2 Secure Sockets Layer

SSL Architecture
SSL Record Protocol
Change Cipher Spec Protocol
Alert Protocol
Handshake Protocol
Cryptographic Computations

6.3 Transport Layer Security

Version Number
Message Authentication Code
Pseudorandom Function
Alert Codes
Cipher Suites
Client Certificate Types
Certificate_Verify and Finished Messages
Cryptographic Computations
Padding

6.4 HTTPS

Connection Initiation
Connection Closure

6.5 Secure Shell (SSH)

Transport Layer Protocol
User Authentication Protocol
Connection Protocol

6.6 Recommended Reading

6.7 Key Terms, Review Questions, and Problems

We cannot enter into alliance with neighboring princes until we are acquainted with their designs.

— The Art of War, Sun Tzu

LEARNING OBJECTIVES

After studying this chapter, you should be able to:

◆ Summarize Web security threats and Web traffic security approaches.

◆ Present an overview of Secure Sockets Layer (SSL).

◆ Understand the differences between Secure Sockets Layer and Transport Layer Security.

◆ Compare the pseudorandom function used in Transport Layer Security with those discussed earlier in the book.

◆ Present an overview of HTTPS (HTTP over SSL).

◆ Present an overview of Secure Shell (SSH).

Virtually all businesses, most government agencies, and many individuals now have Web sites. The number of individuals and companies with Internet access is expanding rapidly and all of these have graphical Web browsers. As a result, businesses are enthusiastic about setting up facilities on the Web for electronic commerce. But the reality is that the Internet and the Web are extremely vulnerable to compromises of various sorts. As businesses wake up to this reality, the demand for secure Web services grows.

The topic of Web security is a broad one and can easily fill a book. In this chapter, we begin with a discussion of the general requirements for Web security and then focus on three standardized schemes that are becoming increasingly important as part of Web commerce and that focus on security at the transport layer: SSL/TLS, HTTPS, and SSH.

6.1 WEB SECURITY CONSIDERATIONS

The World Wide Web is fundamentally a client/server application running over the Internet and TCP/IP intranets. As such, the security tools and approaches discussed so far in this book are relevant to the issue of Web security. However, the following characteristics of Web usage suggest the need for tailored security tools:

- Although Web browsers are very easy to use, Web servers are relatively easy to configure and manage, and Web content is increasingly easy to develop, the underlying software is extraordinarily complex. This complex software may hide many potential security flaws. The short history of the Web is filled with examples of new and upgraded systems, properly installed, that are vulnerable to a variety of security attacks.

- A Web server can be exploited as a launching pad into the corporation's or agency's entire computer complex. Once the Web server is subverted, an attacker may be able to gain access to data and systems not part of the Web itself but connected to the server at the local site.

- Casual and untrained (in security matters) users are common clients for Web-based services. Such users are not necessarily aware of the security risks that exist and do not have the tools or knowledge to take effective countermeasures.

Web Security Threats

Table 6.1 provides a summary of the types of security threats faced when using the Web. One way to group these threats is in terms of passive and active attacks. Passive attacks include eavesdropping on network traffic between browser and server and gaining access to information on a Web site that is supposed to be restricted. Active attacks include impersonating another user, altering messages in transit between client and server, and altering information on a Web site.

Another way to classify Web security threats is in terms of the location of the threat: Web server, Web browser, and network traffic between browser and server. Issues of server and browser security fall into the category of computer system security; Part Six of this book addresses the issue of system security in general but is also applicable to Web system security. Issues of traffic security fall into the category of network security and are addressed in this chapter.

Table 6.1 A Comparison of Threats on the Web

	Threats	**Consequences**	**Countermeasures**
Integrity	• Modification of user data • Trojan horse browser • Modification of memory • Modification of message traffic in transit	• Loss of information • Compromise of machine • Vulnerability to all other threats	Cryptographic checksums
Confidentiality	• Eavesdropping on the net • Theft of info from server • Theft of data from client • Info about network configuration • Info about which client talks to server	• Loss of information • Loss of privacy	Encryption, Web proxies
Denial of Service	• Killing of user threads • Flooding machine with bogus requests • Filling up disk or memory • Isolating machine by DNS attacks	• Disruptive • Annoying • Prevent user from getting work done	Difficult to prevent
Authentication	• Impersonation of legitimate users • Data forgery	• Misrepresentation of user • Belief that false information is valid	Cryptographic techniques

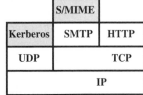

| (a) Network level | (b) Transport level | (c) Application level |

Figure 6.1 Relative Location of Security Facilities in the TCP/IP Protocol Stack

Web Traffic Security Approaches

A number of approaches to providing Web security are possible. The various approaches that have been considered are similar in the services they provide and, to some extent, in the mechanisms that they use, but they differ with respect to their scope of applicability and their relative location within the TCP/IP protocol stack.

Figure 6.1 illustrates this difference. One way to provide Web security is to use IP security (IPsec) (Figure 6.1a). The advantage of using IPsec is that it is transparent to end users and applications and provides a general-purpose solution. Furthermore, IPsec includes a filtering capability so that only selected traffic need incur the overhead of IPsec processing.

Another relatively general-purpose solution is to implement security just above TCP (Figure 6.1b). The foremost example of this approach is the Secure Sockets Layer (SSL) and the follow-on Internet standard known as Transport Layer Security (TLS). At this level, there are two implementation choices. For full generality, SSL (or TLS) could be provided as part of the underlying protocol suite and therefore be transparent to applications. Alternatively, SSL can be embedded in specific packages. For example, Netscape and Microsoft Explorer browsers come equipped with SSL, and most Web servers have implemented the protocol.

Application-specific security services are embedded within the particular application. Figure 6.1c shows examples of this architecture. The advantage of this approach is that the service can be tailored to the specific needs of a given application.

6.2 SECURE SOCKETS LAYER

One of the most widely used security services is the Secure Sockets Layer (SSL) and the follow-on Internet standard known as Transport Layer Security (TLS), the latter defined in RFC 5246. SSL is a general-purpose service implemented as a set of protocols that rely on TCP. At this level, there are two implementation choices. For full generality, SSL (or TLS) could be provided as part of the underlying protocol suite and therefore be transparent to applications. Alternatively, SSL can be embedded in specific packages. For example, most browsers come equipped with SSL, and most Web servers have implemented the protocol.

This section is devoted to a discussion of SSLv3, and next section describes the principal differences between SSLv3 and TLS.

SSL Architecture

SSL is designed to make use of TCP to provide a reliable end-to-end secure service. SSL is not a single protocol but rather two layers of protocols, as illustrated in Figure 6.2.

The SSL Record Protocol provides basic security services to various higher-layer protocols. In particular, the Hypertext Transfer Protocol (HTTP), which provides the transfer service for Web client/server interaction, can operate on top of SSL. Three higher-layer protocols are defined as part of SSL: the Handshake Protocol, The Change Cipher Spec Protocol, and the Alert Protocol. These SSL-specific protocols are used in the management of SSL exchanges and are examined later in this section.

Two important SSL concepts are the SSL session and the SSL connection, which are defined in the specification as follows.

- **Connection:** A connection is a transport (in the OSI layering model definition) that provides a suitable type of service. For SSL, such connections are peer-to-peer relationships. The connections are transient. Every connection is associated with one session.
- **Session:** An SSL session is an association between a client and a server. Sessions are created by the Handshake Protocol. Sessions define a set of cryptographic security parameters which can be shared among multiple connections. Sessions are used to avoid the expensive negotiation of new security parameters for each connection.

Between any pair of parties (applications such as HTTP on client and server), there may be multiple secure connections. In theory, there may also be multiple simultaneous sessions between parties, but this feature is not used in practice.

There are a number of states associated with each session. Once a session is established, there is a current operating state for both read and write (i.e., receive and send). In addition, during the Handshake Protocol, pending read and write states are created. Upon successful conclusion of the Handshake Protocol, the pending states become the current states.

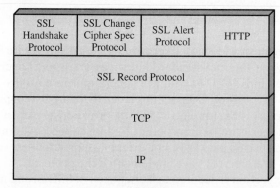

SSL Handshake Protocol	SSL Change Cipher Spec Protocol	SSL Alert Protocol	HTTP
SSL Record Protocol			
TCP			
IP			

Figure 6.2   SSL Protocol Stack

A session state is defined by the following parameters.

- **Session identifier:** An arbitrary byte sequence chosen by the server to identify an active or resumable session state.
- **Peer certificate:** An X509.v3 certificate of the peer. This element of the state may be null.
- **Compression method:** The algorithm used to compress data prior to encryption.
- **Cipher spec:** Specifies the bulk data encryption algorithm (such as null, AES, etc.) and a hash algorithm (such as MD5 or SHA-1) used for MAC calculation. It also defines cryptographic attributes such as the hash_size.
- **Master secret:** 48-byte secret shared between the client and the server.
- **Is resumable:** A flag indicating whether the session can be used to initiate new connections.

A connection state is defined by the following parameters.

- **Server and client random:** Byte sequences that are chosen by the server and client for each connection.
- **Server write MAC secret:** The secret key used in MAC operations on data sent by the server.
- **Client write MAC secret:** The secret key used in MAC operations on data sent by the client.
- **Server write key:** The secret encryption key for data encrypted by the server and decrypted by the client.
- **Client write key:** The symmetric encryption key for data encrypted by the client and decrypted by the server.
- **Initialization vectors:** When a block cipher in CBC mode is used, an initialization vector (IV) is maintained for each key. This field is first initialized by the SSL Handshake Protocol. Thereafter, the final ciphertext block from each record is preserved for use as the IV with the following record.
- **Sequence numbers:** Each party maintains separate sequence numbers for transmitted and received messages for each connection. When a party sends or receives a change cipher spec message, the appropriate sequence number is set to zero. Sequence numbers may not exceed $2^{64} - 1$.

SSL Record Protocol

The SSL Record Protocol provides two services for SSL connections:

- **Confidentiality:** The Handshake Protocol defines a shared secret key that is used for conventional encryption of SSL payloads.
- **Message Integrity:** The Handshake Protocol also defines a shared secret key that is used to form a message authentication code (MAC).

Figure 6.3 SSL Record Protocol Operation

Figure 6.3 indicates the overall operation of the SSL Record Protocol. The Record Protocol takes an application message to be transmitted, fragments the data into manageable blocks, optionally compresses the data, applies a MAC, encrypts, adds a header, and transmits the resulting unit in a TCP segment. Received data are decrypted, verified, decompressed, and reassembled before being delivered to higher-level users.

The first step is **fragmentation**. Each upper-layer message is fragmented into blocks of 2^{14} bytes (16384 bytes) or less. Next, **compression** is optionally applied. Compression must be lossless and may not increase the content length by more than 1024 bytes.[1] In SSLv3 (as well as the current version of TLS), no compression algorithm is specified, so the default compression algorithm is null.

The next step in processing is to compute a **message authentication code** over the compressed data. For this purpose, a shared secret key is used. The calculation is defined as

```
hash(MAC_write_secret ‖ pad_2 ‖
     hash(MAC_write_secret ‖ pad_1 ‖ seq_num ‖
     SSLCompressed.type ‖ SSLCompressed.length ‖
     SSLCompressed.fragment))
```

where

‖	= concatenation
MAC_write_secret	= shared secret key
hash	= cryptographic hash algorithm; either MD5 or SHA-1

---

[1]Of course, one hopes that compression shrinks rather than expands the data. However, for very short blocks, it is possible, because of formatting conventions, that the compression algorithm will actually provide output that is longer than the input.

pad_1	= the byte 0x36 (0011 0110) repeated 48 times (384 bits) for MD5 and 40 times (320 bits) for SHA-1
pad_2	= the byte 0x5C (0101 1100) repeated 48 times for MD5 and 40 times for SHA-1
seq_num	= the sequence number for this message
SSLCompressed.type	= the higher-level protocol used to process this fragment
SSLCompressed.length	= the length of the compressed fragment
SSLCompressed.fragment	= the compressed fragment (if compression is not used, this is the plaintext fragment)

This is very similar to the HMAC algorithm defined in Chapter 3. The difference is that the two pads are concatenated in SSLv3 and are XORed in HMAC. The SSLv3 MAC algorithm is based on the original Internet draft for HMAC, which used concatenation. The final version of HMAC (defined in RFC 2104) uses the XOR.

Next, the compressed message plus the MAC are **encrypted** using symmetric encryption. Encryption may not increase the content length by more than 1024 bytes, so that the total length may not exceed 2^{14} + 2048. The following encryption algorithms are permitted:

Block Cipher		Stream Cipher	
Algorithm	**Key Size**	**Algorithm**	**Key Size**
AES	128, 256	RC4-40	40
IDEA	128	RC4-128	128
RC2-40	40		
DES-40	40		
DES	56		
3DES	168		
Fortezza	80		

Fortezza can be used in a smart card encryption scheme.

For stream encryption, the compressed message plus the MAC are encrypted. Note that the MAC is computed before encryption takes place and that the MAC is then encrypted along with the plaintext or compressed plaintext.

For block encryption, padding may be added after the MAC prior to encryption. The padding is in the form of a number of padding bytes followed by a one-byte indication of the length of the padding. The total amount of padding is the smallest amount such that the total size of the data to be encrypted (plaintext plus MAC plus padding) is a multiple of the cipher's block length. An example is a plaintext (or compressed text if compression is used) of 58 bytes, with a MAC of 20 bytes (using SHA-1), that is encrypted using a block length of 8 bytes (e.g., DES). With the padding-length byte, this yields a total of 79 bytes. To make the total an integer multiple of 8, one byte of padding is added.

The final step of SSL Record Protocol processing is to prepare a header consisting of the following fields:

- **Content Type (8 bits):** The higher-layer protocol used to process the enclosed fragment.
- **Major Version (8 bits):** Indicates major version of SSL in use. For SSLv3, the value is 3.
- **Minor Version (8 bits):** Indicates minor version in use. For SSLv3, the value is 0.
- **Compressed Length (16 bits):** The length in bytes of the plaintext fragment (or compressed fragment if compression is used). The maximum value is $2^{14} + 2048$.

The content types that have been defined are `change_cipher_spec`, `alert`, `handshake`, and `application_data`. The first three are the SSL-specific protocols, discussed next. Note that no distinction is made among the various applications (e.g., HTTP) that might use SSL; the content of the data created by such applications is opaque to SSL.

Figure 6.4 illustrates the SSL record format.

Change Cipher Spec Protocol

The Change Cipher Spec Protocol is one of the three SSL-specific protocols that use the SSL Record Protocol, and it is the simplest. This protocol consists of a single message (Figure 6.5a), which consists of a single byte with the value 1. The sole purpose of this message is to cause the pending state to be copied into the current state, which updates the cipher suite to be used on this connection.

Alert Protocol

The Alert Protocol is used to convey SSL-related alerts to the peer entity. As with other applications that use SSL, alert messages are compressed and encrypted, as specified by the current state.

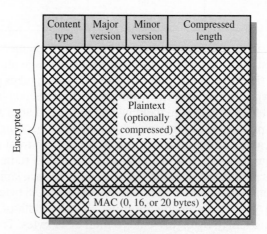

Figure 6.4   SSL Record Format

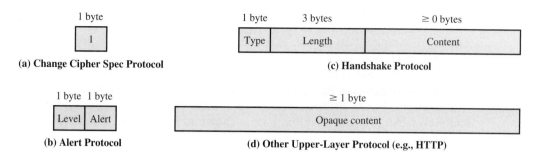

Figure 6.5 SSL Record Protocol Payload

Each message in this protocol consists of two bytes (Figure 6.5b). The first byte takes the value warning (1) or fatal (2) to convey the severity of the message. If the level is fatal, SSL immediately terminates the connection. Other connections on the same session may continue, but no new connections on this session may be established. The second byte contains a code that indicates the specific alert. First, we list those alerts that are always fatal (definitions from the SSL specification):

- **unexpected_message:** An inappropriate message was received.
- **bad_record_mac:** An incorrect MAC was received.
- **decompression_failure:** The decompression function received improper input (e.g., unable to decompress or decompress to greater than maximum allowable length).
- **handshake_failure:** Sender was unable to negotiate an acceptable set of security parameters given the options available.
- **illegal_parameter:** A field in a handshake message was out of range or inconsistent with other fields.

The remaining alerts are the following.

- **close_notify:** Notifies the recipient that the sender will not send any more messages on this connection. Each party is required to send a **close_ notify** alert before closing the write side of a connection.
- **no_certificate:** May be sent in response to a certificate request if no appropriate certificate is available.
- **bad_certificate:** A received certificate was corrupt (e.g., contained a signature that did not verify).
- **unsupported_certificate:** The type of the received certificate is not supported.
- **certificate_revoked:** A certificate has been revoked by its signer.
- **certificate_expired:** A certificate has expired.
- **certificate_unknown:** Some other unspecified issue arose in processing the certificate, rendering it unacceptable.

Handshake Protocol

The most complex part of SSL is the Handshake Protocol. This protocol allows the server and client to authenticate each other and to negotiate an encryption and MAC algorithm and cryptographic keys to be used to protect data sent in an SSL record. The Handshake Protocol is used before any application data is transmitted.

The Handshake Protocol consists of a series of messages exchanged by client and server. All of these have the format shown in Figure 6.5c. Each message has three fields:

- **Type (1 byte):** Indicates one of ten messages. Table 6.2 lists the defined message types.
- **Length (3 bytes):** The length of the message in bytes.
- **Content (≥ 0 bytes):** The parameters associated with this message; these are listed in Table 6.2.

Figure 6.6 shows the initial exchange needed to establish a logical connection between client and server. The exchange can be viewed as having four phases.

PHASE 1. ESTABLISH SECURITY CAPABILITIES   This phase is used to initiate a logical connection and to establish the security capabilities that will be associated with it. The exchange is initiated by the client, which sends a **client_hello message** with the following parameters:

- **Version:** The highest SSL version understood by the client.
- **Random:** A client-generated random structure consisting of a 32-bit time-stamp and 28 bytes generated by a secure random number generator. These values serve as nonces and are used during key exchange to prevent replay attacks.
- **Session ID:** A variable-length session identifier. A nonzero value indicates that the client wishes to update the parameters of an existing connection or to

Table 6.2   SSL Handshake Protocol Message Types

Message Type	Parameters
hello_request	null
client_hello	version, random, session id, cipher suite, compression method
server_hello	version, random, session id, cipher suite, compression method
certificate	chain of X.509v3 certificates
server_key_exchange	parameters, signature
certificate_request	type, authorities
server_done	null
certificate_verify	signature
client_key_exchange	parameters, signature
finished	hash value

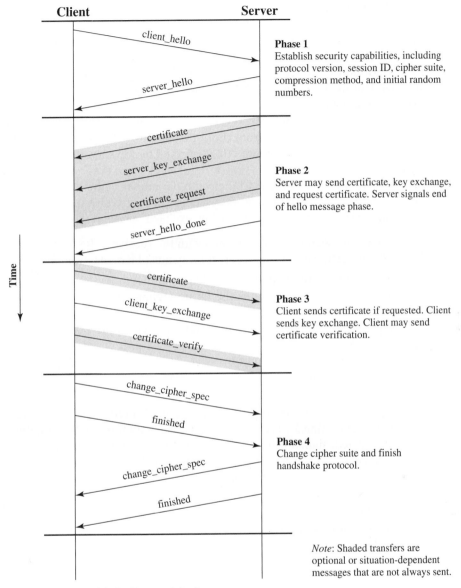

Figure 6.6   Handshake Protocol Action

create a new connection on this session. A zero value indicates that the client wishes to establish a new connection on a new session.

- **CipherSuite:** This is a list that contains the combinations of cryptographic algorithms supported by the client, in decreasing order of preference. Each element of the list (each cipher suite) defines both a key exchange algorithm and a CipherSpec; these are discussed subsequently.

- **Compression Method:** This is a list of the compression methods the client supports.

After sending the `client_hello` message, the client waits for the `server_hello` message, which contains the same parameters as the `client_hello` message. For the `server_hello` message, the following conventions apply. The Version field contains the lower of the versions suggested by the client and the highest supported by the server. The Random field is generated by the server and is independent of the client's Random field. If the SessionID field of the client was nonzero, the same value is used by the server; otherwise the server's SessionID field contains the value for a new session. The CipherSuite field contains the single cipher suite selected by the server from those proposed by the client. The Compression field contains the compression method selected by the server from those proposed by the client.

The first element of the CipherSuite parameter is the key exchange method (i.e., the means by which the cryptographic keys for conventional encryption and MAC are exchanged). The following key exchange methods are supported.

- **RSA:** The secret key is encrypted with the receiver's RSA public key. A public-key certificate for the receiver's key must be made available.

- **Fixed Diffie-Hellman:** This is a Diffie-Hellman key exchange in which the server's certificate contains the Diffie-Hellman public parameters signed by the certificate authority (CA). That is, the public-key certificate contains the Diffie-Hellman public-key parameters. The client provides its Diffie-Hellman public-key parameters either in a certificate, if client authentication is required, or in a key exchange message. This method results in a fixed secret key between two peers based on the Diffie-Hellman calculation using the fixed public keys.

- **Ephemeral Diffie-Hellman:** This technique is used to create ephemeral (temporary, one-time) secret keys. In this case, the Diffie-Hellman public keys are exchanged, signed using the sender's private RSA or DSS key. The receiver can use the corresponding public key to verify the signature. Certificates are used to authenticate the public keys. This would appear to be the most secure of the three Diffie-Hellman options, because it results in a temporary, authenticated key.

- **Anonymous Diffie-Hellman:** The base Diffie-Hellman algorithm is used with no authentication. That is, each side sends its public Diffie-Hellman parameters to the other with no authentication. This approach is vulnerable to man-in-the-middle attacks, in which the attacker conducts anonymous Diffie-Hellman with both parties.

- **Fortezza:** The technique defined for the Fortezza scheme.

Following the definition of a key exchange method is the CipherSpec, which includes the following fields.

- **CipherAlgorithm:** Any of the algorithms mentioned earlier: RC4, RC2, DES, 3DES, DES40, IDEA, or Fortezza

- **MACAlgorithm:** MD5 or SHA-1

- **CipherType:** Stream or Block

- **IsExportable:** True or False
- **HashSize:** 0, 16 (for MD5), or 20 (for SHA-1) bytes
- **Key Material:** A sequence of bytes that contain data used in generating the write keys
- **IV Size:** The size of the Initialization Value for Cipher Block Chaining (CBC) encryption

PHASE 2. SERVER AUTHENTICATION AND KEY EXCHANGE The server begins this phase by sending its certificate if it needs to be authenticated; the message contains one or a chain of X.509 certificates. The **certificate message** is required for any agreed-on key exchange method except anonymous Diffie-Hellman. Note that if fixed Diffie-Hellman is used, this certificate message functions as the server's key exchange message because it contains the server's public Diffie-Hellman parameters.

Next, a `server_key_exchange message` may be sent if it is required. It is not required in two instances: (1) The server has sent a certificate with fixed Diffie-Hellman parameters or (2) a RSA key exchange is to be used. The `server_key_exchange` message is needed for the following:

- **Anonymous Diffie-Hellman:** The message content consists of the two global Diffie-Hellman values (a prime number and a primitive root of that number) plus the server's public Diffie-Hellman key (see Figure 3.12).
- **Ephemeral Diffie-Hellman:** The message content includes the three Diffie-Hellman parameters provided for anonymous Diffie-Hellman plus a signature of those parameters.
- **RSA key exchange (in which the server is using RSA but has a signature-only RSA key):** Accordingly, the client cannot simply send a secret key encrypted with the server's public key. Instead, the server must create a temporary RSA public/private key pair and use the `server_key_exchange` message to send the public key. The message content includes the two parameters of the temporary RSA public key (exponent and modulus; see Figure 3.10) plus a signature of those parameters.
- **Fortezza**

Some further details about the signatures are warranted. As usual, a signature is created by taking the hash of a message and encrypting it with the sender's private key. In this case, the hash is defined as

```
hash(ClientHello.random || ServerHello.random ||
ServerParams)
```

So the hash covers not only the Diffie-Hellman or RSA parameters but also the two nonces from the initial hello messages. This ensures against replay attacks and misrepresentation. In the case of a DSS signature, the hash is performed using the SHA-1 algorithm. In the case of an RSA signature, both an MD5 and an SHA-1 hash are calculated, and the concatenation of the two hashes (36 bytes) is encrypted with the server's private key.

Next, a nonanonymous server (server not using anonymous Diffie-Hellman) can request a certificate from the client. The **certificate_request message** includes two parameters: certificate_type and certificate_authorities. The certificate type indicates the public-key algorithm and its use:

- RSA, signature only
- DSS, signature only
- RSA for fixed Diffie-Hellman; in this case the signature is used only for authentication, by sending a certificate signed with RSA
- DSS for fixed Diffie-Hellman; again, used only for authentication
- RSA for ephemeral Diffie-Hellman
- DSS for ephemeral Diffie-Hellman
- Fortezza

The second parameter in the certificate_request message is a list of the distinguished names of acceptable certificate authorities.

The final message in phase 2, and one that is always required, is the **server_done message**, which is sent by the server to indicate the end of the server hello and associated messages. After sending this message, the server will wait for a client response. This message has no parameters.

PHASE 3. CLIENT AUTHENTICATION AND KEY EXCHANGE Upon receipt of the server_done message, the client should verify that the server provided a valid certificate (if required) and check that the server_hello parameters are acceptable. If all is satisfactory, the client sends one or more messages back to the server.

If the server has requested a certificate, the client begins this phase by sending a **certificate message**. If no suitable certificate is available, the client sends a no_certificate alert instead.

Next is the **client_key_exchange message**, which must be sent in this phase. The content of the message depends on the type of key exchange, as follows.

- **RSA:** The client generates a 48-byte *pre-master secret* and encrypts with the public key from the server's certificate or temporary RSA key from a server_key_exchange message. Its use to compute a *master secret* is explained later.
- **Ephemeral or Anonymous Diffie-Hellman:** The client's public Diffie-Hellman parameters are sent.
- **Fixed Diffie-Hellman:** The client's public Diffie-Hellman parameters were sent in a certificate message, so the content of this message is null.
- **Fortezza:** The client's Fortezza parameters are sent.

Finally, in this phase, the client may send a **certificate_verify message** to provide explicit verification of a client certificate. This message is only sent following any client certificate that has signing capability (i.e., all certificates except

those containing fixed Diffie-Hellman parameters). This message signs a hash code based on the preceding messages, defined as

```
CertificateVerify.signature.md5_hash=
    MD5(master_secret ‖ pad_2 ‖ MD5(handshake_messages ‖
        master_secret ‖ pad_1));
CertificateVerify.signature.sha_hash=
    SHA(master_secret ‖ pad_2 ‖ SHA(handshake_messages ‖
        master_secret ‖ pad_1));
```

where pad_1 and pad_2 are the values defined earlier for the MAC, **handshake_ messages** refers to all Handshake Protocol messages sent or received starting at client_hello but not including this message, and master_secret is the calculated secret whose construction is explained later in this section. If the user's private key is DSS, then it is used to encrypt the SHA-1 hash. If the user's private key is RSA, it is used to encrypt the concatenation of the MD5 and SHA-1 hashes. In either case, the purpose is to verify the client's ownership of the private key for the client certificate. Even if someone is misusing the client's certificate, he or she would be unable to send this message.

PHASE 4. FINISH This phase completes the setting up of a secure connection. The client sends a change_cipher_spec message and copies the pending CipherSpec into the current CipherSpec. Note that this message is not considered part of the Handshake Protocol but is sent using the Change Cipher Spec Protocol. The client then immediately sends the **finished message** under the new algorithms, keys, and secrets. The finished message verifies that the key exchange and authentication processes were successful. The content of the finished message is the concatenation of two hash values:

```
MD5(master_secret ‖ pad2 ‖ MD5(handshake_messages ‖
    Sender ‖ master_secret ‖ pad1))
SHA(master_secret ‖ pad2 ‖ SHA(handshake_messages ‖
    Sender ‖ master_secret ‖ pad1))
```

where Sender is a code that identifies that the sender is the client and handshake_messages is all of the data from all handshake messages up to but not including this message.

In response to these two messages, the server sends its own change_ cipher_spec message, transfers the pending to the current CipherSpec, and sends its finished message. At this point, the handshake is complete and the client and server may begin to exchange application-layer data.

Cryptographic Computations

Two further items are of interest: (1) the creation of a shared master secret by means of the key exchange and (2) the generation of cryptographic parameters from the master secret.

Master Secret Creation The shared master secret is a one-time 48-byte value (384 bits) generated for this session by means of secure key exchange. The creation is in two stages. First, a `pre_master_secret` is exchanged. Second, the `master_secret` is calculated by both parties. For `pre_master_secret` exchange, there are two possibilities.

- **RSA:** A 48-byte `pre_master_secret` is generated by the client, encrypted with the server's public RSA key, and sent to the server. The server decrypts the ciphertext using its private key to recover the pre_master_secret.
- **Diffie-Hellman:** Both client and server generate a Diffie-Hellman public key. After these are exchanged, each side performs the Diffie-Hellman calculation to create the shared `pre_master_secret`.

Both sides now compute the `master_secret` as

```
master_secret = MD5(pre_master_secret || SHA('A' ||
                    pre_master_secret || ClientHello.random ||
                    ServerHello.random)) ||
                MD5(pre_master_secret || SHA('BB' ||
                    pre_master_secret || ClientHello.random ||
                    ServerHello.random)) ||
                MD5(pre_master_secret || SHA('CCC' ||
                    pre_master_secret || ClientHello.random ||
                    ServerHello.random))
```

where `ClientHello.random` and `ServerHello.random` are the two nonce values exchanged in the initial hello messages.

Generation of Cryptographic Parameters CipherSpecs require a client write MAC secret, a server write MAC secret, a client write key, a server write key, a client write IV, and a server write IV, which are generated from the master secret in that order. These parameters are generated from the master secret by hashing the master secret into a sequence of secure bytes of sufficient length for all needed parameters.

The generation of the key material from the master secret uses the same format for generation of the master secret from the pre-master secret as

```
key_block = MD5(master_secret || SHA('A' || master_secret ||
                ServerHello.random || ClientHello.random)) ||
            MD5(master_secret || SHA('BB' || master_secret ||
                ServerHello.random || ClientHello.random)) ||
            MD5(master_secret || SHA('CCC' || master_secret ||
                ServerHello.random || ClientHello.random)) || ...
```

until enough output has been generated. The result of this algorithmic structure is a pseudorandom function. We can view the `master_secret` as the pseudorandom seed value to the function. The client and server random numbers can be viewed as salt values to complicate cryptanalysis (see Chapter 11 for a discussion of the use of salt values).

6.3   TRANSPORT LAYER SECURITY

TLS is an IETF standardization initiative whose goal is to produce an Internet standard version of SSL. TLS is defined as a Proposed Internet Standard in RFC 5246. RFC 5246 is very similar to SSLv3. In this section, we highlight the differences.

Version Number

The TLS Record Format is the same as that of the SSL Record Format (Figure 6.4), and the fields in the header have the same meanings. The one difference is in version values. For the current version of TLS, the major version is 3 and the minor version is 3.

Message Authentication Code

There are two differences between the SSLv3 and TLS MAC schemes: the actual algorithm and the scope of the MAC calculation. TLS makes use of the HMAC algorithm defined in RFC 2104. Recall from Chapter 3 that HMAC is defined as

$$\text{HMAC}_K(M) = \text{H}[(K^+ \oplus \text{opad}) \parallel \text{H}[(K^+ \oplus \text{ipad}) \parallel M]]$$

where

H = embedded hash function (for TLS, either MD5 or SHA-1)

M = message input to HMAC

K^+ = secret key padded with zeros on the left so that the result is equal to the block length of the hash code (for MD5 and SHA-1, block length = 512 bits)

ipad = 00110110 (36 in hexadecimal) repeated 64 times (512 bits)
opad = 01011100 (5C in hexadecimal) repeated 64 times (512 bits)

SSLv3 uses the same algorithm, except that the padding bytes are concatenated with the secret key rather than being XORed with the secret key padded to the block length. The level of security should be about the same in both cases.

For TLS, the MAC calculation encompasses the fields indicated in the following expression:

```
MAC(MAC_write_secret,seq_num ‖ TLSCompressed.type ‖
    TLSCompressed.version ‖ TLSCompressed.length ‖
    TLSCompressed.fragment)
```

The MAC calculation covers all of the fields covered by the SSLv3 calculation, plus the field TLSCompressed.version, which is the version of the protocol being employed.

Pseudorandom Function

TLS makes use of a pseudorandom function referred to as PRF to expand secrets into blocks of data for purposes of key generation or validation. The objective is to make use of a relatively small shared secret value but to generate longer blocks of

Figure 6.7 TLS Function P_hash(secret, seed)

data in a way that is secure from the kinds of attacks made on hash functions and MACs. The PRF is based on the data expansion function (Figure 6.7) given as

```
P_hash(secret, seed) = HMAC_hash(secret,A(1) ‖ seed) ‖
                       HMAC_hash(secret,A(2) ‖ seed) ‖
                       HMAC_hash(secret,A(3) ‖ seed) ‖ . . .
```

where A() is defined as

```
A(0) = seed
A(i) = HMAC_hash(secret, A(i − 1))
```

The data expansion function makes use of the HMAC algorithm with either MD5 or SHA-1 as the underlying hash function. As can be seen, P_hash can be iterated as many times as necessary to produce the required quantity of data. For example, if P_SHA-1 was used to generate 64 bytes of data, it would have to be iterated four times, producing 80 bytes of data of which the last 16 would be discarded. In this case, P_MD5 would also have to be iterated four times, producing exactly 64 bytes of data. Note that each iteration involves two executions of HMAC—each of which in turn involves two executions of the underlying hash algorithm.

To make PRF as secure as possible, it uses two hash algorithms in a way that should guarantee its security if either algorithm remains secure. PRF is defined as

```
PRF(secret, label, seed) = P_hash(S1, label ‖ seed)
```

PRF takes as input a secret value, an identifying label, and a seed value and produces an output of arbitrary length.

Alert Codes

TLS supports all of the alert codes defined in SSLv3 with the exception of no_certificate. A number of additional codes are defined in TLS; of these, the following are always fatal.

- **record_overflow:** A TLS record was received with a payload (ciphertext) whose length exceeds $2^{14} + 2048$ bytes, or the ciphertext decrypted to a length of greater than $2^{14} + 1024$ bytes.
- **unknown_ca:** A valid certificate chain or partial chain was received, but the certificate was not accepted because the CA certificate could not be located or could not be matched with a known, trusted CA.
- **access_denied:** A valid certificate was received, but when access control was applied, the sender decided not to proceed with the negotiation.
- **decode_error:** A message could not be decoded, because either a field was out of its specified range or the length of the message was incorrect.
- **protocol_version:** The protocol version the client attempted to negotiate is recognized but not supported.
- **insufficient_security:** Returned instead of handshake_failure when a negotiation has failed specifically because the server requires ciphers more secure than those supported by the client.
- **unsupported_extension:** Sent by clients that receive an extended server hello containing an extension not in the corresponding client hello.
- **internal_error:** An internal error unrelated to the peer or the correctness of the protocol makes it impossible to continue.
- **decrypt_error:** A handshake cryptographic operation failed, including being unable to verify a signature, decrypt a key exchange, or validate a finished message.

The remaining alerts include the following.

- **user_canceled:** This handshake is being canceled for some reason unrelated to a protocol failure.
- **no_renegotiation:** Sent by a client in response to a hello request or by the server in response to a client hello after initial handshaking. Either of these messages would normally result in renegotiation, but this alert indicates that the sender is not able to renegotiate. This message is always a warning.

Cipher Suites

There are several small differences between the cipher suites available under SSLv3 and under TLS:

- **Key Exchange:** TLS supports all of the key exchange techniques of SSLv3 with the exception of Fortezza.
- **Symmetric Encryption Algorithms:** TLS includes all of the symmetric encryption algorithms found in SSLv3, with the exception of Fortezza.

Client Certificate Types

TLS defines the following certificate types to be requested in a `certificate_request` message: `rsa_sign`, `dss_sign`, `rsa_fixed_dh`, and `dss_fixed_dh`. These are all defined in SSLv3. In addition, SSLv3 includes `rsa_ephemeral_dh`, `dss_ephemeral_dh`, and `fortezza_kea`. Ephemeral Diffie-Hellman involves signing the Diffie-Hellman parameters with either RSA or DSS. For TLS, the `rsa_sign` and `dss_sign` types are used for that function; a separate signing type is not needed to sign Diffie-Hellman parameters. TLS does not include the Fortezza scheme.

`certificate_verify` and Finished Messages

In the TLS `certificate_verify` message, the MD5 and SHA-1 hashes are calculated only over `handshake_messages`. Recall that for SSLv3, the hash calculation also included the master secret and pads. These extra fields were felt to add no additional security.

As with the finished message in SSLv3, the finished message in TLS is a hash based on the shared `master_secret`, the previous handshake messages, and a label that identifies client or server. The calculation is somewhat different. For TLS, we have

```
PRF(master_secret,finished_label,MD5(handshake_messages)‖
    SHA-1(handshake_messages))
```

where `finished_label` is the string "client finished" for the client and "server finished" for the server.

Cryptographic Computations

The `pre_master_secret` for TLS is calculated in the same way as in SSLv3. As in SSLv3, the `master_secret` in TLS is calculated as a hash function of the `pre_master_secret` and the two hello random numbers. The form of the TLS calculation is different from that of SSLv3 and is defined as

```
master_secret = PRF(pre_master_secret,"master secret",
                ClientHello.random‖ServerHello.random)
```

The algorithm is performed until 48 bytes of pseudorandom output are produced.

The calculation of the key block material (MAC secret keys, session encryption keys, and IVs) is defined as

```
key_block = PRF(master_secret, "key expansion",
            SecurityParameters.server_random ||
            SecurityParameters.client_random)
```

until enough output has been generated. As with SSLv3, the `key_block` is a function of the `master_secret` and the client and server random numbers, but for TLS, the actual algorithm is different.

Padding

In SSL, the padding added prior to encryption of user data is the minimum amount required so that the total size of the data to be encrypted is a multiple of the cipher's block length. In TLS, the padding can be any amount that results in a total that is a multiple of the cipher's block length, up to a maximum of 255 bytes. For example, if the plaintext (or compressed text if compression is used) plus MAC plus padding. length byte is 79 bytes long, then the padding length (in bytes) can be 1, 9, 17, and so on, up to 249. A variable padding length may be used to frustrate attacks based on an analysis of the lengths of exchanged messages.

6.4 HTTPS

HTTPS (HTTP over SSL) refers to the combination of HTTP and SSL to implement secure communication between a Web browser and a Web server. The HTTPS capability is built into all modern Web browsers. Its use depends on the Web server supporting HTTPS communication. For example, some search engines do not support HTTPS. Google provides HTTPS as an option: https://google.com.

The principal difference seen by a user of a Web browser is that URL (uniform resource locator) addresses begin with https:// rather than http://. A normal HTTP connection uses port 80. If HTTPS is specified, port 443 is used, which invokes SSL.

When HTTPS is used, the following elements of the communication are encrypted:

- URL of the requested document
- Contents of the document
- Contents of browser forms (filled in by browser user)
- Cookies sent from browser to server and from server to browser
- Contents of HTTP header

HTTPS is documented in RFC 2818, *HTTP Over TLS*. There is no fundamental change in using HTTP over either SSL or TLS, and both implementations are referred to as HTTPS.

Connection Initiation

For HTTPS, the agent acting as the HTTP client also acts as the TLS client. The client initiates a connection to the server on the appropriate port and then sends the TLS ClientHello to begin the TLS handshake. When the TLS handshake has finished, the client may then initiate the first HTTP request. All HTTP data is to be sent as TLS application data. Normal HTTP behavior, including retained connections, should be followed.

There are three levels of awareness of a connection in HTTPS. At the HTTP level, an HTTP client requests a connection to an HTTP server by sending a connection request to the next lowest layer. Typically, the next lowest layer is TCP, but it also may be TLS/SSL. At the level of TLS, a session is established between a TLS client and a TLS server. This session can support one or more connections at any time. As we have seen, a TLS request to establish a connection begins with the establishment of a TCP connection between the TCP entity on the client side and the TCP entity on the server side.

Connection Closure

An HTTP client or server can indicate the closing of a connection by including the following line in an HTTP record: `Connection: close`. This indicates that the connection will be closed after this record is delivered.

The closure of an HTTPS connection requires that TLS close the connection with the peer TLS entity on the remote side, which will involve closing the underlying TCP connection. At the TLS level, the proper way to close a connection is for each side to use the TLS alert protocol to send a `close_notify` alert. TLS implementations must initiate an exchange of closure alerts before closing a connection. A TLS implementation may, after sending a closure alert, close the connection without waiting for the peer to send its closure alert, generating an "incomplete close". Note that an implementation that does this may choose to reuse the session. This should only be done when the application knows (typically through detecting HTTP message boundaries) that it has received all the message data that it cares about.

HTTP clients also must be able to cope with a situation in which the underlying TCP connection is terminated without a prior `close_notify` alert and without a `Connection: close` indicator. Such a situation could be due to a programming error on the server or a communication error that causes the TCP connection to drop. However, the unannounced TCP closure could be evidence of some sort of attack. So the HTTPS client should issue some sort of security warning when this occurs.

6.5 SECURE SHELL (SSH)

Secure Shell (SSH) is a protocol for secure network communications designed to be relatively simple and inexpensive to implement. The initial version, SSH1 was focused on providing a secure remote logon facility to replace TELNET and other remote logon schemes that provided no security. SSH also provides a more

Figure 6.8   SSH Protocol Stack

general client/server capability and can be used for such network functions as file transfer and e-mail. A new version, SSH2, fixes a number of security flaws in the original scheme. SSH2 is documented as a proposed standard in IETF RFCs 4250 through 4256.

SSH client and server applications are widely available for most operating systems. It has become the method of choice for remote login and X tunneling and is rapidly becoming one of the most pervasive applications for encryption technology outside of embedded systems.

SSH is organized as three protocols that typically run on top of TCP (Figure 6.8):

- **Transport Layer Protocol:** Provides server authentication, data confidentiality, and data integrity with forward secrecy (i.e., if a key is compromised during one session, the knowledge does not affect the security of earlier sessions). The transport layer may optionally provide compression.
- **User Authentication Protocol:** Authenticates the user to the server.
- **Connection Protocol:** Multiplexes multiple logical communications channels over a single, underlying SSH connection.

Transport Layer Protocol

HOST KEYS Server authentication occurs at the transport layer, based on the server possessing a public/private key pair. A server may have multiple host keys using multiple different asymmetric encryption algorithms. Multiple hosts may share the same host key. In any case, the server host key is used during key exchange to authenticate the identity of the host. For this to be possible, the client must have a priori knowledge of the server's public host key. RFC 4251 dictates two alternative trust models that can be used:

1. The client has a local database that associates each host name (as typed by the user) with the corresponding public host key. This method requires no centrally administered infrastructure and no third-party coordination. The downside is that the database of name-to-key associations may become burdensome to maintain.

2. The host name-to-key association is certified by a trusted certification authority (CA). The client only knows the CA root key and can verify the validity of all host keys certified by accepted CAs. This alternative eases the maintenance problem, since ideally, only a single CA key needs to be securely stored on the client. On the other hand, each host key must be appropriately certified by a central authority before authorization is possible.

PACKET EXCHANGE Figure 6.9 illustrates the sequence of events in the SSH Transport Layer Protocol. First, the client establishes a TCP connection to the server. This is done via the TCP protocol and is not part of the Transport Layer Protocol. Once the connection is established, the client and server exchange data,

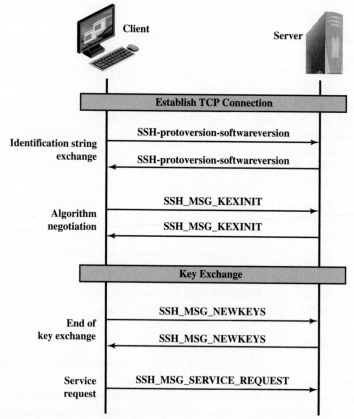

Figure 6.9 SSH Transport Layer Protocol Packet Exchanges

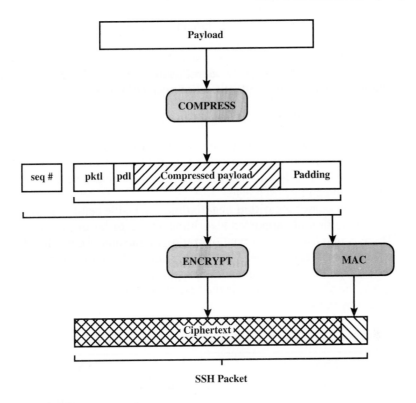

pktl = packet length
pdl = padding length

Figure 6.10   SSH Transport Layer Protocol Packet Formation

referred to as packets, in the data field of a TCP segment. Each packet is in the following format (Figure 6.10).

- **Packet length:** Length of the packet in bytes, not including the packet length and MAC fields.
- **Padding length:** Length of the random padding field.
- **Payload:** Useful contents of the packet. Prior to algorithm negotiation, this field is uncompressed. If compression is negotiated, then in subsequent packets, this field is compressed.
- **Random padding:** Once an encryption algorithm has been negotiated, this field is added. It contains random bytes of padding so that that total length of the packet (excluding the MAC field) is a multiple of the cipher block size, or 8 bytes for a stream cipher.
- **Message authentication code (MAC):** If message authentication has been negotiated, this field contains the MAC value. The MAC value is computed over the entire packet plus a sequence number, excluding the MAC field. The sequence number is an implicit 32-bit packet sequence that is initialized to zero for the first packet and incremented for every packet. The sequence number is not included in the packet sent over the TCP connection.

Once an encryption algorithm has been negotiated, the entire packet (excluding the MAC field) is encrypted after the MAC value is calculated.

The SSH Transport Layer packet exchange consists of a sequence of steps (Figure 6.9). The first step, the **identification string exchange**, begins with the client sending a packet with an identification string of the form:

```
SSH-protoversion-softwareversion SP comments CR LF
```

where SP, CR, and LF are space character, carriage return, and line feed, respectively. An example of a valid string is SSH-2.0-billsSSH_3.6.3q3<CR><LF>. The server responds with its own identification string. These strings are used in the Diffie-Hellman key exchange.

Next comes **algorithm negotiation**. Each side sends an SSH_MSG_KEXINIT containing lists of supported algorithms in the order of preference to the sender. There is one list for each type of cryptographic algorithm. The algorithms include key exchange, encryption, MAC algorithm, and compression algorithm. Table 6.3 shows the allowable options for encryption, MAC, and compression. For each category, the algorithm chosen is the first algorithm on the client's list that is also supported by the server.

Table 6.3   SSH Transport Layer Cryptographic Algorithms

Cipher	
`3des-cbc*`	Three-key 3DES in CBC mode
`blowfish-cbc`	Blowfish in CBC mode
`twofish256-cbc`	Twofish in CBC mode with a 256-bit key
`twofish192-cbc`	Twofish with a 192-bit key
`twofish128-cbc`	Twofish with a 128-bit key
`aes256-cbc`	AES in CBC mode with a 256-bit key
`aes192-cbc`	AES with a 192-bit key
`aes128-cbc**`	AES with a 128-bit key
`Serpent256-cbc`	Serpent in CBC mode with a 256-bit key
`Serpent192-cbc`	Serpent with a 192-bit key
`Serpent128-cbc`	Serpent with a 128-bit key
`arcfour`	RC4 with a 128-bit key
`cast128-cbc`	CAST-128 in CBC mode

MAC algorithm	
`hmac-sha1*`	HMAC-SHA1; digest length = key length = 20
`hmac-sha1-96**`	First 96 bits of HMAC-SHA1; digest length = 12; key length = 20
`hmac-md5`	HMAC-MD5; digest length = key length = 16
`hmac-md5-96`	First 96 bits of HMAC-MD5; digest length = 12; key length = 16

Compression algorithm	
`none*`	No compression
`zlib`	Defined in RFC 1950 and RFC 1951

* = Required
** = Recommended

The next step is **key exchange**. The specification allows for alternative methods of key exchange, but at present, only two versions of Diffie-Hellman key exchange are specified. Both versions are defined in RFC 2409 and require only one packet in each direction. The following steps are involved in the exchange. In this, C is the client; S is the server; p is a large safe prime; g is a generator for a subgroup of $GF(p)$; q is the order of the subgroup; V_S is S's identification string; V_C is C's identification string; K_S is S's public host key; I_C is C's SSH_MSG_KEXINIT message and I_S is S's SSH_MSG_KEXINIT message that have been exchanged before this part begins. The values of p, g, and q are known to both client and server as a result of the algorithm selection negotiation. The hash function hash() is also decided during algorithm negotiation.

1. C generates a random number $x(1 < x < q)$ and computes $e = g^x \bmod p$. C sends e to S.

2. S generates a random number $y(0 < y < q)$ and computes $f = g^y \bmod p$. S receives e. It computes $K = e^y \bmod p$, $H = \text{hash}(\text{V\_C} \| \text{V\_S} \| \text{I\_C} \| \text{I\_S} \| \text{K\_S} \| e \| f \| K)$, and signature s on H with its private host key. S sends $(\text{K\_S} \| f \| s)$ to C. The signing operation may involve a second hashing operation.

3. C verifies that K_S really is the host key for S (e.g., using certificates or a local database). C is also allowed to accept the key without verification; however, doing so will render the protocol insecure against active attacks (but may be desirable for practical reasons in the short term in many environments). C then computes $K = f^x \bmod p$, $H = \text{hash}(\text{V\_C} \| \text{V\_S} \| \text{I\_C} \| \text{I\_S} \| \text{K\_S} \| e \| f \| K)$, and verifies the signature s on H.

As a result of these steps, the two sides now share a master key K. In addition, the server has been authenticated to the client, because the server has used its private key to sign its half of the Diffie-Hellman exchange. Finally, the hash value H serves as a session identifier for this connection. Once computed, the session identifier is not changed, even if the key exchange is performed again for this connection to obtain fresh keys.

The **end of key exchange** is signaled by the exchange of SSH_MSG_NEWKEYS packets. At this point, both sides may start using the keys generated from K, as discussed subsequently.

The final step is **service request**. The client sends an SSH_MSG_SERVICE_REQUEST packet to request either the User Authentication or the Connection Protocol. Subsequent to this, all data is exchanged as the payload of an SSH Transport Layer packet, protected by encryption and MAC.

KEY GENERATION The keys used for encryption and MAC (and any needed IVs) are generated from the shared secret key K, the hash value from the key exchange H, and the session identifier, which is equal to H unless there has been a subsequent key exchange after the initial key exchange. The values are computed as follows.

- Initial IV client to server: $\text{HASH}(K \| H \| \text{"A"} \| \text{session\_id})$
- Initial IV server to client: $\text{HASH}(K \| H \| \text{"B"} \| \text{session\_id})$
- Encryption key client to server: $\text{HASH}(K \| H \| \text{"C"} \| \text{session\_id})$

- Encryption key server to client: $HASH(K \| H \| "D" \| session\_id)$
- Integrity key client to server: $HASH(K \| H \| "E" \| session\_id)$
- Integrity key server to client: $HASH(K \| H \| "F" \| session\_id)$

where HASH() is the hash function determined during algorithm negotiation.

User Authentication Protocol

The User Authentication Protocol provides the means by which the client is authenticated to the server.

MESSAGE TYPES AND FORMATS Three types of messages are always used in the User Authentication Protocol. Authentication requests from the client have the format:

byte	SSH_MSG_USERAUTH_REQUEST (50)
string	user name
string	service name
string	method name
...	method specific fields

where user name is the authorization identity the client is claiming, service name is the facility to which the client is requesting access (typically the SSH Connection Protocol), and method name is the authentication method being used in this request. The first byte has decimal value 50, which is interpreted as SSH_MSG_USERAUTH_REQUEST.

If the server either (1) rejects the authentication request or (2) accepts the request but requires one or more additional authentication methods, the server sends a message with the format:

byte	SSH_MSG_USERAUTH_FAILURE (51)
name-list	authentications that can continue
boolean	partial success

where the name-list is a list of methods that may productively continue the dialog. If the server accepts authentication, it sends a single byte message: SSH_MSG_USERAUTH_SUCCESS (52).

MESSAGE EXCHANGE The message exchange involves the following steps.

1. The client sends a SSH_MSG_USERAUTH_REQUEST with a requested method of none.

2. The server checks to determine if the user name is valid. If not, the server returns SSH_MSG_USERAUTH_FAILURE with the partial success value of false. If the user name is valid, the server proceeds to step 3.

3. The server returns SSH_MSG_USERAUTH_FAILURE with a list of one or more authentication methods to be used.

4. The client selects one of the acceptable authentication methods and sends a SSH_MSG_USERAUTH_REQUEST with that method name and the required

method-specific fields. At this point, there may be a sequence of exchanges to perform the method.

5. If the authentication succeeds and more authentication methods are required, the server proceeds to step 3, using a partial success value of true. If the authentication fails, the server proceeds to step 3, using a partial success value of false.

6. When all required authentication methods succeed, the server sends a `SSH_MSG_USERAUTH_SUCCESS` message, and the Authentication Protocol is over.

AUTHENTICATION METHODS The server may require one or more of the following authentication methods.

- **publickey:** The details of this method depend on the public-key algorithm chosen. In essence, the client sends a message to the server that contains the client's public key, with the message signed by the client's private key. When the server receives this message, it checks whether the supplied key is acceptable for authentication and, if so, it checks whether the signature is correct.

- **password:** The client sends a message containing a plaintext password, which is protected by encryption by the Transport Layer Protocol.

- **hostbased:** Authentication is performed on the client's host rather than the client itself. Thus, a host that supports multiple clients would provide authentication for all its clients. This method works by having the client send a signature created with the private key of the client host. Thus, rather than directly verifying the user's identity, the SSH server verifies the identity of the client host—and then believes the host when it says the user has already authenticated on the client side.

Connection Protocol

The SSH Connection Protocol runs on top of the SSH Transport Layer Protocol and assumes that a secure authentication connection is in use.[2] That secure authentication connection, referred to as a **tunnel,** is used by the Connection Protocol to multiplex a number of logical channels.

CHANNEL MECHANISM All types of communication using SSH, such as a terminal session, are supported using separate channels. Either side may open a channel. For each channel, each side associates a unique channel number, which need not be the same on both ends. Channels are flow controlled using a window mechanism. No data may be sent to a channel until a message is received to indicate that window space is available.

---

[2]RFC 4254, *The Secure Shell (SSH) Connection Protocol*, states that the Connection Protocol runs on top of the Transport Layer Protocol and the User Authentication Protocol. RFC 4251, *SSH Protocol Architecture*, states that the Connection Protocol runs over the User Authentication Protocol. In fact, the Connection Protocol runs over the Transport Layer Protocol, but assumes that the User Authentication Protocol has been previously invoked.

The life of a channel progresses through three stages: opening a channel, data transfer, and closing a channel.

When either side wishes to **open a new channel,** it allocates a local number for the channel and then sends a message of the form:

byte	SSH_MSG_CHANNEL_OPEN
string	channel type
uint32	sender channel
uint32	initial window size
uint32	maximum packet size
....	channel type specific data follows

where uint32 means unsigned 32-bit integer. The channel type identifies the application for this channel, as described subsequently. The sender channel is the local channel number. The initial window size specifies how many bytes of channel data can be sent to the sender of this message without adjusting the window. The maximum packet size specifies the maximum size of an individual data packet that can be sent to the sender. For example, one might want to use smaller packets for interactive connections to get better interactive response on slow links.

If the remote side is able to open the channel, it returns a SSH_MSG_CHANNEL_OPEN_CONFIRMATION message, which includes the sender channel number, the recipient channel number, and window and packet size values for incoming traffic. Otherwise, the remote side returns a SSH_MSG_CHANNEL_OPEN_FAILURE message with a reason code indicating the reason for failure.

Once a channel is open, **data transfer** is performed using a SSH_MSG_CHANNEL_DATA message, which includes the recipient channel number and a block of data. These messages, in both directions, may continue as long as the channel isopen.

When either side wishes to **close a channel,** it sends a SSH_MSG_CHANNEL_CLOSE message, which includes the recipient channel number.

Figure 6.11 provides an example of Connection Protocol Message Exchange.

CHANNEL TYPES Four channel types are recognized in the SSH Connection Protocol specification.

- **session:** The remote execution of a program. The program may be a shell, an application such as file transfer or e-mail, a system command, or some built-in subsystem. Once a session channel is opened, subsequent requests are used to start the remote program.
- **x11:** This refers to the X Window System, a computer software system and network protocol that provides a graphical user interface (GUI) for networked computers. X allows applications to run on a network server but to be displayed on a desktop machine.
- **forwarded-tcpip:** This is remote port forwarding, as explained in the next subsection.
- **direct-tcpip:** This is local port forwarding, as explained in the next subsection.

Figure 6.11 Example of SSH Connection Protocol Message Exchange

PORT FORWARDING One of the most useful features of SSH is port forwarding. In essence, port forwarding provides the ability to convert any insecure TCP connection into a secure SSH connection. This is also referred to as SSH tunneling. We need to know what a port is in this context. A **port** is an identifier of a user of TCP. So, any application that runs on top of TCP has a port number. Incoming TCP traffic is delivered to the appropriate application on the basis of the port number. An application may employ multiple port numbers. For example, for the Simple Mail Transfer Protocol (SMTP), the server side generally listens on port 25, so an incoming SMTP request uses TCP and addresses the data to destination port 25. TCP recognizes that this is the SMTP server address and routes the data to the SMTP server application.

Figure 6.12 illustrates the basic concept behind port forwarding. We have a client application that is identified by port number x and a server application identified by port number y. At some point, the client application invokes the local TCP entity and requests a connection to the remote server on port y. The local TCP

Figure 6.12 SSH Transport Layer Packet Exchanges

entity negotiates a TCP connection with the remote TCP entity, such that the connection links local port x to remote port y.

To secure this connection, SSH is configured so that the SSH Transport Layer Protocol establishes a TCP connection between the SSH client and server entities, with TCP port numbers a and b, respectively. A secure SSH tunnel is established over this TCP connection. Traffic from the client at port x is redirected to the local SSH entity and travels through the tunnel where the remote SSH entity delivers the data to the server application on port y. Traffic in the other direction is similarly redirected.

SSH supports two types of port forwarding: local forwarding and remote forwarding. **Local forwarding** allows the client to set up a "hijacker" process. This will intercept selected application-level traffic and redirect it from an unsecured TCP connection to a secure SSH tunnel. SSH is configured to listen on selected ports. SSH grabs all traffic using a selected port and sends it through an SSH tunnel. On the other end, the SSH server sends the incoming traffic to the destination port dictated by the client application.

The following example should help clarify local forwarding. Suppose you have an e-mail client on your desktop and use it to get e-mail from your mail server via the Post Office Protocol (POP). The assigned port number for POP3 is port 110. We can secure this traffic in the following way:

1. The SSH client sets up a connection to the remote server.
2. Select an unused local port number, say 9999, and configure SSH to accept traffic from this port destined for port 110 on the server.
3. The SSH client informs the SSH server to create a connection to the destination, in this case mailserver port 110.
4. The client takes any bits sent to local port 9999 and sends them to the server inside the encrypted SSH session. The SSH server decrypts the incoming bits and sends the plaintext to port 110.
5. In the other direction, the SSH server takes any bits received on port 110 and sends them inside the SSH session back to the client, who decrypts and sends them to the process connected to port 9999.

With **remote forwarding,** the user's SSH client acts on the server's behalf. The client receives traffic with a given destination port number, places the traffic on the correct port and sends it to the destination the user chooses. A typical example of remote forwarding is the following. You wish to access a server at work from your home computer. Because the work server is behind a firewall, it will not accept an SSH request from your home computer. However, from work you can set up an SSH tunnel using remote forwarding. This involves the following steps.

1. From the work computer, set up an SSH connection to your home computer. The firewall will allow this, because it is a protected outgoing connection.
2. Configure the SSH server to listen on a local port, say 22, and to deliver data across the SSH connection addressed to remote port, say 2222.
3. You can now go to your home computer, and configure SSH to accept traffic on port 2222.
4. You now have an SSH tunnel that can be used for remote logon to the work server.

6.6 RECOMMENDED READING

[RESC01] is a good detailed treatment of SSL and TLS. [BARR05] provides a thorough treatment of SSH. The original version (SSH-1) of SSH was introduced in [YLON96].

BARR05 Barrett, D.; Silverman, R.; and Byrnes, R. *SSH The Secure Shell: The Definitive Guide.* Sebastopol, CA: O'Reilly, 2005.

RESC01 Rescorla, E. *SSL and TLS: Designing and Building Secure Systems.* Reading, MA: Addison-Wesley, 2001.

YLON96 Ylonen, T. "SSH - Secure Login Connections over the Internet." *Proceedings, Sixth USENIX Security Symposium,* July 1996.

6.7 KEY TERMS, REVIEW QUESTIONS, AND PROBLEMS

Key Terms

Alert protocol	HTTPS (HTTP over SSL)	Secure Socket Layer (SSL)
Change Cipher Spec protocol	Master Secret	Transport Layer Security
Handshake protocol	Secure Shell (SSH)	(TLS)

Review Questions

6.1 What characteristics of Web usage suggest the need for tailored security tools?

6.2 What is IPsec? List the advantages of IPSec.

6.3 What is SSL? What are the two implementation choices for SSL?

6.4 Explain the SSL's two layer protocol stack.

6.5 List the parameters that define an SSL connection state.

6.6 Briefly explain the operation of SSL Record Protocol.

6.7 Explain briefly the fields of the SSL Record Protocol header.

6.8 What are the two differences between the SSLv3 and TSL MAC schemes?

6.9 What is the purpose of a pseudorandom function in TSL?

6.10 What is HTTPS? What elements of the communication are encrypted in HTTPS?

Problems

6.1 What is a Change Cipher Spec Protocol? How it is used by the client and server while setting up a secure connection?

6.2 What will be the padding length (in bytes) in TSL if the plaintext and MAC and padding length byte are 79 bytes long in total?

6.3 Consider the following threats to Web security and describe how each is countered by a particular feature of SSL.

a. Brute-Force Cryptanalytic Attack: An exhaustive search of the key space for a conventional encryption algorithm.

b. Known Plaintext Dictionary Attack: Many messages will contain predictable plaintext, such as the HTTP GET command. An attacker constructs a dictionary containing every possible encryption of the known-plaintext message. When an encrypted message is intercepted, the attacker takes the portion containing the encrypted known plaintext and looks up the ciphertext in the dictionary. The ciphertext should match against an entry that was encrypted with the same secret key. If there are several matches, each of these can be tried against the full ciphertext to determine the right one. This attack is especially effective against small key sizes (e.g., 40-bit keys).

c. Replay Attack: Earlier SSL handshake messages are replayed.

d. Man-in-the-Middle Attack: An attacker interposes during key exchange, acting as the client to the server and as the server to the client.

e. Password Sniffing: Passwords in HTTP or other application traffic are eavesdropped.

f. IP Spoofing: Uses forged IP addresses to fool a host into accepting bogus data.

g. IP Hijacking: An active, authenticated connection between two hosts is disrupted and the attacker takes the place of one of the hosts.

h. SYN Flooding: An attacker sends TCP SYN messages to request a connection but does not respond to the final message to establish the connection fully. The attacked TCP module typically leaves the "half-open connection" around for a few minutes. Repeated SYN messages can clog the TCP module.

6.4 Based on what you have learned in this chapter, is it possible in SSL for the receiver to reorder SSL record blocks that arrive out of order? If so, explain how it can be done. If not, why not?

6.5 What is port forwarding? What are the different types of port forwarding supported by SSH?

CHAPTER 7

WIRELESS NETWORK SECURITY

7.1 Wireless Security

Wireless Network Threats
Wireless Security Measures

7.2 Mobile Device Security

Security Threats
Mobile Device Security Strategy

7.3 IEEE 802.11 Wireless LAN Overview

The Wi-Fi Alliance
IEEE 802 Protocol Architecture
IEEE 802.11 Network Components and Architectural Model
IEEE 802.11 Services

7.4 IEEE 802.11i Wireless LAN Security

IEEE 802.11i Services
IEEE 802.11i Phases of Operation
Discovery Phase
Authentication Phase
Key Management Phase
Protected Data Transfer Phase
The IEEE 802.11i Pseudorandom Function

7.5 Recommended Reading

7.6 Key Terms, Review Questions, and Problems

Investigators have published numerous reports of birds taking turns vocalizing; the bird spoken to gave its full attention to the speaker and never vocalized at the same time, as if the two were holding a conversation.

Researchers and scholars who have studied the data on avian communication carefully write (a) the communication code of birds, such as crows, has not been broken by any means; (b) probably all birds have wider vocabularies than anyone realizes; and (c) greater complexity and depth are recognized in avian communication as research progresses.

— *The Human Nature of Birds*, Theodore Barber

LEARNING OBJECTIVES

After studying this chapter, you should be able to:

◆ Present an overview of security threats and countermeasures for wireless networks.

◆ Understand the unique security threats posed by the use of mobile devices with enterprise networks.

◆ Describe the principal elements in a mobile device security strategy.

◆ Understand the essential elements of the IEEE 802.11 wireless LAN standard.

◆ Summarize the various components of the IEEE 802.11i wireless LAN security architecture.

This chapter begins with a general overview of wireless security issues. We then focus on the relatively new area of mobile device security, examining threats and countermeasures for mobile devices used in the enterprise. Then, we look at the IEEE 802.11i standard for wireless LAN security. This standard is part of IEEE 802.11, also referred to as Wi-Fi. We begin the discussion with an overview of IEEE 802.11, and then we look in some detail at IEEE 802.11i.

7.1 WIRELESS SECURITY

Wireless networks, and the wireless devices that use them, introduce a host of security problems over and above those found in wired networks. Some of the key factors contributing to the higher security risk of wireless networks compared to wired networks include the following [MA10]:

• **Channel:** Wireless networking typically involves broadcast communications, which is far more susceptible to eavesdropping and jamming than wired networks. Wireless networks are also more vulnerable to active attacks that exploit vulnerabilities in communications protocols.

| Endpoint | Wireless medium | Access point |

Figure 7.1 Wireless Networking Components

- **Mobility:** Wireless devices are, in principal and usually in practice, far more portable and mobile than wired devices. This mobility results in a number of risks, described subsequently.

- **Resources:** Some wireless devices, such as smartphones and tablets, have sophisticated operating systems but limited memory and processing resources with which to counter threats, including denial of service and malware.

- **Accessibility:** Some wireless devices, such as sensors and robots, may be left unattended in remote and/or hostile locations. This greatly increases their vulnerability to physical attacks.

In simple terms, the wireless environment consists of three components that provide point of attack (Figure 7.1). The wireless client can be a cell phone, a Wi-Fi–enabled laptop or tablet, a wireless sensor, a Bluetooth device, and so on. The wireless access point provides a connection to the network or service. Examples of access points are cell towers, Wi-Fi hotspots, and wireless access points to wired local or wide area networks. The transmission medium, which carries the radio waves for data transfer, is also a source of vulnerability.

Wireless Network Threats

[CHOI08] lists the following security threats to wireless networks:

- **Accidental association:** Company wireless LANs or wireless access points to wired LANs in close proximity (e.g., in the same or neighboring buildings) may create overlapping transmission ranges. A user intending to connect to one LAN may unintentionally lock on to a wireless access point from a neighboring network. Although the security breach is accidental, it nevertheless exposes resources of one LAN to the accidental user.

- **Malicious association:** In this situation, a wireless device is configured to appear to be a legitimate access point, enabling the operator to steal passwords from legitimate users and then penetrate a wired network through a legitimate wireless access point.

- **Ad hoc networks:** These are peer-to-peer networks between wireless computers with no access point between them. Such networks can pose a security threat due to a lack of a central point of control.

- **Nontraditional networks:** Nontraditional networks and links, such as personal network Bluetooth devices, barcode readers, and handheld PDAs, pose a security risk in terms of both eavesdropping and spoofing.

- **Identity theft (MAC spoofing):** This occurs when an attacker is able to eavesdrop on network traffic and identify the MAC address of a computer with network privileges.

- **Man-in-the middle attacks:** This type of attack is described in Chapter 3 in the context of the Diffie-Hellman key exchange protocol. In a broader sense, this attack involves persuading a user and an access point to believe that they are talking to each other when in fact the communication is going through an intermediate attacking device. Wireless networks are particularly vulnerable to such attacks.

- **Denial of service (DoS):** This type of attack is discussed in detail in Chapter 10. In the context of a wireless network, a DoS attack occurs when an attacker continually bombards a wireless access point or some other accessible wireless port with various protocol messages designed to consume system resources. The wireless environment lends itself to this type of attack, because it is so easy for the attacker to direct multiple wireless messages at the target.

- **Network injection:** A network injection attack targets wireless access points that are exposed to nonfiltered network traffic, such as routing protocol messages or network management messages. An example of such an attack is one in which bogus reconfiguration commands are used to affect routers and switches to degrade network performance.

Wireless Security Measures

Following [CHOI08], we can group wireless security measures into those dealing with wireless transmissions, wireless access points, and wireless networks (consisting of wireless routers and endpoints).

SECURING WIRELESS TRANSMISSIONS The principal threats to wireless transmission are eavesdropping, altering or inserting messages, and disruption. To deal with eavesdropping, two types of countermeasures are appropriate:

- **Signal-hiding techniques:** Organizations can take a number of measures to make it more difficult for an attacker to locate their wireless access points, including turning off service set identifier (SSID) broadcasting by wireless access points; assigning cryptic names to SSIDs; reducing signal strength to the lowest level that still provides requisite coverage; and locating wireless access points in the interior of the building, away from windows and exterior walls. Greater security can be achieved by the use of directional antennas and of signal-shielding techniques.

- **Encryption:** Encryption of all wireless transmission is effective against eavesdropping to the extent that the encryption keys are secured.

The use of encryption and authentication protocols is the standard method of countering attempts to alter or insert transmissions.

The methods discussed in Chapter 10 for dealing with DoS apply to wireless transmissions. Organizations can also reduce the risk of unintentional DoS attacks. Site surveys can detect the existence of other devices using the same frequency range, to help determine where to locate wireless access points. Signal strengths can be adjusted and shielding used in an attempt to isolate a wireless environment from competing nearby transmissions.

Securing Wireless Access Points The main threat involving wireless access points is unauthorized access to the network. The principal approach for preventing such access is the IEEE 802.1X standard for port-based network access control. The standard provides an authentication mechanism for devices wishing to attach to a LAN or wireless network. The use of 802.1X can prevent rogue access points and other unauthorized devices from becoming insecure backdoors.

Section 5.3 provides an introduction to 802.1X.

Securing Wireless Networks [CHOI08] recommends the following techniques for wireless network security:

1. Use encryption. Wireless routers are typically equipped with built-in encryption mechanisms for router-to-router traffic.

2. Use antivirus and antispyware software, and a firewall. These facilities should be enabled on all wireless network endpoints.

3. Turn off identifier broadcasting. Wireless routers are typically configured to broadcast an identifying signal so that any device within range can learn of the router's existence. If a network is configured so that authorized devices know the identity of routers, this capability can be disabled, so as to thwart attackers.

4. Change the identifier on your router from the default. Again, this measure thwarts attackers who will attempt to gain access to a wireless network using default router identifiers.

5. Change your router's pre-set password for administration. This is another prudent step.

6. Allow only specific computers to access your wireless network. A router can be configured to only communicate with approved MAC addresses. Of course, MAC addresses can be spoofed, so this is just one element of a security strategy.

7.2 MOBILE DEVICE SECURITY

Prior to the widespread use of smartphones, the dominant paradigm for computer and network security in organizations was as follows. Corporate IT was tightly controlled. User devices were typically limited to Windows PCs. Business applications were controlled by IT and either run locally on endpoints or on physical servers in data centers. Network security was based upon clearly defined perimeters that separated trusted internal networks from the untrusted Internet. Today, there have been massive changes in each of these assumptions. An organization's networks must accommodate the following:

- **Growing use of new devices:** Organizations are experiencing significant growth in employee use of mobile devices. In many cases, employees are allowed to use a combination of endpoint devices as part of their day-to-day activities.

- **Cloud-based applications:** Applications no longer run solely on physical servers in corporate data centers. Quite the opposite, applications can run anywhere—on traditional physical servers, on mobile virtual servers, or in the cloud. Additionally, end users can now take advantage of a wide variety of cloud-based applications and IT services for personal and professional use. Facebook can be used for an employee's personal profiles or as a component of a corporate marketing campaign. Employees depend upon Skype to speak with friends abroad or for legitimate business video conferencing. Dropbox and Box can be used to distribute documents between corporate and personal devices for mobility and user productivity.

- **De-perimeterization:** Given new device proliferation, application mobility, and cloud-based consumer and corporate services, the notion of a static network perimeter is all but gone. Now there are a multitude of network perimeters around devices, applications, users, and data. These perimeters have also become quite dynamic as they must adapt to various environmental conditions such as user role, device type, server virtualization mobility, network location, and time-of-day.

- **External business requirements:** The enterprise must also provide guests, third-party contractors, and business partners network access using various devices from a multitude of locations.

The central element in all of these changes is the mobile computing device. Mobile devices have become an essential element for organizations as part of the overall network infrastructure. Mobile devices such as smartphones, tablets, and memory sticks provide increased convenience for individuals as well as the potential for increased productivity in the workplace. Because of their widespread use and unique characteristics, security for mobile devices is a pressing and complex issue. In essence, an organization needs to implement a security policy through a combination of security features built into the mobile devices and additional security controls provided by network components that regulate the use of the mobile devices.

Security Threats

Mobile devices need additional, specialized protection measures beyond those implemented for other client devices, such as desktop and laptop devices that are used only within the organization's facilities and on the organization's networks. SP 800-14 (*Guidelines for Managing and Securing Mobile Devices in the Enterprise*, July 2012) lists seven major security concerns for mobile devices. We examine each of these in turn.

Lack of Physical Security Controls Mobile devices are typically under the complete control of the user, and are used and kept in a variety of locations outside the organization's control, including off premises. Even if a device is required to remain on premises, the user may move the device within the organization between secure and nonsecured locations. Thus, theft and tampering are realistic threats.

The security policy for mobile devices must be based on the assumption that any mobile device may be stolen or at least accessed by a malicious party. The threat is twofold: A malicious party may attempt to recover sensitive data from the device itself, or may use the device to gain access to the organization's resources.

USE OF UNTRUSTED MOBILE DEVICES In addition to company-issued and company-controlled mobile devices, virtually all employees will have personal smartphones and/or tablets. The organization must assume that these devices are not trustworthy. That is, the devices may not employ encryption and either the user or a third party may have installed a bypass to the built-in restrictions on security, operating system use, and so on.

USE OF UNTRUSTED NETWORKS If a mobile device is used on premises, it can connect to organization resources over the organization's own in-house wireless networks. However, for off-premises use, the user will typically access organizational resources via Wi-Fi or cellular access to the Internet and from the Internet to the organization. Thus, traffic that includes an off-premises segment is potentially susceptible to eavesdropping or man-in-the-middle types of attacks. Thus, the security policy must be based on the assumption that the networks between the mobile device and the organization are not trustworthy.

USE OF APPLICATIONS CREATED BY UNKNOWN PARTIES By design, it is easy to find and install third-party applications on mobile devices. This poses the obvious risk of installing malicious software. An organization has several options for dealing with this threat, as described subsequently.

INTERACTION WITH OTHER SYSTEMS A common feature found on smartphones and tablets is the ability to automatically synchronize data, apps, contacts, photos, and so on with other computing devices and with cloud-based storage. Unless an organization has control of all the devices involved in synchronization, there is considerable risk of the organization's data being stored in an unsecured location, plus the risk of the introduction of malware.

USE OF UNTRUSTED CONTENT Mobile devices may access and use content that other computing devices do not encounter. An example is the Quick Response (QR) code, which is a two-dimensional barcode. QR codes are designed to be captured by a mobile device camera and used by the mobile device. The QR code translates to a URL, so that a malicious QR code could direct the mobile device to malicious Web sites.

USE OF LOCATION SERVICES The GPS capability on mobile devices can be used to maintain a knowledge of the physical location of the device. While this feature might be useful to an organization as part of a presence service, it creates security risks. An attacker can use the location information to determine where the device and user are located, which may be of use to the attacker.

Mobile Device Security Strategy

With the threats listed in the preceding discussion in mind, we outline the principal elements of a mobile device security strategy. They fall into three categories: device security, client/server traffic security, and barrier security (Figure 7.2).

Mobile device is
configured with
security mechanisms and
parameters to conform to
organization security policy

Traffic is encrypted;
uses SSL or IPsec
VPN tunnel

Mobile device configuration server

Application/ database server

Authentication/ access control server

Firewall

Authentication
and access control
protocols used to
verify device and user
and establish limits
on access

Firewall limits
scope of data
and application
access

Figure 7.2   Mobile Device Security Elements

DEVICE SECURITY A number of organizations will supply mobile devices for employee use and preconfigure those devices to conform to the enterprise security policy. However, many organizations will find it convenient or even necessary to adopt a bring-your-own-device (BYOD) policy that allows the personal mobile devices of employees to have access to corporate resources. IT managers should be able to inspect each device before allowing network access. IT will want to establish configuration guidelines for operating systems and applications. For example, "rooted" or "jail-broken" devices are not permitted on the network, and mobile devices cannot store corporate contacts on local storage. Whether a device is owned by the organization or BYOD, the organization should configure the device with security controls, including the following:

- Enable auto-lock, which causes the device to lock if it has not been used for a given amount of time, requiring the user to re-enter a four-digit PIN or a password to re-activate the device.
- Enable password or PIN protection. The PIN or password is needed to unlock the device. In addition, it can be configured so that e-mail and other data on the device are encrypted using the PIN or password and can only be retrieved with the PIN or password.
- Avoid using auto-complete features that remember user names or passwords.
- Enable remote wipe.

- Ensure that SSL protection is enabled, if available.
- Make sure that software, including operating systems and applications, is up to date.
- Install antivirus software as it becomes available.
- Either sensitive data should be prohibited from storage on the mobile device or it should be encrypted.
- IT staff should also have the ability to remotely access devices, wipe the device of all data, and then disable the device in the event of loss or theft.
- The organization may prohibit all installation of third-party applications, implement whitelisting to prohibit installation of all unapproved applications, or implement a secure sandbox that isolates the organization's data and applications from all other data and applications on the mobile device. Any application that is on an approved list should be accompanied by a digital signature and a public-key certificate from an approved authority.
- The organization can implement and enforce restrictions on what devices can synchronize and on the use of cloud-based storage.
- To deal with the threat of untrusted content, security responses can include training of personnel on the risks inherent in untrusted content and disabling camera use on corporate mobile devices.
- To counter the threat of malicious use of location services, the security policy can dictate that such service is disabled on all mobile devices.

TRAFFIC SECURITY Traffic security is based on the usual mechanisms for encryption and authentication. All traffic should be encrypted and travel by secure means, such as SSL or IPv6. Virtual private networks (VPNs) can be configured so that all traffic between the mobile device and the organization's network is via a VPN.

A strong authentication protocol should be used to limit the access from the device to the resources of the organization. Often, a mobile device has a single device-specific authenticator, because it is assumed that the device has only one user. A preferable strategy is to have a two-layer authentication mechanism, which involves authenticating the device and then authenticating the user of the device.

BARRIER SECURITY The organization should have security mechanisms to protect the network from unauthorized access. The security strategy can also include firewall policies specific to mobile device traffic. Firewall policies can limit the scope of data and application access for all mobile devices. Similarly, intrusion detection and intrusion prevention systems can be configured to have tighter rules for mobile device traffic.

7.3 IEEE 802.11 WIRELESS LAN OVERVIEW

IEEE 802 is a committee that has developed standards for a wide range of local area networks (LANs). In 1990, the IEEE 802 Committee formed a new working group, IEEE 802.11, with a charter to develop a protocol and transmission specifications for wireless LANs (WLANs). Since that time, the demand for

Table 7.1   IEEE 802.11 Terminology

Access point (AP)	Any entity that has station functionality and provides access to the distribution system via the wireless medium for associated stations.
Basic service set (BSS)	A set of stations controlled by a single coordination function.
Coordination function	The logical function that determines when a station operating within a BSS is permitted to transmit and may be able to receive PDUs.
Distribution system (DS)	A system used to interconnect a set of BSSs and integrated LANs to create an ESS.
Extended service set (ESS)	A set of one or more interconnected BSSs and integrated LANs that appear as a single BSS to the LLC layer at any station associated with one of these BSSs.
MAC protocol data unit (MPDU)	The unit of data exchanged between two peer MAC entities using the services of the physical layer.
MAC service data unit (MSDU)	Information that is delivered as a unit between MAC users.
Station	Any device that contains an IEEE 802.11 conformant MAC and physical layer.

WLANs at different frequencies and data rates has exploded. Keeping pace with this demand, the IEEE 802.11 working group has issued an ever-expanding list of standards. Table 7.1 briefly defines key terms used in the IEEE 802.11 standard.

The Wi-Fi Alliance

The first 802.11 standard to gain broad industry acceptance was 802.11b. Although 802.11b products are all based on the same standard, there is always a concern whether products from different vendors will successfully interoperate. To meet this concern, the Wireless Ethernet Compatibility Alliance (WECA), an industry consortium, was formed in 1999. This organization, subsequently renamed the Wi-Fi (Wireless Fidelity) Alliance, created a test suite to certify interoperability for 802.11b products. The term used for certified 802.11b products is *Wi-Fi*. Wi-Fi certification has been extended to 802.11g products. The Wi-Fi Alliance has also developed a certification process for 802.11a products, called *Wi-Fi5*. The Wi-Fi Alliance is concerned with a range of market areas for WLANs, including enterprise, home, and hot spots.

More recently, the Wi-Fi Alliance has developed certification procedures for IEEE 802.11 security standards, referred to as Wi-Fi Protected Access (WPA). The most recent version of WPA, known as WPA2, incorporates all of the features of the IEEE 802.11i WLAN security specification.

IEEE 802 Protocol Architecture

Before proceeding, we need to briefly preview the IEEE 802 protocol architecture. IEEE 802.11 standards are defined within the structure of a layered set of protocols. This structure, used for all IEEE 802 standards, is illustrated in Figure 7.3.

Figure 7.3   IEEE 802.11 Protocol Stack

PHYSICAL LAYER   The lowest layer of the IEEE 802 reference model is the **physical layer**, which includes such functions as encoding/decoding of signals and bit transmission/reception. In addition, the physical layer includes a specification of the transmission medium. In the case of IEEE 802.11, the physical layer also defines frequency bands and antenna characteristics.

MEDIA ACCESS CONTROL   All LANs consist of collections of devices that share the network's transmission capacity. Some means of controlling access to the transmission medium is needed to provide an orderly and efficient use of that capacity. This is the function of a **media access control (MAC)** layer. The MAC layer receives data from a higher-layer protocol, typically the Logical Link Control (LLC) layer, in the form of a block of data known as the **MAC service data unit (MSDU)**. In general, the MAC layer performs the following functions:

- On transmission, assemble data into a frame, known as a **MAC protocol data unit (MPDU)** with address and error-detection fields.
- On reception, disassemble frame, and perform address recognition and error detection.
- Govern access to the LAN transmission medium.

The exact format of the MPDU differs somewhat for the various MAC protocols in use. In general, all of the MPDUs have a format similar to that of Figure 7.4. The fields of this frame are as follows.

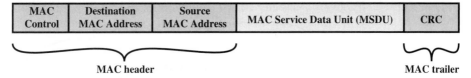

Figure 7.4   General IEEE 802 MPDU Format

- **MAC Control:** This field contains any protocol control information needed for the functioning of the MAC protocol. For example, a priority level could be indicated here.
- **Destination MAC Address:** The destination physical address on the LAN for this MPDU.
- **Source MAC Address:** The source physical address on the LAN for this MPDU.
- **MAC Service Data Unit:** The data from the next higher layer.
- **CRC:** The cyclic redundancy check field; also known as the Frame Check Sequence (FCS) field. This is an error-detecting code, such as that which is used in other data-link control protocols. The CRC is calculated based on the bits in the entire MPDU. The sender calculates the CRC and adds it to the frame. The receiver performs the same calculation on the incoming MPDU and compares that calculation to the CRC field in that incoming MPDU. If the two values don't match, then one or more bits have been altered in transit.

The fields preceding the MSDU field are referred to as the **MAC header**, and the field following the MSDU field is referred to as the **MAC trailer**. The header and trailer contain control information that accompany the data field and that are used by the MAC protocol.

LOGICAL LINK CONTROL In most data-link control protocols, the data-link protocol entity is responsible not only for detecting errors using the CRC, but for recovering from those errors by retransmitting damaged frames. In the LAN protocol architecture, these two functions are split between the MAC and LLC layers. The MAC layer is responsible for detecting errors and discarding any frames that contain errors. The LLC layer optionally keeps track of which frames have been successfully received and retransmits unsuccessful frames.

IEEE 802.11 Network Components and Architectural Model

Figure 7.5 illustrates the model developed by the 802.11 working group. The smallest building block of a wireless LAN is a **basic service set (BSS)**, which consists of wireless stations executing the same MAC protocol and competing for access to the same shared wireless medium. A BSS may be isolated, or it may connect to a backbone **distribution system (DS)** through an **access point (AP)**. The AP functions as a bridge and a relay point. In a BSS, client stations do not communicate directly with one another. Rather, if one station in the BSS wants to communicate with another station in the same BSS, the MAC frame is first sent from the originating station to

Figure 7.5   IEEE 802.11 Extended Service Set

the AP and then from the AP to the destination station. Similarly, a MAC frame from a station in the BSS to a remote station is sent from the local station to the AP and then relayed by the AP over the DS on its way to the destination station. The BSS generally corresponds to what is referred to as a cell in the literature. The DS can be a switch, a wired network, or a wireless network.

When all the stations in the BSS are mobile stations that communicate directly with one another (not using an AP), the BSS is called an **independent BSS (IBSS)**. An IBSS is typically an ad hoc network. In an IBSS, the stations all communicate directly, and no AP is involved.

A simple configuration is shown in Figure 7.5, in which each station belongs to a single BSS; that is, each station is within wireless range only of other stations within the same BSS. It is also possible for two BSSs to overlap geographically, so that a single station could participate in more than one BSS. Furthermore, the association between a station and a BSS is dynamic. Stations may turn off, come within range, and go out of range.

An **extended service set (ESS)** consists of two or more basic service sets interconnected by a distribution system. The extended service set appears as a single logical LAN to the logical link control (LLC) level.

IEEE 802.11 Services

IEEE 802.11 defines nine services that need to be provided by the wireless LAN to achieve functionality equivalent to that which is inherent to wired LANs. Table 7.2 lists the services and indicates two ways of categorizing them.

Table 7.2   IEEE 802.11 Services

Service	Provider	Used to support
Association	Distribution system	MSDU delivery
Authentication	Station	LAN access and security
Deauthentication	Station	LAN access and security
Disassociation	Distribution system	MSDU delivery
Distribution	Distribution system	MSDU delivery
Integration	Distribution system	MSDU delivery
MSDU delivery	Station	MSDU delivery
Privacy	Station	LAN access and security
Reassociation	Distribution system	MSDU delivery

1. The service provider can be either the station or the DS. Station services are implemented in every 802.11 station, including AP stations. Distribution services are provided between BSSs; these services may be implemented in an AP or in another special-purpose device attached to the distribution system.

2. Three of the services are used to control IEEE 802.11 LAN access and confidentiality. Six of the services are used to support delivery of MSDUs between stations. If the MSDU is too large to be transmitted in a single MPDU, it may be fragmented and transmitted in a series of MPDUs.

Following the IEEE 802.11 document, we next discuss the services in an order designed to clarify the operation of an IEEE 802.11 ESS network. **MSDU delivery**, which is the basic service, already has been mentioned. Services related to security are introduced in Section 7.4.

DISTRIBUTION OF MESSAGES WITHIN A DS   The two services involved with the distribution of messages within a DS are distribution and integration. **Distribution** is the primary service used by stations to exchange MPDUs when the MPDUs must traverse the DS to get from a station in one BSS to a station in another BSS. For example, suppose a frame is to be sent from station 2 (STA 2) to station 7 (STA 7) in Figure 7.5. The frame is sent from STA 2 to AP 1, which is the AP for this BSS. The AP gives the frame to the DS, which has the job of directing the frame to the AP associated with STA 7 in the target BSS. AP 2 receives the frame and forwards it to STA 7. How the message is transported through the DS is beyond the scope of the IEEE 802.11 standard.

If the two stations that are communicating are within the same BSS, then the distribution service logically goes through the single AP of that BSS.

The **integration** service enables transfer of data between a station on an IEEE 802.11 LAN and a station on an integrated IEEE 802.x LAN. The term *integrated* refers to a wired LAN that is physically connected to the DS and whose stations may be logically connected to an IEEE 802.11 LAN via the integration service. The integration service takes care of any address translation and media conversion logic required for the exchange of data.

ASSOCIATION-RELATED SERVICES The primary purpose of the MAC layer is to transfer MSDUs between MAC entities; this purpose is fulfilled by the distribution service. For that service to function, it requires information about stations within the ESS that is provided by the association-related services. Before the distribution service can deliver data to or accept data from a station, that station must be *associated*. Before looking at the concept of association, we need to describe the concept of mobility. The standard defines three transition types, based on mobility:

- **No transition:** A station of this type is either stationary or moves only within the direct communication range of the communicating stations of a single BSS.
- **BSS transition:** This is defined as a station movement from one BSS to another BSS within the same ESS. In this case, delivery of data to the station requires that the addressing capability be able to recognize the new location of the station.
- **ESS transition:** This is defined as a station movement from a BSS in one ESS to a BSS within another ESS. This case is supported only in the sense that the station can move. Maintenance of upper-layer connections supported by 802.11 cannot be guaranteed. In fact, disruption of service is likely to occur.

To deliver a message within a DS, the distribution service needs to know where the destination station is located. Specifically, the DS needs to know the identity of the AP to which the message should be delivered in order for that message to reach the destination station. To meet this requirement, a station must maintain an association with the AP within its current BSS. Three services relate to this requirement:

- **Association:** Establishes an initial association between a station and an AP. Before a station can transmit or receive frames on a wireless LAN, its identity and address must be known. For this purpose, a station must establish an association with an AP within a particular BSS. The AP can then communicate this information to other APs within the ESS to facilitate routing and delivery of addressed frames.
- **Reassociation:** Enables an established association to be transferred from one AP to another, allowing a mobile station to move from one BSS to another.
- **Disassociation:** A notification from either a station or an AP that an existing association is terminated. A station should give this notification before leaving an ESS or shutting down. However, the MAC management facility protects itself against stations that disappear without notification.

7.4 IEEE 802.11i WIRELESS LAN SECURITY

There are two characteristics of a wired LAN that are not inherent in a wireless LAN.

1. In order to transmit over a wired LAN, a station must be physically connected to the LAN. On the other hand, with a wireless LAN, any station within radio

range of the other devices on the LAN can transmit. In a sense, there is a form of authentication with a wired LAN in that it requires some positive and presumably observable action to connect a station to a wired LAN.

2. Similarly, in order to receive a transmission from a station that is part of a wired LAN, the receiving station also must be attached to the wired LAN. On the other hand, with a wireless LAN, any station within radio range can receive. Thus, a wired LAN provides a degree of privacy, limiting reception of data to stations connected to the LAN.

These differences between wired and wireless LANs suggest the increased need for robust security services and mechanisms for wireless LANs. The original 802.11 specification included a set of security features for privacy and authentication that were quite weak. For privacy, 802.11 defined the **Wired Equivalent Privacy (WEP)** algorithm. The privacy portion of the 802.11 standard contained major weaknesses. Subsequent to the development of WEP, the 802.11i task group has developed a set of capabilities to address the WLAN security issues. In order to accelerate the introduction of strong security into WLANs, the Wi-Fi Alliance promulgated **Wi-Fi Protected Access (WPA)** as a Wi-Fi standard. WPA is a set of security mechanisms that eliminates most 802.11 security issues and was based on the current state of the 802.11i standard. The final form of the 802.11i standard is referred to as ***Robust Security Network (RSN)***. The Wi-Fi Alliance certifies vendors in compliance with the full 802.11i specification under the WPA2 program.

The RSN specification is quite complex, and occupies 145 pages of the 2012 IEEE 802.11 standard. In this section, we provide an overview.

IEEE 802.11i Services

The 802.11i RSN security specification defines the following services.

- **Authentication:** A protocol is used to define an exchange between a user and an AS that provides mutual authentication and generates temporary keys to be used between the client and the AP over the wireless link.
- **Access control:**[1] This function enforces the use of the authentication function, routes the messages properly, and facilitates key exchange. It can work with a variety of authentication protocols.
- **Privacy with message integrity:** MAC-level data (e.g., an LLC PDU) are encrypted along with a message integrity code that ensures that the data have not been altered.

Figure 7.6a indicates the security protocols used to support these services, while Figure 7.6b lists the cryptographic algorithms used for these services.

---

[1]In this context, we are discussing access control as a security function. This is a different function than media access control (MAC) as described in Section 7.3. Unfortunately, the literature and the standards use the term *access control* in both contexts.

(a) Services and protocols

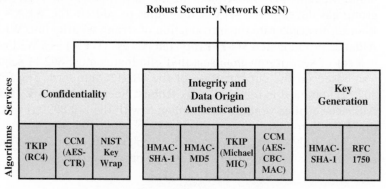

(b) Cryptographic algorithms

CBC-MAC	= Cipher Block Chaining Message Authentication Code (MAC)
CCM	= Counter Mode with Cipher Block Chaining Message Authentication Code
CCMP	= Counter Mode with Cipher Block Chaining MAC Protocol
TKIP	= Temporal Key Integrity Protocol

Figure 7.6 Elements of IEEE 802.11i

IEEE 802.11i Phases of Operation

The operation of an IEEE 802.11i RSN can be broken down into five distinct phases of operation. The exact nature of the phases will depend on the configuration and the end points of the communication. Possibilities include (see Figure 7.5):

1. Two wireless stations in the same BSS communicating via the access point (AP) for that BSS.

2. Two wireless stations (STAs) in the same ad hoc IBSS communicating directly with each other.

3. Two wireless stations in different BSSs communicating via their respective APs across a distribution system.

4. A wireless station communicating with an end station on a wired network via its AP and the distribution system.

IEEE 802.11i security is concerned only with secure communication between the STA and its AP. In case 1 in the preceding list, secure communication is assured if each STA establishes secure communications with the AP. Case 2 is similar, with the AP functionality residing in the STA. For case 3, security is not provided across the distribution system at the level of IEEE 802.11, but only within each BSS. End-to-end security (if required) must be provided at a higher layer. Similarly, in case 4, security is only provided between the STA and its AP.

With these considerations in mind, Figure 7.7 depicts the five phases of operation for an RSN and maps them to the network components involved. One new component is the authentication server (AS). The rectangles indicate the exchange of sequences of MPDUs. The five phases are defined as follows.

- **Discovery:** An AP uses messages called Beacons and Probe Responses to advertise its IEEE 802.11i security policy. The STA uses these to identify an AP for a WLAN with which it wishes to communicate. The STA associates with the AP, which it uses to select the cipher suite and authentication mechanism when the Beacons and Probe Responses present a choice.

- **Authentication:** During this phase, the STA and AS prove their identities to each other. The AP blocks non-authentication traffic between the STA and AS until the authentication transaction is successful. The AP does not participate in the authentication transaction other than forwarding traffic between the STA and AS.

Figure 7.7   IEEE 802.11i Phases of Operation

- **Key generation and distribution:** The AP and the STA perform several operations that cause cryptographic keys to be generated and placed on the AP and the STA. Frames are exchanged between the AP and STA only.

- **Protected data transfer:** Frames are exchanged between the STA and the end station through the AP. As denoted by the shading and the encryption module icon, secure data transfer occurs between the STA and the AP only; security is not provided end-to-end.

- **Connection termination:** The AP and STA exchange frames. During this phase, the secure connection is torn down and the connection is restored to the original state.

Discovery Phase

We now look in more detail at the RSN phases of operation, beginning with the discovery phase, which is illustrated in the upper portion of Figure 7.8. The purpose of this phase is for an STA and an AP to recognize each other, agree on a set of security capabilities, and establish an association for future communication using those security capabilities.

SECURITY CAPABILITIES During this phase, the STA and AP decide on specific techniques in the following areas:

- Confidentiality and MPDU integrity protocols for protecting unicast traffic (traffic only between this STA and AP)
- Authentication method
- Cryptography key management approach

Confidentiality and integrity protocols for protecting multicast/broadcast traffic are dictated by the AP, since all STAs in a multicast group must use the same protocols and ciphers. The specification of a protocol, along with the chosen key length (if variable) is known as a *cipher suite*. The options for the confidentiality and integrity cipher suite are

- WEP, with either a 40-bit or 104-bit key, which allows backward compatibility with older IEEE 802.11 implementations
- TKIP
- CCMP
- Vendor-specific methods

The other negotiable suite is the authentication and key management (AKM) suite, which defines (1) the means by which the AP and STA perform mutual authentication and (2) the means for deriving a root key from which other keys may be generated. The possible AKM suites are

- IEEE 802.1X
- Pre-shared key (no explicit authentication takes place and mutual authentication is implied if the STA and AP share a unique secret key)
- Vendor-specific methods

Figure 7.8 IEEE 802.11i Phases of Operation: Capability Discovery, Authentication, and Association

MPDU EXCHANGE The discovery phase consists of three exchanges.

- **Network and security capability discovery:** During this exchange, STAs discover the existence of a network with which to communicate. The AP either periodically broadcasts its security capabilities (not shown in figure), indicated by RSN IE (Robust Security Network Information Element), in a specific channel through the Beacon frame; or responds to a station's Probe Request through a Probe Response frame. A wireless station may discover available access points and corresponding security capabilities by either passively monitoring the Beacon frames or actively probing every channel.

- **Open system authentication:** The purpose of this frame sequence, which provides no security, is simply to maintain backward compatibility with the

IEEE 802.11 state machine, as implemented in existing IEEE 802.11 hardware. In essence, the two devices (STA and AP) simply exchange identifiers.

- **Association:** The purpose of this stage is to agree on a set of security capabilities to be used. The STA then sends an Association Request frame to the AP. In this frame, the STA specifies one set of matching capabilities (one authentication and key management suite, one pairwise cipher suite, and one group-key cipher suite) from among those advertised by the AP. If there is no match in capabilities between the AP and the STA, the AP refuses the Association Request. The STA blocks it too, in case it has associated with a rogue AP or someone is inserting frames illicitly on its channel. As shown in Figure 7.8, the IEEE 802.1X controlled ports are blocked, and no user traffic goes beyond the AP. The concept of blocked ports is explained subsequently.

Authentication Phase

As was mentioned, the authentication phase enables mutual authentication between an STA and an authentication server (AS) located in the DS. Authentication is designed to allow only authorized stations to use the network and to provide the STA with assurance that it is communicating with a legitimate network.

IEEE 802.1X ACCESS CONTROL APPROACH IEEE 802.11i makes use of another standard that was designed to provide access control functions for LANs. The standard is IEEE 802.1X, Port-Based Network Access Control. The authentication protocol that is used, the Extensible Authentication Protocol (EAP), is defined in the IEEE 802.1X standard. IEEE 802.1X uses the terms *supplicant*, *authenticator*, and *authentication server* (AS). In the context of an 802.11 WLAN, the first two terms correspond to the wireless station and the AP. The AS is typically a separate device on the wired side of the network (i.e., accessible over the DS) but could also reside directly on the authenticator.

Before a supplicant is authenticated by the AS using an authentication protocol, the authenticator only passes control or authentication messages between the supplicant and the AS; the 802.1X control channel is unblocked, but the 802.11 data channel is blocked. Once a supplicant is authenticated and keys are provided, the authenticator can forward data from the supplicant, subject to predefined access control limitations for the supplicant to the network. Under these circumstances, the data channel is unblocked.

As indicated in Figure 5.5, 802.1X uses the concepts of controlled and uncontrolled ports. Ports are logical entities defined within the authenticator and refer to physical network connections. For a WLAN, the authenticator (the AP) may have only two physical ports: one connecting to the DS and one for wireless communication within its BSS. Each logical port is mapped to one of these two physical ports. An uncontrolled port allows the exchange of PDUs between the supplicant and the other AS, regardless of the authentication state of the supplicant. A controlled port allows the exchange of PDUs between a supplicant and other systems on the LAN only if the current state of the supplicant authorizes such an exchange. IEEE 802.1X is covered in more detail in Chapter 5.

The 802.1X framework, with an upper-layer authentication protocol, fits nicely with a BSS architecture that includes a number of wireless stations and an AP. However, for an IBSS, there is no AP. For an IBSS, 802.11i provides a more complex solution that, in essence, involves pairwise authentication between stations on the IBSS.

MPDU EXCHANGE The lower part of Figure 7.8 shows the MPDU exchange dictated by IEEE 802.11 for the authentication phase. We can think of authentication phase as consisting of the following three phases.

- **Connect to AS:** The STA sends a request to its AP (the one with which it has an association) for connection to the AS. The AP acknowledges this request and sends an access request to the AS.
- **EAP exchange:** This exchange authenticates the STA and AS to each other. A number of alternative exchanges are possible, as explained subsequently.
- **Secure key delivery:** Once authentication is established, the AS generates a master session key (MSK), also known as the Authentication, Authorization, and Accounting (AAA) key and sends it to the STA. As explained subsequently, all the cryptographic keys needed by the STA for secure communication with its AP are generated from this MSK. IEEE 802.11i does not prescribe a method for secure delivery of the MSK but relies on EAP for this. Whatever method is used, it involves the transmission of an MPDU containing an encrypted MSK from the AS, via the AP, to the AS.

EAP EXCHANGE As mentioned, there are a number of possible EAP exchanges that can be used during the authentication phase. Typically, the message flow between STA and AP employs the EAP over LAN (EAPOL) protocol, and the message flow between the AP and AS uses the Remote Authentication Dial In User Service (RADIUS) protocol, although other options are available for both STA-to-AP and AP-to-AS exchanges. [FRAN07] provides the following summary of the authentication exchange using EAPOL and RADIUS.

1. The EAP exchange begins with the AP issuing an EAP-Request/Identity frame to the STA.
2. The STA replies with an EAP-Response/Identity frame, which the AP receives over the uncontrolled port. The packet is then encapsulated in RADIUS over EAP and passed on to the RADIUS server as a RADIUS-Access-Request packet.
3. The AAA server replies with a RADIUS-Access-Challenge packet, which is passed on to the STA as an EAP-Request. This request is of the appropriate authentication type and contains relevant challenge information.
4. The STA formulates an EAP-Response message and sends it to the AS. The response is translated by the AP into a Radius-Access-Request with the response to the challenge as a data field. Steps 3 and 4 may be repeated multiple times, depending on the EAP method in use. For TLS tunneling methods, it is common for authentication to require 10 to 20 round trips.

5. The AAA server grants access with a Radius-Access-Accept packet. The AP issues an EAP-Success frame. (Some protocols require confirmation of the EAP success inside the TLS tunnel for authenticity validation.) The controlled port is authorized, and the user may begin to access the network.

Note from Figure 7.8 that the AP controlled port is still blocked to general user traffic. Although the authentication is successful, the ports remain blocked until the temporal keys are installed in the STA and AP, which occurs during the 4-Way Handshake.

Key Management Phase

During the key management phase, a variety of cryptographic keys are generated and distributed to STAs. There are two types of keys: pairwise keys used for communication between an STA and an AP and group keys used for multicast communication. Figure 7.9, based on [FRAN07], shows the two key hierarchies, and Table 7.3 defines the individual keys.

PAIRWISE KEYS Pairwise keys are used for communication between a pair of devices, typically between an STA and an AP. These keys form a hierarchy beginning with a master key from which other keys are derived dynamically and used for a limited period of time.

At the top level of the hierarchy are two possibilities. A **pre-shared key (PSK)** is a secret key shared by the AP and a STA and installed in some fashion outside the scope of IEEE 802.11i. The other alternative is the **master session key (MSK)**, also known as the AAAK, which is generated using the IEEE 802.1X protocol during the authentication phase, as described previously. The actual method of key generation depends on the details of the authentication protocol used. In either case (PSK or MSK), there is a unique key shared by the AP with each STA with which it communicates. All the other keys derived from this master key are also unique between an AP and an STA. Thus, each STA, at any time, has one set of keys, as depicted in the hierarchy of Figure 7.9a, while the AP has one set of such keys for each of its STAs.

The **pairwise master key (PMK)** is derived from the master key. If a PSK is used, then the PSK is used as the PMK; if a MSK is used, then the PMK is derived from the MSK by truncation (if necessary). By the end of the authentication phase, marked by the 802.1X EAP Success message (Figure 7.8), both the AP and the STA have a copy of their shared PMK.

The PMK is used to generate the **pairwise transient key (PTK)**, which in fact consists of three keys to be used for communication between an STA and AP after they have been mutually authenticated. To derive the PTK, the HMAC-SHA-1 function is applied to the PMK, the MAC addresses of the STA and AP, and nonces generated when needed. Using the STA and AP addresses in the generation of the PTK provides protection against session hijacking and impersonation; using nonces provides additional random keying material.

The three parts of the PTK are as follows.

* **EAP Over LAN (EAPOL) Key Confirmation Key (EAPOL-KCK):** Supports the integrity and data origin authenticity of STA-to-AP control frames during

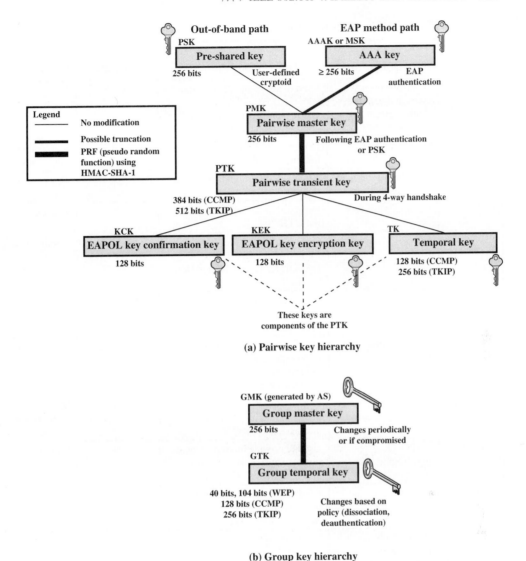

Figure 7.9 IEEE 802.11i Key Hierarchies

operational setup of an RSN. It also performs an access control function: proof-of-possession of the PMK. An entity that possesses the PMK is authorized to use the link.

- **EAPOL Key Encryption Key (EAPOL-KEK):** Protects the confidentiality of keys and other data during some RSN association procedures.
- **Temporal Key (TK):** Provides the actual protection for user traffic.

GROUP KEYS Group keys are used for multicast communication in which one STA sends MPDU's to multiple STAs. At the top level of the group key hierarchy is the **group master key (GMK)**. The GMK is a key-generating key used with other inputs

Table 7.3 IEEE 802.11i Keys for Data Confidentiality and Integrity Protocols

Abbreviation	Name	Description / Purpose	Size (bits)	Type
AAA Key	Authentication, Accounting, and Authorization Key	Used to derive the PMK. Used with the IEEE 802.1X authentication and key management approach. Same as MMSK.	≥ 256	Key generation key, root key
PSK	Pre-shared Key	Becomes the PMK in pre-shared key environments.	256	Key generation key, root key
PMK	Pairwise Master Key	Used with other inputs to derive the PTK.	256	Key generation key
GMK	Group Master Key	Used with other inputs to derive the GTK.	128	Key generation key
PTK	Pair-wise Transient Key	Derived from the PMK. Comprises the EAPOL-KCK, EAPOL-KEK, and TK and (for TKIP) the MIC key.	512 (TKIP) 384 (CCMP)	Composite key
TK	Temporal Key	Used with TKIP or CCMP to provide confidentiality and integrity protection for unicast user traffic.	256 (TKIP) 128 (CCMP)	Traffic key
GTK	Group Temporal Key	Derived from the GMK. Used to provide confidentiality and integrity protection for multicast/broadcast user traffic.	256 (TKIP) 128 (CCMP) 40,104 (WEP)	Traffic key
MIC Key	Message Integrity Code Key	Used by TKIP's Michael MIC to provide integrity protection of messages.	64	Message integrity key
EAPOL-KCK	EAPOL-Key Confirmation Key	Used to provide integrity protection for key material distributed during the 4-Way Handshake.	128	Message integrity key
EAPOL-KEK	EAPOL-Key Encryption Key	Used to ensure the confidentiality of the GTK and other key material in the 4-Way Handshake.	128	Traffic key / key encryption key
WEP Key	Wired Equivalent Privacy Key	Used with WEP.	40,104	Traffic key

to derive the **group temporal key (GTK)**. Unlike the PTK, which is generated using material from both AP and STA, the GTK is generated by the AP and transmitted to its associated STAs. Exactly how this GTK is generated is undefined. IEEE 802.11i, however, requires that its value is computationally indistinguishable from random. The GTK is distributed securely using the pairwise keys that are already established. The GTK is changed every time a device leaves the network.

PAIRWISE KEY DISTRIBUTION The upper part of Figure 7.10 shows the MPDU exchange for distributing pairwise keys. This exchange is known as the **4-way handshake**. The STA and AP use this handshake to confirm the existence of the PMK, verify the selection of the cipher suite, and derive a fresh PTK for the following data session. The four parts of the exchange are as follows.

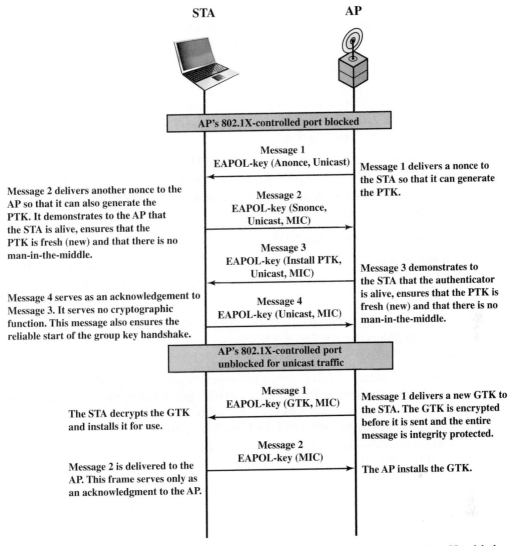

STA　　　　　　　**AP**

AP's 802.1X-controlled port blocked

Message 1
EAPOL-key (Anonce, Unicast)

Message 1 delivers a nonce to
the STA so that it can generate
the PTK.

Message 2 delivers another nonce to the
AP so that it can also generate the
PTK. It demonstrates to the AP that
the STA is alive, ensures that the
PTK is fresh (new) and that there is no
man-in-the-middle.

Message 2
EAPOL-key (Snonce,
Unicast, MIC)

Message 3
EAPOL-key (Install PTK,
Unicast, MIC)

Message 3 demonstrates to
the STA that the authenticator
is alive, ensures that the PTK is
fresh (new) and that there is no
man-in-the-middle.

Message 4 serves as an acknowledgement to
Message 3. It serves no cryptographic
function. This message also ensures the
reliable start of the group key handshake.

Message 4
EAPOL-key (Unicast, MIC)

AP's 802.1X-controlled port
unblocked for unicast traffic

Message 1
EAPOL-key (GTK, MIC)

Message 1 delivers a new GTK to
the STA. The GTK is encrypted
before it is sent and the entire
message is integrity protected.

The STA decrypts the GTK
and installs it for use.

Message 2
EAPOL-key (MIC)

Message 2 is delivered to the
AP. This frame serves only as
an acknowledgment to the AP.

The AP installs the GTK.

Figure 7.10　IEEE 802.11i Phases of Operation: Four-Way Handshake and Group Key Handshake

- **AP → STA:** Message includes the MAC address of the AP and a nonce
  (Anonce)
- **STA → AP:** The STA generates its own nonce (Snonce) and uses both nonces
  and both MAC addresses, plus the PMK, to generate a PTK. The STA then
  sends a message containing its MAC address and Snonce, enabling the AP to
  generate the same PTK. This message includes a message integrity code (MIC)[2]
  using HMAC-MD5 or HMAC-SHA-1-128. The key used with the MIC is KCK.

---

[2]While *MAC* is commonly used in cryptography to refer to a Message Authentication Code, the term
MIC is used instead in connection with 802.11i because *MAC* has another standard meaning, Media
Access Control, in networking.

- **AP → STA:** The AP is now able to generate the PTK. The AP then sends a message to the STA, containing the same information as in the first message, but this time including a MIC.

- **STA → AP:** This is merely an acknowledgment message, again protected by a MIC.

GROUP KEY DISTRIBUTION   For group key distribution, the AP generates a GTK and distributes it to each STA in a multicast group. The two-message exchange with each STA consists of the following:

- **AP → STA:** This message includes the GTK, encrypted either with RC4 or with AES. The key used for encryption is A MIC value is appended.

- **STA → AP:** The STA acknowledges receipt of the GTK. This message includes a MIC value.

Protected Data Transfer Phase

IEEE 802.11i defines two schemes for protecting data transmitted in 802.11 MPDUs: the Temporal Key Integrity Protocol (TKIP), and the Counter Mode-CBC MAC Protocol (CCMP).

TKIP   TKIP is designed to require only software changes to devices that are implemented with the older wireless LAN security approach called Wired Equivalent Privacy (WEP). TKIP provides two services:

- **Message integrity:** TKIP adds a message integrity code (MIC) to the 802.11 MAC frame after the data field. The MIC is generated by an algorithm, called Michael, that computes a 64-bit value using as input the source and destination MAC address values and the Data field, plus key material.

- **Data confidentiality:** Data confidentiality is provided by encrypting the MPDU plus MIC value using RC4.

The 256-bit TK (Figure 7.9) is employed as follows. Two 64-bit keys are used with the Michael message digest algorithm to produce a message integrity code. One key is used to protect STA-to-AP messages, and the other key is used to protect AP-to-STA messages. The remaining 128 bits are truncated to generate the RC4 key used to encrypt the transmitted data.

For additional protection, a monotonically increasing TKIP sequence counter (TSC) is assigned to each frame. The TSC serves two purposes. First, the TSC is included with each MPDU and is protected by the MIC to protect against replay attacks. Second, the TSC is combined with the session TK to produce a dynamic encryption key that changes with each transmitted MPDU, thus making cryptanalysis more difficult.

CCMP   CCMP is intended for newer IEEE 802.11 devices that are equipped with the hardware to support this scheme. As with TKIP, CCMP provides two services:

- **Message integrity:** CCMP uses the cipher block chaining message authentication code (CBC-MAC), described in Chapter 3.

- **Data confidentiality:** CCMP uses the CTR block cipher mode of operation with AES for encryption. CTR is described in Chapter 2.

The same 128-bit AES key is used for both integrity and confidentiality. The scheme uses a 48-bit packet number to construct a nonce to prevent replay attacks.

The IEEE 802.11i Pseudorandom Function

At a number of places in the IEEE 802.11i scheme, a pseudorandom function (PRF) is used. For example, it is used to generate nonces, to expand pairwise keys, and to generate the GTK. Best security practice dictates that different pseudorandom number streams be used for these different purposes. However, for implementation efficiency, we would like to rely on a single pseudorandom number generator function.

The PRF is built on the use of HMAC-SHA-1 to generate a pseudorandom bit stream. Recall that HMAC-SHA-1 takes a message (block of data) and a key of length at least 160 bits and produces a 160-bit hash value. SHA-1 has the property that the change of a single bit of the input produces a new hash value with no apparent connection to the preceding hash value. This property is the basis for pseudorandom number generation.

The IEEE 802.11i PRF takes four parameters as input and produces the desired number of random bits. The function is of the form PRF(K, A, B, Len), where

K = a secret key

A = a text string specific to the application (e.g., nonce generation or pairwise key expansion)

B = some data specific to each case

Len = desired number of pseudorandom bits

For example, for the pairwise transient key for CCMP:

```
PTK = PRF(PMK,"Pairwise key expansion",min(AP-
      Addr,STA-Addr) ‖ max(AP-Addr,STA-Addr) ‖ min
      (Anonce,Snonce) ‖ max(Anonce,Snonce),384)
```

So, in this case, the parameters are

K = PMK

A = the text string "Pairwise key expansion"

B = a sequence of bytes formed by concatenating the two MAC addresses and the two nonces

Len = 384 bits

Similarly, a nonce is generated by

```
Nonce = PRF(Random Number,"InitCounter",MAC ‖ Time, 256)
```

$$R = \text{HMAC-SHA-1}(K, A \parallel 0 \parallel B \parallel i)$$

Figure 7.11 IEEE 802.11i Pseudorandom Function

where **Time** is a measure of the network time known to the nonce generator. The group temporal key is generated by

```
GTK = PRF(GMK,"Group key expansion", MAC ‖ Gnonce, 256)
```

Figure 7.11 illustrates the function $PRF(K, A, B, Len)$. The parameter K serves as the key input to HMAC. The message input consists of four items concatenated together: the parameter A, a byte with value 0, the parameter B, and a counter i. The counter is initialized to 0. The HMAC algorithm is run once, producing a 160-bit hash value. If more bits are required, HMAC is run again with the same inputs, except that i is incremented each time until the necessary number of bits is generated. We can express the logic as

```
PRF(K, A, B, Len)
  R ← null string
  for i ← 0 to ((Len + 159)/160 - 1) do
  R ← R‖HMAC-SHA-1(K, A‖0‖B‖i)
  Return Truncate-to-Len(R, Len)
```

7.5 RECOMMENDED READING

[SOUP12] provides a good overview of mobile device threats and countermeasures. [BECH11] is a useful analysis of smartphone security issues.

The IEEE 802.11 and Wi-Fi specifications are covered in more detail in [STAL11]. [FRAN07] is an excellent, detailed treatment of IEEE 802.11i. [CHEN05a] provides an overview of IEEE 802.11i.

BECH11 Becher, M., et al. "Mobile Security Catching Up? Revealing the Nuts and Bolts of the Security of Mobile Devices." *IEEE Symposium on Security and Privacy*, May 2011.

CHEN05a Chen, J.; Jiang, M.; and Liu, Y. "Wireless LAN Security and IEEE 802.11i." *IEEE Wireless Communications*, February 2005.

FRAN07 Frankel, S.; Eydt, B.; Owens, L.; and Scarfone, K. *Establishing Wireless Robust Security Networks: A Guide to IEEE 802.11i.* NIST Special Publication SP 800-97, February 2007.

SOUP12 Souppaya, M.; and Scarfone, K. *Guidelines for Managing and Securing Mobile Devices in the Enterprise.* NIST Special Publication SP 800-124, July 2012.

STAL11 Stallings, W. *Data and Computer Communications, Ninth Edition.* Upper Saddle River, NJ: Prentice Hall, 2011.

7.6 KEY TERMS, REVIEW QUESTIONS, AND PROBLEMS

Key Terms

4-way handshake	IEEE 802.11i	pseudorandom function
access point (AP)	independent BSS (IBSS)	Robust Security Network
Alert Protocol	logical link control	(RSN)
basic service set (BSS)	(LLC)	Temporal Key Integrity
Counter Mode-CBC MAC	media access control (MAC)	Protocol (TKIP)
Protocol (CCMP)	MAC protocol data unit	Wired Equivalent Privacy
distribution system (DS)	(MPDU)	(WEP)
extended service set (ESS)	MAC service data unit	Wireless LAN (WLAN)
group keys	(MSDU)	Wi-Fi
Handshake Protocol	message integrity code (MIC)	Wi-Fi Protected Access
IEEE 802.1X	Michael	(WPA)
IEEE 802.11	pairwise keys	

Review Questions

7.1 Which factors of wireless networks are of higher security risk compared to wired network?

7.2 List the security threats to wireless networks.

7.3 Identify at least five security measures for wireless network security.

7.4 Briefly explain an IEEE 802.11 protocol stack.

7.5 Differentiate between IEEE 802.11's basic service set and the extended service set.

7.6 What is WEP? What are the different security improvements for WEP?

7.7 What are the different security services defined by an IEEE 802.11i RSN?

7.8 Explain the five different phases of operation of an IEEE 802.11i RSN.

Problems

7.1 In IEEE 802.11, open system authentication simply consists of two communications. An authentication is requested by the client, which contains the station ID (typically the MAC address). This is followed by an authentication response from the AP/router containing a success or failure message. An example of when a failure may occur is if the client's MAC address is explicitly excluded in the AP/router configuration.
   a. What are the benefits of this authentication scheme?
   b. What are the security vulnerabilities of this authentication scheme?

7.2 Prior to the introduction of IEEE 802.11i, the security scheme for IEEE 802.11 was Wired Equivalent Privacy (WEP). WEP assumed all devices in the network share a secret key. The purpose of the authentication scenario is for the STA to prove that it possesses the secret key. Authentication proceeds as shown in Figure 7.12. The STA sends a message to the AP requesting authentication. The AP issues a challenge, which is a sequence of 128 random bytes sent as plaintext. The STA encrypts the challenge with the shared key and returns it to the AP. The AP decrypts the incoming value and compares it to the challenge that it sent. If there is a match, the AP confirms that authentication has succeeded.
   a. What are the benefits of this authentication scheme?
   b. This authentication scheme is incomplete. What is missing and why is this important? *Hint:* The addition of one or two messages would fix the problem.
   c. What is a cryptographic weakness of this scheme?

7.3 For WEP, data integrity and data confidentiality are achieved using the RC4 stream encryption algorithm. The transmitter of an MPDU performs the following steps, referred to as encapsulation:
   1. The transmitter selects an initial vector (IV) value.
   2. The IV value is concatenated with the WEP key shared by transmitter and receiver to form the seed, or key input, to RC4.
   3. A 32-bit cyclic redundancy check (CRC) is computed over all the bits of the MAC data field and appended to the data field. The CRC is a common error-detection code used in data link control protocols. In this case, the CRC serves as a integrity check value (ICV).

Figure 7.12 WEP Authentication

4. The result of step 3 is encrypted using RC4 to form the ciphertext block.
5. The plaintext IV is prepended to the ciphertext block to form the encapsulated MPDU for transmission.
   a. Draw a block diagram that illustrates the encapsulation process.
   b. Describe the steps at the receiver end to recover the plaintext and perform the integrity check.
   c. Draw a block diagram that illustrates part b.

7.4 A potential weakness of the CRC as an integrity check is that it is a linear function. This means that you can predict which bits of the CRC are changed if a single bit of the message is changed. Furthermore, it is possible to determine which combination of bits could be flipped in the message so that the net result is no change in the CRC. Thus, there are a number of combinations of bit flippings of the plaintext message that leave the CRC unchanged, so message integrity is defeated. However, in WEP, if an attacker does not know the encryption key, the attacker does not have access to the plaintext, only to the ciphertext block. Does this mean that the ICV is protected from the bit flipping attack? Explain.

CHAPTER 8

ELECTRONIC MAIL SECURITY

8.1 Pretty Good Privacy

Notation
Operational Description

8.2 S/MIME

RFC 5322
Multipurpose Internet Mail Extensions
S/MIME Functionality
S/MIME Messages
S/MIME Certificate Processing
Enhanced Security Services

8.3 DomainKeys Identified Mail

Internet Mail Architecture
E-mail Threats
DKIM Strategy
DKIM Functional Flow

8.4 Recommended Reading

8.5 Key Terms, Review Questions, and Problems

Despite the refusal of VADM Poindexter and LtCol North to appear, the Board's access to other sources of information filled much of this gap. The FBI provided documents taken from the files of the National Security Advisor and relevant NSC staff members, including messages from the PROF system between VADM Poindexter and LtCol North. The PROF messages were conversations by computer, written at the time events occurred and presumed by the writers to be protected from disclosure. In this sense, they provide a first-hand, contemporaneous account of events.

—The Tower Commission Report to President Reagan on the
Iran-Contra Affair, 1987

LEARNING OBJECTIVES

After studying this chapter, you should be able to:

◆ Present an overview of the operation of PGP (Pretty Good Privacy).

◆ Present an overview of MIME (Multipurpose Internet Mail Extension).

◆ Understand the functionality of S/MIME (Secure/Multipurpose Internet Mail Extension) and the security threats it addresses.

◆ Summarize the key functional components of the Internet mail architecture.

◆ Understand the role of DKIM (DomainKeys Identified Mail).

In virtually all distributed environments, electronic mail is the most heavily used network-based application. Users expect to be able to, and do, send e-mail to others who are connected directly or indirectly to the Internet, regardless of host operating system or communications suite. With the explosively growing reliance on e-mail, there grows a demand for authentication and confidentiality services. Two schemes stand out as approaches that enjoy widespread use: Pretty Good Privacy (PGP) and S/MIME. Both are examined in this chapter. The chapter closes with a discussion of DomainKeys Identified Mail.

8.1 PRETTY GOOD PRIVACY

PGP is a remarkable phenomenon. Largely the effort of a single person, Phil Zimmermann, PGP provides a confidentiality and authentication service that can be used for electronic mail and file storage applications. In essence, Zimmermann has done the following:

1. Selected the best available cryptographic algorithms as building blocks.

2. Integrated these algorithms into a general-purpose application that is independent of operating system and processor and that is based on a small set of easy-to-use commands.

3. Made the package and its documentation, including the source code, freely available via the Internet, bulletin boards, and commercial networks such as AOL (America On Line).

4. Entered into an agreement with a company (Viacrypt, now Network Associates) to provide a fully compatible, low-cost commercial version of PGP.

PGP has grown explosively and is now widely used. A number of reasons can be cited for this growth.

1. It is available free worldwide in versions that run on a variety of platforms, including Windows, UNIX, Macintosh, and many more. In addition, the commercial version satisfies users who want a product that comes with vendor support.

2. It is based on algorithms that have survived extensive public review and are considered extremely secure. Specifically, the package includes RSA, DSS, and Diffie-Hellman for public-key encryption; CAST-128, IDEA, and 3DES for symmetric encryption; and SHA-1 for hash coding.

3. It has a wide range of applicability, from corporations that wish to select and enforce a standardized scheme for encrypting files and messages to individuals who wish to communicate securely with others worldwide over the Internet and other networks.

4. It was not developed by, nor is it controlled by, any governmental or standards organization. For those with an instinctive distrust of "the establishment," this makes PGP attractive.

5. PGP is now on an Internet standards track (RFC 3156; *MIME Security with OpenPGP*). Nevertheless, PGP still has an aura of an antiestablishment endeavor.

We begin with an overall look at the operation of PGP. Appendix H examines how cryptographic keys are created and stored, and address the vital issue of public-key management.

Notation

Most of the notation used in this chapter has been used before, but a few terms are new. It is perhaps best to summarize those at the beginning. The following symbols are used.

K_s = session key used in symmetric encryption scheme

PR_a = private key of user A, used in public-key encryption scheme

PU_a = public key of user A, used in public-key encryption scheme

EP = public-key encryption

DP = public-key decryption

EC = symmetric encryption

DC = symmetric decryption

H = hash function

|| = concatenation

Z   = compression using ZIP algorithm
R64 = conversion to radix 64 ASCII format[1]

The PGP documentation often uses the term *secret key* to refer to a key paired with a public key in a public-key encryption scheme. As was mentioned earlier, this practice risks confusion with a secret key used for symmetric encryption. Hence, we use the term *private key* instead.

Operational Description

The actual operation of PGP, as opposed to the management of keys, consists of four services: authentication, confidentiality, compression, and e-mail compatibility (Table 8.1). We examine each of these in turn.

AUTHENTICATION Figure 8.1a illustrates the digital signature service provided by PGP. This is the digital signature scheme discussed in Chapter 4 and illustrated in Figure 4.5. The sequence is as follows.

1. The sender creates a message.
2. SHA-1 is used to generate a 160-bit hash code of the message.
3. The hash code is encrypted with RSA using the sender's private key, and the result is prepended to the message.
4. The receiver uses RSA with the sender's public key to decrypt and recover the hash code.
5. The receiver generates a new hash code for the message and compares it with the decrypted hash code. If the two match, the message is accepted as authentic.

Table 8.1   Summary of PGP Services

Function	Algorithms Used	Description
Digital signature	DSS/SHA or RSA/SHA	A hash code of a message is created using SHA-1. This message digest is encrypted using DSS or RSA with the sender's private key and included with the message.
Message encryption	CAST or IDEA or Three-key Triple DES with Diffie-Hellman or RSA	A message is encrypted using CAST-128 or IDEA or 3DES with a one-time session key generated by the sender. The session key is encrypted using Diffie-Hellman or RSA with the recipient's public key and included with the message.
Compression	ZIP	A message may be compressed for storage or transmission using ZIP.
E-mail compatibility	Radix-64 conversion	To provide transparency for e-mail applications, an encrypted message may be converted to an ASCII string using radix-64 conversion.

---

[1]The American Standard Code for Information Interchange (ASCII) is described in Appendix I.

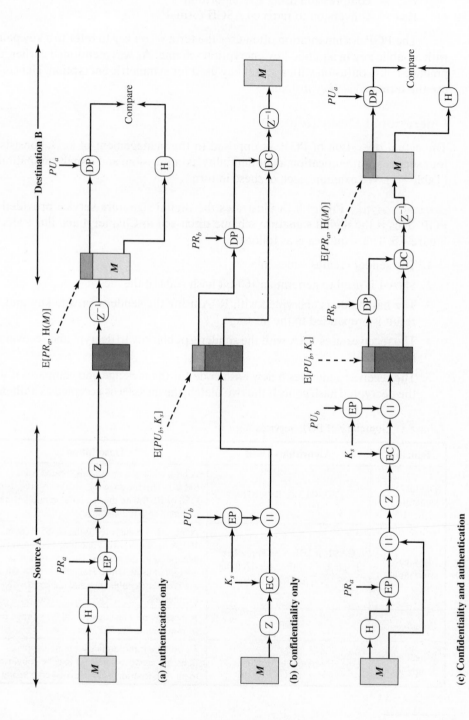

(a) Authentication only

(b) Confidentiality only

(c) Confidentiality and authentication

Figure 8.1   PGP Cryptographic Functions

The combination of SHA-1 and RSA provides an effective digital signature scheme. Because of the strength of RSA, the recipient is assured that only the possessor of the matching private key can generate the signature. Because of the strength of SHA-1, the recipient is assured that no one else could generate a new message that matches the hash code and, hence, the signature of the original message.

As an alternative, signatures can be generated using DSS/SHA-1.

Although signatures normally are found attached to the message or file that they sign, this is not always the case: Detached signatures are supported. A detached signature may be stored and transmitted separately from the message it signs. This is useful in several contexts. A user may wish to maintain a separate signature log of all messages sent or received. A detached signature of an executable program can detect subsequent virus infection. Finally, detached signatures can be used when more than one party must sign a document, such as a legal contract. Each person's signature is independent and therefore is applied only to the document. Otherwise, signatures would have to be nested, with the second signer signing both the document and the first signature, and so on.

CONFIDENTIALITY Another basic service provided by PGP is confidentiality, which is provided by encrypting messages to be transmitted or to be stored locally as files. In both cases, the symmetric encryption algorithm CAST-128 may be used. Alternatively, IDEA or 3DES may be used. The 64-bit cipher feedback (CFB) mode is used.

As always, one must address the problem of key distribution. In PGP, each symmetric key is used only once. That is, a new key is generated as a random 128-bit number for each message. Thus, although this is referred to in the documentation as a session key, it is in reality a one-time key. Because it is to be used only once, the session key is bound to the message and transmitted with it. To protect the key, it is encrypted with the receiver's public key. Figure 8.1b illustrates the sequence, which can be described as follows.

1. The sender generates a message and a random 128-bit number to be used as a session key for this message only.
2. The message is encrypted using CAST-128 (or IDEA or 3DES) with the session key.
3. The session key is encrypted with RSA using the recipient's public key and is prepended to the message.
4. The receiver uses RSA with its private key to decrypt and recover the session key.
5. The session key is used to decrypt the message.

As an alternative to the use of RSA for key encryption, PGP provides an option referred to as *Diffie-Hellman*. As was explained in Chapter 3, Diffie-Hellman is a key exchange algorithm. In fact, PGP uses a variant of Diffie-Hellman that does provide encryption/decryption, known as ElGamal.

Several observations may be made. First, to reduce encryption time, the combination of symmetric and public-key encryption is used in preference to simply using RSA or ElGamal to encrypt the message directly: CAST-128 and the other symmetric algorithms are substantially faster than RSA or ElGamal. Second, the use of the public-key algorithm solves the session-key distribution problem, because only the recipient is able to recover the session key that is bound to the message. Note that we do not need a session-key exchange protocol of the type discussed in Chapter 4, because we are not beginning an ongoing session. Rather, each message is a one-time independent event with its own key. Furthermore, given the store-and-forward nature of electronic mail, the use of handshaking to assure that both sides have the same session key is not practical. Finally, the use of one-time symmetric keys strengthens what is already a strong symmetric encryption approach. Only a small amount of plaintext is encrypted with each key, and there is no relationship among the keys. Thus, to the extent that the public-key algorithm is secure, the entire scheme is secure. To this end, PGP provides the user with a range of key size options from 768 to 3072 bits (the DSS key for signatures is limited to 1024 bits).

CONFIDENTIALITY AND AUTHENTICATION As Figure 8.1c illustrates, both services may be used for the same message. First, a signature is generated for the plaintext message and prepended to the message. Then the plaintext message plus signature is encrypted using CAST-128 (or IDEA or 3DES), and the session key is encrypted using RSA (or ElGamal). This sequence is preferable to the opposite: encrypting the message and then generating a signature for the encrypted message. It is generally more convenient to store a signature with a plaintext version of a message. Furthermore, for purposes of third-party verification, if the signature is performed first, a third party need not be concerned with the symmetric key when verifying the signature.

In summary, when both services are used, the sender first signs the message with its own private key, then encrypts the message with a session key, and finally encrypts the session key with the recipient's public key.

COMPRESSION As a default, PGP compresses the message after applying the signature but before encryption. This has the benefit of saving space both for e-mail transmission and for file storage.

The placement of the compression algorithm, indicated by Z for compression and Z^{-1} for decompression in Figure 8.1, is critical.

1. The signature is generated before compression for two reasons:

    a. It is preferable to sign an uncompressed message so that one can store only the uncompressed message together with the signature for future verification. If one signed a compressed document, then it would be necessary either to store a compressed version of the message for later verification or to recompress the message when verification is required.

    b. Even if one were willing to generate dynamically a recompressed message for verification, PGP's compression algorithm presents a difficulty. The algorithm is not deterministic; various implementations of the algorithm achieve different tradeoffs in running speed versus compression ratio and, as a result, produce different compressed forms. However, these different compression algorithms are interoperable because any version of the algorithm can correctly decompress the output of any other version. Applying the hash function and signature after compression would constrain all PGP implementations to the same version of the compression algorithm.

2. Message encryption is applied after compression to strengthen cryptographic security. Because the compressed message has less redundancy than the original plaintext, cryptanalysis is more difficult.

The compression algorithm used is ZIP, which is described in Appendix G.

E-MAIL COMPATIBILITY When PGP is used, at least part of the block to be transmitted is encrypted. If only the signature service is used, then the message digest is encrypted (with the sender's private key). If the confidentiality service is used, the message plus signature (if present) are encrypted (with a one-time symmetric key). Thus, part or all of the resulting block consists of a stream of arbitrary 8-bit octets. However, many electronic mail systems only permit the use of blocks consisting of ASCII text. To accommodate this restriction, PGP provides the service of converting the raw 8-bit binary stream to a stream of printable ASCII characters.

The scheme used for this purpose is radix-64 conversion. Each group of three octets of binary data is mapped into four ASCII characters. This format also appends a CRC to detect transmission errors. See Appendix K for a description.

The use of radix 64 expands a message by 33%. Fortunately, the session key and signature portions of the message are relatively compact, and the plaintext message has been compressed. In fact, the compression should be more than enough to compensate for the radix-64 expansion. For example, [HELD96] reports an average compression ratio of about 2.0 using ZIP. If we ignore the relatively small signature and key components, the typical overall effect of compression and expansion of a file of length X would be $1.33 \times 0.5 \times X = 0.665 \times X$. Thus, there is still an overall compression of about one-third.

One noteworthy aspect of the radix-64 algorithm is that it blindly converts the input stream to radix-64 format regardless of content, even if the input happens to be ASCII text. Thus, if a message is signed but not encrypted and the conversion is applied to the entire block, the output will be unreadable to the casual observer, which provides a certain level of confidentiality. As an option, PGP can be configured to convert to radix-64 format only the signature portion of signed plaintext messages. This enables the human recipient to read the message without using PGP. PGP would still have to be used to verify the signature.

Figure 8.2 shows the relationship among the four services so far discussed. On transmission (if it is required), a signature is generated using a hash code of the uncompressed plaintext. Then the plaintext (plus signature if present) is compressed. Next, if confidentiality is required, the block (compressed plaintext or compressed signature plus plaintext) is encrypted and prepended with the public-key-encrypted symmetric encryption key. Finally, the entire block is converted to radix-64 format.

On reception, the incoming block is first converted back from radix-64 format to binary. Then, if the message is encrypted, the recipient recovers the session key and decrypts the message. The resulting block is then decompressed. If the message is signed, the recipient recovers the transmitted hash code and compares it to its own calculation of the hash code.

Figure 8.2 Transmission and Reception of PGP Messages

(a) Generic transmission diagram (from A)

(b) Generic reception diagram (to B)

8.2 S/MIME

Secure/Multipurpose Internet Mail Extension (S/MIME) is a security enhancement to the MIME Internet e-mail format standard based on technology from RSA Data Security. Although both PGP and S/MIME are on an IETF standards track, it appears likely that S/MIME will emerge as the industry standard for commercial and organizational use, while PGP will remain the choice for personal e-mail security for many users. S/MIME is defined in a number of documents—most importantly RFCs 3370, 3850, 3851, and 3852.

To understand S/MIME, we need first to have a general understanding of the underlying e-mail format that it uses, namely MIME. But to understand the significance of MIME, we need to go back to the traditional e-mail format standard, RFC 822, which is still in common use. The most recent version of this format specification is RFC 5322 (*Internet Message Format*). Accordingly, this section first provides an introduction to these two earlier standards and then moves on to a discussion of S/MIME.

RFC 5322

RFC 5322 defines a format for text messages that are sent using electronic mail. It has been the standard for Internet-based text mail messages and remains in common use. In the RFC 5322 context, messages are viewed as having an envelope and contents. The envelope contains whatever information is needed to accomplish transmission and delivery. The contents compose the object to be delivered to the recipient. The RFC 5322 standard applies only to the contents. However, the content standard includes a set of header fields that may be used by the mail system to create the envelope, and the standard is intended to facilitate the acquisition of such information by programs.

The overall structure of a message that conforms to RFC 5322 is very simple. A message consists of some number of header lines (*the header*) followed by unrestricted text (*the body*). The header is separated from the body by a blank line. Put differently, a message is ASCII text, and all lines up to the first blank line are assumed to be header lines used by the user agent part of the mail system.

A header line usually consists of a keyword, followed by a colon, followed by the keyword's arguments; the format allows a long line to be broken up into several lines. The most frequently used keywords are *From*, *To*, *Subject*, and *Date*. Here is an example message:

```
Date: October 8, 2009 2:15:49 PM EDT
From: "William Stallings" <ws@shore.net>
Subject: The Syntax in RFC 5322
To: Smith@Other-host.com
Cc: Jones@Yet-Another-Host.com

Hello. This section begins the actual
message body, which is delimited from the
message heading by a blank line.
```

Another field that is commonly found in RFC 5322 headers is *Message-ID*. This field contains a unique identifier associated with this message.

Multipurpose Internet Mail Extensions

Multipurpose Internet Mail Extension (MIME) is an extension to the RFC 5322 framework that is intended to address some of the problems and limitations of the use of Simple Mail Transfer Protocol (SMTP), defined in RFC 821, or some other mail transfer protocol and RFC 5322 for electronic mail. [PARZ06] lists the following limitations of the SMTP/5322 scheme.

1. SMTP cannot transmit executable files or other binary objects. A number of schemes are in use for converting binary files into a text form that can be used by SMTP mail systems, including the popular UNIX UUencode/UUdecode scheme. However, none of these is a standard or even a *de facto* standard.

2. SMTP cannot transmit text data that includes national language characters, because these are represented by 8-bit codes with values of 128 decimal or higher, and SMTP is limited to 7-bit ASCII.

3. SMTP servers may reject mail message over a certain size.

4. SMTP gateways that translate between ASCII and the character code EBCDIC do not use a consistent set of mappings, resulting in translation problems.

5. SMTP gateways to X.400 electronic mail networks cannot handle nontextual data included in X.400 messages.

6. Some SMTP implementations do not adhere completely to the SMTP standards defined in RFC 821. Common problems include:
   - Deletion, addition, or reordering of carriage return and linefeed
   - Truncating or wrapping lines longer than 76 characters
   - Removal of trailing white space (tab and space characters)
   - Padding of lines in a message to the same length
   - Conversion of tab characters into multiple space characters

MIME is intended to resolve these problems in a manner that is compatible with existing RFC 5322 implementations. The specification is provided in RFCs 2045 through 2049.

OVERVIEW The MIME specification includes the following elements.

1. Five new message header fields are defined, which may be included in an RFC 5322 header. These fields provide information about the body of the message.

2. A number of content formats are defined, thus standardizing representations that support multimedia electronic mail.

3. Transfer encodings are defined that enable the conversion of any content format into a form that is protected from alteration by the mail system.

In this subsection, we introduce the five message header fields. The next two subsections deal with content formats and transfer encodings.

The five header fields defined in MIME are

- **MIME-Version:** Must have the parameter value 1.0. This field indicates that the message conforms to RFCs 2045 and 2046.
- **Content-Type:** Describes the data contained in the body with sufficient detail that the receiving user agent can pick an appropriate agent or mechanism to represent the data to the user or otherwise deal with the data in an appropriate manner.
- **Content-Transfer-Encoding:** Indicates the type of transformation that has been used to represent the body of the message in a way that is acceptable for mail transport.
- **Content-ID:** Used to identify MIME entities uniquely in multiple contexts.
- **Content-Description:** A text description of the object with the body; this is useful when the object is not readable (e.g., audio data).

Any or all of these fields may appear in a normal RFC 5322 header. A compliant implementation must support the MIME-Version, Content-Type, and Content-Transfer-Encoding fields; the Content-ID and Content-Description fields are optional and may be ignored by the recipient implementation.

MIME CONTENT TYPES The bulk of the MIME specification is concerned with the definition of a variety of content types. This reflects the need to provide standardized ways of dealing with a wide variety of information representations in a multimedia environment.

Table 8.2 lists the content types specified in RFC 2046. There are seven different major types of content and a total of 15 subtypes. In general, a content type declares the general type of data, and the subtype specifies a particular format for that type of data.

For the **text type** of body, no special software is required to get the full meaning of the text aside from support of the indicated character set. The primary subtype is *plain text*, which is simply a string of ASCII characters or ISO 8859 characters. The *enriched* subtype allows greater formatting flexibility.

The **multipart type** indicates that the body contains multiple, independent parts. The Content-Type header field includes a parameter (called a boundary) that defines the delimiter between body parts. This boundary should not appear in any parts of the message. Each boundary starts on a new line and consists of two hyphens followed by the boundary value. The final boundary, which indicates the end of the last part, also has a suffix of two hyphens. Within each part, there may be an optional ordinary MIME header.

Here is a simple example of a multipart message containing two parts—both consisting of simple text (taken from RFC 2046).

```
From: Nathaniel Borenstein <nsb@bellcore.com>
To: Ned Freed <ned@innosoft.com>
Subject: Sample message
```

```
MIME-Version: 1.0
Content-type: multipart/mixed; boundary="simple boundary"
```

This is the preamble. It is to be ignored, though it is a handy place for mail composers to include an explanatory note to non-MIME conformant readers.

—simple boundary

This is implicitly typed plain ASCII text. It does NOT end with a linebreak.

—simple boundary

```
Content-type: text/plain; charset=us-ascii
```

This is explicitly typed plain ASCII text. It DOES end with a linebreak.

—simple boundary—

This is the epilogue. It is also to be ignored.

There are four subtypes of the multipart type, all of which have the same overall syntax. The **multipart/mixed subtype** is used when there are multiple independent body parts that need to be bundled in a particular order. For the **multipart/ parallel subtype**, the order of the parts is not significant. If the recipient's system is appropriate, the multiple parts can be presented in parallel. For example, a picture

Table 8.2   MIME Content Types

Type	Subtype	Description
Text	Plain	Unformatted text; may be ASCII or ISO 8859.
	Enriched	Provides greater format flexibility.
Multipart	Mixed	The different parts are independent but are to be transmitted together. They should be presented to the receiver in the order that they appear in the mail message.
	Parallel	Differs from Mixed only in that no order is defined for delivering the parts to the receiver.
	Alternative	The different parts are alternative versions of the same information. They are ordered in increasing faithfulness to the original, and the recipient's mail system should display the "best" version to the user.
	Digest	Similar to Mixed, but the default type/subtype of each part is message/rfc822.
Message	rfc822	The body is itself an encapsulated message that conforms to RFC 822.
	Partial	Used to allow fragmentation of large mail items, in a way that is transparent to the recipient.
	External-body	Contains a pointer to an object that exists elsewhere.
Image	jpeg	The image is in JPEG format, JFIF encoding.
	gif	The image is in GIF format.
Video	mpeg	MPEG format.
Audio	Basic	Single-channel 8-bit ISDN mu-law encoding at a sample rate of 8 kHz.
Application	PostScript	Adobe Postscript format.
	octet-stream	General binary data consisting of 8-bit bytes.

or text part could be accompanied by a voice commentary that is played while the picture or text is displayed.

For the **multipart/alternative subtype**, the various parts are different representations of the same information. The following is an example:

```
From: Nathaniel Borenstein <nsb@bellcore.com>
To: Ned Freed <ned@innosoft.com>
Subject: Formatted text mail
MIME-Version: 1.0
Content-Type: multipart/alternative;
boundary = boundary42

    —boundary42
Content-Type: text/plain; charset = us-ascii
    ...plain text version of message goes here....

    —boundary42
Content-Type: text/enriched
    ...RFC 1896 text/enriched version of same message
goes here...

    —boundary42—
```

In this subtype, the body parts are ordered in terms of increasing preference. For this example, if the recipient system is capable of displaying the message in the text/enriched format, this is done; otherwise, the plain text format is used.

The **multipart/digest subtype** is used when each of the body parts is interpreted as an RFC 5322 message with headers. This subtype enables the construction of a message whose parts are individual messages. For example, the moderator of a group might collect e-mail messages from participants, bundle these messages, and send them out in one encapsulating MIME message.

The **message type** provides a number of important capabilities in MIME. The **message/rfc822 subtype** indicates that the body is an entire message, including header and body. Despite the name of this subtype, the encapsulated message may be not only a simple RFC 5322 message but also any MIME message.

The **message/partial subtype** enables fragmentation of a large message into a number of parts, which must be reassembled at the destination. For this subtype, three parameters are specified in the Content-Type: Message/Partial field: an *id* common to all fragments of the same message, a *sequence number* unique to each fragment, and the *total* number of fragments.

The **message/external-body subtype** indicates that the actual data to be conveyed in this message are not contained in the body. Instead, the body contains the information needed to access the data. As with the other message types, the message/external-body subtype has an outer header and an encapsulated message with its own header. The only necessary field in the outer header is the Content-Type field, which identifies this as a message/external-body subtype. The inner header is the message header for the encapsulated message. The Content-Type field in the outer header must include an access-type parameter, which indicates the method of access, such as FTP (file transfer protocol).

The **application type** refers to other kinds of data, typically either uninterpreted binary data or information to be processed by a mail-based application.

MIME TRANSFER ENCODINGS The other major component of the MIME specification, in addition to content type specification, is a definition of transfer encodings for message bodies. The objective is to provide reliable delivery across the largest range of environments.

The MIME standard defines two methods of encoding data. The Content-Transfer-Encoding field can actually take on six values, as listed in Table 8.3. However, three of these values (7bit, 8bit, and binary) indicate that no encoding has been done but provide some information about the nature of the data. For SMTP transfer, it is safe to use the 7bit form. The 8bit and binary forms may be usable in other mail transport contexts. Another Content-Transfer-Encoding value is x-token, which indicates that some other encoding scheme is used for which a name is to be supplied. This could be a vendor-specific or application-specific scheme. The two actual encoding schemes defined are quoted-printable and base64. Two schemes are defined to provide a choice between a transfer technique that is essentially human readable and one that is safe for all types of data in a way that is reasonably compact.

The **quoted-printable** transfer encoding is useful when the data consists largely of octets that correspond to printable ASCII characters. In essence, it represents nonsafe characters by the hexadecimal representation of their code and introduces reversible (soft) line breaks to limit message lines to 76 characters.

The **base64 transfer encoding**, also known as radix-64 encoding, is a common one for encoding arbitrary binary data in such a way as to be invulnerable to the processing by mail-transport programs. It is also used in PGP and is described in Appendix K.

A MULTIPART EXAMPLE Figure 8.3, taken from RFC 2045, is the outline of a complex multipart message. The message has five parts to be displayed serially: two introductory plain text parts, an embedded multipart message, a richtext part, and

Table 8.3 MIME Transfer Encodings

7bit	The data are all represented by short lines of ASCII characters.
8bit	The lines are short, but there may be non-ASCII characters (octets with the high-order bit set).
binary	Not only may non-ASCII characters be present, but the lines are not necessarily short enough for SMTP transport.
quoted-printable	Encodes the data in such a way that if the data being encoded are mostly ASCII text, the encoded form of the data remains largely recognizable by humans.
base64	Encodes data by mapping 6-bit blocks of input to 8-bit blocks of output, all of which are printable ASCII characters.
x-token	A named nonstandard encoding.

MIME-Version: 1.0
From: Nathaniel Borenstein <nsb@bellcore.com>
To: Ned Freed <ned@innosoft.com>
Subject: A multipart example
Content-Type: multipart/mixed;
   boundary=unique-boundary-1

This is the preamble area of a multipart message. Mail readers that understand multipart format should ignore this preamble. If you are reading this text, you might want to consider changing to a mail reader that understands how to properly display multipart messages.

--unique-boundary-1

   ...Some text appears here...
[Note that the preceding blank line means no header fields were given and this is text, with charset US ASCII. It could have been done with explicit typing as in the next part.]

--unique-boundary-1
Content-type: text/plain; charset=US-ASCII

This could have been part of the previous part, but illustrates explicit versus implicit typing of body parts.

--unique-boundary-1
Content-Type: multipart/parallel;   boundary=unique-boundary-2

--unique-boundary-2
Content-Type: audio/basic
Content-Transfer-Encoding: base64

   ... base64-encoded 8000 Hz single-channel mu-law-format audio data goes here....

--unique-boundary-2
Content-Type: image/jpeg
Content-Transfer-Encoding: base64

   ... base64-encoded image data goes here....

--unique-boundary-2--

--unique-boundary-1
Content-type: text/enriched

This is <bold><italic>richtext.</italic></bold> <smaller>as defined in RFC 1896</smaller>

Isn't it <bigger><bigger>cool?</bigger></bigger>

--unique-boundary-1
Content-Type: message/rfc822

From: (mailbox in US-ASCII)
To: (address in US-ASCII)
Subject: (subject in US-ASCII)
Content-Type: Text/plain; charset=ISO-8859-1
Content-Transfer-Encoding: Quoted-printable

   ... Additional text in ISO-8859-1 goes here ...

--unique-boundary-1--

Figure 8.3 Example MIME Message Structure

a closing encapsulated text message in a non-ASCII character set. The embedded multipart message has two parts to be displayed in parallel: a picture and an audio fragment.

CANONICAL FORM   An important concept in MIME and S/MIME is that of canonical form. Canonical form is a format, appropriate to the content type, that is standardized for use between systems. This is in contrast to native form, which is a format that may be peculiar to a particular system. Table 8.4, from RFC 2049, should help clarify this matter.

S/MIME Functionality

In terms of general functionality, S/MIME is very similar to PGP. Both offer the ability to sign and/or encrypt messages. In this subsection, we briefly summarize S/MIME capability. We then look in more detail at this capability by examining message formats and message preparation.

FUNCTIONS   S/MIME provides the following functions.

- **Enveloped data:** This consists of encrypted content of any type and encrypted-content encryption keys for one or more recipients.
- **Signed data:** A digital signature is formed by taking the message digest of the content to be signed and then encrypting that with the private key of the signer. The content plus signature are then encoded using base64 encoding. A signed data message can only be viewed by a recipient with S/MIME capability.
- **Clear-signed data:** As with signed data, a digital signature of the content is formed. However, in this case, only the digital signature is encoded using

Table 8.4   Native and Canonical Form

Native Form	The body to be transmitted is created in the system's native format. The native character set is used and, where appropriate, local end-of-line conventions are used as well. The body may be a UNIX-style text file, or a Sun raster image, or a VMS indexed file, or audio data in a system-dependent format stored only in memory, or anything else that corresponds to the local model for the representation of some form of information. Fundamentally, the data is created in the "native" form that corresponds to the type specified by the media type.
Canonical Form	The entire body, including "out-of-band" information such as record lengths and possibly file attribute information, is converted to a universal canonical form. The specific media type of the body as well as its associated attributes dictate the nature of the canonical form that is used. Conversion to the proper canonical form may involve character set conversion, transformation of audio data, compression, or various other operations specific to the various media types. If character set conversion is involved, however, care must be taken to understand the semantics of the media type, which may have strong implications for any character set conversion (e.g., with regard to syntactically meaningful characters in a text subtype other than "plain").

base64. As a result, recipients without S/MIME capability can view the message content, although they cannot verify the signature.

- **Signed and enveloped data:** Signed-only and encrypted-only entities may be nested, so that encrypted data may be signed and signed data or clear-signed data may be encrypted.

CRYPTOGRAPHIC ALGORITHMS Table 8.5 summarizes the cryptographic algorithms used in S/MIME. S/MIME uses the following terminology taken from RFC 2119 (*Key Words for use in RFCs to Indicate Requirement Levels*) to specify the requirement level:

- **MUST:** The definition is an absolute requirement of the specification. An implementation must include this feature or function to be in conformance with the specification.

- **SHOULD:** There may exist valid reasons in particular circumstances to ignore this feature or function, but it is recommended that an implementation include the feature or function.

S/MIME incorporates three public-key algorithms. The Digital Signature Standard (DSS) described in Chapter 3 is the preferred algorithm for digital signature. S/MIME lists Diffie-Hellman as the preferred algorithm for encrypting session keys; in fact, S/MIME uses a variant of Diffie-Hellman that does provide encryption/decryption, known as ElGamal. As an alternative, RSA, described in Chapter 3, can be used for both signatures and session key encryption. These are the same algorithms used in PGP and provide a high level of security. For the hash function used to create the digital signature, the specification requires the 160-bit SHA-1 but recommends receiver support for the 128-bit MD5 for backward

Table 8.5   Cryptographic Algorithms Used in S/MIME

Function	Requirement
Create a message digest to be used in forming a digital signature.	MUST support SHA-1. Receiver SHOULD support MD5 for backward compatibility.
Encrypt message digest to form a digital signature.	Sending and receiving agents MUST support DSS. Sending agents SHOULD support RSA encryption. Receiving agents SHOULD support verification of RSA signatures with key sizes 512 bits to 1024 bits.
Encrypt session key for transmission with a message.	Sending and receiving agents SHOULD support Diffie-Hellman. Sending and receiving agents MUST support RSA encryption with key sizes 512 bits to 1024 bits.
Encrypt message for transmission with a one-time session key.	Sending and receiving agents MUST support encryption with tripleDES. Sending agents SHOULD support encryption with AES. Sending agents SHOULD support encryption with RC2/40.
Create a message authentication code.	Receiving agents MUST support HMAC with SHA-1. Sending agents SHOULD support HMAC with SHA-1.

compatibility with older versions of S/MIME. As we discussed in Chapter 3, there is justifiable concern about the security of MD5, so SHA-1 is clearly the preferred alternative.

For message encryption, three-key triple DES (tripleDES) is recommended, but compliant implementations must support 40-bit RC2. The latter is a weak encryption algorithm but allows compliance with U.S. export controls.

The S/MIME specification includes a discussion of the procedure for deciding which content encryption algorithm to use. In essence, a sending agent has two decisions to make. First, the sending agent must determine if the receiving agent is capable of decrypting using a given encryption algorithm. Second, if the receiving agent is only capable of accepting weakly encrypted content, the sending agent must decide if it is acceptable to send using weak encryption. To support this decision process, a sending agent may announce its decrypting capabilities in order of preference for any message that it sends out. A receiving agent may store that information for future use.

The following rules, in the following order, should be followed by a sending agent.

1. If the sending agent has a list of preferred decrypting capabilities from an intended recipient, it SHOULD choose the first (highest preference) capability on the list that it is capable of using.

2. If the sending agent has no such list of capabilities from an intended recipient but has received one or more messages from the recipient, then the outgoing message SHOULD use the same encryption algorithm as was used on the last signed and encrypted message received from that intended recipient.

3. If the sending agent has no knowledge about the decryption capabilities of the intended recipient and is willing to risk that the recipient may not be able to decrypt the message, then the sending agent SHOULD use triple DES.

4. If the sending agent has no knowledge about the decryption capabilities of the intended recipient and is not willing to risk that the recipient may not be able to decrypt the message, then the sending agent MUST use RC2/40.

If a message is to be sent to multiple recipients and a common encryption algorithm cannot be selected for all, then the sending agent will need to send two messages. However, in that case, it is important to note that the security of the message is made vulnerable by the transmission of one copy with lower security.

S/MIME Messages

S/MIME makes use of a number of new MIME content types, which are shown in Table 8.6. All of the new application types use the designation PKCS. This refers to a set of public-key cryptography specifications issued by RSA Laboratories and made available for the S/MIME effort.

We examine each of these in turn after first looking at the general procedures for S/MIME message preparation.

Table 8.6   S/MIME Content Types

Type	Subtype	smime Parameter	Description
Multipart	Signed		A clear-signed message in two parts: one is the message and the other is the signature.
Application	`pkcs7-mime`	`signedData`	A signed S/MIME entity.
	`pkcs7-mime`	`envelopedData`	An encrypted S/MIME entity.
	`pkcs7-mime`	`degenerate signedData`	An entity containing only public-key certificates.
	`pkcs7-mime`	`CompressedData`	A compressed S/MIME entity.
	`pkcs7-signature`	`signedData`	The content type of the signature subpart of a multipart/signed message.

SECURING A MIME ENTITY S/MIME secures a MIME entity with a signature, encryption, or both. A MIME entity may be an entire message (except for the RFC 5322 headers), or if the MIME content type is multipart, then a MIME entity is one or more of the subparts of the message. The MIME entity is prepared according to the normal rules for MIME message preparation. Then the MIME entity plus some security-related data, such as algorithm identifiers and certificates, are processed by S/MIME to produce what is known as a PKCS object. A PKCS object is then treated as message content and wrapped in MIME (provided with appropriate MIME headers). This process should become clear as we look at specific objects and provide examples.

In all cases, the message to be sent is converted to canonical form. In particular, for a given type and subtype, the appropriate canonical form is used for the message content. For a multipart message, the appropriate canonical form is used for each subpart.

The use of transfer encoding requires special attention. For most cases, the result of applying the security algorithm will be to produce an object that is partially or totally represented in arbitrary binary data. This will then be wrapped in an outer MIME message, and transfer encoding can be applied at that point, typically base64. However, in the case of a multipart signed message (described in more detail later), the message content in one of the subparts is unchanged by the security process. Unless that content is 7bit, it should be transfer encoded using base64 or quoted-printable so that there is no danger of altering the content to which the signature was applied.

We now look at each of the S/MIME content types.

ENVELOPEDDATA An `application/pkcs7-mime` subtype is used for one of four categories of S/MIME processing, each with a unique smime-type parameter. In all cases, the resulting entity (referred to as an *object*) is represented in a form known as Basic Encoding Rules (BER), which is defined in ITU-T Recommendation X.209. The BER format consists of arbitrary octet strings and is therefore binary data. Such an object should be transfer encoded with base64 in the outer MIME message. We first look at envelopedData.

The steps for preparing an envelopedData MIME entity are

1. Generate a pseudorandom session key for a particular symmetric encryption algorithm (RC2/40 or triple DES).

2. For each recipient, encrypt the session key with the recipient's public RSA key.

3. For each recipient, prepare a block known as `RecipientInfo` that contains an identifier of the recipient's public-key certificate,[2] an identifier of the algorithm used to encrypt the session key, and the encrypted session key.

4. Encrypt the message content with the session key.

The `RecipientInfo` blocks followed by the encrypted content constitute the `envelopedData`. This information is then encoded into base64. A sample message (excluding the RFC 5322 headers) is

```
Content-Type: application/pkcs7-mime; smime-type=enveloped-
        data; name=smime.p7m
Content-Transfer-Encoding: base64
Content-Disposition: attachment; filename=smime.p7m
```

rfvbnj756tbBghyHhHUujhJhjH77n8HHGT9HG4VQpfyF467GhIGfHfYT6
7n8HHGghyHhHUujhJh4VQpfyF467GhIGfHfYGTrfvbnjT6jH7756tbB9H
f8HHGTrfvhJhjH776tbB9HG4VQbnj7567GhIGfHfYT6ghyHhHUujpfyF4
OGhIGfHfQbnj756YT64V

To recover the encrypted message, the recipient first strips off the base64 encoding. Then the recipient's private key is used to recover the session key. Finally, the message content is decrypted with the session key.

SIGNEDDATA The `signedData` smime-type can be used with one or more signers. For clarity, we confine our description to the case of a single digital signature. The steps for preparing a signedData MIME entity are

1. Select a message digest algorithm (SHA or MD5).

2. Compute the message digest (hash function) of the content to be signed.

3. Encrypt the message digest with the signer's private key.

4. Prepare a block known as `SignerInfo` that contains the signer's public-key certificate, an identifier of the message digest algorithm, an identifier of the algorithm used to encrypt the message digest, and the encrypted message digest.

The `signedData` entity consists of a series of blocks, including a message digest algorithm identifier, the message being signed, and `SignerInfo`. The `signedData` entity may also include a set of public-key certificates sufficient to constitute a chain from a recognized root or top-level certification authority to the signer. This information is then encoded into base64. A sample message (excluding the RFC 5322 headers) is

---

[2]This is an X.509 certificate, discussed later in this section.

```
Content-Type: application/pkcs7-mime; smime-type=
        signed-data; name=smime.p7m
Content-Transfer-Encoding: base64
Content-Disposition: attachment; filename=smime.p7m
```

```
567GhIGfHfYT6ghyHhHUujpfyF4f8HHGTrfvhJhjH776tbB9HG4VQbnj7
77n8HHGT9HG4VQpfyF467GhIGfHfYT6rfvbnj756tbBghyHhHUujhJhjH
HUujhJh4VQpfyF467GhIGfHfYGTrfvbnjT6jH7756tbB9H7n8HHGghyHh
6YT64V0GhIGfHfQbnj75
```

To recover the signed message and verify the signature, the recipient first strips off the base64 encoding. Then the signer's public key is used to decrypt the message digest. The recipient independently computes the message digest and compares it to the decrypted message digest to verify the signature.

CLEAR SIGNING Clear signing is achieved using the multipart content type with a signed subtype. As was mentioned, this signing process does not involve transforming the message to be signed, so that the message is sent "in the clear." Thus, recipients with MIME capability but not S/MIME capability are able to read the incoming message.

A multipart/signed message has two parts. The first part can be any MIME type but must be prepared so that it will not be altered during transfer from source to destination. This means that if the first part is not 7bit, then it needs to be encoded using base64 or quoted-printable. Then this part is processed in the same manner as signedData, but in this case an object with signedData format is created that has an empty message content field. This object is a detached signature. It is then transfer encoded using base64 to become the second part of the multipart/signed message. This second part has a MIME content type of application and a subtype of pkcs7-signature. Here is a sample message:

```
Content-Type: multipart/signed;
    protocol="application/pkcs7-signature";
    micalg=sha1; boundary=boundary42
```

```
—boundary42
Content-Type: text/plain
```

```
This is a clear-signed message.
```

```
—boundary42
Content-Type: application/pkcs7-signature; name=smime.p7s
Content-Transfer-Encoding: base64
Content-Disposition: attachment; filename=smime.p7s
```

```
ghyHhHUujhJhjH77n8HHGTrfvbnj756tbB9HG4VQpfyF467GhIGfHfYT6
4VQpfyF467GhIGfHfYT6jH77n8HHGghyHhHUujhJh756tbB9HGTrfvbnj
n8HHGTrfvhJhjH776tbB9HG4VQbnj7567GhIGfHfYT6ghyHhHUujpfyF4
7GhIGfHfYT64VQbnj756
```

```
—boundary42—
```

The protocol parameter indicates that this is a two-part clear-signed entity. The `micalg` parameter indicates the type of message digest used. The receiver can verify the signature by taking the message digest of the first part and comparing this to the message digest recovered from the signature in the second part.

REGISTRATION REQUEST Typically, an application or user will apply to a certification authority for a public-key certificate. The application/pkcs10 S/MIME entity is used to transfer a certification request. The certification request includes `certification RequestInfo` block, followed by an identifier of the public-key encryption algorithm, followed by the signature of the `certificationRequestInfo` block made using the sender's private key. The `certificationRequestInfo` block includes a name of the certificate subject (the entity whose public key is to be certified) and a bit-string representation of the user's public key.

CERTIFICATES-ONLY MESSAGE A message containing only certificates or a certificate revocation list (CRL) can be sent in response to a registration request. The message is an application/pkcs7-mime type/subtype with an smime-type parameter of degenerate. The steps involved are the same as those for creating a `signedData` message, except that there is no message content and the `signerInfo` field is empty.

S/MIME Certificate Processing

S/MIME uses public-key certificates that conform to version 3 of X.509 (see Chapter 4). The key-management scheme used by S/MIME is in some ways a hybrid between a strict X.509 certification hierarchy and PGP's web of trust. As with the PGP model, S/MIME managers and/or users must configure each client with a list of trusted keys and with certificate revocation lists. That is, the responsibility is local for maintaining the certificates needed to verify incoming signatures and to encrypt outgoing messages. On the other hand, the certificates are signed by certification authorities.

USER AGENT ROLE An S/MIME user has several key-management functions to perform.

- **Key generation:** The user of some related administrative utility (e.g., one associated with LAN management) MUST be capable of generating separate Diffie-Hellman and DSS key pairs and SHOULD be capable of generating RSA key pairs. Each key pair MUST be generated from a good source of nondeterministic random input and be protected in a secure fashion. A user agent SHOULD generate RSA key pairs with a length in the range of 768 to 1024 bits and MUST NOT generate a length of less than 512 bits.
- **Registration:** A user's public key must be registered with a certification authority in order to receive an X.509 public-key certificate.
- **Certificate storage and retrieval:** A user requires access to a local list of certificates in order to verify incoming signatures and to encrypt outgoing messages. Such a list could be maintained by the user or by some local administrative entity on behalf of a number of users.

VeriSign Certificates There are several companies that provide certification authority (CA) services. For example, Nortel has designed an enterprise CA solution and can provide S/MIME support within an organization. There are a number of Internet-based CAs, including VeriSign, GTE, and the U.S. Postal Service. Of these, the most widely used is the VeriSign CA service, a brief description of which we now provide.

VeriSign provides a CA service that is intended to be compatible with S/MIME and a variety of other applications. VeriSign issues X.509 certificates with the product name VeriSign Digital ID. As of early 1998, over 35,000 commercial Web sites were using VeriSign Server Digital IDs, and over a million consumer Digital IDs had been issued to users of Netscape and Microsoft browsers.

The information contained in a Digital ID depends on the type of Digital ID and its use. At a minimum, each Digital ID contains

- Owner's public key
- Owner's name or alias
- Expiration date of the Digital ID
- Serial number of the Digital ID
- Name of the certification authority that issued the Digital ID
- Digital signature of the certification authority that issued the Digital ID

Digital IDs can also contain other user-supplied information, including

- Address
- E-mail address
- Basic registration information (country, zip code, age, and gender)

VeriSign provides three levels, or classes, of security for public-key certificates, as summarized in Table 8.7. A user requests a certificate online at VeriSign's Web site or other participating Web sites. Class 1 and Class 2 requests are processed on line, and in most cases take only a few seconds to approve. Briefly, the following procedures are used.

- For Class 1 Digital IDs, VeriSign confirms the user's e-mail address by sending a PIN and Digital ID pick-up information to the e-mail address provided in the application.
- For Class 2 Digital IDs, VeriSign verifies the information in the application through an automated comparison with a consumer database in addition to performing all of the checking associated with a Class 1 Digital ID. Finally, confirmation is sent to the specified postal address alerting the user that a Digital ID has been issued in his or her name.
- For Class 3 Digital IDs, VeriSign requires a higher level of identity assurance. An individual must prove his or her identity by providing notarized credentials or applying in person.

Table 8.7   VeriSign Public-Key Certificate Classes

	Class 1	Class 2	Class 3
Summary of Confirmation of Identity	Automated unambiguous name and e-mail address search.	Same as Class 1, plus automated enrollment information check and automated address check.	Same as Class 1, plus personal presence and ID documents plus Class 2 automated ID check for individuals; business records (or filings) for organizations.
IA Private Key Protection	PCA: trustworthy hardware; CA: trustworthy software or trustworthy hardware.	PCA and CA: trustworthy hardware.	PCA and CA: trustworthy hardware.
Certificate Applicant and Subscriber Private Key Protection	Encryption software (PIN protected) recommended but not required.	Encryption software (PIN protected) required.	Encryption software (PIN protected) required; hardware token recommended but not required.
Applications Implemented or Contemplated by Users	Web-browsing and certain e-mail usage.	Individual and intra- and inter-company e-mail, online subscriptions, password replacement, and software validation.	E-banking, corp. database access, personal banking, membership-based online services, content integrity services, e-commerce server, software validation; authentication of LRAAs; and strong encryption for certain servers.

IA   = Issuing Authority
CA   = Certification Authority
PCA   = VeriSign public primary certification authority
PIN   = Personal Identification Number
LRAA = Local Registration Authority Administrator

Enhanced Security Services

As of this writing, three enhanced security services have been proposed in an Internet draft. The details of these may change, and additional services may be added. The three services are

- **Signed receipts:** A signed receipt may be requested in a `SignedData` object. Returning a signed receipt provides proof of delivery to the originator of a message and allows the originator to demonstrate to a third party that the recipient received the message. In essence, the recipient signs the entire original message plus the original (sender's) signature and appends the new signature to form a new S/MIME message.

- **Security labels:** A security label may be included in the authenticated attributes of a `SignedData` object. A security label is a set of security information regarding the sensitivity of the content that is protected by S/MIME encapsulation. The labels may be used for access control, by indicating which users are permitted access to an object. Other uses include priority (secret, confidential, restricted, and so on) or role based, describing which kind of people can see the information (e.g., patient's health-care team, medical billing agents, etc.).

- **Secure mailing lists:** When a user sends a message to multiple recipients, a certain amount of per-recipient processing is required, including the use of each recipient's public key. The user can be relieved of this work by employing the services of an S/MIME Mail List Agent (MLA). An MLA can take a single incoming message, perform the recipient-specific encryption for each recipient, and forward the message. The originator of a message need only send the message to the MLA with encryption performed using the MLA's public key.

8.3 DOMAINKEYS IDENTIFIED MAIL

DomainKeys Identified Mail (DKIM) is a specification for cryptographically signing e-mail messages, permitting a signing domain to claim responsibility for a message in the mail stream. Message recipients (or agents acting in their behalf) can verify the signature by querying the signer's domain directly to retrieve the appropriate public key and thereby can confirm that the message was attested to by a party in possession of the private key for the signing domain. DKIM is a proposed Internet Standard (RFC 4871: *DomainKeys Identified Mail (DKIM) Signatures*). DKIM has been widely adopted by a range of e-mail providers, including corporations, government agencies, gmail, yahoo, and many Internet Service Providers (ISPs).

This section provides an overview of DKIM. Before beginning our discussion of DKIM, we introduce the standard Internet mail architecture. Then we look at the threat that DKIM is intended to address, and finally provide an overview of DKIM operation.

Internet Mail Architecture

To understand the operation of DKIM, it is useful to have a basic grasp of the Internet mail architecture, which is currently defined in RFC 5598. This subsection provides an overview of the basic concepts.

At its most fundamental level, the Internet mail architecture consists of a user world in the form of Message User Agents (MUA), and the transfer world, in the form of the Message Handling Service (MHS), which is composed of Message Transfer Agents (MTA). The MHS accepts a message from one user and delivers it to one or more other users, creating a virtual MUA-to-MUA exchange environment. This architecture involves three types of interoperability. One is directly between users: messages must be formatted by the MUA on behalf of the message author so that the message can be displayed to the message recipient by the destination MUA. There are also interoperability requirements between the MUA and the MHS—first when a message is posted from an MUA to the MHS and later when it is delivered from the MHS to the destination MUA. Interoperability is required among the MTA components along the transfer path through the MHS.

Figure 8.4 illustrates the key components of the Internet mail architecture, which include the following.

- **Message User Agent (MUA):** Operates on behalf of user actors and user applications. It is their representative within the e-mail service. Typically, this function is housed in the user's computer and is referred to as a client e-mail

Figure 8.4 Function Modules and Standardized Protocols Used Between Them

program or a local network e-mail server. The author MUA formats a message and performs initial submission into the MHS via a MSA. The recipient MUA processes received mail for storage and/or display to the recipient user.

- **Mail Submission Agent (MSA):** Accepts the message submitted by an MUA and enforces the policies of the hosting domain and the requirements of Internet standards. This function may be located together with the MUA or as a separate functional model. In the latter case, the Simple Mail Transfer Protocol (SMTP) is used between the MUA and the MSA.

- **Message Transfer Agent (MTA):** Relays mail for one application-level hop. It is like a packet switch or IP router in that its job is to make routing assessments and to move the message closer to the recipients. Relaying is performed by a sequence of MTAs until the message reaches a destination MDA. An MTA also adds trace information to the message header. SMTP is used between MTAs and between an MTA and an MSA or MDA.

- **Mail Delivery Agent (MDA):** Responsible for transferring the message from the MHS to the MS.

- **Message Store (MS):** An MUA can employ a long-term MS. An MS can be located on a remote server or on the same machine as the MUA. Typically, an MUA retrieves messages from a remote server using POP (Post Office Protocol) or IMAP (Internet Message Access Protocol).

Two other concepts need to be defined. An **administrative management domain (ADMD)** is an Internet e-mail provider. Examples include a department that operates a local mail relay (MTA), an IT department that operates an enterprise mail relay, and an ISP that operates a public shared e-mail service. Each ADMD can have different operating policies and trust-based decision making. One obvious example is the distinction between mail that is exchanged within an organization and mail that is exchanged between independent organizations. The rules for handling the two types of traffic tend to be quite different.

The **Domain Name System (DNS)** is a directory lookup service that provides a mapping between the name of a host on the Internet and its numerical address.

E-mail Threats

RFC 4686 (*Analysis of Threats Motivating DomainKeys Identified Mail*) describes the threats being addressed by DKIM in terms of the characteristics, capabilities, and location of potential attackers.

CHARACTERISTICS   RFC 4686 characterizes the range of attackers on a spectrum of three levels of threat.

1. At the low end are attackers who simply want to send e-mail that a recipient does not want to receive. The attacker can use one of a number of commercially available tools that allow the sender to falsify the origin address of messages. This makes it difficult for the receiver to filter spam on the basis of originating address or domain.

2. At the next level are professional senders of bulk spam mail. These attackers often operate as commercial enterprises and send messages on behalf of third parties. They employ more comprehensive tools for attack, including Mail Transfer Agents (MTAs) and registered domains and networks of compromised computers (zombies) to send messages and (in some cases) to harvest addresses to which to send.

3. The most sophisticated and financially motivated senders of messages are those who stand to receive substantial financial benefit, such as from an e-mail-based fraud scheme. These attackers can be expected to employ all of the above mechanisms and additionally may attack the Internet infrastructure itself, including DNS cache-poisoning attacks and IP routing attacks.

CAPABILITIES   RFC 4686 lists the following as capabilities that an attacker might have.

1. Submit messages to MTAs and Message Submission Agents (MSAs) at multiple locations in the Internet.

2. Construct arbitrary Message Header fields, including those claiming to be mailing lists, resenders, and other mail agents.

3. Sign messages on behalf of domains under their control.

4. Generate substantial numbers of either unsigned or apparently signed messages that might be used to attempt a denial-of-service attack.

5. Resend messages that may have been previously signed by the domain.

6. Transmit messages using any envelope information desired.

7. Act as an authorized submitter for messages from a compromised computer.

8. Manipulation of IP routing. This could be used to submit messages from specific IP addresses or difficult-to-trace addresses, or to cause diversion of messages to a specific domain.

9. Limited influence over portions of DNS using mechanisms such as cache poisoning. This might be used to influence message routing or to falsify advertisements of DNS-based keys or signing practices.

10. Access to significant computing resources, for example, through the conscription of worm-infected "zombie" computers. This could allow the "bad actor" to perform various types of brute-force attacks.

11. Ability to eavesdrop on existing traffic, perhaps from a wireless network.

LOCATION DKIM focuses primarily on attackers located outside of the administrative units of the claimed originator and the recipient. These administrative units frequently correspond to the protected portions of the network adjacent to the originator and recipient. It is in this area that the trust relationships required for authenticated message submission do not exist and do not scale adequately to be practical. Conversely, within these administrative units, there are other mechanisms (such as authenticated message submission) that are easier to deploy and more likely to be used than DKIM. External "bad actors" are usually attempting to exploit the "any-to-any" nature of e-mail that motivates most recipient MTAs to accept messages from anywhere for delivery to their local domain. They may generate messages without signatures, with incorrect signatures, or with correct signatures from domains with little traceability. They may also pose as mailing lists, greeting cards, or other agents that legitimately send or resend messages on behalf of others.

DKIM Strategy

DKIM is designed to provide an e-mail authentication technique that is transparent to the end user. In essence, a user's e-mail message is signed by a private key of the administrative domain from which the e-mail originates. The signature covers all of the content of the message and some of the RFC 5322 message headers. At the receiving end, the MDA can access the corresponding public key via a DNS and verify the signature, thus authenticating that the message comes from the claimed administrative domain. Thus, mail that originates from somewhere else but claims to come from a given domain will not pass the authentication test and can be rejected. This approach differs from that of S/MIME and PGP, which use the originator's private key to sign the content of the message. The motivation for DKIM is based on the following reasoning.[3]

1. S/MIME depends on both the sending and receiving users employing S/MIME. For almost all users, the bulk of incoming mail does not use S/MIME, and the bulk of the mail the user wants to send is to recipients not using S/MIME.

---

[3]The reasoning is expressed in terms of the use of S/MIME. The same argument applies to PGP.

2. S/MIME signs only the message content. Thus, RFC 5322 header information concerning origin can be compromised.

3. DKIM is not implemented in client programs (MUAs) and is therefore transparent to the user; the user need take no action.

4. DKIM applies to all mail from cooperating domains.

5. DKIM allows good senders to prove that they did send a particular message and to prevent forgers from masquerading as good senders.

Figure 8.5 is a simple example of the operation of DKIM. We begin with a message generated by a user and transmitted into the MHS to an MSA that is within the user's administrative domain. An e-mail message is generated by an e-mail client program. The content of the message, plus selected RFC 5322 headers, is signed by the e-mail provider using the provider's private key. The signer is associated with a domain, which could be a corporate local network, an ISP, or a public e-mail facility such as gmail. The signed message then passes through the Internet via a sequence of MTAs. At the destination, the MDA retrieves the public key for the incoming signature and verifies the signature before passing the message on to the destination e-mail client. The default signing algorithm is RSA with SHA-256. RSA with SHA-1 also may be used.

DNS = domain name system
MDA = mail delivery agent
MSA = mail submission agent
MTA = message transfer agent
MUA = message user agent

Figure 8.5   Simple Example of DKIM Deployment

DKIM Functional Flow

Figure 8.6 provides a more detailed look at the elements of DKIM operation. Basic message processing is divided between a signing Administrative Management Domain (ADMD) and a verifying ADMD. At its simplest, this is between the originating ADMD and the delivering ADMD, but it can involve other ADMDs in the handling path.

Signing is performed by an authorized module within the signing ADMD and uses private information from a Key Store. Within the originating ADMD, this might be performed by the MUA, MSA, or an MTA. Verifying is performed by an authorized module within the verifying ADMD. Within a delivering ADMD, verifying might be performed by an MTA, MDA, or MUA. The module verifies the signature or determines whether a particular signature was required. Verifying the signature uses public information from the Key Store. If the signature passes,

Figure 8.6 DKIM Functional Flow

reputation information is used to assess the signer and that information is passed to the message filtering system. If the signature fails or there is no signature using the author's domain, information about signing practices related to the author can be retrieved remotely and/or locally, and that information is passed to the message filtering system. For example, if the sender (e.g., gmail) uses DKIM but no DKIM signature is present, then the message may be considered fraudulent.

The signature is inserted into the RFC 5322 message as an additional header entry, starting with the keyword `Dkim-Signature`. You can view examples from your own incoming mail by using the View Long Headers (or similar wording) option for an incoming message. Here is an example:

```
Dkim-Signature:      v=1; a=rsa-sha256; c=relaxed/relaxed;
                     d=gmail.com; s=gamma; h=domainkey-signa-
                     ture:mime-version:received:date:message-
                     id:subject  :from:to:content-type:con-
                     tent-transfer-encoding;
                     bh=5mZvQDyCRuyLb1Y28K4zgS2MPOemFToDBgvbJ
                     7GO90s=;
                     b=PcUvPSDygb4ya5Dyj1rbZGp/VyRiScuaz7TTG
                     J5qW5slM+klzv6kcfYdGDHzEVJW+Z
                     FetuPfF1ETOVhELtwH0zjSccOyPkEiblOf6gILO
                     bm3DDRm3Ys1/FVrbhVOlA+/jH9Aei
                     uIIw/5iFnRbSH6qPDVv/beDQqAWQfA/wF705k=
```

Before a message is signed, a process known as canonicalization is performed on both the header and body of the RFC 5322 message. Canonicalization is necessary to deal with the possibility of minor changes in the message made en route, including character encoding, treatment of trailing white space in message lines, and the "folding" and "unfolding" of header lines. The intent of canonicalization is to make a minimal transformation of the message (for the purpose of signing; the message itself is not changed, so the canonicalization must be performed again by the verifier) that will give it its best chance of producing the same canonical value at the receiving end. DKIM defines two header canonicalization algorithms ("simple" and "relaxed") and two for the body (with the same names). The simple algorithm tolerates almost no modification, while the relaxed tolerates common modifications.

The signature includes a number of fields. Each field begins with a tag consisting of a tag code followed by an equals sign and ends with a semicolon. The fields include the following:

- **v** = DKIM version.
- **a** = Algorithm used to generate the signature; must be either rsa-sha1 or rsa-sha256.
- **c** = Canonicalization method used on the header and the body.
- **d** = A domain name used as an identifier to refer to the identity of a responsible person or organization. In DKIM, this identifier is called the Signing Domain IDentifier (SDID). In our example, this field indicates that the sender is using a gmail address.

- **s** = In order that different keys may be used in different circumstances for the same signing domain (allowing expiration of old keys, separate departmental signing, or the like), DKIM defines a selector (a name associated with a key), which is used by the verifier to retrieve the proper key during signature verification.

- **h** = Signed Header fields. A colon-separated list of header field names that identify the header fields presented to the signing algorithm. Note that in our example above, the signature covers the domainkey-signature field. This refers to an older algorithm (since replaced by DKIM) that is still in use.

- **bh** = The hash of the canonicalized body part of the message. This provides additional information for diagnosing signature verification failures.

- **b** = The signature data in base64 format; this is the encrypted hash code.

8.4 RECOMMENDED READING

[LEIB07] provides an overview of DKIM.

> **LEIB07**   Leiba, B., and Fenton, J. "DomainKeys Identified Mail (DKIM): Using Digital Signatures for Domain Verification." *Proceedings of Fourth Conference on E-mail and Anti-Spam (CEAS 07)*, 2007.

8.5 KEY TERMS, REVIEW QUESTIONS, AND PROBLEMS

Key Terms

detached signature DomainKeys Identified Mail (DKIM) electronic mail	Multipurpose Internet Mail Extensions (MIME) Pretty Good Privacy (PGP) radix 64	session key S/MIME trust ZIP

Review Questions

8.1 What is PGP? Briefly explain its operation.

8.2 Name the encryption algorithms used by PGP to provide confidentiality.

8.3 How does the public-key algorithm solve the session-key distribution problem in PGP?

8.4 Why is message encryption applied after compression in PGP?

8.5 How is radix-64 expansion compensated for in an email application?

8.6 What are the disadvantages of the radix-64 algorithm in an email application?

8.7 What are the limitations of SMTP defined in RFC 821?

8.8 Briefly explain five MIME message header fields.

8.9 What are the different content types of the MIME specifications?

8.10 What are the different functions provided by S/MIME?

Problems

8.1 PGP makes use of the cipher feedback (CFB) mode of CAST-128, whereas most symmetric encryption applications (other than key encryption) use the cipher block chaining (CBC) mode. We have

$$\text{CBC: } C_i = E(K, [C_{i-1} \oplus P_i]); \quad P_i = C_{i-1} \oplus D(K, C_i)$$

$$\text{CFB: } C_i = P_i \oplus E(K, C_{i-1}); \quad P_i = C_i \oplus E(K, C_{i-1})$$

These two appear to provide equal security. Suggest a reason why PGP uses the CFB mode.

8.2 In the PGP scheme, what is the expected number of session keys generated before a previously created key is produced?

8.3 As discussed in Appendix H, a PGP user may have multiple public keys. So that a recipient knows which public key is being used by a sender, a key ID, consisting of the least significant 64 bits of the public key, is sent with the message. What is the probability that a user with N public keys will have at least one duplicate key ID?

8.4 As discussed in Appendix H, the first 16 bits of the message digest in a PGP signature are translated in the clear. This enables the recipient to determine if the correct public key was used to decrypt the message digest by comparing the plaintext copy of the first two octets with the first two octets of the decrypted digest.
  a. To what extent does this compromise the security of the hash algorithm?
  b. To what extent does it in fact perform its intended function, namely, to help determine if the correct RSA key was used to decrypt the digest?

8.5 For this problem and the next, consult Appendix H. In Figure H.2, each entry in the public-key ring contains an Owner Trust field that indicates the degree of trust associated with this public-key owner. Why is that not enough? That is, if this owner is trusted and this is supposed to be the owner's public key, why is that trust not enough to permit PGP to use this public key?

8.6 What is the basic difference between X.509 and PGP in terms of key hierarchies and key trust?

8.7 Phil Zimmermann chose IDEA, three-key triple DES, and CAST-128 as symmetric encryption algorithms for PGP. Give reasons why each of the following symmetric encryption algorithms described in this book is suitable or unsuitable for PGP: DES, two-key triple DES, and AES.

8.8 Consider radix-64 conversion as a form of encryption. In this case, there is no key. But suppose that an opponent knew only that some form of substitution algorithm was being used to encrypt English text and did not guess that it was R64. How effective would this algorithm be against cryptanalysis?

8.9 Encode the text "plaintext" using the following techniques. Assume characters are stored in 8-bit ASCII with zero parity.
  a. Radix-64
  b. Quoted-printable

CHAPTER 9

IP SECURITY

9.1 IP Security Overview

> Applications of IPsec
> Benefits of IPsec
> Routing Applications
> IPsec Documents
> IPsec Services
> Transport and Tunnel Modes

9.2 IP Security Policy

> Security Associations
> Security Association Database
> Security Policy Database
> IP Traffic Processing

9.3 Encapsulating Security Payload

> ESP Format
> Encryption and Authentication Algorithms
> Padding
> Anti-Replay Service
> Transport and Tunnel Modes

9.4 Combining Security Associations

> Authentication Plus Confidentiality
> Basic Combinations of Security Associations

9.5 Internet Key Exchange

> Key Determination Protocol
> Header and Payload Formats

9.6 Cryptographic Suites

9.7 Recommended Reading

9.8 Key Terms, Review Questions, and Problems

If a secret piece of news is divulged by a spy before the time is ripe, he must be put to death, together with the man to whom the secret was told.

— *The Art of War*, Sun Tzu

LEARNING OBJECTIVES

After studying this chapter, you should be able to:

◆ Present an overview of IP security (IPsec).

◆ Explain the difference between transport mode and tunnel mode.

◆ Understand the concept of security association.

◆ Explain the difference between the security association database and the security policy database.

◆ Summarize the traffic processing functions performed by IPsec for outbound packets and for inbound packets.

◆ Present an overview of Encapsulating Security Payload.

◆ Discuss the alternatives for combining security associations.

◆ Present an overview of Internet Key Exchange.

◆ Summarize the alternative cryptographic suites approved for use with IPsec.

There are application-specific security mechanisms for a number of application areas, including electronic mail (S/MIME, PGP), client/server (Kerberos), Web access (Secure Sockets Layer), and others. However, users have security concerns that cut across protocol layers. For example, an enterprise can run a secure, private IP network by disallowing links to untrusted sites, encrypting packets that leave the premises, and authenticating packets that enter the premises. By implementing security at the IP level, an organization can ensure secure networking not only for applications that have security mechanisms but also for the many security-ignorant applications.

IP-level security encompasses three functional areas: authentication, confidentiality, and key management. The authentication mechanism assures that a received packet was, in fact, transmitted by the party identified as the source in the packet header. In addition, this mechanism assures that the packet has not been altered in transit. The confidentiality facility enables communicating nodes to encrypt messages to prevent eavesdropping by third parties. The key management facility is concerned with the secure exchange of keys.

We begin this chapter with an overview of IP security (IPsec) and an introduction to the IPsec architecture. We then look at each of the three functional areas in detail. Appendix D reviews Internet protocols.

9.1 IP SECURITY OVERVIEW

In 1994, the Internet Architecture Board (IAB) issued a report titled "Security in the Internet Architecture" (RFC 1636). The report identified key areas for security mechanisms. Among these were the need to secure the network infrastructure from unauthorized monitoring and control of network traffic and the need to secure end-user-to-end-user traffic using authentication and encryption mechanisms.

To provide security, the IAB included authentication and encryption as necessary security features in the next-generation IP, which has been issued as IPv6. Fortunately, these security capabilities were designed to be usable both with the current IPv4 and the future IPv6. This means that vendors can begin offering these features now, and many vendors now do have some IPsec capability in their products. The IPsec specification now exists as a set of Internet standards.

Applications of IPsec

IPsec provides the capability to secure communications across a LAN, across private and public WANs, and across the Internet. Examples of its use include:

- **Secure branch office connectivity over the Internet:** A company can build a secure virtual private network over the Internet or over a public WAN. This enables a business to rely heavily on the Internet and reduce its need for private networks, saving costs and network management overhead.

- **Secure remote access over the Internet:** An end user whose system is equipped with IP security protocols can make a local call to an Internet Service Provider (ISP) and gain secure access to a company network. This reduces the cost of toll charges for traveling employees and telecommuters.

- **Establishing extranet and intranet connectivity with partners:** IPsec can be used to secure communication with other organizations, ensuring authentication and confidentiality and providing a key exchange mechanism.

- **Enhancing electronic commerce security:** Even though some Web and electronic commerce applications have built-in security protocols, the use of IPsec enhances that security. IPsec guarantees that all traffic designated by the network administrator is both encrypted and authenticated, adding an additional layer of security to whatever is provided at the application layer.

The principal feature of IPsec that enables it to support these varied applications is that it can encrypt and/or authenticate *all* traffic at the IP level. Thus, all distributed applications (including remote logon, client/server, e-mail, file transfer, Web access, and so on) can be secured.

Figure 9.1 is a typical scenario of IPsec usage. An organization maintains LANs at dispersed locations. Nonsecure IP traffic is conducted on each LAN. For traffic offsite, through some sort of private or public WAN, IPsec protocols are used. These protocols operate in networking devices, such as a router or firewall, that connect each LAN to the outside world. The IPsec networking device will typically encrypt and compress all traffic going into the WAN and decrypt and decompress traffic coming from the WAN; these operations are transparent to workstations and

Figure 9.1 An IP Security Scenario

servers on the LAN. Secure transmission is also possible with individual users who dial into the WAN. Such user workstations must implement the IPsec protocols to provide security.

Benefits of IPsec

Some of the benefits of IPsec:

- When IPsec is implemented in a firewall or router, it provides strong security that can be applied to all traffic crossing the perimeter. Traffic within a company or workgroup does not incur the overhead of security-related processing.
- IPsec in a firewall is resistant to bypass if all traffic from the outside must use IP and the firewall is the only means of entrance from the Internet into the organization.
- IPsec is below the transport layer (TCP, UDP) and so is transparent to applications. There is no need to change software on a user or server system when IPsec is implemented in the firewall or router. Even if IPsec is implemented in end systems, upper-layer software, including applications, is not affected.
- IPsec can be transparent to end users. There is no need to train users on security mechanisms, issue keying material on a per-user basis, or revoke keying material when users leave the organization.

- IPsec can provide security for individual users if needed. This is useful for off-site workers and for setting up a secure virtual subnetwork within an organization for sensitive applications.

Routing Applications

In addition to supporting end users and protecting premises systems and networks, IPsec can play a vital role in the routing architecture required for internetworking. [HUIT98] lists the following examples of the use of IPsec. IPsec can assure that

- A router advertisement (a new router advertises its presence) comes from an authorized router.
- A neighbor advertisement (a router seeks to establish or maintain a neighbor relationship with a router in another routing domain) comes from an authorized router.
- A redirect message comes from the router to which the initial IP packet was sent.
- A routing update is not forged.

Without such security measures, an opponent can disrupt communications or divert some traffic. Routing protocols such as Open Shortest Path First (OSPF) should be run on top of security associations between routers that are defined by IPsec.

IPsec Documents

IPsec encompasses three functional areas: authentication, confidentiality, and key management. The totality of the IPsec specification is scattered across dozens of RFCs and draft IETF documents, making this the most complex and difficult to grasp of all IETF specifications. The best way to grasp the scope of IPsec is to consult the latest version of the IPsec document roadmap, which as of this writing is RFC 6071 [*IP Security (IPsec) and Internet Key Exchange (IKE) Document Roadmap*, February 2011]. The documents can be categorized into the following groups.

- **Architecture:** Covers the general concepts, security requirements, definitions, and mechanisms defining IPsec technology. The current specification is RFC 4301, *Security Architecture for the Internet Protocol*.
- **Authentication Header (AH):** AH is an extension header to provide message authentication. The current specification is RFC 4302, *IP Authentication Header*. Because message authentication is provided by ESP, the use of AH is deprecated. It is included in IPsecv3 for backward compatibility but should not be used in new applications. We do not discuss AH in this chapter.
- **Encapsulating Security Payload (ESP):** ESP consists of an encapsulating header and trailer used to provide encryption or combined encryption/authentication. The current specification is RFC 4303, *IP Encapsulating Security Payload (ESP)*.
- **Internet Key Exchange (IKE):** This is a collection of documents describing the key management schemes for use with IPsec. The main specification is RFC 5996, *Internet Key Exchange (IKEv2) Protocol*, but there are a number of related RFCs.

- **Cryptographic algorithms:** This category encompasses a large set of documents that define and describe cryptographic algorithms for encryption, message authentication, pseudorandom functions (PRFs), and cryptographic key exchange.
- **Other:** There are a variety of other IPsec-related RFCs, including those dealing with security policy and management information base (MIB) content.

IPsec Services

IPsec provides security services at the IP layer by enabling a system to select required security protocols, determine the algorithm(s) to use for the service(s), and put in place any cryptographic keys required to provide the requested services. Two protocols are used to provide security: an authentication protocol designated by the header of the protocol, Authentication Header (AH); and a combined encryption/authentication protocol designated by the format of the packet for that protocol, Encapsulating Security Payload (ESP). RFC 4301 lists the following services:

- Access control
- Connectionless integrity
- Data origin authentication
- Rejection of replayed packets (a form of partial sequence integrity)
- Confidentiality (encryption)
- Limited traffic flow confidentiality

Transport and Tunnel Modes

Both AH and ESP support two modes of use: transport and tunnel mode. The operation of these two modes is best understood in the context of a description of ESP, which is covered in Section 9.3. Here we provide a brief overview.

TRANSPORT MODE Transport mode provides protection primarily for upper-layer protocols. That is, transport mode protection extends to the payload of an IP packet.[1] Examples include a TCP or UDP segment or an ICMP packet, all of which operate directly above IP in a host protocol stack. Typically, transport mode is used for end-to-end communication between two hosts (e.g., a client and a server, or two workstations). When a host runs AH or ESP over IPv4, the payload is the data that normally follow the IP header. For IPv6, the payload is the data that normally follow both the IP header and any IPv6 extensions headers that are present, with the possible exception of the destination options header, which may be included in the protection.

ESP in transport mode encrypts and optionally authenticates the IP payload but not the IP header. AH in transport mode authenticates the IP payload and selected portions of the IP header.

TUNNEL MODE Tunnel mode provides protection to the entire IP packet. To achieve this, after the AH or ESP fields are added to the IP packet, the entire packet plus security fields is treated as the payload of new outer IP packet with a new outer IP

---

[1]In this chapter, the term *IP packet* refers to either an IPv4 datagram or an IPv6 packet.

Table 9.1   Tunnel Mode and Transport Mode Functionality

	Transport Mode SA	**Tunnel Mode SA**
AH	Authenticates IP payload and selected portions of IP header and IPv6 extension headers.	Authenticates entire inner IP packet (inner header plus IP payload) plus selected portions of outer IP header and outer IPv6 extension headers.
ESP	Encrypts IP payload and any IPv6 extension headers following the ESP header.	Encrypts entire inner IP packet.
ESP with Authentication	Encrypts IP payload and any IPv6 extension headers following the ESP header. Authenticates IP payload but not IP header.	Encrypts entire inner IP packet. Authenticates inner IP packet.

header. The entire original, inner, packet travels through a tunnel from one point of an IP network to another; no routers along the way are able to examine the inner IP header. Because the original packet is encapsulated, the new, larger packet may have totally different source and destination addresses, adding to the security. Tunnel mode is used when one or both ends of a security association (SA) are a security gateway, such as a firewall or router that implements IPsec. With tunnel mode, a number of hosts on networks behind firewalls may engage in secure communications without implementing IPsec. The unprotected packets generated by such hosts are tunneled through external networks by tunnel mode SAs set up by the IPsec software in the firewall or secure router at the boundary of the local network.

Here is an example of how tunnel mode IPsec operates. Host A on a network generates an IP packet with the destination address of host B on another network. This packet is routed from the originating host to a firewall or secure router at the boundary of A's network. The firewall filters all outgoing packets to determine the need for IPsec processing. If this packet from A to B requires IPsec, the firewall performs IPsec processing and encapsulates the packet with an outer IP header. The source IP address of this outer IP packet is this firewall, and the destination address may be a firewall that forms the boundary to B's local network. This packet is now routed to B's firewall, with intermediate routers examining only the outer IP header. At B's firewall, the outer IP header is stripped off, and the inner packet is delivered to B.

ESP in tunnel mode encrypts and optionally authenticates the entire inner IP packet, including the inner IP header. AH in tunnel mode authenticates the entire inner IP packet and selected portions of the outer IP header.

Table 9.1 summarizes transport and tunnel mode functionality.

9.2 IP SECURITY POLICY

Fundamental to the operation of IPsec is the concept of a security policy applied to each IP packet that transits from a source to a destination. IPsec policy is determined primarily by the interaction of two databases, the **security association database (SAD)** and the **security policy database (SPD)**. This section provides an

Figure 9.2 IPsec Architecture

overview of these two databases and then summarizes their use during IPsec operation. Figure 9.2 illustrates the relevant relationships.

Security Associations

A key concept that appears in both the authentication and confidentiality mechanisms for IP is the security association (SA). An association is a one-way logical connection between a sender and a receiver that affords security services to the traffic carried on it. If a peer relationship is needed for two-way secure exchange, then two security associations are required.

A security association is uniquely identified by three parameters.

- **Security Parameters Index (SPI):** A 32-bit unsigned integer assigned to this SA and having local significance only. The SPI is carried in AH and ESP headers to enable the receiving system to select the SA under which a received packet will be processed.

- **IP Destination Address:** This is the address of the destination endpoint of the SA, which may be an end-user system or a network system such as a firewall or router.

- **Security Protocol Identifier:** This field from the outer IP header indicates whether the association is an AH or ESP security association.

Hence, in any IP packet, the security association is uniquely identified by the Destination Address in the IPv4 or IPv6 header and the SPI in the enclosed extension header (AH or ESP).

Security Association Database

In each IPsec implementation, there is a nominal[2] Security Association Database that defines the parameters associated with each SA. A security association is normally defined by the following parameters in an SAD entry.

---

[2]Nominal in the sense that the functionality provided by a Security Association Database must be present in any IPsec implementation, but the way in which that functionality is provided is up to the implementer.

- **Security Parameter Index:** A 32-bit value selected by the receiving end of an SA to uniquely identify the SA. In an SAD entry for an outbound SA, the SPI is used to construct the packet's AH or ESP header. In an SAD entry for an inbound SA, the SPI is used to map traffic to the appropriate SA.

- **Sequence Number Counter:** A 32-bit value used to generate the Sequence Number field in AH or ESP headers, described in Section 9.3 (required for all implementations).

- **Sequence Counter Overflow:** A flag indicating whether overflow of the Sequence Number Counter should generate an auditable event and prevent further transmission of packets on this SA (required for all implementations).

- **Anti-Replay Window:** Used to determine whether an inbound AH or ESP packet is a replay, described in Section 9.3 (required for all implementations).

- **AH Information:** Authentication algorithm, keys, key lifetimes, and related parameters being used with AH (required for AH implementations).

- **ESP Information:** Encryption and authentication algorithm, keys, initialization values, key lifetimes, and related parameters being used with ESP (required for ESP implementations).

- **Lifetime of this Security Association:** A time interval or byte count after which an SA must be replaced with a new SA (and new SPI) or terminated, plus an indication of which of these actions should occur (required for all implementations).

- **IPsec Protocol Mode:** Tunnel, transport, or wildcard.

- **Path MTU:** Any observed path maximum transmission unit (maximum size of a packet that can be transmitted without fragmentation) and aging variables (required for all implementations).

The key management mechanism that is used to distribute keys is coupled to the authentication and privacy mechanisms only by way of the Security Parameters Index (SPI). Hence, authentication and privacy have been specified independent of any specific key management mechanism.

IPsec provides the user with considerable flexibility in the way in which IPsec services are applied to IP traffic. As we will see later, SAs can be combined in a number of ways to yield the desired user configuration. Furthermore, IPsec provides a high degree of granularity in discriminating between traffic that is afforded IPsec protection and traffic that is allowed to bypass IPsec, as in the former case relating IP traffic to specific SAs.

Security Policy Database

The means by which IP traffic is related to specific SAs (or no SA in the case of traffic allowed to bypass IPsec) is the nominal Security Policy Database (SPD). In its simplest form, an SPD contains entries, each of which defines a subset of IP traffic and points to an SA for that traffic. In more complex environments, there may be multiple entries that potentially relate to a single SA or multiple SAs associated with a single SPD entry. The reader is referred to the relevant IPsec documents for a full discussion.

Each SPD entry is defined by a set of IP and upper-layer protocol field values, called *selectors*. In effect, these selectors are used to filter outgoing traffic in order to map it into a particular SA. Outbound processing obeys the following general sequence for each IP packet.

1. Compare the values of the appropriate fields in the packet (the selector fields) against the SPD to find a matching SPD entry, which will point to zero or more SAs.
2. Determine the SA if any for this packet and its associated SPI.
3. Do the required IPsec processing (i.e., AH or ESP processing).

The following selectors determine an SPD entry:

- **Remote IP Address:** This may be a single IP address, an enumerated list or range of addresses, or a wildcard (mask) address. The latter two are required to support more than one destination system sharing the same SA (e.g., behind a firewall).
- **Local IP Address:** This may be a single IP address, an enumerated list or range of addresses, or a wildcard (mask) address. The latter two are required to support more than one source system sharing the same SA (e.g., behind a firewall).
- **Next Layer Protocol:** The IP protocol header (IPv4, IPv6, or IPv6 Extension) includes a field (Protocol for IPv4, Next Header for IPv6 or IPv6 Extension) that designates the protocol operating over IP. This is an individual protocol number, ANY, or for IPv6 only, OPAQUE. If AH or ESP is used, then this IP protocol header immediately precedes the AH or ESP header in the packet.
- **Name:** A user identifier from the operating system. This is not a field in the IP or upper-layer headers but is available if IPsec is running on the same operating system as the user.
- **Local and Remote Ports:** These may be individual TCP or UDP port values, an enumerated list of ports, or a wildcard port.

Table 9.2 provides an example of an SPD on a host system (as opposed to a network system such as a firewall or router). This table reflects the following

Table 9.2   Host SPD Example

Protocol	Local IP	Port	Remote IP	Port	Action	Comment
UDP	1.2.3.101	500	*	500	BYPASS	IKE
ICMP	1.2.3.101	*	*	*	BYPASS	Error messages
*	1.2.3.101	*	1.2.3.0/24	*	PROTECT: ESP intransport-mode	Encrypt intranet traffic
TCP	1.2.3.101	*	1.2.4.10	80	PROTECT: ESP intransport-mode	Encrypt to server
TCP	1.2.3.101	*	1.2.4.10	443	BYPASS	TLS: avoid double encryption
*	1.2.3.101	*	1.2.4.0/24	*	DISCARD	Others in DMZ
*	1.2.3.101	*	*	*	BYPASS	Internet

configuration: A local network configuration consists of two networks. The basic corporate network configuration has the IP network number 1.2.3.0/24. The local configuration also includes a secure LAN, often known as a DMZ, that is identified as 1.2.4.0/24. The DMZ is protected from both the outside world and the rest of the corporate LAN by firewalls. The host in this example has the IP address 1.2.3.10, and it is authorized to connect to the server 1.2.4.10 in the DMZ.

The entries in the SPD should be self-explanatory. For example, UDP port 500 is the designated port for IKE. Any traffic from the local host to a remote host for purposes of an IKE exchange bypasses the IPsec processing.

IP Traffic Processing

IPsec is executed on a packet-by-packet basis. When IPsec is implemented, each outbound IP packet is processed by the IPsec logic before transmission, and each inbound packet is processed by the IPsec logic after reception and before passing the packet contents on to the next higher layer (e.g., TCP or UDP). We look at the logic of these two situations in turn.

OUTBOUND PACKETS Figure 9.3 highlights the main elements of IPsec processing for outbound traffic. A block of data from a higher layer, such as TCP, is passed

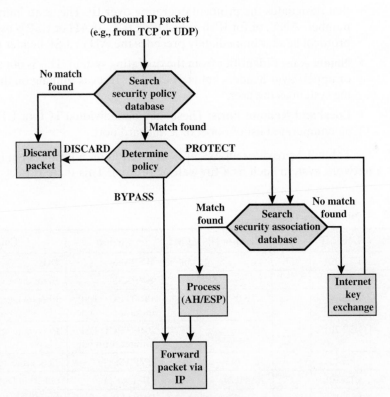

Figure 9.3 Processing Model for Outbound Packets

down to the IP layer and an IP packet is formed, consisting of an IP header and an IP body. Then the following steps occur:

1. IPsec searches the SPD for a match to this packet.

2. If no match is found, then the packet is discarded and an error message is generated.

3. If a match is found, further processing is determined by the first matching entry in the SPD. If the policy for this packet is DISCARD, then the packet is discarded. If the policy is BYPASS, then there is no further IPsec processing; the packet is forwarded to the network for transmission.

4. If the policy is PROTECT, then a search is made of the SAD for a matching entry. If no entry is found, then IKE is invoked to create an SA with the appropriate keys and an entry is made in the SA.

5. The matching entry in the SAD determines the processing for this packet. Either encryption, authentication, or both can be performed, and either transport or tunnel mode can be used. The packet is then forwarded to the network for transmission.

INBOUND PACKETS Figure 9.4 highlights the main elements of IPsec processing for inbound traffic. An incoming IP packet triggers the IPsec processing. The following steps occur:

1. IPsec determines whether this is an unsecured IP packet or one that has ESP or AH headers/trailers, by examining the IP Protocol field (IPv4) or Next Header field (IPv6).

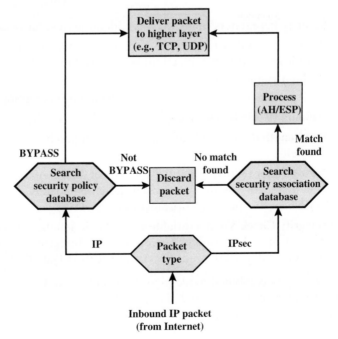

Figure 9.4 Processing Model for Inbound Packets

2. If the packet is unsecured, IPsec searches the SPD for a match to this packet. If the first matching entry has a policy of BYPASS, the IP header is processed and stripped off and the packet body is delivered to the next higher layer, such as TCP. If the first matching entry has a policy of PROTECT or DISCARD, or if there is no matching entry, the packet is discarded.

3. For a secured packet, IPsec searches the SAD. If no match is found, the packet is discarded. Otherwise, IPsec applies the appropriate ESP or AH processing. Then, the IP header is processed and stripped off and the packet body is delivered to the next higher layer, such as TCP.

9.3 ENCAPSULATING SECURITY PAYLOAD

ESP can be used to provide confidentiality, data origin authentication, connection-less integrity, an anti-replay service (a form of partial sequence integrity), and (limited) traffic flow confidentiality. The set of services provided depends on options selected at the time of Security Association (SA) establishment and on the location of the implementation in a network topology.

ESP can work with a variety of encryption and authentication algorithms, including authenticated encryption algorithms such as GCM.

ESP Format

Figure 9.5a shows the top-level format of an ESP packet. It contains the following fields.

- **Security Parameters Index (32 bits):** Identifies a security association.
- **Sequence Number (32 bits):** A monotonically increasing counter value; this provides an anti-replay function, as discussed for AH.
- **Payload Data (variable):** This is a transport-level segment (transport mode) or IP packet (tunnel mode) that is protected by encryption.
- **Padding (0–255 bytes):** The purpose of this field is discussed later.
- **Pad Length (8 bits):** Indicates the number of pad bytes immediately preceding this field.
- **Next Header (8 bits):** Identifies the type of data contained in the payload data field by identifying the first header in that payload (e.g., an extension header in IPv6, or an upper-layer protocol such as TCP).
- **Integrity Check Value (variable):** A variable-length field (must be an integral number of 32-bit words) that contains the Integrity Check Value computed over the ESP packet minus the Authentication Data field.

When any combined mode algorithm is employed, the algorithm itself is expected to return both decrypted plaintext and a pass/fail indication for the integrity check. For combined mode algorithms, the ICV that would normally appear at the end of the ESP packet (when integrity is selected) may be omitted. When the ICV is omitted and integrity is selected, it is the responsibility of the combined mode

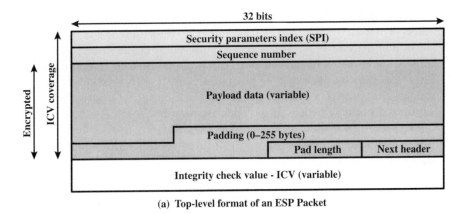

(a) Top-level format of an ESP Packet

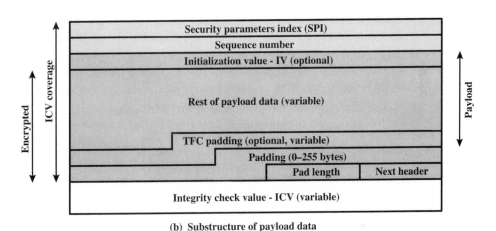

(b) Substructure of payload data

Figure 9.5 ESP Packet Format

algorithm to encode within the Payload Data an ICV-equivalent means of verifying the integrity of the packet.

Two additional fields may be present in the payload (Figure 9.5b). An **initialization value (IV)**, or nonce, is present if this is required by the encryption or authenticated encryption algorithm used for ESP. If tunnel mode is being used, then the IPsec implementation may add **traffic flow confidentiality (TFC)** padding after the Payload Data and before the Padding field, as explained subsequently.

Encryption and Authentication Algorithms

The Payload Data, Padding, Pad Length, and Next Header fields are encrypted by the ESP service. If the algorithm used to encrypt the payload requires cryptographic synchronization data, such as an initialization vector (IV), then these data may be carried explicitly at the beginning of the Payload Data field. If included, an IV is usually not encrypted, although it is often referred to as being part of the ciphertext.

The ICV field is optional. It is present only if the integrity service is selected and is provided by either a separate integrity algorithm or a combined mode algorithm that uses an ICV. The ICV is computed after the encryption is performed. This order of processing facilitates rapid detection and rejection of replayed or bogus packets by the receiver prior to decrypting the packet, hence potentially reducing the impact of denial of service (DoS) attacks. It also allows for the possibility of parallel processing of packets at the receiver that is decryption can take place in parallel with integrity checking. Note that because the ICV is not protected by encryption, a keyed integrity algorithm must be employed to compute the ICV.

Padding

The Padding field serves several purposes:

- If an encryption algorithm requires the plaintext to be a multiple of some number of bytes (e.g., the multiple of a single block for a block cipher), the Padding field is used to expand the plaintext (consisting of the Payload Data, Padding, Pad Length, and Next Header fields) to the required length.

- The ESP format requires that the Pad Length and Next Header fields be right aligned within a 32-bit word. Equivalently, the ciphertext must be an integer multiple of 32 bits. The Padding field is used to assure this alignment.

- Additional padding may be added to provide partial traffic-flow confidentiality by concealing the actual length of the payload.

Anti-Replay Service

A **replay attack** is one in which an attacker obtains a copy of an authenticated packet and later transmits it to the intended destination. The receipt of duplicate, authenticated IP packets may disrupt service in some way or may have some other undesired consequence. The Sequence Number field is designed to thwart such attacks. First, we discuss sequence number generation by the sender, and then we look at how it is processed by the recipient.

When a new SA is established, the **sender** initializes a sequence number counter to 0. Each time that a packet is sent on this SA, the sender increments the counter and places the value in the Sequence Number field. Thus, the first value to be used is 1. If anti-replay is enabled (the default), the sender must not allow the sequence number to cycle past $2^{32} - 1$ back to zero. Otherwise, there would be multiple valid packets with the same sequence number. If the limit of $2^{32} - 1$ is reached, the sender should terminate this SA and negotiate a new SA with a new key.

Because IP is a connectionless, unreliable service, the protocol does not guarantee that packets will be delivered in order and does not guarantee that all packets will be delivered. Therefore, the IPsec authentication document dictates that the **receiver** should implement a window of size W, with a default of $W = 64$. The right edge of the window represents the highest sequence number, N, so far received for a valid packet. For any packet with a sequence number in the range from $N - W + 1$ to N that has been correctly received (i.e., properly authenticated), the

Figure 9.6 Anti-replay Mechanism

corresponding slot in the window is marked (Figure 9.6). Inbound processing proceeds as follows when a packet is received:

1. If the received packet falls within the window and is new, the MAC is checked. If the packet is authenticated, the corresponding slot in the window is marked.

2. If the received packet is to the right of the window and is new, the MAC is checked. If the packet is authenticated, the window is advanced so that this sequence number is the right edge of the window, and the corresponding slot in the window is marked.

3. If the received packet is to the left of the window or if authentication fails, the packet is discarded; this is an auditable event.

Transport and Tunnel Modes

Figure 9.7 shows two ways in which the IPsec ESP service can be used. In the upper part of the figure, encryption (and optionally authentication) is provided directly between two hosts. Figure 9.7b shows how tunnel mode operation can be used to set up a **virtual private network**. In this example, an organization has four private networks interconnected across the Internet. Hosts on the internal networks use the Internet for transport of data but do not interact with other Internet-based hosts. By terminating the tunnels at the security gateway to each internal network, the configuration allows the hosts to avoid implementing the security capability. The former technique is supported by a transport mode SA, while the latter technique uses a tunnel mode SA.

In this section, we look at the scope of ESP for the two modes. The considerations are somewhat different for IPv4 and IPv6. We use the packet formats of Figure 9.8a as a starting point.

TRANSPORT MODE ESP Transport mode ESP is used to encrypt and optionally authenticate the data carried by IP (e.g., a TCP segment), as shown in Figure 9.8b. For this mode using IPv4, the ESP header is inserted into the IP packet immediately prior to the transport-layer header (e.g., TCP, UDP, ICMP), and an ESP

(a) Transport-level security

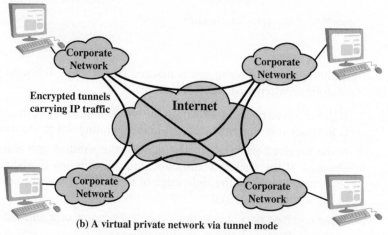

(b) A virtual private network via tunnel mode

Figure 9.7 Transport-Mode versus Tunnel-Mode Encryption

trailer (Padding, Pad Length, and Next Header fields) is placed after the IP packet. If authentication is selected, the ESP Authentication Data field is added after the ESP trailer. The entire transport-level segment plus the ESP trailer are encrypted. Authentication covers all of the ciphertext plus the ESP header.

In the context of IPv6, ESP is viewed as an end-to-end payload; that is, it is not examined or processed by intermediate routers. Therefore, the ESP header appears after the IPv6 base header and the hop-by-hop, routing, and fragment extension headers. The destination options extension header could appear before or after the ESP header, depending on the semantics desired. For IPv6, encryption covers the entire transport-level segment plus the ESP trailer plus the destination options extension header if it occurs after the ESP header. Again, authentication covers the ciphertext plus the ESP header.

Transport mode operation may be summarized as follows.

1. At the source, the block of data consisting of the ESP trailer plus the entire transport-layer segment is encrypted and the plaintext of this block is replaced with its ciphertext to form the IP packet for transmission. Authentication is added if this option is selected.

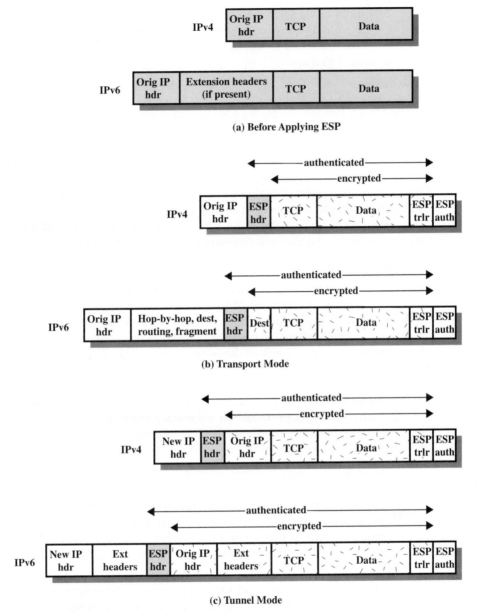

Figure 9.8 Scope of ESP Encryption and Authentication

2. The packet is then routed to the destination. Each intermediate router needs to examine and process the IP header plus any plaintext IP extension headers but does not need to examine the ciphertext.

3. The destination node examines and processes the IP header plus any plaintext IP extension headers. Then, on the basis of the SPI in the ESP header, the destination node decrypts the remainder of the packet to recover the plaintext transport-layer segment.

Transport mode operation provides confidentiality for any application that uses it, thus avoiding the need to implement confidentiality in every individual application. One drawback to this mode is that it is possible to do traffic analysis on the transmitted packets.

TUNNEL MODE ESP   Tunnel mode ESP is used to encrypt an entire IP packet (Figure 9.8c). For this mode, the ESP header is prefixed to the packet and then the packet plus the ESP trailer is encrypted. This method can be used to counter traffic analysis.

Because the IP header contains the destination address and possibly source routing directives and hop-by-hop option information, it is not possible simply to transmit the encrypted IP packet prefixed by the ESP header. Intermediate routers would be unable to process such a packet. Therefore, it is necessary to encapsulate the entire block (ESP header plus ciphertext plus Authentication Data, if present) with a new IP header that will contain sufficient information for routing but not for traffic analysis.

Whereas the transport mode is suitable for protecting connections between hosts that support the ESP feature, the tunnel mode is useful in a configuration that includes a firewall or other sort of security gateway that protects a trusted network from external networks. In this latter case, encryption occurs only between an external host and the security gateway or between two security gateways. This relieves hosts on the internal network of the processing burden of encryption and simplifies the key distribution task by reducing the number of needed keys. Further, it thwarts traffic analysis based on ultimate destination.

Consider a case in which an external host wishes to communicate with a host on an internal network protected by a firewall, and in which ESP is implemented in the external host and the firewalls. The following steps occur for transfer of a transport-layer segment from the external host to the internal host.

1. The source prepares an inner IP packet with a destination address of the target internal host. This packet is prefixed by an ESP header; then the packet and ESP trailer are encrypted and Authentication Data may be added. The resulting block is encapsulated with a new IP header (base header plus optional extensions such as routing and hop-by-hop options for IPv6) whose destination address is the firewall; this forms the outer IP packet.

2. The outer packet is routed to the destination firewall. Each intermediate router needs to examine and process the outer IP header plus any outer IP extension headers but does not need to examine the ciphertext.

3. The destination firewall examines and processes the outer IP header plus any outer IP extension headers. Then, on the basis of the SPI in the ESP header, the destination node decrypts the remainder of the packet to recover the plaintext inner IP packet. This packet is then transmitted in the internal network.

4. The inner packet is routed through zero or more routers in the internal network to the destination host.

Figure 9.9 shows the protocol architecture for the two modes.

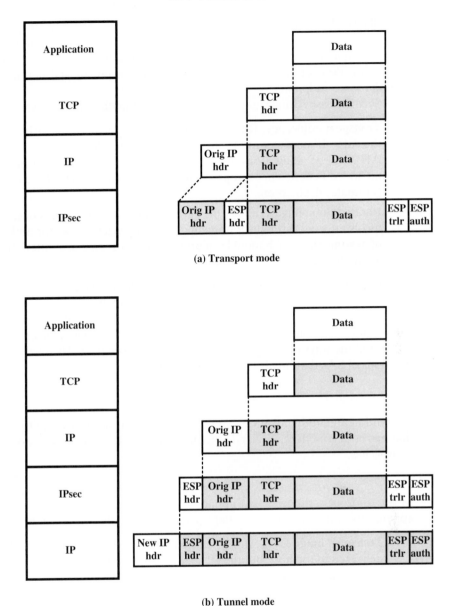

(a) Transport mode

(b) Tunnel mode

Figure 9.9   Protocol Operation for ESP

9.4 COMBINING SECURITY ASSOCIATIONS

An individual SA can implement either the AH or ESP protocol but not both. Sometimes a particular traffic flow will call for the services provided by both AH and ESP. Further, a particular traffic flow may require IPsec services between hosts and, for that same flow, separate services between security gateways, such as firewalls. In all of these cases, multiple SAs must be employed for the same traffic flow to achieve the desired IPsec services. The term *security association bundle* refers to a sequence of SAs through which traffic must be processed to provide a desired set of IPsec services. The SAs in a bundle may terminate at different endpoints or at the same endpoints.

Security associations may be combined into bundles in two ways:

- **Transport adjacency:** Refers to applying more than one security protocol to the same IP packet without invoking tunneling. This approach to combining AH and ESP allows for only one level of combination; further nesting yields no added benefit since the processing is performed at one IPsec instance: the (ultimate) destination.

- **Iterated tunneling:** Refers to the application of multiple layers of security protocols effected through IP tunneling. This approach allows for multiple levels of nesting, since each tunnel can originate or terminate at a different IPsec site along the path.

The two approaches can be combined, for example, by having a transport SA between hosts travel part of the way through a tunnel SA between security gateways.

One interesting issue that arises when considering SA bundles is the order in which authentication and encryption may be applied between a given pair of endpoints and the ways of doing so. We examine that issue next. Then we look at combinations of SAs that involve at least one tunnel.

Authentication Plus Confidentiality

Encryption and authentication can be combined in order to transmit an IP packet that has both confidentiality and authentication between hosts. We look at several approaches.

ESP WITH AUTHENTICATION OPTION This approach is illustrated in Figure 9.8. In this approach, the user first applies ESP to the data to be protected and then appends the authentication data field. There are actually two subcases:

- **Transport mode ESP:** Authentication and encryption apply to the IP payload delivered to the host, but the IP header is not protected.

- **Tunnel mode ESP:** Authentication applies to the entire IP packet delivered to the outer IP destination address (e.g., a firewall), and authentication is performed at that destination. The entire inner IP packet is protected by the privacy mechanism for delivery to the inner IP destination.

For both cases, authentication applies to the ciphertext rather than the plaintext.

TRANSPORT ADJACENCY Another way to apply authentication after encryption is to use two bundled transport SAs, with the inner being an ESP SA and the outer being an AH SA. In this case, ESP is used without its authentication option. Because the inner SA is a transport SA, encryption is applied to the IP payload. The resulting packet consists of an IP header (and possibly IPv6 header extensions) followed by an ESP. AH is then applied in transport mode, so that authentication covers the ESP plus the original IP header (and extensions) except for mutable fields. The advantage of this approach over simply using a single ESP SA with the ESP authentication option is that the authentication covers more fields, including the source and destination IP addresses. The disadvantage is the overhead of two SAs versus one SA.

TRANSPORT-TUNNEL BUNDLE The use of authentication prior to encryption might be preferable for several reasons. First, because the authentication data are protected by encryption, it is impossible for anyone to intercept the message and alter the authentication data without detection. Second, it may be desirable to store the authentication information with the message at the destination for later reference. It is more convenient to do this if the authentication information applies to the un-encrypted message; otherwise the message would have to be reencrypted to verify the authentication information.

One approach to applying authentication before encryption between two hosts is to use a bundle consisting of an inner AH transport SA and an outer ESP tunnel SA. In this case, authentication is applied to the IP payload plus the IP header (and extensions) except for mutable fields. The resulting IP packet is then processed in tunnel mode by ESP; the result is that the entire, authenticated inner packet is encrypted and a new outer IP header (and extensions) is added.

Basic Combinations of Security Associations

The IPsec Architecture document lists four examples of combinations of SAs that must be supported by compliant IPsec hosts (e.g., workstation, server) or security gateways (e.g., firewall, router). These are illustrated in Figure 9.10. The lower part of each case in the figure represents the physical connectivity of the elements; the upper part represents logical connectivity via one or more nested SAs. Each SA can be either AH or ESP. For host-to-host SAs, the mode may be either transport or tunnel; otherwise it must be tunnel mode.

Case 1. All security is provided between end systems that implement IPsec. For any two end systems to communicate via an SA, they must share the appropriate secret keys. Among the possible combinations are

a. AH in transport mode

b. ESP in transport mode

c. ESP followed by AH in transport mode (an ESP SA inside an AH SA)

d. Any one of a, b, or c inside an AH or ESP in tunnel mode

We have already discussed how these various combinations can be used to support authentication, encryption, authentication before encryption, and authentication after encryption.

Case 2. Security is provided only between gateways (routers, firewalls, etc.) and no hosts implement IPsec. This case illustrates simple virtual private network support. The security architecture document specifies that only a single tunnel SA is needed for this case. The tunnel could support AH, ESP, or ESP with the authentication option. Nested tunnels are not required, because the IPsec services apply to the entire inner packet.

One or More SAs

Router

Host*

Local Intranet

Router

Internet

Local Intranet

Host*

(a) Case 1

Tunnel SA

Security Gateway*

Host

Local Intranet

Internet

Security Gateway*

Local Intranet

Host

(b) Case 2

Tunnel SA

One or Two SAs

Security Gateway*

Host*

Local Intranet

Security Gateway*

Internet

Local Intranet

Host*

(c) Case 3

Tunnel SA

One or Two SAs

Security Gateway*

Host*

Local Intranet

Host*

Internet

Security Gateway*

Local Intranet

Host*

(d) Case 4

* = implements IPsec

Figure 9.10 Basic Combinations of Security Associations

Case 3. This builds on case 2 by adding end-to-end security. The same combinations discussed for cases 1 and 2 are allowed here. The gateway-to-gateway tunnel provides either authentication, confidentiality, or both for all traffic between end systems. When the gateway-to-gateway tunnel is ESP, it also provides a limited form of traffic confidentiality. Individual hosts can implement any additional IPsec services required for given applications or given users by means of end-to-end SAs.

Case 4. This provides support for a remote host that uses the Internet to reach an organization's firewall and then to gain access to some server or workstation behind the firewall. Only tunnel mode is required between the remote host and the firewall. As in case 1, one or two SAs may be used between the remote host and the local host.

9.5 INTERNET KEY EXCHANGE

The key management portion of IPsec involves the determination and distribution of secret keys. A typical requirement is four keys for communication between two applications: transmit and receive pairs for both integrity and confidentiality. The IPsec Architecture document mandates support for two types of key management:

- **Manual:** A system administrator manually configures each system with its own keys and with the keys of other communicating systems. This is practical for small, relatively static environments.

- **Automated:** An automated system enables the on-demand creation of keys for SAs and facilitates the use of keys in a large distributed system with an evolving configuration.

The default automated key management protocol for IPsec is referred to as ISAKMP/Oakley and consists of the following elements:

- **Oakley Key Determination Protocol:** Oakley is a key exchange protocol based on the Diffie-Hellman algorithm but providing added security. Oakley is generic in that it does not dictate specific formats.

- **Internet Security Association and Key Management Protocol (ISAKMP):** ISAKMP provides a framework for Internet key management and provides the specific protocol support, including formats, for negotiation of security attributes.

ISAKMP by itself does not dictate a specific key exchange algorithm; rather, ISAKMP consists of a set of message types that enable the use of a variety of key exchange algorithms. Oakley is the specific key exchange algorithm mandated for use with the initial version of ISAKMP.

In IKEv2, the terms Oakley and ISAKMP are no longer used, and there are significant differences from the use of Oakley and ISAKMP in IKEv1. Nevertheless, the basic functionality is the same. In this section, we describe the IKEv2 specification.

Key Determination Protocol

IKE key determination is a refinement of the Diffie-Hellman key exchange algorithm. Recall that Diffie-Hellman involves the following interaction between users A and B. There is prior agreement on two global parameters: q, a large prime number; and α, a primitive root of q. A selects a random integer X_A as its private key and transmits to B its public key $Y_A = \alpha^{X_A} \bmod q$. Similarly, B selects a random integer X_B as its private key and transmits to A its public key $Y_B = \alpha^{X_B} \bmod q$. Each side can now compute the secret session key:

$$K = (Y_B)^{X_A} \bmod q = (Y_A)^{X_B} \bmod q = \alpha^{X_A X_B} \bmod q$$

The Diffie-Hellman algorithm has two attractive features:

- Secret keys are created only when needed. There is no need to store secret keys for a long period of time, exposing them to increased vulnerability.
- The exchange requires no pre-existing infrastructure other than an agreement on the global parameters.

However, there are a number of weaknesses to Diffie-Hellman, as pointed out in [HUIT98].

- It does not provide any information about the identities of the parties.
- It is subject to a man-in-the-middle attack, in which a third party C impersonates B while communicating with A and impersonates A while communicating with B. Both A and B end up negotiating a key with C, which can then listen to and pass on traffic. The man-in-the-middle attack proceeds as

    1. B sends his public key Y_B in a message addressed to A (see Figure 3.13).
    2. The enemy (E) intercepts this message. E saves B's public key and sends a message to A that has B's User ID but E's public key Y_E. This message is sent in such a way that it appears as though it was sent from B's host system. A receives E's message and stores E's public key with B's User ID. Similarly, E sends a message to B with E's public key, purporting to come from A.
    3. B computes a secret key K_1 based on B's private key and Y_E. A computes a secret key K_2 based on A's private key and Y_E. E computes K_1 using E's secret key X_E and Y_B and computers K_2 using X_E and Y_A.
    4. From now on, E is able to relay messages from A to B and from B to A, appropriately changing their encipherment en route in such a way that neither A nor B will know that they share their communication with E.

- It is computationally intensive. As a result, it is vulnerable to a clogging attack, in which an opponent requests a high number of keys. The victim spends considerable computing resources doing useless modular exponentiation rather than real work.

IKE key determination is designed to retain the advantages of Diffie-Hellman, while countering its weaknesses.

FEATURES OF IKE KEY DETERMINATION The IKE key determination algorithm is characterized by five important features:

1. It employs a mechanism known as cookies to thwart clogging attacks.
2. It enables the two parties to negotiate a *group*; this, in essence, specifies the global parameters of the Diffie-Hellman key exchange.
3. It uses nonces to ensure against replay attacks.
4. It enables the exchange of Diffie-Hellman public key values.
5. It authenticates the Diffie-Hellman exchange to thwart man-in-the-middle attacks.

We have already discussed Diffie-Hellman. Let us look at the remainder of these elements in turn. First, consider the problem of clogging attacks. In this attack, an opponent forges the source address of a legitimate user and sends a public Diffie-Hellman key to the victim. The victim then performs a modular exponentiation to compute the secret key. Repeated messages of this type can *clog* the victim's system with useless work. The **cookie exchange** requires that each side send a pseudorandom number, the cookie, in the initial message, which the other side acknowledges. This acknowledgment must be repeated in the first message of the Diffie-Hellman key exchange. If the source address was forged, the opponent gets no answer. Thus, an opponent can only force a user to generate acknowledgments and not to perform the Diffie-Hellman calculation.

IKE mandates that cookie generation satisfy three basic requirements:

1. The cookie must depend on the specific parties. This prevents an attacker from obtaining a cookie using a real IP address and UDP port and then using it to swamp the victim with requests from randomly chosen IP addresses or ports.
2. It must not be possible for anyone other than the issuing entity to generate cookies that will be accepted by that entity. This implies that the issuing entity will use local secret information in the generation and subsequent verification of a cookie. It must not be possible to deduce this secret information from any particular cookie. The point of this requirement is that the issuing entity need not save copies of its cookies, which are then more vulnerable to discovery, but can verify an incoming cookie acknowledgment when it needs to.
3. The cookie generation and verification methods must be fast to thwart attacks intended to sabotage processor resources.

The recommended method for creating the cookie is to perform a fast hash (e.g., MD5) over the IP Source and Destination addresses, the UDP Source and Destination ports, and a locally generated secret value.

IKE key determination supports the use of different **groups** for the Diffie-Hellman key exchange. Each group includes the definition of the two global parameters and the identity of the algorithm. The current specification includes the following groups.

- Modular exponentiation with a 768-bit modulus

$$q = 2^{768} - 2^{704} - 1 + 2^{64} \times (\lfloor 2^{638} \times \pi \rfloor + 149686)$$
$$\alpha = 2$$

- Modular exponentiation with a 1024-bit modulus

$$q = 2^{1024} - 2^{960} - 1 + 2^{64} \times (\lfloor 2^{894} \times \pi \rfloor + 129093)$$
$$\alpha = 2$$

- Modular exponentiation with a 1536-bit modulus
  - Parameters to be determined
- Elliptic curve group over 2^{155}
  - Generator (hexadecimal): X = 7B, Y = 1C8
  - Elliptic curve parameters (hexadecimal): A = 0, Y = 7338F
- Elliptic curve group over 2^{185}
  - Generator (hexadecimal): X = 18, Y = D
  - Elliptic curve parameters (hexadecimal): A = 0, Y = 1EE9

The first three groups are the classic Diffie-Hellman algorithm using modular exponentiation. The last two groups use the elliptic curve analog to Diffie-Hellman, which was described in Chapter 3.

IKE key determination employs **nonces** to ensure against replay attacks. Each nonce is a locally generated pseudorandom number. Nonces appear in responses and are encrypted during certain portions of the exchange to secure their use.

Three different **authentication** methods can be used with IKE key determination:

- **Digital signatures:** The exchange is authenticated by signing a mutually obtainable hash; each party encrypts the hash with its private key. The hash is generated over important parameters, such as user IDs and nonces.

- **Public-key encryption:** The exchange is authenticated by encrypting parameters such as IDs and nonces with the sender's private key.

- **Symmetric-key encryption:** A key derived by some out-of-band mechanism can be used to authenticate the exchange by symmetric encryption of exchange parameters.

IKEv2 Exchanges The IKEv2 protocol involves the exchange of messages in pairs. The first two pairs of exchanges are referred to as the **initial exchanges** (Figure 9.11a). In the first exchange, the two peers exchange information concerning cryptographic algorithms and other security parameters they are willing to use along with nonces and Diffie-Hellman (DH) values. The result of this exchange is to set up a special SA called the IKE SA (see Figure 9.2). This SA defines parameters for a secure channel between the peers over which subsequent message exchanges take place. Thus, all subsequent IKE message exchanges are protected by encryption and message authentication. In the second exchange, the two parties authenticate one another and set up a first IPsec SA to be placed in the SADB and used for

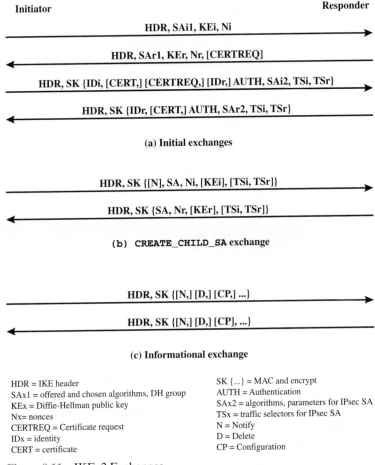

Figure 9.11   IKEv2 Exchanges

protecting ordinary (i.e. non-IKE) communications between the peers. Thus, four messages are needed to establish the first SA for general use.

The **CREATE_CHILD_SA exchange** can be used to establish further SAs for protecting traffic. The **informational exchange** is used to exchange management information, IKEv2 error messages, and other notifications.

Header and Payload Formats

IKE defines procedures and packet formats to establish, negotiate, modify, and delete security associations. As part of SA establishment, IKE defines payloads for exchanging key generation and authentication data. These payload formats provide a consistent framework independent of the specific key exchange protocol, encryption algorithm, and authentication mechanism.

IKE HEADER FORMAT   An IKE message consists of an IKE header followed by one or more payloads. All of this is carried in a transport protocol. The specification dictates that implementations must support the use of UDP for the transport protocol.

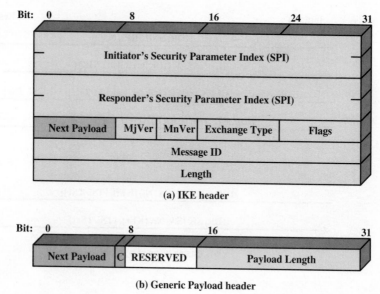

(a) IKE header

(b) Generic Payload header

Figure 9.12 IKE Formats

Figure 9.12a shows the header format for an IKE message. It consists of the following fields.

- **Initiator SPI (64 bits):** A value chosen by the initiator to identify a unique IKE security association (SA).

- **Responder SPI (64 bits):** A value chosen by the responder to identify a unique IKE SA.

- **Next Payload (8 bits):** Indicates the type of the first payload in the message; payloads are discussed in the next subsection.

- **Major Version (4 bits):** Indicates major version of IKE in use.

- **Minor Version (4 bits):** Indicates minor version in use.

- **Exchange Type (8 bits):** Indicates the type of exchange; these are discussed later in this section.

- **Flags (8 bits):** Indicates specific options set for this IKE exchange. Three bits are defined so far. The initiator bit indicates whether this packet is sent by the SA initiator. The version bit indicates whether the transmitter is capable of using a higher major version number than the one currently indicated. The response bit indicates whether this is a response to a message containing the same message ID.

- **Message ID (32 bits):** Used to control retransmission of lost packets and matching of requests and responses.

- **Length (32 bits):** Length of total message (header plus all payloads) in octets.

IKE PAYLOAD TYPES All IKE payloads begin with the same generic payload header shown in Figure 9.12b. The Next Payload field has a value of 0 if this is the last payload in the message; otherwise its value is the type of the next payload. The Payload Length field indicates the length in octets of this payload, including the generic payload header.

The critical bit is 0 if the sender wants the recipient to skip this payload if it does not understand the payload type code in the Next Payload field of the previous payload. It is set to 1 if the sender wants the recipient to reject this entire message if it does not understand the payload type.

Table 9.3 summarizes the payload types defined for IKE and lists the fields, or parameters, that are part of each payload. The **SA payload** is used to begin the establishment of an SA. The payload has a complex, hierarchical structure. The payload may contain multiple proposals. Each proposal may contain multiple protocols. Each protocol may contain multiple transforms. And each transform may contain multiple attributes. These elements are formatted as substructures within the payload as follows.

- **Proposal:** This substructure includes a proposal number, a protocol ID (AH, ESP, or IKE), an indicator of the number of transforms, and then a transform substructure. If more than one protocol is to be included in a proposal, then there is a subsequent proposal substructure with the same proposal number.

- **Transform:** Different protocols support different transform types. The transforms are used primarily to define cryptographic algorithms to be used with a particular protocol.

- **Attribute:** Each transform may include attributes that modify or complete the specification of the transform. An example is key length.

Table 9.3   IKE Payload Types

Type	Parameters
Security Association	Proposals
Key Exchange	DH Group #, Key Exchange Data
Identification	ID Type, ID Data
Certificate	Cert Encoding, Certificate Data
Certificate Request	Cert Encoding, Certification Authority
Authentication	Auth Method, Authentication Data
Nonce	Nonce Data
Notify	Protocol-ID, SPI Size, Notify Message Type, SPI, Notification Data
Delete	Protocol-ID, SPI Size, # of SPIs, SPI (one or more)
Vendor ID	Vendor ID
Traffic Selector	Number of TSs, Traffic Selectors
Encrypted	IV, Encrypted IKE payloads, Padding, Pad Length, ICV
Configuration	CFG Type, Configuration Attributes
Extensible Authentication Protocol	EAP Message

The **Key Exchange payload** can be used for a variety of key exchange techniques, including Oakley, Diffie-Hellman, and the RSA-based key exchange used by PGP. The Key Exchange data field contains the data required to generate a session key and is dependent on the key exchange algorithm used.

The **Identification payload** is used to determine the identity of communicating peers and may be used for determining authenticity of information. Typically the ID Data field will contain an IPv4 or IPv6 address.

The **Certificate payload** transfers a public-key certificate. The Certificate Encoding field indicates the type of certificate or certificate-related information, which may include the following:

- PKCS #7 wrapped X.509 certificate
- PGP certificate
- DNS signed key
- X.509 certificate—signature
- X.509 certificate—key exchange
- Kerberos tokens
- Certificate Revocation List (CRL)
- Authority Revocation List (ARL)
- SPKI certificate

At any point in an IKE exchange, the sender may include a **Certificate Request** payload to request the certificate of the other communicating entity. The payload may list more than one certificate type that is acceptable and more than one certificate authority that is acceptable.

The **Authentication** payload contains data used for message authentication purposes. The authentication method types so far defined are RSA digital signature, shared-key message integrity code, and DSS digital signature.

The **Nonce** payload contains random data used to guarantee liveness during an exchange and to protect against replay attacks.

The **Notify** payload contains either error or status information associated with this SA or this SA negotiation. The following table lists the IKE notify messages.

Error Messages	Status Messages
Unsupported Critical Payload	Initial Contact
	Set Window Size
Invalid IKE SPI	Additional TS Possible
Invalid Major Version	IPCOMP Supported
Invalid Syntax	NAT Detection Source IP
Invalid Payload Type	NAT Detection Destination IP
Invalid Message ID	Cookie
Invalid SPI	Use Transport Mode

Error Messages	Status Messages
No Proposal Chosen	HTTP Cert Lookup Supported
Invalid KE Payload	Rekey SA
Authentication Failed	ESP TFC Padding Not Supported
Single Pair Required	Non First Fragments Also
No Additional SAS	
Internal Address Failure	
Failed CP Required	
TS Unacceptable	
Invalid Selectors	

The **Delete** payload indicates one or more SAs that the sender has deleted from its database and that therefore are no longer valid.

The **Vendor ID** payload contains a vendor-defined constant. The constant is used by vendors to identify and recognize remote instances of their implementations. This mechanism allows a vendor to experiment with new features while maintaining backward compatibility.

The **Traffic Selector** payload allows peers to identify packet flows for processing by IPsec services.

The **Encrypted** payload contains other payloads in encrypted form. The encrypted payload format is similar to that of ESP. It may include an IV if the encryption algorithm requires it and an ICV if authentication is selected.

The **Configuration** payload is used to exchange configuration information between IKE peers.

The **Extensible Authentication Protocol (EAP)** payload allows IKE SAs to be authenticated using EAP, which was discussed in Chapter 5.

9.6 CRYPTOGRAPHIC SUITES

The IPsecv3 and IKEv3 protocols rely on a variety of types of cryptographic algorithms. To promote interoperability, two RFCs define recommended suites of cryptographic algorithms and parameters for various applications.

RFC 4308 defines two cryptographic suites for establishing virtual private networks. Suite VPN-A matches the commonly used corporate VPN security used in older IKEv1 implementations at the time of the issuance of IKEv2 in 2005. Suite VPN-B provides stronger security and is recommended for new VPNs that implement IPsecv3 and IKEv2.

Table 9.4a lists the algorithms and parameters for the two suites. There are several points to note about these two suites. For symmetric cryptography, VPN-A

Table 9.4 Cryptographic Suites for IPsec

	VPN-A	**VPN-B**
ESP encryption	3DES-CBC	AES-CBC (128-bit key)
ESP integrity	HMAC-SHA1-96	AES-XCBC-MAC-96
IKE encryption	3DES-CBC	AES-CBC (128-bit key)
IKE PRF	HMAC-SHA1	AES-XCBC-PRF-128
IKE Integrity	HMAC-SHA1-96	AES-XCBC-MAC-96
IKE DH group	1024-bit MODP	2048-bit MODP

(a) Virtual private networks (RFC 4308)

	GCM-128	**GCM-256**	**GMAC-128**	**GMAC-256**
ESP encryption/ Integrity	AES-GCM (128-bit key)	AES-GCM (256-bit key)	Null	Null
ESP integrity	Null	Null	AES-GMAC (128-bit key)	AES-GMAC (256-bit key)
IKE encryption	AES-CBC (128-bit key)	AES-CBC (256-bit key)	AES-CBC (128-bit key)	AES-CBC (256-bit key)
IKE PRF	HMAC-SHA-256	HMAC-SHA-384	HMAC-SHA-256	HMAC-SHA-384
IKE Integrity	HMAC-SHA-256-128	HMAC-SHA-384-192	HMAC-SHA-256-128	HMAC-SHA-384-192
IKE DH group	256-bit random ECP	384-bit random ECP	256-bit random ECP	384-bit random ECP

(b) NSA Suite B (RFC 4869)

relies on 3DES and HMAC, while VPN-B relies exclusively on AES. Three types of secret-key algorithms are used:

- **Encryption:** For encryption, the cipher block chaining (CBC) mode is used.
- **Message authentication:** For message authentication, VPN-A relies on HMAC with SHA-1 with the output truncated to 96 bits. VPN-B relies on a variant of CMAC with the output truncated to 96 bits.
- **Pseudorandom function:** IKEv2 generates pseudorandom bits by repeated use of the MAC used for message authentication.

RFC 6379 defines four optional cryptographic suites that are compatible with the United States National Security Agency's Suite B specifications. In 2005, the NSA issued Suite B, which defined the algorithms and strengths needed to protect both sensitive but unclassified (SBU) and classified information for use in its Cryptographic Modernization program [LATT09]. The four suites defined in RFC 4869 provide choices for ESP and IKE. The four suites are differentiated by the choice of cryptographic algorithm strengths and a choice of whether ESP is to provide both confidentiality and integrity or integrity only. All of the suites offer greater protection than the two VPN suites defined in RFC 4308.

Table 9.4b lists the algorithms and parameters for the two suites. As with RFC 4308, three categories of secret key algorithms are listed:

- **Encryption:** For ESP, authenticated encryption is provided using the Galois/Counter Mode (GCM) with either 128-bit or 256-bit AES keys. GCM is a block cipher mode of operation based on the counter mode described in Chapter 2. GCM provides both encryption and authentication. For IKE encryption, CBC is used, as it was for the VPN suites.
- **Message authentication:** For ESP, if only authentication is required, then GMAC is used, GMAC is the authentication portion of GMC. For IKE, message authentication is provided using HMAC with one of the SHA-3 hash functions.
- **Pseudorandom function:** As with the VPN suites, IKEv2 in these suites generates pseudorandom bits by repeated use of the MAC used for message authentication.

For the Diffie-Hellman algorithm, the use of elliptic curve groups modulo a prime is specified. For authentication, elliptic curve digital signatures are listed. The original IKEv2 documents used RSA-based digital signatures. Equivalent or greater strength can be achieved using ECC with fewer key bits.

9.7 RECOMMENDED READING

IPv6 and IPv4 are covered in more detail in [STAL11]. [CHEN98] provides a good discussion of an IPsec design. [FRAN05] is a more comprehensive treatment of IPsec. [PATE06] is a useful overview of IPsecv3 and IKEv2 with an emphasis on cryptographic aspects.

CHEN98   Cheng, P., et al. "A Security Architecture for the Internet Protocol." *IBM Systems Journal,* Number 1, 1998.

FRAN05   Frankel, S., et al. *Guide to IPsec VPNs.* NIST SP 800-77, 2005.

PATE06   Paterson, K. "A Cryptographic Tour of the IPsec Standards." " *Cryptology ePrint Archive: Report 2006/097,* April 2006.

STAL11   Stallings, W. *Data and Computer Communications, Ninth Edition.* Upper Saddle River, NJ: Prentice Hall, 2011.

9.8 KEY TERMS, REVIEW QUESTIONS, AND PROBLEMS

Key Terms

anti-replay service	Internet Key Exchange (IKE)	security association (SA)
Authentication Header (AH)	IP Security (IPsec)	transport mode
Encapsulating Security	IPv4	tunnel mode
Payload (ESP)	IPv6	
Internet Security Association	Oakley key determination	
and Key Management	protocol	
Protocol (ISAKMP)	replay attack	

Review Questions

9.1 What are the advantages of implementing security at the IP level?

9.2 What is IPsec? What are its benefits?

9.3 How is IPsec important for internetworking routing?

9.4 Explain using an example how tunnel mode IPsec operates.

9.5 Define the SAP associated with each SA.

9.6 Explain how outbound IP packets are processed by IPsec.

9.7 What are the basic approaches to bundling SAs?

9.8 What are the advantages of the Encapsulating Security Payload?

Problems

9.1 Explain the anti-replay mechanism shown in Fig. 9.6.

9.2 Draw a figure similar to Figure 9.8 for AH.

9.3 List the major security services provided by AH and ESP, respectively.

9.4 In discussing AH processing, it was mentioned that not all of the fields in an IP header are included in MAC calculation.
   a. For each of the fields in the IPv4 header, indicate whether the field is immutable, mutable but predictable, or mutable (zeroed prior to ICV calculation).
   b. Do the same for the IPv6 header.
   c. Do the same for the IPv6 extension headers.
   In each case, justify your decision for each field.

9.5 Suppose that the current replay window spans from 120 to 530.
   a. If the next incoming authenticated packet has sequence number 105, what will the receiver do with the packet, and what will be the parameters of the window after that?
   b. If instead the next incoming authenticated packet has sequence number 440, what will the receiver do with the packet, and what will be the parameters of the window after that?
   c. If instead the next incoming authenticated packet has sequence number 540, what will the receiver do with the packet, and what will be the parameters of the window after that?

9.6 When tunnel mode is used, a new outer IP header is constructed. For both IPv4 and IPv6, indicate the relationship of each outer IP header field and each extension header in the outer packet to the corresponding field or extension header of the inner IP packet. That is, indicate which outer values are derived from inner values and which are constructed independently of the inner values.

9.7 End-to-end authentication and encryption are desired between two hosts. Draw figures similar to Figure 9.8 that show each of the following.
   a. Transport adjacency with encryption applied before authentication.
   b. A transport SA bundled inside a tunnel SA with encryption applied before authentication.
   c. A transport SA bundled inside a tunnel SA with authentication applied before encryption.

9.8 The IPsec architecture document states that when two transport mode SAs are bundled to allow both AH and ESP protocols on the same end-to-end flow, only one ordering of security protocols seems appropriate: performing the ESP protocol before performing the AH protocol. Why is this approach recommended rather than authentication before encryption?

9.9 What is meant by key management for IPsec? Describe automated key management protocol for IPsec.

9.10 What are the five important features of IKE key determination?

CHAPTER 10

MALICIOUS SOFTWARE

10.1   Types of Malicious Software (Malware)

10.2   Propagation—Infected Content—Viruses

10.3   Propagation—Vulnerability Exploit—Worms

10.4   Propagation—Social Engineering—Spam E-mail, Trojans

10.5   Payload—System Corruption

10.6   Payload—Attack Agent—Zombie, Bots

10.7   Payload—Information Theft—Keyloggers, Phishing, Spyware

10.8   Payload—Stealthing—Backdoors, Rootkits

10.9   Countermeasures

10.10 Distributed Denial of Service Attacks

10.11 Recommended Reading

10.12 Key Terms, Review Questions, and Problems

What is the concept of defense: The parrying of a blow. What is its characteristic feature: Awaiting the blow.

— *On War*, Carl Von Clausewitz

LEARNING OBJECTIVES

After studying this chapter, you should be able to:

◆ Describe three broad mechanisms malware uses to propagate.

◆ Understand the basic operation of viruses, worms, and trojans.

◆ Describe four broad categories of malware payloads.

◆ Understand the different threats posed by bots, spyware, and rootkits.

◆ Describe some malware countermeasure elements.

◆ Describe three locations for malware detection mechanisms.

Malicious software, or **malware**, arguably constitutes one of the most significant categories of threats to computer systems. [SOUP12a] defines malware as "a program that is covertly inserted into another program with the intent to destroy data, run destructive or intrusive programs, or otherwise compromise the confidentiality, integrity, or availability of the victim's data, applications, or operating system." Hence, we are concerned with the threat malware poses to application programs, to utility programs, such as editors and compilers, and to kernel-level programs. We are also concerned with its use on compromised or malicious Web sites and servers, or in especially crafted spam e-mails or other messages, which aim to trick users into revealing sensitive personal information.

This chapter[1] examines the wide spectrum of malware threats and countermeasures. We begin with a survey of various types of malware and offer a broad classification based first on the means malware uses to spread or **propagate**, and then on the variety of actions or **payloads** used once the malware has reached a target. Propagation mechanisms include those used by viruses, worms, and trojans. Payloads include system corruption, bots, phishing, spyware, and rootkits. The discussion then includes a review of countermeasure approaches. Finally, distributed denial-of-service (DDoS) attacks are reviewed.

10.1 TYPES OF MALICIOUS SOFTWARE (MALWARE)

The terminology in this area presents problems because of a lack of universal agreement on all of the terms and because some of the categories overlap. Table 10.1 is a useful guide to some of the terms in use.

---

[1] I am indebted to Lawrie Brown of the Australian Defence Force Academy, who contributed substantially to this chapter.

Table 10.1 Terminology for Malicious Software

Name	Description
Virus	Malware that, when executed, tries to replicate itself into other executable code; when it succeeds the code is said to be infected. When the infected code is executed, the virus also executes.
Worm	A computer program that can run independently and can propagate a complete working version of itself onto other hosts on a network.
Logic bomb	A program inserted into software by an intruder. A logic bomb lies dormant until a pre-defined condition is met; the program then triggers an unauthorized act.
Trojan horse	A computer program that appears to have a useful function, but also has a hidden and potentially malicious function that evades security mechanisms, sometimes by exploiting legitimate authorizations of a system entity that invokes the Trojan horse program.
Backdoor (trapdoor)	Any mechanism that bypasses a normal security check; it may allow unauthorized access to functionality.
Mobile code	Software (e.g., script, macro, or other portable instruction) that can be shipped unchanged to a heterogeneous collection of platforms and execute with identical semantics.
Exploits	Code specific to a single vulnerability or set of vulnerabilities.
Downloaders	Program that installs other items on a machine that is under attack. Usually, a downloader is sent in an e-mail.
Auto-rooter	Malicious hacker tools used to break into new machines remotely.
Kit (virus generator)	Set of tools for generating new viruses automatically.
Spammer programs	Used to send large volumes of unwanted e-mail.
Flooders	Used to attack networked computer systems with a large volume of traffic to carry out a denial-of-service (DoS) attack.
Keyloggers	Captures keystrokes on a compromised system.
Rootkit	Set of hacker tools used after attacker has broken into a computer system and gained root-level access.
Zombie, bot	Program activated on an infected machine that is activated to launch attacks on other machines.
Spyware	Software that collects information from a computer and transmits it to another system.
Adware	Advertising that is integrated into software. It can result in pop-up ads or redirection of a browser to a commercial site.

A Broad Classification of Malware

Although a range of schemes can be used, one useful approach classifies malware into two broad categories, based first on how it spreads or propagates to reach the desired targets and then on the actions or payloads it performs once a target is reached.

Propagation mechanisms include infection of existing executable or interpreted content by viruses that is subsequently spread to other systems; exploit of software vulnerabilities either locally or over a network by worms or drive-by-downloads to allow the malware to replicate; and social engineering attacks that convince users to bypass security mechanisms to install trojans or to respond to phishing attacks.

Earlier approaches to malware classification distinguished between those that need a host program, being parasitic code such as viruses, and those that are independent, self-contained programs run on the system such as worms, trojans, and bots. Another distinction used was between malware that does not replicate, such as trojans and spam e-mail, and malware that does, including viruses and worms.

Payload actions performed by malware once it reaches a target system can include corruption of system or data files; theft of service in order to make the system a zombie agent of attack as part of a botnet; theft of information from the system, especially of logins, passwords, or other personal details by keylogging or spyware programs; and stealthing where the malware hides its presence on the system from attempts to detect and block it.

While early malware tended to use a single means of propagation to deliver a single payload, as it evolved we see a growth of blended malware that incorporates a range of both propagation mechanisms and payloads that increase its ability to spread, hide, and perform a range of actions on targets. A **blended attack** uses multiple methods of infection or propagation, to maximize the speed of contagion and the severity of the attack. Some malware even support an update mechanism that allows it to change the range of propagation and payload mechanisms utilized once it is deployed.

In the following sections, we survey these various categories of malware, and then follow with a discussion of appropriate countermeasures.

Attack Kits

Initially, the development and deployment of malware required considerable technical skill by software authors. This changed with the development of virus-creation toolkits in the early 1990s, and then later of more general attack kits in the 2000s, that greatly assisted in the development and deployment of malware [FOSS10]. These toolkits, often known as **crimeware**, now include a variety of propagation mechanisms and payload modules that even novices can combine, select, and deploy. They can also easily be customized with the latest discovered vulnerabilities in order to exploit the window of opportunity between the publication of a weakness and the widespread deployment of patches to close it. These kits greatly enlarged the population of attackers able to deploy malware. Although the malware created with such toolkits tends to be less sophisticated than that designed from scratch, the sheer number of new variants that can be generated by attackers using these toolkits creates a significant problem for those defending systems against them.

The Zeus crimeware toolkit is a prominent, recent example of such an attack kit, which was used to generate a wide range of very effective, stealthed malware that facilitates a range of criminal activities, in particular capturing and exploiting banking credentials [BINS10].

Attack Sources

Another significant malware development over the last couple of decades is the change from attackers being individuals, often motivated to demonstrate their technical competence to their peers, to more organized and dangerous attack sources. These include politically motivated attackers, criminals, and organized crime; organizations that sell their services to companies and nations; and national government agencies. This has significantly changed the resources available and motivation behind the rise of malware, and indeed has led to development of a large underground economy involving the sale of attack kits, access to compromised hosts, and to stolen information.

10.2 PROPAGATION—INFECTED CONTENT—VIRUSES

The first category of malware propagation concerns parasitic software fragments that attach themselves to some existing executable content. The fragment may be machine code that infects some existing application, utility, or system program, or even the code used to boot a computer system. More recently, the fragment has been some form of scripting code, typically used to support active content within data files such as Microsoft Word documents, Excel spreadsheets, or Adobe PDF documents.

The Nature of Viruses

A computer virus is a piece of software that can "infect" other programs, or indeed any type of executable content, by modifying them. The modification includes injecting the original code with a routine to make copies of the virus code, which can then go on to infect other content.

A computer virus carries in its instructional code the recipe for making perfect copies of itself. The typical virus becomes embedded in a program, or carrier of executable content, on a computer. Then, whenever the infected computer comes into contact with an uninfected piece of code, a fresh copy of the virus passes into the new location. Thus, the infection can spread from computer to computer, aided by unsuspecting users, who exchange these programs or carrier files on disk or USB stick, or who send them to one another over a network. In a network environment, the ability to access documents, applications, and system services on other computers provides a perfect culture for the spread of such viral code.

A virus that attaches to an executable program can do anything that the program is permitted to do. It executes secretly when the host program is run. Once the virus code is executing, it can perform any function, such as erasing files and programs, that is allowed by the privileges of the current user. One reason viruses dominated the malware scene in earlier years was the lack of user authentication and access controls on personal computer systems at that time. This enabled a virus to infect any executable content on the system. The significant quantity of programs shared on floppy disk also enabled its easy, if somewhat slow, spread. The inclusion of tighter access controls on modern operating systems significantly hinders the ease of infection of such traditional, machine-executable code, viruses. This resulted in the development of macro viruses that exploit the active content supported by some document types, such as Microsoft Word or Excel files, or Adobe PDF documents. Such documents are easily modified and shared by users as part of their normal system use and are not protected by the same access controls as programs. Currently, a viral mode of infection is typically one of several propagation mechanisms used by contemporary malware, which may also include worm and Trojan capabilities.

A computer virus, and more generally many contemporary types of malware, includes one or more variants of each of these components:

- **Infection mechanism:** The means by which a virus spreads or propagates, enabling it to replicate. The mechanism is also referred to as the **infection vector**.
- **Trigger:** The event or condition that determines when the payload is activated or delivered, sometimes known as a **logic bomb**.
- **Payload:** What the virus does, besides spreading. The payload may involve damage or benign but noticeable activity.

During its lifetime, a typical virus goes through the following four phases:

- **Dormant phase:** The virus is idle. The virus will eventually be activated by some event, such as a date, the presence of another program or file, or the capacity of the disk exceeding some limit. Not all viruses have this stage.
- **Propagation phase:** The virus places a copy of itself into other programs or into certain system areas on the disk. The copy may not be identical to the propagating version; viruses often morph to evade detection. Each infected program will now contain a clone of the virus, which will itself enter a propagation phase.
- **Triggering phase:** The virus is activated to perform the function for which it was intended. As with the dormant phase, the triggering phase can be caused by a variety of system events, including a count of the number of times that this copy of the virus has made copies of itself.
- **Execution phase:** The function is performed. The function may be harmless, such as a message on the screen, or damaging, such as the destruction of programs and data files.

Most viruses that infect executable program files carry out their work in a manner that is specific to a particular operating system and, in some cases, specific to a particular hardware platform. Thus, they are designed to take advantage of the details and weaknesses of particular systems. Macro viruses, though, target specific document types, which are often supported on a variety of systems.

EXECUTABLE VIRUS STRUCTURE Traditional machine-executable virus code can be prepended or postpended to some executable program, or it can be embedded into the program in some other fashion. The key to its operation is that the infected program, when invoked, will first execute the virus code and then execute the original code of the program.

A very general depiction of virus structure is shown in Figure 10.1a. In this case, the virus code, V, is prepended to infected programs, and it is assumed that the entry point to the program, when invoked, is the first line of the program.

The infected program begins with the virus code and works as follows. The first line of code labels the program, which then begins execution with the main action block of the virus. The second line is a special marker that is used by the virus to determine whether or not a potential victim program has already been infected with this virus. When the program is invoked, control is immediately transferred to the main virus program. The virus program may first seek

```
program V                          program CV
1234567;                           1234567;

procedure attach-to-program;       procedure attach-to-program;
begin                              begin
    repeat                             repeat
       file := get-random-program;        file := get-random-program;
       until first-program-line ≠ 1234567;  until first-program-line ≠ 1234567;
       prepend V to file;                 compress file;   (* t₁ *)
end;                                      prepend CV to file;  (* t₂ *)
                                   end;
procedure execute-payload;
begin                              procedure (* main action block *)
    (* perform payload actions *)      if ask-permission then attach-to-program;
end;                                   uncompress rest of this file into tempfile;  (* t₃ *)
                                       execute tempfile;  (* t₄ *)
procedure trigger-condition;       end;
begin
    (* return true if trigger condition is true *)
end;

begin (* main action block *)
    attach-to-program;
    if trigger-condition then execute-payload;
    goto main;
end;
```

(a) A simple virus   (b) A compression virus

Figure 10.1   Example Virus Logic

out uninfected executable files and infect them. Next, the virus may execute its payload if the required trigger conditions, if any, are met. Finally, the virus transfers control to the original program. If the infection phase of the program is reasonably rapid, a user is unlikely to notice any difference between the execution of an infected and an uninfected program.

A virus such as the one just described is easily detected because an infected version of a program is longer than the corresponding uninfected one. A way to thwart such a simple means of detecting a virus is to compress the executable file so that both the infected and uninfected versions are of identical length. Figure 10.1b shows in general terms the logic required. The key lines in this virus are labeled with times, and Figure 10.2 illustrates the operation. We begin at time t_0, with program P_1', which is program P_1 infected with virus CV, and a clean program P_2, which is not infected with CV. When P_1 is invoked, control passes to its virus, which performs the following steps:

t_1 For each uninfected file P_2 that is found, the virus first compresses that file to produce P_2', which is shorter than the original program by the size of the virus CV.

t_2 A copy of CV is prepended to the compressed program.

t_3 The compressed version of the original infected program, P_1' is uncompressed.

t_4 The uncompressed original program P_1 is executed.

In this example, the virus does nothing other than propagate. As previously mentioned, the virus may also include one or more payloads.

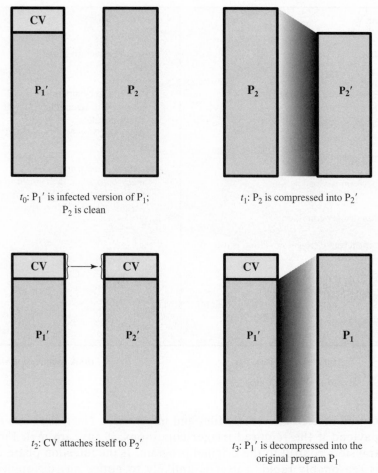

t_0: P_1' is infected version of P_1; P$_2$ is clean

t_1: P_2 is compressed into P_2'

t_2: CV attaches itself to P_2'

t_3: P_1' is decompressed into the original program P_1

Figure 10.2   A Compression Virus

Once a virus has gained entry to a system by infecting a single program, it is in a position to potentially infect some or all other executable files on that system when the infected program executes, depending on the access permissions the infected program has. Thus, viral infection can be completely prevented by blocking the virus from gaining entry in the first place. Unfortunately, prevention is extraordinarily difficult because a virus can be part of any program outside a system. Thus, unless one is content to take an absolutely bare piece of iron and write all one's own system and application programs, one is vulnerable. Many forms of infection can also be blocked by denying normal users the right to modify programs on the system.

Viruses Classification

There has been a continuous arms race between virus writers and writers of antivirus software since viruses first appeared. As effective countermeasures are developed for existing types of viruses, newer types are developed. There is no simple or universally agreed-upon classification scheme for viruses. In this section, we follow [AYCO06] and classify viruses along two orthogonal axes: the type of target the virus tries to infect and the method the virus uses to conceal itself from detection by users and antivirus software.

A virus **classification by target** includes the following categories:

- **Boot sector infector:** Infects a master boot record or boot record and spreads when a system is booted from the disk containing the virus.
- **File infector:** Infects files that the operating system or shell consider to be executable.
- **Macro virus:** Infects files with macro or scripting code that is interpreted by an application.
- **Multipartite virus:** Infects files in multiple ways. Typically, the multipartite virus is capable of infecting multiple types of files, so that virus eradication must deal with all of the possible sites of infection.

A virus classification by concealment strategy includes the following categories:

- **Encrypted virus:** A typical approach is as follows. A portion of the virus creates a random encryption key and encrypts the remainder of the virus. The key is stored with the virus. When an infected program is invoked, the virus uses the stored random key to decrypt the virus. When the virus replicates, a different random key is selected. Because the bulk of the virus is encrypted with a different key for each instance, there is no constant bit pattern to observe.
- **Stealth virus:** A form of virus explicitly designed to hide itself from detection by antivirus software. Thus, the entire virus, not just a payload, is hidden. It may use both code mutation, for example, compression, and rootkit techniques to achieve this.
- **Polymorphic virus:** A virus that mutates with every infection, making detection by the "signature" of the virus impossible.
- **Metamorphic virus:** As with a polymorphic virus, a metamorphic virus mutates with every infection. The difference is that a metamorphic virus rewrites itself completely at each iteration, increasing the difficulty of detection. Metamorphic viruses may change their behavior as well as their appearance.

A **polymorphic virus** creates copies during replication that are functionally equivalent but have distinctly different bit patterns, in order to defeat programs that scan for viruses. In this case, the "signature" of the virus will vary with each copy. To achieve this variation, the virus may randomly insert superfluous instructions or interchange the order of independent instructions. A more effective approach is to use encryption. The strategy of the encryption virus is followed. The portion of the virus that is responsible for generating keys and performing encryption/decryption is referred to as the *mutation engine*. The mutation engine itself is altered with each use.

Macro and Scripting Viruses

Macro viruses infect scripting code used to support active content in a variety of user document types. Macro viruses are particularly threatening for a number of reasons:

1. A macro virus is platform independent. Many macro viruses infect active content in commonly used applications, such as macros in Microsoft Word documents or other Microsoft Office documents, or scripting code in Adobe PDF documents. Any hardware platform and operating system that supports these applications can be infected.

2. Macro viruses infect documents, not executable portions of code. Most of the information introduced onto a computer system is in the form of documents rather than programs.

3. Macro viruses are easily spread, as the documents they exploit are shared in normal use. A very common method is by electronic mail.

4. Because macro viruses infect user documents rather than system programs, traditional file system access controls are of limited use in preventing their spread, since users are expected to modify them.

Macro viruses take advantage of support for active content using a scripting or macro language, embedded in a word processing document or other type of file. Typically, users employ macros to automate repetitive tasks and thereby save keystrokes. They are also used to support dynamic content, form validation, and other useful tasks associated with these documents.

Successive releases of MS Office products provide increased protection against macro viruses. For example, Microsoft offers an optional Macro Virus Protection tool that detects suspicious Word files and alerts the customer to the potential risk of opening a file with macros. Various antivirus product vendors have also developed tools to detect and remove macro viruses. As in other types of viruses, the arms race continues in the field of macro viruses, but they no longer are the predominant virus threat.

Another possible host for macro virus–style malware is in Adobe's PDF documents. These can support a range of embedded components, including Javascript and other types of scripting code. Although recent PDF viewers include measures to warn users when such code is run, the message the user is shown can be manipulated to trick them into permitting its execution. If this occurs, the code could potentially act as a virus to infect other PDF documents the user can access on his or her system. Alternatively, it can install a Trojan, or act as a worm, as we discuss later [STEV11].

10.3 PROPAGATION—VULNERABILITY EXPLOIT—WORMS

A worm is a program that actively seeks out more machines to infect, and then each infected machine serves as an automated launching pad for attacks on other machines. Worm programs exploit software vulnerabilities in client or server programs to gain access to each new system. They can use network connections to spread from system to system. They can also spread through shared media, such as USB drives or CD and DVD data disks. E-mail worms spread in macro or script code included in documents attached to e-mail or to instant messenger file transfers. Upon activation, the worm may replicate and propagate again. In addition to propagation, the worm usually carries some form of payload, such as those we discuss later.

To replicate itself, a worm uses some means to access remote systems. These include the following:

- **Electronic mail or instant messenger facility:** A worm e-mails a copy of itself to other systems or sends itself as an attachment via an of instant message service, so that its code is run when the e-mail or attachment is received or viewed.

- **File sharing:** A worm either creates a copy of itself or infects other suitable files as a virus on removable media such as a USB drive; it then executes when the drive is connected to another system using the autorun mechanism by exploiting some software vulnerability or when a user opens the infected file on the target system.

- **Remote execution capability:** A worm executes a copy of itself on another system, either by using an explicit remote execution facility or by exploiting a program flaw in a network service to subvert its operations.

- **Remote file access or transfer capability:** A worm uses a remote file access or transfer service to another system to copy itself from one system to the other, where users on that system may then execute it.

- **Remote login capability:** A worm logs onto a remote system as a user and then uses commands to copy itself from one system to the other, where it then executes.

The new copy of the worm program is then run on the remote system where, in addition to any payload functions that it performs on that system, it continues to propagate.

A worm typically uses the same phases as a computer virus: dormant, propagation, triggering, and execution. The propagation phase generally performs the following functions:

- Search for appropriate access mechanisms to other systems to infect by examining host tables, address books, buddy lists, trusted peers, and other similar repositories of remote system access details; by scanning possible target host addresses; or by searching for suitable removable media devices to use.

- Use the access mechanisms found to transfer a copy of itself to the remote system and cause the copy to be run.

The worm may also attempt to determine whether a system has previously been infected before copying itself to the system. In a multiprogramming system, it can also disguise its presence by naming itself as a system process or using some other name that may not be noticed by a system operator. More recent worms can even inject their code into existing processes on the system and run using additional threads in that process, to further disguise their presence.

Target Discovery

The first function in the propagation phase for a network worm is for it to search for other systems to infect, a process known as **scanning** or **fingerprinting**. For such worms, which exploit software vulnerabilities in remotely accessible network services, it must identify potential systems running the vulnerable service, and then infect them. Then, typically, the worm code now installed on the infected machines repeats the same scanning process, until a large distributed network of infected machines is created.

[MIRK04] lists the following types of network address scanning strategies that such a worm can use:

- **Random:** Each compromised host probes random addresses in the IP address space, using a different seed. This technique produces a high volume of Internet traffic, which may cause generalized disruption even before the actual attack is launched.

- **Hit list:** The attacker first compiles a long list of potential vulnerable machines. This can be a slow process done over a long period to avoid detection that an attack is underway. Once the list is compiled, the attacker begins infecting machines on the list. Each infected machine is provided with a portion of the list to scan. This strategy results in a very short scanning period, which may make it difficult to detect that infection is taking place.

- **Topological:** This method uses information contained on an infected victim machine to find more hosts to scan.

- **Local subnet:** If a host is infected behind a firewall, that host then looks for targets in its own local network. The host uses the subnet address structure to find other hosts that would otherwise be protected by the firewall.

Worm Propagation Model

A well-designed worm can spread rapidly and infect massive numbers of hosts. It is useful to have a general model for the rate of worm propagation. Computer viruses and worms exhibit similar self-replication and propagation behavior to biological viruses. Thus we can look to classic epidemic models for understanding computer virus and worm propagation behavior. A simplified, classic epidemic model can be expressed as follows:

$$\frac{dI(t)}{dt} = \beta I(t)S(t)$$

where

$I(t)$ = number of individuals infected as of time t

$S(t)$ = number of susceptible individuals (susceptible to infection but not yet infected) at time t

β = infection rate

N = size of the population, $N = I(t) + S(t)$

Figure 10.3 shows the dynamics of worm propagation using this model. Propagation proceeds through three phases. In the initial phase, the number of hosts

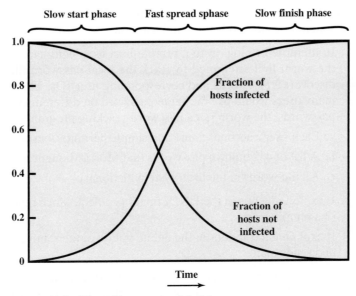

Figure 10.3   Worm Propagation Model

increases exponentially. To see that this is so, consider a simplified case in which a worm is launched from a single host and infects two nearby hosts. Each of these hosts infects two more hosts, and so on. This results in exponential growth. After a time, infecting hosts waste some time attacking already-infected hosts, which reduces the rate of infection. During this middle phase, growth is approximately linear, but the rate of infection is rapid. When most vulnerable computers have been infected, the attack enters a slow finish phase as the worm seeks out those remaining hosts that are difficult to identify.

Clearly, the objective in countering a worm is to catch the worm in its slow start phase, at a time when few hosts have been infected.

Zou and others [ZOU05] describe a model for worm propagation based on an analysis of network worm attacks at that time. The speed of propagation and the total number of hosts infected depend on a number of factors, including the mode of propagation, the vulnerability or vulnerabilities exploited, and the degree of similarity to preceding attacks. For the latter factor, an attack that is a variation of a recent previous attack may be countered more effectively than a more novel attack. Zou's model agrees closely with Figure 10.3.

The Morris Worm

The earliest significant worm infection was released onto the Internet by Robert Morris in 1988 [ORMA03]. The Morris worm was designed to spread on UNIX systems and used a number of different techniques for propagation. When a copy began execution, its first task was to discover other hosts known to this host that would allow entry from this host. The worm performed this task by examining a variety of lists and tables, including system tables that declared which other machines were trusted by this host, users' mail forwarding files, tables by which users gave themselves permission for access to remote accounts, and from a program that reported the status of network connections. For each discovered host, the worm tried a number of methods for gaining access:

1. It attempted to log on to a remote host as a legitimate user. In this method, the worm first attempted to crack the local password file and then used the discovered passwords and corresponding user IDs. The assumption was that many users would use the same password on different systems. To obtain the passwords, the worm ran a password-cracking program that tried
   a. Each user's account name and simple permutations of it
   b. A list of 432 built-in passwords that Morris thought to be likely candidates[2]
   c. All the words in the local system dictionary
2. It exploited a bug in the UNIX finger protocol, which reports the whereabouts of a remote user.
3. It exploited a trapdoor in the debug option of the remote process that receives and sends mail.

If any of these attacks succeeded, the worm achieved communication with the operating system command interpreter. It then sent this interpreter a short bootstrap program, issued a command to execute that program, and then logged off. The bootstrap program then called back the parent program and downloaded the remainder of the worm. The new worm was then executed.

State of Worm Technology

The state of the art in worm technology includes the following:

- **Multiplatform:** Newer worms are not limited to Windows machines but can attack a variety of platforms, especially the popular varieties of UNIX, or exploit macro or scripting languages supported in popular document types.
- **Multiexploit:** New worms penetrate systems in a variety of ways, using exploits against Web servers, browsers, e-mail, file sharing, and other network-based applications, or via shared media.
- **Ultrafast spreading:** Exploit various techniques to optimize the rate of spread of a worm to maximize its likelihood of locating as many vulnerable machines as possible in a short time period.
- **Polymorphic:** To evade detection, skip past filters, and foil real-time analysis, worms adopt the virus polymorphic technique. Each copy of the worm has new code generated on the fly using functionally equivalent instructions and encryption techniques.
- **Metamorphic:** In addition to changing their appearance, metamorphic worms have a repertoire of behavior patterns that are unleashed at different stages of propagation.
- **Transport vehicles:** Because worms can rapidly compromise a large number of systems, they are ideal for spreading a wide variety of malicious payloads,

---

[2]The complete list is provided at this book's Premium Content Web site.

such as distributed denial-of-service bots, rootkits, spam e-mail generators, and spyware.

- **Zero-day exploit:** To achieve maximum surprise and distribution, a worm should exploit an unknown vulnerability that is only discovered by the general network community when the worm is launched.

Mobile Code

Mobile code refers to programs (e.g., script, macro, or other portable instruction) that can be shipped unchanged to a heterogeneous collection of platforms and execute with identical semantics [JANS08].

Mobile code is transmitted from a remote system to a local system and then executed on the local system without the user's explicit instruction. Mobile code often acts as a mechanism for a virus, worm, or Trojan horse to be transmitted to the user's workstation. In other cases, mobile code takes advantage of vulnerabilities to perform its own exploits, such as unauthorized data access or root compromise. Popular vehicles for mobile code include Java applets, ActiveX, JavaScript, and VBScript. The most common ways of using mobile code for malicious operations on local system are cross-site scripting, interactive and dynamic Web sites, e-mail attachments, and downloads from untrusted sites or of untrusted software.

Client-Side Vulnerabilities and Drive-by-Downloads

Another approach to exploiting software vulnerabilities involves the exploit of bugs in user applications to install malware. One common approach to this exploits browser vulnerabilities so that when the user views a Web page controlled by the attacker, it contains code that exploits the browser bug to download and install malware on the system without the user's knowledge or consent. This is known as a **drive-by-download** and is a common exploit in recent attack kits. In most cases this malware does not actively propagate as a worm does, but rather waits for unsuspecting users to visit the malicious Web page in order to spread to their systems.

Related variants can exploit bugs in common e-mail clients, such as the Klez mass-mailing worm seen in October 2001, which targeted a bug in the HTML handling in Microsoft's Outlook and Outlook Express programs to automatically run itself. Or, such malware may target common PDF viewers to also download and install malware without the user's consent, when they view a malicious PDF document [STEV11]. Such documents may be spread by spam e-mail or be part of a targeted phishing attack, as we discuss next.

10.4 PROPAGATION—SOCIAL ENGINEERING—SPAM E-MAIL, TROJANS

The final category of malware propagation we consider involves social engineering, "tricking" users to assist in the compromise of their own systems or personal information. This can occur when a user views and responds to some SPAM e-mail or permits the installation and execution of some Trojan horse program or scripting code.

Spam (Unsolicited Bulk) E-Mail

Unsolicited bulk e-mail, commonly known as spam, imposes significant costs on both the network infrastructure needed to relay this traffic and on users who need to filter their legitimate e-mails out of this flood. In response to the explosive growth in spam, there has been the equally rapid growth of the antispam industry, which provides products to detect and filter spam e-mails. This has led to an arms race between the spammers devising techniques to sneak their content through and the defenders taking efforts to block them [KREI09].

While some spam is sent from legitimate mail servers, most recent spam is sent by botnets using compromised user systems, as we discuss in Section 10.6. A significant portion of spam e-mail content is just advertising, trying to convince the recipient to purchase some product online, or used in scams, such as stock scams or money mule job ads. But spam is also a significant carrier of malware. The e-mail may have an attached document, which, if opened, may exploit a software vulnerability to install malware on the user's system, as we discussed in the previous section. Or, it may have an attached Trojan horse program or scripting code that, if run, also installs malware on the user's system. Some trojans avoid the need for user agreement by exploiting a software vulnerability in order to install themselves, as we discuss next. Finally the spam may be used in a phishing attack, typically directing the user either to a fake Web site that mirrors some legitimate service, such as an online banking site, where it attempts to capture the user's login and password details, or to complete some form with sufficient personal details to allow the attacker to impersonate the user in an identity theft. All of these uses make spam e-mails a significant security concern. However, in many cases it requires the user's active choice to view the e-mail and any attached document or to permit the installation of some program, in order for the compromise to occur.

Trojan Horses

A Trojan horse is a useful, or apparently useful, program or utility containing hidden code that, when invoked, performs some unwanted or harmful function.

Trojan horse programs can be used to accomplish functions indirectly that the attacker could not accomplish directly. For example, to gain access to sensitive, personal information stored in the files of a user, an attacker could create a Trojan horse program that, when executed, scans the user's files for the desired sensitive information and sends a copy of it to the attacker via a Web form or e-mail or text message. The author could then entice users to run the program by incorporating it into a game or useful utility program and making it available via a known software distribution site or app store. This approach has been used recently with utilities that "claim" to be the latest antivirus scanner, or security update, for systems, but which are actually malicious trojans, often carrying payloads such as spyware that searches for banking credentials. Hence, users need to take precautions to validate the source of any software they install.

Trojan horses fit into one of three models:

* Continuing to perform the function of the original program and additionally performing a separate malicious activity

- Continuing to perform the function of the original program but modifying the function to perform malicious activity (e.g., a Trojan horse version of a login program that collects passwords) or to disguise other malicious activity (e.g., a Trojan horse version of a process-listing program that does not display certain processes that are malicious)

- Performing a malicious function that completely replaces the function of the original program

Some trojans avoid the requirement for user assistance by exploiting some software vulnerability to enable their automatic installation and execution. In this they share some features of a worm, but unlike it, they do not replicate. A prominent example of such an attack was the Hydraq Trojan used in Operation Aurora in 2009 and early 2010. This exploited a vulnerability in Internet Explorer to install itself and targeted several high-profile companies [SYMA11]. It was typically distributed either by spam e-mail or via a compromised Web site using a "drive-by-download."

10.5 PAYLOAD—SYSTEM CORRUPTION

Once malware is active on the target system, the next concern is what actions it will take on this system, that is, what payload does it carry. Some malware has a nonexistent or nonfunctional payload. Its only purpose, either deliberate or due to accidental early release, is to spread. More commonly, it carries one or more payloads that perform covert actions for the attacker.

An early payload seen in a number of viruses and worms resulted in data destruction on the infected system when certain trigger conditions were met [WEAV03]. A related payload is one that displays unwanted messages or content on the user's system when triggered. More seriously, another variant attempts to inflict real-world damage on the system. All of these actions target the integrity of the computer system's software or hardware, or of the user's data. These changes may not occur immediately, but only when specific trigger conditions are met that satisfy their logic-bomb code.

As an alternative to just destroying data, some malware encrypts the user's data and demands payment in order to access the key needed to recover this information. This is sometimes known as **ransomware**. The PC Cyborg Trojan seen in 1989 was an early example of this. However, around mid-2006 a number of worms and trojans, such as the Gpcode Trojan, that used public-key cryptography with increasingly larger key sizes to encrypt data. The user needed to pay a ransom or to make a purchase from certain sites, in order to receive the key to decrypt this data. While earlier instances used weaker cryptography that could be cracked without paying the ransom, the later versions using public-key cryptography with large key sizes could not be broken this way.

Real-World Damage

A further variant of system corruption payloads aims to cause damage to physical equipment. The infected system is clearly the device most easily targeted. The Chernobyl virus not only corrupts data, it attempts to rewrite the BIOS code used to initially boot the computer. If it is successful, the boot process fails, and the system is unusable until the BIOS chip is either reprogrammed or replaced.

The Stuxnet worm targets some specific industrial control system software as its key payload [CHEN11]. If control systems using certain Siemens industrial control software with a specific configuration of devices are infected, then the worm replaces the original control code with code that deliberately drives the controlled equipment outside its normal operating range, resulting in the failure of the attached equipment. The centrifuges used in the Iranian uranium enrichment program were strongly suspected as the target, with reports of much higher than normal failure rates observed in them over the period when this worm was active. As noted in our earlier discussion, this has raised concerns over the use of sophisticated targeted malware for industrial sabotage.

Logic Bomb

A key component of data-corrupting malware is the logic bomb. The logic bomb is code embedded in the malware that is set to "explode" when certain conditions are met. Examples of conditions that can be used as triggers for a logic bomb are the presence or absence of certain files or devices on the system, a particular day of the week or date, a particular version or configuration of some software, or a particular user running the application. Once triggered, a bomb may alter or delete data or entire files, cause a machine halt, or do some other damage. All of the examples we describe in this section include such code.

10.6 PAYLOAD—ATTACK AGENT—ZOMBIE, BOTS

The next category of payload we discuss is where the malware subverts the computational and network resources of the infected system for use by the attacker. Such a system is known as a bot (robot), zombie, or drone, and secretly takes over another Internet-attached computer and then uses that computer to launch or manage attacks that are difficult to trace to the bot's creator. The bot is typically planted on hundreds or thousands of computers belonging to unsuspecting third parties. The collection of bots often is capable of acting in a coordinated manner; such a collection is referred to as a **botnet**. This type of payload attacks the integrity and availability of the infected system.

Uses of Bots

[HONE05] lists the following uses of bots:

- **Distributed denial-of-service (DDoS) attacks:** A DDoS attack is an attack on a computer system or network that causes a loss of service to users. We examine DDoS attacks in Section 10.10.

- **Spamming:** With the help of a botnet and thousands of bots, an attacker is able to send massive amounts of bulk e-mail (spam).

- **Sniffing traffic:** Bots can also use a packet sniffer to watch for interesting cleartext data passing by a compromised machine. The sniffers are mostly used to retrieve sensitive information like usernames and passwords.

- **Keylogging:** If the compromised machine uses encrypted communication channels (e.g., HTTPS or POP3S), then just sniffing the network packets on the victim's computer is useless because the appropriate key to decrypt the packets is missing. But by using a keylogger, which captures keystrokes on the infected machine, an attacker can retrieve sensitive information.

- **Spreading new malware:** Botnets are used to spread new bots. This is very easy since all bots implement mechanisms to download and execute a file via HTTP or FTP. A botnet with 10,000 hosts that acts as the start base for a worm or mail virus allows very fast spreading and thus causes more harm.

- **Installing advertisement add-ons and browser helper objects (BHOs):** Botnets can also be used to gain financial advantages. This works by setting up a fake Web site with some advertisements: The operator of this Web site negotiates a deal with some hosting companies that pay for clicks on ads. With the help of a botnet, these clicks can be "automated" so that instantly a few thousand bots click on the pop-ups. This process can be further enhanced if the bot hijacks the start-page of a compromised machine so that the "clicks" are executed each time the victim uses the browser.

- **Attacking IRC chat networks:** Botnets are also used for attacks against Internet Relay Chat (IRC) networks. Popular among attackers is the so-called clone attack: In this kind of attack, the controller orders each bot to connect a large number of clones to the victim IRC network. The victim is flooded by service requests from thousands of bots or thousands of channel-joins by these cloned bots. In this way, the victim IRC network is brought down, similar to a DDoS attack.

- **Manipulating online polls/games:** Online polls/games are getting more and more attention and it is rather easy to manipulate them with botnets. Since every bot has a distinct IP address, every vote will have the same credibility as a vote cast by a real person. Online games can be manipulated in a similar way.

Remote Control Facility

The remote control facility is what distinguishes a bot from a worm. A worm propagates itself and activates itself, whereas a bot is controlled from some central facility, at least initially.

A typical means of implementing the remote control facility is on an IRC server. All bots join a specific channel on this server and treat incoming messages as commands. More recent botnets tend to avoid IRC mechanisms and use covert communication channels via protocols such as HTTP. Distributed control mechanisms, using peer-to-peer protocols, are also used, to avoid a single point of failure.

Once a communications path is established between a control module and the bots, the control module can activate the bots. In its simplest form, the control module simply issues command to the bot that causes the bot to execute routines that are already implemented in the bot. For greater flexibility, the control module can issue update commands that instruct the bots to download a file from some Internet location and execute it. The bot in this latter case becomes a more general-purpose tool that can be used for multiple attacks.

10.7 PAYLOAD—INFORMATION THEFT—KEYLOGGERS, PHISHING, SPYWARE

We now consider payloads where the malware gathers data stored on the infected system for use by the attacker. A common target is the user's login and password credentials to banking, gaming, and related sites, which the attacker then uses to impersonate the user to access these sites for gain. Less commonly, the payload may target documents or system configuration details for the purpose of reconnaissance or espionage. These attacks target the confidentiality of this information.

Credential Theft, Keyloggers, and Spyware

Typically, users send their login and password credentials to banking, gaming, and related sites over encrypted communication channels (e.g., HTTPS or POP3S), which protect them from capture by monitoring network packets. To bypass this, an attacker can install a **keylogger**, which captures keystrokes on the infected machine to allow an attacker to monitor this sensitive information. Since this would result in the attacker receiving a copy of all text entered on the compromised machine, keyloggers typically implement some form of filtering mechanism that only returns information close to desired keywords (e.g., "login" or "password" or "paypal.com").

In response to the use of keyloggers, some banking and other sites switched to using a graphical applet to enter critical information, such as passwords. Since these do not use text entered via the keyboard, traditional keyloggers do not capture this information. In response, attackers developed more general **spyware** payloads, which subvert the compromised machine to allow monitoring of a wide range of activity on the system. This may include monitoring the history and content of browsing activity, redirecting certain Web page requests to fake sites controlled by the attacker, dynamically modifying data exchanged between the browser and certain Web sites of interest. All of which can result in significant compromise of the user's personal information.

Phishing and Identity Theft

Another approach used to capture a user's login and password credentials is to include a URL in a spam e-mail that links to a fake Web site controlled by the attacker, but which mimics the login page of some banking, gaming, or similar site. This is normally included in some message suggesting that urgent action is required by the user to authenticate his or her account, to prevent it being locked. If the user is careless, and doesn't realize that he or she is being conned, then following the link and supplying the requested details will certainly result in the attackers exploiting the user's account using the captured credentials.

More generally, such a spam e-mail may direct a user to a fake Web site controlled by the attacker or to complete some enclosed form and return to an e-mail accessible to the attacker, which is used to gather a range of private, personal, information on the user. Given sufficient details, the attacker can then "assume" the user's identity for the purpose of obtaining credit or sensitive access to other resources. This is known as a **phishing** attack, which exploits social engineering to leverage user's trust by masquerading as communications from a trusted source [GOLD10].

Such general spam e-mails are typically widely distributed to very large numbers of users, often via a botnet. While the content will not match appropriate trusted sources for a significant fraction of the recipients, the attackers rely on it reaching sufficient users of the named trusted source, a gullible portion of whom will respond, for it to be profitable.

A more dangerous variant of this is the **spear-phishing** attack. This again is an e-mail claiming to be from a trusted source. However, the recipients are carefully researched by the attacker, and each e-mail is carefully crafted to suit its recipient specifically, often quoting a range of information to convince him or her of its authenticity. This greatly increases the likelihood of the recipient responding as desired by the attacker.

Reconnaissance and Espionage

Credential theft and identity theft are special cases of a more general reconnaissance payload, which aims to obtain certain types of desired information and return this to the attacker. These special cases are certainly the most common; however other targets are known. Operation Aurora in 2009 used a Trojan to gain access to and potentially modify source code repositories at a range of high-tech, security, and defense contractor companies [SYMA11]. The Stuxnet worm discovered in 2010 included capture of hardware and software configuration details in order to determine whether it had compromised the specific desired target systems. Early versions of this worm returned this same information, which was then used to develop the attacks deployed in later versions [CHEN11].

10.8 PAYLOAD—STEALTHING—BACKDOORS, ROOTKITS

The final category of payload we discuss concerns techniques used by malware to hide its presence on the infected system and to provide covert access to that system. This type of payload also attacks the integrity of the infected system.

Backdoor

A **backdoor**, also known as a **trapdoor**, is a secret entry point into a program that allows someone who is aware of the backdoor to gain access without going through the usual security access procedures. The backdoor is code that recognizes some special sequence of input or is triggered by being run from a certain user ID or by an unlikely sequence of events.

A backdoor is usually implemented as a network service listening on some nonstandard port that the attacker can connect to and issue commands through to be run on the compromised system.

It is difficult to implement operating system controls for backdoors in applications. Security measures must focus on the program development and software update activities, and on programs that wish to offer a network service.

Rootkit

A rootkit is a set of programs installed on a system to maintain covert access to that system with administrator (or root)[3] privileges, while hiding evidence of its presence to the greatest extent possible. This provides access to all the functions and services of the operating system. The rootkit alters the host's standard functionality in a malicious and stealthy way. With root access, an attacker has complete control of the system and can add or change programs and files, monitor processes, send and receive network traffic, and get backdoor access on demand.

A rootkit can make many changes to a system to hide its existence, making it difficult for the user to determine that the rootkit is present and to identify what changes have been made. In essence, a rootkit hides by subverting the mechanisms that monitor and report on the processes, files, and registries on a computer.

A rootkit can be classified using the following characteristics:

- **Persistent:** Activates each time the system boots. The rootkit must store code in a persistent store, such as the registry or file system, and configure a method by which the code executes without user intervention. This means it is easier to detect, as the copy in persistent storage can potentially be scanned.

- **Memory based:** Has no persistent code and therefore cannot survive a reboot. However, because it is only in memory, it can be harder to detect.

- **User mode:** Intercepts calls to APIs (application program interfaces) and modifies returned results. For example, when an application performs a directory listing, the return results don't include entries identifying the files associated with the rootkit.

- **Kernel mode:** Can intercept calls to native APIs in kernel mode.[4] The rootkit can also hide the presence of a malware process by removing it from the kernel's list of active processes.

- **Virtual machine based:** This type of rootkit installs a lightweight virtual machine monitor and then runs the operating system in a virtual machine above it. The rootkit can then transparently intercept and modify states and events occurring in the virtualized system.

- **External mode:** The malware is located outside the normal operation mode of the targeted system, in BIOS or system management mode, where it can directly access hardware.

This classification shows a continuing arms race between rootkit authors, who exploit ever more stealthy mechanisms to hide their code, and those who develop mechanisms to harden systems against such subversion or to detect when it has occurred.

---

[3]On UNIX systems, the administrator, or *superuser*, account is called root; hence the term *root access*.
[4]The kernel is the portion of the OS that includes the most heavily used and most critical portions of software. Kernel mode is a privileged mode of execution reserved for the kernel. Typically, kernel mode allows access to regions of main memory that are unavailable to processes executing in a less privileged mode and also enables execution of certain machine instructions that are restricted to the kernel mode.

10.9 COUNTERMEASURES

Malware Countermeasure Approaches

[SOUP12a] lists four main elements of prevention: policy, awareness, vulnerability mitigation, and threat mitigation. Having a suitable policy to address malware prevention provides a basis for implementing appropriate preventative countermeasures.

One of the first countermeasures that should be employed is to ensure all systems are as current as possible, with all patches applied, in order to reduce the number of vulnerabilities that might be exploited on the system. The next is to set appropriate access controls on the applications and data stored on the system, to reduce the number of files that any user can access, and hence potentially infect or corrupt, as a result of them executing some malware code. These measures directly target the key propagation mechanisms used by worms, viruses, and some trojans.

The third common propagation mechanism, which targets users in a social engineering attack, can be countered using appropriate user awareness and training. This aims to equip users to be more aware of these attacks, and less likely to take actions that result in their compromise. [SOUP12a] provides examples of suitable awareness issues.

If prevention fails, then technical mechanisms can be used to support the following threat mitigation options:

- **Detection:** Once the infection has occurred, determine that it has occurred and locate the malware.
- **Identification:** Once detection has been achieved, identify the specific malware that has infected the system.
- **Removal:** Once the specific malware has been identified, remove all traces of malware virus from all infected systems so that it cannot spread further.

If detection succeeds but either identification or removal is not possible, then the alternative is to discard any infected or malicious files and reload a clean backup version. In the case of some particularly nasty infections, this may require a complete wipe of all storage, and rebuild of the infected system from known clean media.

To begin, let us consider some requirements for effective malware countermeasures:

- **Generality:** The approach taken should be able to handle a wide variety of attacks.
- **Timeliness:** The approach should respond quickly so as to limit the number of infected programs or systems and the consequent activity.
- **Resiliency:** The approach should be resistant to evasion techniques employed by attackers to hide the presence of their malware.
- **Minimal denial-of-service costs:** The approach should result in minimal reduction in capacity or service due to the actions of the countermeasure software, and should not significantly disrupt normal operation.

- **Transparency:** The countermeasure software and devices should not require modification to existing (legacy) OSs, application software, and hardware.
- **Global and local coverage:** The approach should be able to deal with attack sources both from outside and inside the enterprise network.

Achieving all these requirements often requires the use of multiple approaches. Detection of the presence of malware can occur in a number of locations. It may occur on the infected system, where some host-based "antivirus" program is running, monitoring data imported into the system, and the execution and behavior of programs running on the system. Or, it may take place as part of the perimeter security mechanisms used in an organization's firewall and intrusion detection systems (IDSs). Lastly, detection may use distributed mechanisms that gather data from both host-based and perimeter sensors, potentially over a large number of networks and organizations, in order to obtain the largest scale view of the movement of malware.

Host-Based Scanners

The first location where antivirus software is used is on each end system. This gives the software the maximum access to information not only on the behavior of the malware as it interacts with the targeted system but also on the smallest overall view of malware activity. The use of antivirus software on personal computers is now widespread, in part caused by the explosive growth in malware volume and activity. Advances in virus and other malware technology, and in antivirus technology and other countermeasures, go hand in hand. Early malware used relatively simple and easily detected code, and hence could be identified and purged with relatively simple antivirus software packages. As the malware arms race has evolved, both the malware code and, necessarily, antivirus software have grown more complex and sophisticated.

[STEP93] identifies four generations of antivirus software:

- **First generation:** Simple scanners
- **Second generation:** Heuristic scanners
- **Third generation:** Activity traps
- **Fourth generation:** Full-featured protection

A **first-generation** scanner requires a malware signature to identify the malware. The signature may contain "wildcards" but matches essentially the same structure and bit pattern in all copies of the malware. Such signature-specific scanners are limited to the detection of known malware. Another type of first-generation scanner maintains a record of the length of programs and looks for changes in length as a result of virus infection.

A **second-generation** scanner does not rely on a specific signature. Rather, the scanner uses heuristic rules to search for probable malware instances. One class of such scanners looks for fragments of code that are often associated with malware. For example, a scanner may look for the beginning of an encryption loop used in a polymorphic virus and discover the encryption key. Once the key is discovered, the scanner can decrypt the malware to identify it, and then remove the infection and return the program to service.

Another second-generation approach is integrity checking. A checksum can be appended to each program. If malware alters or replaces some program without changing the checksum, then an integrity check will catch this change. To counter malware that is sophisticated enough to change the checksum when it alters a program, an encrypted hash function can be used. The encryption key is stored separately from the program so that the malware cannot generate a new hash code and encrypt that. By using a hash function rather than a simpler checksum, the malware is prevented from adjusting the program to produce the same hash code as before. If a protected list of programs in trusted locations is kept, this approach can also detect attempts to replace or install rogue code or programs in these locations.

Third-generation programs are memory-resident programs that identify malware by its actions rather than its structure in an infected program. Such programs the advantage that it is not necessary to develop signatures and heuristics for a wide array of malware. Rather, it is necessary only to identify the small set of actions that indicate that malicious activity is being attempted and then to intervene.

Fourth-generation products are packages consisting of a variety of antivirus techniques used in conjunction. These include scanning and activity trap components. In addition, such a package includes access control capability, which limits the ability of malware to penetrate a system and then limits the ability of a malware to update files in order to propagate.

The arms race continues. With fourth-generation packages, a more comprehensive defense strategy is employed, broadening the scope of defense to more general-purpose computer security measures. These include more sophisticated antivirus approaches. We now highlight two of the most important.

HOST-BASED BEHAVIOR-BLOCKING SOFTWARE   Unlike heuristics or fingerprint-based scanners, **behavior-blocking software** integrates with the operating system of a host computer and monitors program behavior in real time for malicious actions [CONR02, NACH02]. The behavior blocking software then blocks potentially malicious actions before they have a chance to affect the system. Monitored behaviors can include the following:

- Attempts to open, view, delete, and/or modify files
- Attempts to format disk drives and other unrecoverable disk operations
- Modifications to the logic of executable files or macros
- Modification of critical system settings, such as start-up settings
- Scripting of e-mail and instant messaging clients to send executable content
- Initiation of network communications

Because a behavior blocker can block suspicious software in real time, it has an advantage over such established antivirus detection techniques as fingerprinting or heuristics. There are literally trillions of different ways to obfuscate and rearrange the instructions of a virus or worm, many of which will evade detection by a fingerprint scanner or heuristic. But eventually, malicious code must make a well-defined request to the operating system. Given that the behavior blocker can intercept all such requests, it can identify and block malicious actions regardless of how obfuscated the program logic appears to be.

Behavior blocking alone has limitations. Because the malicious code must run on the target machine before all its behaviors can be identified, it can cause harm before it has been detected and blocked. For example, a new item of malware might shuffle a number of seemingly unimportant files around the hard drive before modifying a single file and being blocked. Even though the actual modification was blocked, the user may be unable to locate his or her files, causing a loss to productivity or possibly having worse consequences.

SPYWARE DETECTION AND REMOVAL Although general antivirus products include signatures to detect spyware, the threat this type of malware poses, and its use of stealthing techniques, means that a range of spyware specific detection and removal utilities exist. These specialize in the detection and removal of spyware, and provide more robust capabilities. Thus they complement, and should be used along with, more general antivirus products.

ROOTKIT COUNTERMEASURES Rootkits can be extraordinarily difficult to detect and neutralize, particularly so for kernel-level rootkits. Many of the administrative tools that could be used to detect a rootkit or its traces can be compromised by the rootkit precisely so that it is undetectable.

Countering rootkits requires a variety of network- and computer-level security tools. Both network- and host-based IDSs can look for the code signatures of known rootkit attacks in incoming traffic. Host-based antivirus software can also be used to recognize the known signatures.

Of course, there are always new rootkits and modified versions of existing rootkits that display novel signatures. For these cases, a system needs to look for behaviors that could indicate the presence of a rootkit, such as the interception of system calls or a keylogger interacting with a keyboard driver. Such behavior detection is far from straightforward. For example, antivirus software typically intercepts system calls.

Another approach is to do some sort of file integrity check. An example of this is RootkitRevealer, a freeware package from SysInternals. The package compares the results of a system scan using APIs with the actual view of storage using instructions that do not go through an API. Because a rootkit conceals itself by modifying the view of storage seen by administrator calls, RootkitRevealer catches the discrepancy.

If a kernel-level rootkit is detected, the only secure and reliable way to recover is to do an entire new OS install on the infected machine.

Perimeter Scanning Approaches

The next location where antivirus software is used is on an organization's firewall and IDS. It is typically included in e-mail and Web proxy services running on these systems. It may also be included in the traffic analysis component of an IDS. This gives the antivirus software access to malware in transit over a network connection to any of the organization's systems, providing a larger-scale view of malware activity. This software may also include intrusion prevention measures, blocking the flow of any suspicious traffic, thus preventing it reaching and compromising some target system, either inside or outside the organization.

However, this approach is limited to scanning the malware content, as it does not have access to any behavior observed when it runs on an infected system. Two types of monitoring software may be used:

- **Ingress monitors:** These are located at the border between the enterprise network and the Internet. They can be part of the ingress-filtering software of a border router or external firewall or a separate passive monitor. A honeypot can also capture incoming malware traffic. An example of a detection technique for an ingress monitor is to look for incoming traffic to unused local IP addresses.

- **Egress monitors:** These can be located at the egress point of individual LANs on the enterprise network as well as at the border between the enterprise network and the Internet. In the former case, the egress monitor can be part of the egress-filtering software of a LAN router or switch. As with ingress monitors, the external firewall or a honeypot can house the monitoring software. Indeed, the two types of monitors can be collocated. The egress monitor is designed to catch the source of a malware attack by monitoring outgoing traffic for signs of scanning or other suspicious behavior.

Perimeter monitoring can also assist in detecting and responding to botnet activity by detecting abnormal traffic patterns associated with this activity. Once bots are activated and an attack is underway, such monitoring can be used to detect the attack. However, the primary objective is to try to detect and disable the botnet during its construction phase, using the various scanning techniques we have just discussed, identifying and blocking the malware that is used to propagate this type of payload.

PERIMETER WORM COUNTERMEASURES There is considerable overlap in techniques for dealing with viruses and worms. Once a worm is resident on a machine, antivirus software can be used to detect it, and possibly remove it. In addition, because worm propagation generates considerable network activity, perimeter network activity and usage monitoring can form the basis of a worm defense. Following [JHI07], we list six classes of worm defense that address the network activity it may generate:

A. **Signature-based worm scan filtering:** This type of approach generates a worm signature, which is then used to prevent worm scans from entering/leaving a network/host. Typically, this approach involves identifying suspicious flows and generating a worm signature. This approach is vulnerable to the use of polymorphic worms: Either the detection software misses the worm or, if it is sufficiently sophisticated to deal with polymorphic worms, the scheme may take a long time to react. [NEWS05] is an example of this approach.

B. **Filter-based worm containment:** This approach is similar to class A but focuses on worm content rather than a scan signature. The filter checks a message to determine if it contains worm code. An example is Vigilante [COST05], which relies on collaborative worm detection at end hosts. This approach can be quite effective but requires efficient detection algorithms and rapid alert dissemination.

C. **Payload-classification-based worm containment:** These network-based techniques examine packets to see if they contain a worm. Various anomaly detection techniques can be used, but care is needed to avoid high levels of false positives or negatives. An example of this approach, which looks for exploit code in network flows, is reported in [CHIN05]. This approach does not generate signatures based on byte patterns but rather looks for control and data flow structures that suggest an exploit.

D. **Threshold random walk (TRW) scan detection:** TRW exploits randomness in picking destinations to connect to as a way of detecting if a scanner is in operation [JUNG04]. TRW is suitable for deployment in high-speed, low-cost network devices. It is effective against the common behavior seen in worm scans.

E. **Rate limiting:** This class limits the rate of scanlike traffic from an infected host. Various strategies can be used, including limiting the number of new machines a host can connect to in a window of time, detecting a high connection failure rate, and limiting the number of unique IP addresses a host can scan in a window of time. [CHEN04] is an example. This class of countermeasures may introduce longer delays for normal traffic. This class is also not suited for slow, stealthy worms that spread slowly to avoid detection based on activity level.

F. **Rate halting:** This approach immediately blocks outgoing traffic when a threshold is exceeded either in outgoing connection rate or in diversity of connection attempts [JHI07]. The approach must include measures to quickly unblock mistakenly blocked hosts in a transparent way. Rate halting can integrate with a signature- or filter-based approach so that once a signature or filter is generated, every blocked host can be unblocked. Rate halting appears to offer a very effective countermeasure. As with rate limiting, rate-halting techniques are not suitable for slow, stealthy worms.

Distributed Intelligence Gathering Approaches

The final location where antivirus software is used is in a distributed configuration. It gathers data from a large number of both host-based and perimeter sensors, relays this intelligence to a central analysis system able to correlate and analyze the data, which can then return updated signatures and behavior patterns to enable all of the coordinated systems to respond and defend against malware attacks. A number of such systems have been proposed. We discuss one such approach in the remainder of this section.

Figure 10.4 shows an example of a distributed worm countermeasure architecture (based on [SIDI05]). The system works as follows (numbers in figure refer to numbers in the following list):

1. Sensors deployed at various network locations detect a potential worm. The sensor logic can also be incorporated in IDS sensors.

2. The sensors send alerts to a central server, which correlates and analyzes the incoming alerts. The correlation server determines the likelihood that a worm attack is being observed and the key characteristics of the attack.

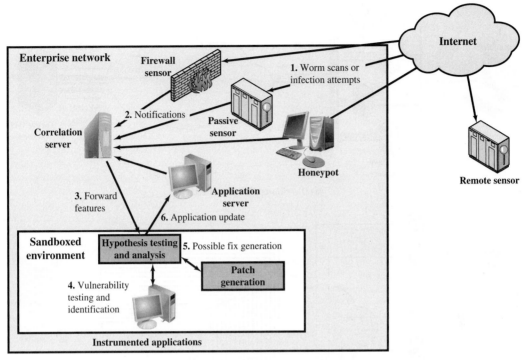

Figure 10.4   Placement of Worm Monitors

3. The server forwards its information to a protected environment, where the potential worm may be sandboxed for analysis and testing.

4. The protected system tests the suspicious software against an appropriately instrumented version of the targeted application to identify the vulnerability.

5. The protected system generates one or more software patches and tests these.

6. If the patch is not susceptible to the infection and does not compromise the application's functionality, the system sends the patch to the application host to update the targeted application.

10.10 DISTRIBUTED DENIAL OF SERVICE ATTACKS

A denial-of-service (DoS) attack is an attempt to prevent legitimate users of a service from using that service. When this attack comes from a single host or network node, then it is simply referred to as a DoS attack. A more serious threat is posed by a DDoS attack. DDoS attacks make computer systems inaccessible by flooding servers, networks, or even end-user systems with useless traffic so that legitimate users can no longer gain access to those resources. In a typical DDoS attack, a large number of compromised hosts are amassed to send useless packets.

This section is concerned with DDoS attacks. First, we look at the nature and types of attacks. Next, we examine methods by which an attacker is able to recruit a network of hosts for attack launch. Finally, this section looks at countermeasures.

(a) Distributed SYN flood attack

(b) Distributed ICMP attack

Figure 10.5   Examples of Simple DDoS Attacks

DDoS Attack Description

A DDoS attack attempts to consume the target's resources so that it cannot provide service. One way to classify DDoS attacks is in terms of the type of resource that is consumed. Broadly speaking, the resource consumed is either an internal host resource on the target system or data transmission capacity in the local network to which the target is attacked.

A simple example of an **internal resource attack** is the SYN flood attack. Figure 10.5a shows the steps involved:

1. The attacker takes control of multiple hosts over the Internet, instructing them to contact the target Web server.

2. The slave hosts begin sending TCP/IP SYN (synchronize/initialization) packets, with erroneous return IP address information, to the target.

3. Each SYN packet is a request to open a TCP connection. For each such packet, the Web server responds with a SYN/ACK (synchronize/acknowledge) packet, trying to establish a TCP connection with a TCP entity at a

spurious IP address. The Web server maintains a data structure for each SYN request waiting for a response back and becomes bogged down as more traffic floods in. The result is that legitimate connections are denied while the victim machine is waiting to complete bogus "half-open" connections.

The TCP state data structure is a popular internal resource target but by no means the only one. [CERT01] gives the following examples:

1. An intruder may attempt to use up available data structures that are used by the OS to manage processes, such as process table entries and process control information entries. The attack can be quite simple, such as a program that forks new processes repeatedly.

2. An intruder may attempt to allocate to itself large amounts of disk space by a variety of straightforward means. These include generating numerous emails, forcing errors that trigger audit trails, and placing files in shareable areas.

Figure 10.5b illustrates an example of an **attack that consumes data transmission resources**. The following steps are involved:

1. The attacker takes control of multiple hosts over the Internet, instructing them to send ICMP ECHO packets[5] with the target's spoofed IP address to a group of hosts that act as reflectors, as described subsequently.

2. Nodes at the bounce site receive multiple spoofed requests and respond by sending echo reply packets to the target site.

3. The target's router is flooded with packets from the bounce site, leaving no data transmission capacity for legitimate traffic.

Another way to classify DDoS attacks is as either direct or reflector DDoS attacks. In a **direct DDoS attack** (Figure 10.6a), the attacker is able to implant zombie software on a number of sites distributed throughout the Internet. Often, the DDoS attack involves two levels of zombie machines: master zombies and slave zombies. The hosts of both machines have been infected with malicious code. The attacker coordinates and triggers the master zombies, which in turn coordinate and trigger the slave zombies. The use of two levels of zombies makes it more difficult to trace the attack back to its source and provides for a more resilient network of attackers.

A **reflector DDoS attack** adds another layer of machines (Figure 10.6b). In this type of attack, the slave zombies construct packets requiring a response that contain the target's IP address as the source IP address in the packet's IP header. These packets are sent to uninfected machines known as reflectors. The uninfected machines respond with packets directed at the target machine. A reflector DDoS attack can easily involve more machines and more traffic than a direct DDoS attack and hence be more damaging. Further, tracing back the attack or filtering out the attack packets is more difficult because the attack comes from widely dispersed uninfected machines.

---

[5]The Internet Control Message Protocol (ICMP) is an IP-level protocol for the exchange of control packets between a router and a host or between hosts. The ECHO packet requires the recipient to respond with an echo reply to check that communication is possible between entities.

Figure 10.6   Types of Flooding-Based DDoS Attacks

Constructing the Attack Network

The first step in a DDoS attack is for the attacker to infect a number of machines with zombie software that will ultimately be used to carry out the attack. The essential ingredients in this phase of the attack are the following:

1. Software that can carry out the DDoS attack. The software must be able to run on a large number of machines, must be able to conceal its existence,

must be able to communicate with the attacker or have some sort of time-triggered mechanism, and must be able to launch the intended attack toward the target.

2. A vulnerability in a large number of systems. The attacker must become aware of a vulnerability that many system administrators and individual users have failed to patch and that enables the attacker to install the zombie software.

3. A strategy for locating vulnerable machines, a process known as scanning.

In the scanning process, the attacker first seeks out a number of vulnerable machines and infects them. Then, typically, the zombie software that is installed in the infected machines repeats the same scanning process, until a large distributed network of infected machines is created. [MIRK04] lists the following types of scanning strategies:

- **Random:** Each compromised host probes random addresses in the IP address space, using a different seed. This technique produces a high volume of Internet traffic, which may cause generalized disruption even before the actual attack is launched.

- **Hit list:** The attacker first compiles a long list of potential vulnerable machines. This can be a slow process done over a long period to avoid detection that an attack is underway. Once the list is compiled, the attacker begins infecting machines on the list. Each infected machine is provided with a portion of the list to scan. This strategy results in a very short scanning period, which may make it difficult to detect that infection is taking place.

- **Topological:** This method uses information contained on an infected victim machine to find more hosts to scan.

- **Local subnet:** If a host is infected behind a firewall, that host then looks for targets in its own local network. The host uses the subnet address structure to find other hosts that would otherwise be protected by the firewall.

DDoS Countermeasures

In general, there are three lines of defense against DDoS attacks [CHAN02]:

- **Attack prevention and preemption (before the attack):** These mechanisms enable the victim to endure attack attempts without denying service to legitimate clients. Techniques include enforcing policies for resource consumption and providing backup resources available on demand. In addition, prevention mechanisms modify systems and protocols on the Internet to reduce the possibility of DDoS attacks.

- **Attack detection and filtering (during the attack):** These mechanisms attempt to detect the attack as it begins and respond immediately. This minimizes the impact of the attack on the target. Detection involves looking for suspicious patterns of behavior. Response involves filtering out packets likely to be part of the attack.

- **Attack source traceback and identification (during and after the attack):** This is an attempt to identify the source of the attack as a first step in preventing future attacks. However, this method typically does not yield results fast enough, if at all, to mitigate an ongoing attack.

The challenge in coping with DDoS attacks is the sheer number of ways in which they can operate. Thus, DDoS countermeasures must evolve with the threat.

10.11 RECOMMENDED READING

For a thorough understanding of viruses, the book to read is [SZOR05]. Another excellent treatment is [AYCO06]. Good overview articles on viruses and worms are [CASS01], [KEPH97], and [NACH97]. [WEAV03] supplies a comprehensive survey of worm characteristics.

[HOLZ05] and [MCLA04] provide overviews of bots. [LEVI06], [LEVI04], [GEER06], and [EMBL08] describe various types of rootkits and their operation.

[SOUP12a] provides guidance on malware prevention and handling.

AYCO06 Aycock, J. *Computer Viruses and Malware.* New York: Springer, 2006.

CASS01 Cass, S. "Anatomy of Malice." *IEEE Spectrum*, November 2001.

EMBL08 Embleton, S.; Sparks, S.; and Zou, C. "SMM Rootkits: A New Breed of OS-Independent Malware." *Proceedings of the 4th International Conference on Security and Privacy in Communication Networks*, ACM, September 2008.

GEER06 Geer, D. "Hackers Get to the Root of the Problem." *Computer*, May 2006.

HOLZ05 Holz, T. "A Short Visit to the Bot Zoo." *IEEE Security and Privacy*, May–June 2005.

KEPH97 Kephart, J.; Sorkin, G.; Chess, D.; and White, S. "Fighting Computer Viruses." *Scientific American*, November 1997.

LEVI04 Levine, J.; Grizzard, J.; and Owen, H. "A Methodology to Detect and Characterize Kernel Level Rootkit Exploits Involving Redirection of the System Call Table." *Proceedings, Second IEEE International Information Assurance Workshop*, 2004.

LEVI06 Levine, J.; Grizzard, J.; and Owen, H. "Detecting and Categorizing Kernel-Level Rootkits to Aid Future Detection." *IEEE Security and Privacy*, January–February 2006.

MCLA04 McLaughlin, L. "Bot Software Spreads, Causes New Worries." *IEEE Distributed Systems Online*, June 2004.

NACH97 Nachenberg, C. "Computer Virus-Antivirus Coevolution." *Communications of the ACM*, January 1997.

SOUP12a Soup, M., and Scar, K. *Guide to Malware Incident Prevention and Handling for Desktops and Laptops*, NIST Special Publication 800-83 (Draft), July 2012.

SZOR05 Szor, P. *The Art of Computer Virus Research and Defense.* Reading, MA: Addison-Wesley, 2005.

WEAV03 Weaver, N., et al. "A Taxonomy of Computer Worms." *The First ACM Workshop on Rapid Malcode (WORM)*, 2003.

10.12 KEY TERMS, REVIEW QUESTIONS, AND PROBLEMS

Key Terms

adware	e-mail virus	reflector DDoS attack
attack kit	flooders	rootkit
backdoor	keyloggers	scanning
behavior-blocking software	logic bomb	spear-phishing
blended attack	macro virus	spyware
boot sector infector	malicious software	stealth virus
bot	malware	trapdoor
botnet	metamorphic virus	Trojan horse
crimeware	mobile code	virus
direct DDoS attack	parasitic virus	worm
distributed denial of service	phishing	zombie
(DDoS)	polymorphic virus	zero-day exploit
downloader	ransomware	
drive-by-download		

Review Questions

10.1 What are three broad mechanisms that malware can use to propagate?

10.2 What are four broad categories of payloads that malware may carry?

10.3 What are typical phases of operation of a virus or worm?

10.4 What mechanisms can a virus use to conceal itself?

10.5 What is the difference between machine-executable and macro viruses?

10.6 What means can a worm use to access remote systems to propagate?

10.7 What is a "drive-by-download" and how does it differ from a worm?

10.8 What is a "logic bomb"?

10.9 Differentiate among the following: a backdoor, a bot, a keylogger, spyware, and a rootkit? Can they all be present in the same malware?

10.10 List some of the different levels in a system that a rootkit may use.

10.11 Describe some malware countermeasure elements.

10.12 List three places malware mitigation mechanisms may be located.

10.13 Briefly describe the four generations of antivirus software.

10.14 How does behavior-blocking software work?

10.15 What is a distributed denial-of-service system?

Problems

10.1 There is a flaw in the virus program of Figure 10.1a. What is it?

10.2 The question arises as to whether it is possible to develop a program that can analyze a piece of software to determine if it is a virus. Consider that we have a program D that is supposed to be able to do that. That is, for any program P, if we run D(P), the result returned is TRUE (P is a virus) or FALSE (P is not a virus). Now consider the following program:

```
Program CV :=
    { . . .
    main-program :=
        {if D(CV) then goto next:
                else infect-executable;
        }
    next:
    }
```

In the preceding program, infect-executable is a module that scans memory for executable programs and replicates itself in those programs. Determine if D can correctly decide whether CV is a virus.

10.3 The following code fragments show a sequence of virus instructions and a metamorphic version of the virus. Describe the effect produced by the metamorphic code.

Original Code	Metamorphic Code
mov eax, 5	mov eax, 5
add eax, ebx	push ecx
call [eax]	pop ecx
	add eax, ebx
	swap eax, ebx
	swap ebx, eax
	call [eax]
	nop

10.4 The list of passwords used by the Morris worm is provided at this book's Premium Content Web site.
   a. The assumption has been expressed by many people that this list represents words commonly used as passwords. Does this seem likely? Justify your answer.
   b. If the list does not reflect commonly used passwords, suggest some approaches that Morris may have used to construct the list.

10.5 What type of malware is the following code fragment?

```
legitimate code
if data is Friday the 13th;
    crash_computer();
legitimate code
```

10.6 Consider the following fragment in an authentication program and determine what type of malicious software this is.

```
username = read_username();
password = read_password();
if username is "133t h4ck0r"
    return ALLOW_LOGIN;
if username and password are valid
    return ALLOW_LOGIN
else return DENY_LOGIN
```

10.7 Assume you have found a USB memory stick in your work parking area. What threats might this pose to your work computer should you just plug the memory stick in and examine its contents? In particular, consider whether each of the malware propagation mechanisms we discuss could use such a memory stick for transport. What steps could you take to mitigate these threats and safely determine the contents of the memory stick?

10.8   Suppose you observe that your home PC is responding very slowly to information requests from the net. And then you further observe that your network gateway shows high levels of network activity, even though you have closed your e-mail client, Web browser, and other programs that access the net. What types of malware could cause these symptoms? Discuss how the malware might have gained access to your system. What steps can you take to check whether this has occurred? If you do identify malware on your PC, how can you restore it to safe operation?

10.9   Suppose that while trying to access a collection of short videos on some Web site, you see a popup window stating that you need to install this custom codec in order to view the videos. What threat might this pose to your computer system if you approve this installation request?

10.10   Suppose you have a new smartphone and are excited about the range of apps available for it. You read about a really interesting new game that is available for your phone. You do a quick Web search for it and see that a version is available from one of the free marketplaces. When you download and start to install this app, you are asked to approve the access permissions granted to it. You see that it wants permission to "Send SMS messages" and to "Access your address-book." Should you be suspicious that a game wants these types of permissions? What threat might the app pose to your smartphone? Should you grant these permissions and proceed to install it? What types of malware might it be?

10.11   Assume you receive an e-mail that appears to come from a senior manager of your company, with a subject indicating that it concerns a project that you are currently working on. When you view the e-mail, you see that it asks you to review the attached revised press release, supplied as a PDF document, to check that all details are correct before management releases it. When you attempt to open the PDF, the viewer pops up a dialog labeled "Launch File," indicating that "the file and its viewer application are set to be launched by this PDF file." In the section of this dialog labeled "File" there are a number of blank lines and finally the text "Click the 'Open' button to view this document." You also note that there is a vertical scroll-bar visible for this region. What type of threat might this pose to your computer system should you indeed select the "Open" button? How could you check your suspicions without threatening your system? What type of attack is this type of message associated with? How many people are likely to have received this particular e-mail?

10.12   Assume you receive an e-mail that appears to come from your bank, with your bank logo in it and with the following contents:

> "Dear Customer, Our records show that your Internet Banking access has been blocked due to too many login attempts with invalid information such as incorrect access number, password, or security number. We urge you to restore your account access immediately and avoid permanent closure of your account, by clicking on this link to restore your account. Thank you from your customer service team."

What form of attack is this e-mail attempting? What is the most likely mechanism used to distribute this e-mail? How should you respond to such e-mails?

10.13   Suppose you receive a letter from a finance company stating that your loan payments are in arrears and that action is required to correct this. However, as far as you know, you have never applied for, or received, a loan from this company! What may have occurred that led to this loan being created? What type of malware, and on which computer systems, might have provided the necessary information to an attacker that enabled him or her to successfully obtain this loan?

10.14   Suggest some methods of attacking the worm countermeasure architecture, discussed in Section 10.9, that could be used by worm creators. Suggest some possible countermeasures to these methods.

CHAPTER 11

INTRUDERS

11.1 Intruders

Intruder Behavior Patterns
Intrusion Techniques

11.2 Intrusion Detection

Audit Records
Statistical Anomaly Detection
Rule-Based Intrusion Detection
The Base-Rate Fallacy
Distributed Intrusion Detection
Honeypots
Intrusion Detection Exchange Format

11.3 Password Management

The Vulnerability of Passwords
The Use of Hashed Passwords
User Password Choices
Password Selection Strategies
Bloom Filter

11.4 Recommended Reading

11.5 Key Terms, Review Questions, and Problems

"Badges? We ain't got no badges! We don't need no badges! I don't have to show you any stinking badges!!"

— The Treasure of the Sierra Madre, 1948

LEARNING OBJECTIVES

After studying this chapter, you should be able to:

◆ Distinguish among various types of intruder behavior patterns.

◆ Understand the basic principles of and requirements for intrusion detection.

◆ Discuss the key features of intrusion detection systems.

◆ Define the intrusion detection exchange format.

◆ Explain the purpose of honeypots.

◆ Explain the mechanism by which hashed passwords are used for user authentication.

◆ Understand the use of the Bloom filter in password management.

A significant security problem for networked systems is hostile, or at least unwanted, trespass by users or software. User trespass can take the form of unauthorized logon to a machine or, in the case of an authorized user, acquisition of privileges or performance of actions beyond those that have been authorized. Software trespass can take the form of a virus, worm, or Trojan horse.

All these attacks relate to network security because system entry can be achieved by means of a network. However, these attacks are not confined to network-based attacks. A user with access to a local terminal may attempt trespass without using an intermediate network. A virus or Trojan horse may be introduced into a system by means of an optical disc. Only the worm is a uniquely network phenomenon. Thus, system trespass is an area in which the concerns of network security and computer security overlap.

Because the focus of this book is network security, we do not attempt a comprehensive analysis of either the attacks or the security countermeasures related to system trespass. Instead, in this Part we present a broad overview of these concerns.

This chapter covers the subject of intruders. First, we examine the nature of the attack and then look at strategies intended for prevention and, failing that, detection. Next we examine the related topic of password management.

11.1 INTRUDERS

One of the two most publicized threats to security is the intruder (the other is viruses), often referred to as a hacker or cracker. In an important early study of intrusion, Anderson [ANDE80] identified three classes of intruders:

- **Masquerader:** An individual who is not authorized to use the computer and who penetrates a system's access controls to exploit a legitimate user's account

- **Misfeasor:** A legitimate user who accesses data, programs, or resources for which such access is not authorized, or who is authorized for such access but misuses his or her privileges

- **Clandestine user:** An individual who seizes supervisory control of the system and uses this control to evade auditing and access controls or to suppress audit collection

The masquerader is likely to be an outsider, the misfeasor generally is an insider, and the clandestine user can be either an outsider or an insider.

Intruder attacks range from the benign to the serious. At the benign end of the scale, there are many people who simply wish to explore internets and see what is out there. At the serious end are individuals who are attempting to read privileged data, perform unauthorized modifications to data, or disrupt the system.

[GRAN04] lists the following examples of intrusion:

- Performing a remote root compromise of an e-mail server
- Defacing a Web server
- Guessing and cracking passwords
- Copying a database containing credit card numbers
- Viewing sensitive data, including payroll records and medical information, without authorization
- Running a packet sniffer on a workstation to capture usernames and passwords
- Using a permission error on an anonymous FTP server to distribute pirated software and music files
- Dialing into an unsecured modem and gaining internal network access
- Posing as an executive, calling the help desk, resetting the executive's e-mail password, and learning the new password
- Using an unattended, logged-in workstation without permission

Intruder Behavior Patterns

The techniques and behavior patterns of intruders are constantly shifting, to exploit newly discovered weaknesses and to evade detection and countermeasures. Even so, intruders typically follow one of a number of recognizable behavior patterns, and these patterns typically differ from those of ordinary users. In the following, we look at three broad examples of intruder behavior patterns, to give the reader some feel for the challenge facing the security administrator.

HACKERS Traditionally, those who hack into computers do so for the thrill of it or for status. The hacking community is a strong meritocracy in which status is determined by level of competence. Thus, attackers often look for targets of opportunity and then share the information with others. A typical example is a break-in at a large financial institution reported in [RADC04]. The intruder took advantage of the fact that the corporate network was running unprotected services, some of which were not even needed. In this case, the key to the break-in was the pcAnywhere application. The manufacturer, Symantec, advertises this program as a remote control solution that enables secure connection to remote devices. But the attacker had an easy time gaining access to pcAnywhere; the administrator used the same three-letter username and password for the program. In this case, there was no intrusion detection system on the 700-node corporate network. The intruder was only discovered when a vice-president walked into her office and saw the cursor moving files around on her Windows workstation.

Benign intruders might be tolerable, although they do consume resources and may slow performance for legitimate users. However, there is no way in advance to know whether an intruder will be benign or malign. Consequently, even for systems with no particularly sensitive resources, there is a motivation to control this problem.

Intrusion detection systems (IDSs) and intrusion prevention systems (IPSs) are designed to counter this type of hacker threat. In addition to using such systems, organizations can consider restricting remote logons to specific IP addresses and/or use virtual private network technology.

One of the results of the growing awareness of the intruder problem has been the establishment of a number of computer emergency response teams (CERTs). These cooperative ventures collect information about system vulnerabilities and disseminate it to systems managers. Hackers also routinely read CERT reports. Thus, it is important for system administrators to quickly insert all software patches to discovered vulnerabilities. Unfortunately, given the complexity of many IT systems, and the rate at which patches are released, this is increasingly difficult to achieve without automated updating. Even then, there are problems caused by incompatibilities resulting from the updated software. Hence the need for multiple layers of defense in managing security threats to IT systems.

CRIMINALS Organized groups of hackers have become a widespread and common threat to Internet-based systems. These groups can be in the employ of a corporation or government but often are loosely affiliated gangs of hackers. Typically, these gangs are young, often Eastern European, Russian, or southeast Asian hackers who do business on the Web [ANTE06]. They meet in underground forums with names like DarkMarket.org and theftservices.com to trade tips and data and coordinate attacks. A common target is a credit card file at an e-commerce server. Attackers attempt to gain root access. The card numbers are used by organized crime gangs to purchase expensive items and are then posted to carder sites, where others can access and use the account numbers; this obscures usage patterns and complicates investigation.

Whereas traditional hackers look for targets of opportunity, criminal hackers usually have specific targets, or at least classes of targets in mind. Once a site is penetrated, the attacker acts quickly, scooping up as much valuable information as possible and exiting.

IDSs and IPSs can also be used for these types of attackers, but may be less effective because of the quick in-and-out nature of the attack. For e-commerce sites, database encryption should be used for sensitive customer information, especially credit cards. For hosted e-commerce sites (provided by an outsider service), the e-commerce organization should make use of a dedicated server (not used to support multiple customers) and closely monitor the provider's security services.

INSIDER ATTACKS Insider attacks are among the most difficult to detect and prevent. Employees already have access and knowledge about the structure and content of corporate databases. Insider attacks can be motivated by revenge or simply a feeling of entitlement. An example of the former is the case of Kenneth Patterson, fired from his position as data communications manager for American Eagle Outfitters. Patterson disabled the company's ability to process credit card purchases during five days of the holiday season of 2002. As for a sense of entitlement, there have always been many employees who felt entitled to take extra office supplies for home use, but this now extends to corporate data. An example is that of a vice-president of sales for a stock analysis firm who quit to go to a competitor. Before she left, she copied the customer database to take with her. The offender reported feeling no animus toward her former employee; she simply wanted the data because it would be useful to her.

Although IDS and IPS facilities can be useful in countering insider attacks, other more direct approaches are of higher priority. Examples include the following:

- Enforce least privilege, only allowing access to the resources employees need to do their job.
- Set logs to see what users access and what commands they are entering.
- Protect sensitive resources with strong authentication.
- Upon termination, delete employee's computer and network access.
- Upon termination, make a mirror image of employee's hard drive before reissuing it. That evidence might be needed if your company information turns up at a competitor.

In this section, we look at the techniques used for intrusion. Then we examine ways to detect intrusion.

Intrusion Techniques

The objective of the intruder is to gain access to a system or to increase the range of privileges accessible on a system. Most initial attacks use system or software vulnerabilities that allow a user to execute code that opens a backdoor into the system. Alternatively, the intruder attempts to acquire information that should have been protected. In some cases, this information is in the form of a user password. With knowledge of some other user's password, an intruder can log in to a system and exercise all the privileges accorded to the legitimate user.

Typically, a system must maintain a file that associates a password with each authorized user. If such a file is stored with no protection, then it is an easy matter to gain access to it and learn passwords. The password file can be protected in one of two ways:

- **One-way function:** The system stores only the value of a function based on the user's password. When the user presents a password, the system transforms that password and compares it with the stored value. In practice, the system usually performs a one-way transformation (not reversible), in which the password is used to generate a key for the one-way function and in which a fixed-length output is produced.
- **Access control:** Access to the password file is limited to one or a very few accounts.

If one or both of these countermeasures are in place, some effort is needed for a potential intruder to learn passwords. On the basis of a survey of the literature and interviews with a number of password crackers, [ALVA90] reports the following techniques for learning passwords:

1. Try default passwords used with standard accounts that are shipped with the system. Many administrators do not bother to change these defaults.
2. Exhaustively try all short passwords (those of one to three characters).
3. Try words in the system's online dictionary or a list of likely passwords. Examples of the latter are readily available on hacker bulletin boards.
4. Collect information about users, such as their full names, the names of their spouse and children, pictures in their office, and books in their office that are related to hobbies.
5. Try users' phone numbers, Social Security numbers, and room numbers.
6. Try all legitimate license plate numbers for this state.
7. Use a Trojan horse (described in Chapter 10) to bypass restrictions on access.
8. Tap the line between a remote user and the host system.

The first six methods are various ways of guessing a password. If an intruder has to verify the guess by attempting to log in, it is a tedious and easily countered means of attack. For example, a system can simply reject any login after three password attempts, thus requiring the intruder to reconnect to the host to try again. Under these circumstances, it is not practical to try more than a handful of passwords. However, the intruder is unlikely to try such crude methods. For example, if an intruder can gain access with a low level of privileges to an encrypted password file, then the strategy would be to capture that file and then use the encryption mechanism of that particular system at leisure until a valid password that provided greater privileges was discovered.

Guessing attacks are feasible, and indeed highly effective, when a large number of guesses can be attempted automatically and each guess verified, without the guessing process being detectable. Later in this chapter, we have much to say about thwarting guessing attacks.

The seventh method of attack listed earlier, the Trojan horse, can be particularly difficult to counter. An example of a program that bypasses access controls has been cited in [ALVA90]. A low-privilege user produced a game program and invited the system operator to use it in his or her spare time. The program did indeed play a game, but in the background it also contained code to copy the password file, which was unencrypted but access protected, into the user's file. Because the game was running under the operator's high-privilege mode, it was able to gain access to the password file.

The eighth attack listed, line tapping, is a matter of physical security.

Other intrusion techniques do not require learning a password. Intruders can get access to a system by exploiting attacks such as buffer overflows on a program that runs with certain privileges. Privilege escalation can be done this way as well.

We turn now to a discussion of the two principal countermeasures: detection and prevention. Detection is concerned with learning of an attack, either before or after its success. Prevention is a challenging security goal and an uphill battle at all times. The difficulty stems from the fact that the defender must attempt to thwart all possible attacks, whereas the attacker is free to try to find the weakest link in the defense chain and attack at that point.

11.2 INTRUSION DETECTION

Inevitably, the best intrusion prevention system will fail. A system's second line of defense is intrusion detection, and this has been the focus of much research in recent years. This interest is motivated by a number of considerations, including the following:

1. If an intrusion is detected quickly enough, the intruder can be identified and ejected from the system before any damage is done or any data are compromised. Even if the detection is not sufficiently timely to preempt the intruder, the sooner that the intrusion is detected, the less the amount of damage and the more quickly that recovery can be achieved.

2. An effective intrusion detection system can serve as a deterrent, so acting to prevent intrusions.

3. Intrusion detection enables the collection of information about intrusion techniques that can be used to strengthen the intrusion prevention facility.

Intrusion detection is based on the assumption that the behavior of the intruder differs from that of a legitimate user in ways that can be quantified. Of course, we cannot expect that there will be a crisp, exact distinction between an attack by an intruder and the normal use of resources by an authorized user. Rather, we must expect that there will be some overlap.

Figure 11.1 suggests, in very abstract terms, the nature of the task confronting the designer of an intrusion detection system. Although the typical behavior of an intruder differs from the typical behavior of an authorized user, there is an overlap in these behaviors. Thus, a loose interpretation of intruder behavior, which will catch more intruders, will also lead to a number of **false positives**, or authorized users identified as intruders. On the other hand, an attempt to limit false positives by a tight interpretation of intruder behavior will lead to an increase in **false negatives**, or intruders not identified as intruders. Thus, there is an element of compromise and art in the practice of intrusion detection.

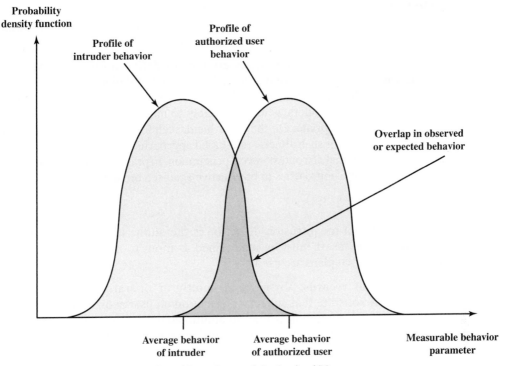

Figure 11.1   Profiles of Behavior of Intruders and Authorized Users

In Anderson's study [ANDE80], it was postulated that one could, with reasonable confidence, distinguish between a masquerader and a legitimate user. Patterns of legitimate user behavior can be established by observing past history, and significant deviation from such patterns can be detected. Anderson suggests that the task of detecting a misfeasor (legitimate user performing in an unauthorized fashion) is more difficult, in that the distinction between abnormal and normal behavior may be small. Anderson concluded that such violations would be undetectable solely through the search for anomalous behavior. However, misfeasor behavior might nevertheless be detectable by intelligent definition of the class of conditions that suggest unauthorized use. Finally, the detection of the clandestine user was felt to be beyond the scope of purely automated techniques. These observations, which were made in 1980, remain true today.

[PORR92] identifies the following approaches to intrusion detection:

1. **Statistical anomaly detection:** Involves the collection of data relating to the behavior of legitimate users over a period of time. Then statistical tests are applied to observed behavior to determine with a high level of confidence whether that behavior is not legitimate user behavior.

   a. Threshold detection: This approach involves defining thresholds, independent of user, for the frequency of occurrence of various events.

   b. Profile based: A profile of the activity of each user is developed and used to detect changes in the behavior of individual accounts.

2. **Rule-based detection:** Involves an attempt to define a set of rules or attack patterns that can be used to decide that a given behavior is that of an intruder. This is often referred to as **signature detection**.

In essence, anomaly approaches attempt to define normal, or expected, behavior, whereas signature-based approaches attempt to define proper behavior.

In terms of the types of attackers listed earlier, statistical anomaly detection is effective against masqueraders, who are unlikely to mimic the behavior patterns of the accounts they appropriate. On the other hand, such techniques may be unable to deal with misfeasors. For such attacks, rule-based approaches may be able to recognize events and sequences that, in context, reveal penetration. In practice, a system may exhibit a combination of both approaches to be effective against a broad range of attacks.

Audit Records

A fundamental tool for intrusion detection is the audit record. Some record of ongoing activity by users must be maintained as input to an intrusion detection system. Basically, two plans are used:

- **Native audit records:** Virtually all multiuser operating systems include accounting software that collects information on user activity. The advantage of using this information is that no additional collection software is needed. The disadvantage is that the native audit records may not contain the needed information or may not contain it in a convenient form.

- **Detection-specific audit records:** A collection facility can be implemented that generates audit records containing only that information required by the intrusion detection system. One advantage of such an approach is that it could be made vendor independent and ported to a variety of systems. The disadvantage is the extra overhead involved in having, in effect, two accounting packages running on a machine.

A good example of detection-specific audit records is one developed by Dorothy Denning [DENN87]. Each audit record contains the following fields:

- **Subject:** A subject initiates actions. A subject could be a user or a process acting on behalf of users or groups of users. Subjects may be grouped into different access classes, and these classes may overlap.

- **Action:** An action initiated by a subject refers to some object; for example, login, read, perform I/O, execute.

- **Object:** Actions are performed on or with objects. Examples include files, programs, messages, records, terminals, printers, and user- or program-created structures. When a subject is the recipient of an action, such as electronic mail, then that subject is considered an object. Objects may be grouped by type. Object granularity may vary by object type and by environment. For example, database actions may be audited for the database as a whole or at the record level.

- **Exception-Condition:** If an exception condition occurs, this field contains identifying information.

- **Resource-Usage:** This is a list, in which each item gives the amount used of some resource (e.g., number of lines printed or displayed, number of records read or written, processor time, I/O units used, session elapsed time).
- **Time-Stamp:** The time stamp specifies the data and time of an action.

Most user operations are made up of a number of elementary actions. For example, a file copy involves the execution of the user command, which includes doing access validation and setting up the copy, plus the read from one file, plus the write to another file. Consider the command

```
COPY GAME.EXE TO <Libray>GAME.EXE
```

issued by Smith to copy an executable file GAME from the current directory to the <Library> directory. The following audit records may be generated:

Smith	execute	*<Library>COPY.EXE*	0	CPU = 00002	11058721678

Smith	read	*<Smith>GAME.EXE*	0	RECORDS = 0	11058721679

Smith	execute	*<Library>COPY.EXE*	write-viol	RECORDS = 0	11058721680

In this case, the copy is aborted because Smith does not have write permission to <Library>.

The decomposition of a user operation into elementary actions has three advantages:

1. Because objects are the protectable entities in a system, the use of elementary actions enables an audit of all behavior affecting an object. Thus, the system can detect attempted subversions of access controls (by noting an abnormality in the number of exception conditions returned) and can detect successful subversions by noting an abnormality in the set of objects accessible to the subject.

2. Single-object, single-action audit records simplify the model and the implementation.

3. Because of the simple, uniform structure of the detection-specific audit records, it may be relatively easy to obtain this information or at least part of it by a straightforward mapping from existing native audit records to the detection-specific audit records.

Statistical Anomaly Detection

As was mentioned, statistical anomaly detection techniques fall into two broad categories: threshold detection and profile-based systems. Threshold detection involves counting the number of occurrences of a specific event type over an interval of time. If the count surpasses what is considered a reasonable number that one might expect to occur, then intrusion is assumed.

Threshold analysis, by itself, is a crude and ineffective detector of even moderately sophisticated attacks. Both the threshold and the time interval must be determined. Because of the variability across users, such thresholds are likely to generate either a lot of false positives or a lot of false negatives. However, simple threshold detectors may be useful in conjunction with more sophisticated techniques.

Profile-based anomaly detection focuses on characterizing the past behavior of individual users or related groups of users and then detecting significant deviations. A profile may consist of a set of parameters, so that deviation on just a single parameter may not be sufficient in itself to signal an alert.

The foundation of this approach is an analysis of audit records. The audit records provide input to the intrusion detection function in two ways. First, the designer must decide on a number of quantitative metrics that can be used to measure user behavior. An analysis of audit records over a period of time can be used to determine the activity profile of the average user. Thus, the audit records serve to define typical behavior. Second, current audit records are the input used to detect intrusion. That is, the intrusion detection model analyzes incoming audit records to determine deviation from average behavior.

Examples of metrics that are useful for profile-based intrusion detection are the following:

- **Counter:** A nonnegative integer that may be incremented but not decremented until it is reset by management action. Typically, a count of certain event types is kept over a particular period of time. Examples include the number of logins by a single user during an hour, the number of times a given command is executed during a single user session, and the number of password failures during a minute.

- **Gauge:** A nonnegative integer that may be incremented or decremented. Typically, a gauge is used to measure the current value of some entity. Examples include the number of logical connections assigned to a user application and the number of outgoing messages queued for a user process.

- **Interval timer:** The length of time between two related events. An example is the length of time between successive logins to an account.

- **Resource utilization:** Quantity of resources consumed during a specified period. Examples include the number of pages printed during a user session and total time consumed by a program execution.

Given these general metrics, various tests can be performed to determine whether current activity fits within acceptable limits. [DENN87] lists the following approaches that may be taken:

- Mean and standard deviation
- Multivariate
- Markov process
- Time series
- Operational

The simplest statistical test is to measure the **mean and standard deviation** of a parameter over some historical period. This gives a reflection of the average behavior and its variability. The use of mean and standard deviation is applicable to a wide variety of counters, timers, and resource measures. But these measures, by themselves, are typically too crude for intrusion detection purposes.

The **mean and standard deviation** of a parameter are simple measures to calculate. Taken over a given period of time, these values provide a measure average behavior and its variability. These two calculations can be applied to a variety of counters, timers, and resource measures. However, these two measures are inadequate, by themselves, for effective intrusion detection.

A **multivariate** calculation determines a correlate between two or more variables. Intruder behavior may be characterized with greater confidence by considering such correlations (for example, processor time and resource usage, or login frequency and session elapsed time).

A **Markov process** estimates transition probabilities among various states. As an example, this model might be used to look at transitions between certain commands.

A **time series** model observes and calculates values based on a sequence of events over time. Such models can be used to detect a series of actions that happens to rapidly or too slowly. A variety of statistical tests can be applied to characterize abnormal timing.

An **operational model** can be used to characterize what is considered abnormal, as opposed to performing an automated analysis of past audit records. Typically, fixed limits are defined and intrusion is suspected for an observation that is outside the limits. This type of approach works best where intruder behavior can be deduced from certain types of activities. For example, a large number of login attempts over a short period suggests an attempted intrusion.

As an example of the use of these various metrics and models, Table 11.1 shows various measures considered or tested for the Stanford Research Institute (SRI) Intrusion Detection System (IDES) [ANDE95, JAVI91] and the follow-on program Emerald [NEUM99].

The main advantage of the use of statistical profiles is that a prior knowledge of security flaws is not required. The detector program learns what is "normal" behavior and then looks for deviations. The approach is not based on system-dependent characteristics and vulnerabilities. Thus, it should be readily portable among a variety of systems.

Rule-Based Intrusion Detection

Rule-based techniques detect intrusion by observing events in the system and applying a set of rules that lead to a decision regarding whether a given pattern of activity is or is not suspicious. In very general terms, we can characterize all approaches as focusing on either anomaly detection or penetration identification, although there is some overlap in these approaches.

Rule-based anomaly detection is similar in terms of its approach and strengths to statistical anomaly detection. With the rule-based approach, historical audit records are analyzed to identify usage patterns and to automatically generate rules

Table 11.1 Measures That May Be Used for Intrusion Detection

Measure	Model	Type of Intrusion Detected
Login and Session Activity		
Login frequency by day and time	Mean and standard deviation	Intruders may be likely to log in during off-hours
Frequency of login at different locations	Mean and standard deviation	Intruders may log in from a location that a particular user rarely or never uses
Time since last login	Operational	Break in on a "dead" account
Elapsed time per session	Mean and standard deviation	Significant deviations might indicate masquerader
Quantity of output to location	Mean and standard deviation	Excessive amounts of data transmitted to remote locations could signify leakage of sensitive data
Session resource utilization	Mean and standard deviation	Unusual processor or I/O levels could signal an intruder
Password failures at login	Operational	Attempted break-in by password guessing
Failures to login from specified terminals	Operational	Attempted break-in
Command or Program Execution Activity		
Execution frequency	Mean and standard deviation	May detect intruders, who are likely to use different commands, or a successful penetration by a legitimate user, who has gained access to privileged commands
Program resource utilization	Mean and standard deviation	An abnormal value might suggest injection of a virus or Trojan horse, which performs side-effects that increase I/O or processor utilization
Execution denials	Operational model	May detect penetration attempt by individual user who seeks higher privileges
File Access Activity		
Read, write, create, delete frequency	Mean and standard deviation	Abnormalities for read and write access for individual users may signify masquerading or browsing
Records read, written	Mean and standard deviation	Abnormality could signify an attempt to obtain sensitive data by inference and aggregation
Failure count for read, write, create, delete	Operational	May detect users who persistently attempt to access unauthorized files

that describe those patterns. Rules may represent past behavior patterns of users, programs, privileges, time slots, terminals, and so on. Current behavior is then observed, and each transaction is matched against the set of rules to determine if it conforms to any historically observed pattern of behavior.

As with statistical anomaly detection, rule-based anomaly detection does not require knowledge of security vulnerabilities within the system. Rather, the scheme is based on observing past behavior and, in effect, assuming that the future will be like the past. In order for this approach to be effective, a rather large database of rules will be needed. For example, a scheme described in [VACC89] contains anywhere from 10^4 to 10^6 rules.

Rule-based penetration identification takes a very different approach to intrusion detection. The key feature of such systems is the use of rules for identifying known penetrations or penetrations that would exploit known weaknesses. Rules can also be defined that identify suspicious behavior, even when the behavior is within the bounds of established patterns of usage. Typically, the rules used in these systems are specific to the machine and operating system. The most fruitful approach to developing such rules is to analyze attack tools and scripts collected on the Internet. These rules can be supplemented with rules generated by knowledgeable security personnel. In this latter case, the normal procedure is to interview system administrators and security analysts to collect a suite of known penetration scenarios and key events that threaten the security of the target system.

A simple example of the type of rules that can be used is found in NIDX, an early system that used heuristic rules that can be used to assign degrees of suspicion to activities [BAUE88]. Example heuristics are the following:

1. Suspicious activity: A user accesses the personal directory of another user and attempts to read files in that directory.

2. Suspicious activity: A user accesses the personal directory of another user and attempts to write or create files in that directory.

3. Expected activity: A user logs in after hours and accesses the same file he or she accessed during business hours.

4. Suspicious activity: A user opens a disk devices directly rather than relying on higher-level operating system utilities.

5. Suspicious activity: A user is logged onto one system twice at the same time.

6. Suspicious activity: A user makes copies of system programs.

The penetration identification scheme used in IDES is representative of the strategy followed. Audit records are examined as they are generated, and they are matched against the rule base. If a match is found, then the user's *suspicion rating* is increased. If enough rules are matched, then the rating will pass a threshold that results in the reporting of an anomaly.

The IDES approach is based on an examination of audit records. A weakness of this plan is its lack of flexibility. For a given penetration scenario, there may be a number of alternative audit record sequences that could be produced, each varying from the others slightly or in subtle ways. It may be difficult to pin down all these variations in explicit rules. Another method is to develop a higher-level model independent of specific audit records. An example of this is a state transition model known as USTAT [VIGN02, ILGU95]. USTAT deals in general actions rather than the detailed specific actions recorded by the UNIX auditing mechanism. USTAT is implemented on a SunOS system that provides audit records on 239 events. Of these, only 28 are used by a preprocessor, which maps these onto 10 general actions (Table 11.2). Using just these actions and the parameters that are invoked with each action, a state transition diagram is developed that characterizes

Table 11.2   USTAT Actions Versus SunOS Event Types

USTAT Action	SunOS Event Type
Read	open_r, open_rc, open_rtc, open_rwc, open_rwtc, open_rt, open_rw, open_rwt
Write	truncate, ftruncate, creat, open_rtc, open_rwc, open_rwtc, open_rt, open_rw, open_rwt, open_w, open_wt, open_wc, open_wct
Create	mkdir, creat, open_rc, open_rtc, open_rwc, open_rwtc, open_wc, open_wtc, mknod
Delete	rmdir, unlink
Execute	exec, execve
Exit	exit
Modify_Owner	chown, fchown
Modify_Perm	chmod, fchmod
Rename	rename
Hardlink	link

suspicious activity. Because a number of different auditable events map into a smaller number of actions, the rule-creation process is simpler. Furthermore, the state transition diagram model is easily modified to accommodate newly learned intrusion behaviors.

The Base–Rate Fallacy

To be of practical use, an intrusion detection system should detect a substantial percentage of intrusions while keeping the false alarm rate at an acceptable level. If only a modest percentage of actual intrusions are detected, the system provides a false sense of security. On the other hand, if the system frequently triggers an alert when there is no intrusion (a false alarm), then either system managers will begin to ignore the alarms or much time will be wasted analyzing the false alarms.

Unfortunately, because of the nature of the probabilities involved, it is very difficult to meet the standard of high rate of detections with a low rate of false alarms. In general, if the actual numbers of intrusions is low compared to the number of legitimate uses of a system, then the false alarm rate will be high unless the test is extremely discriminating. This is an example of a phenomenon known as the **base-rate fallacy**. A study of existing intrusion detection systems, reported in [AXEL00], indicated that current systems have not overcome the problem of the base-rate fallacy. See Appendix J for a brief background on the mathematics of this problem.

Distributed Intrusion Detection

Traditionally, work on intrusion detection systems focused on single-system stand-alone facilities. The typical organization, however, needs to defend a distributed collection of hosts supported by a LAN or internetwork. Although it is possible to mount a defense by using stand-alone intrusion detection systems on each host, a more effective defense can be achieved by coordination and cooperation among intrusion detection systems across the network.

Porras points out the following major issues in the design of a distributed intrusion detection system [PORR92]:

- A distributed intrusion detection system may need to deal with different audit record formats. In a heterogeneous environment, different systems will employ different native audit collection systems and, if using intrusion detection, may employ different formats for security-related audit records.
- One or more nodes in the network will serve as collection and analysis points for the data from the systems on the network. Thus, either raw audit data or summary data must be transmitted across the network. Therefore, there is a requirement to assure the integrity and confidentiality of these data. Integrity is required to prevent an intruder from masking his or her activities by altering the transmitted audit information. Confidentiality is required because the transmitted audit information could be valuable.
- Either a centralized or decentralized architecture can be used. With a centralized architecture, there is a single central point of collection and analysis of all audit data. This eases the task of correlating incoming reports but creates a potential bottleneck and single point of failure. With a decentralized architecture, there are more than one analysis centers, but these must coordinate their activities and exchange information.

A good example of a distributed intrusion detection system is one developed at the University of California at Davis [HEBE92, SNAP91]. A similar approach has been taken for a project at Purdue [SPAF00, BALA98]. Figure 11.2 shows the overall architecture, which consists of three main components:

- **Host agent module:** An audit collection module operating as a background process on a monitored system. Its purpose is to collect data on security-related events on the host and transmit these to the central manager.
- **LAN monitor agent module:** Operates in the same fashion as a host agent module except that it analyzes LAN traffic and reports the results to the central manager.
- **Central manager module:** Receives reports from LAN monitor and host agents, and processes and correlates these reports to detect intrusion.

The scheme is designed to be independent of any operating system or system auditing implementation. Figure 11.3 shows the general approach that is taken. The agent captures each audit record produced by the native audit collection system. A filter is applied that retains only those records that are of security interest. These records are then reformatted into a standardized format referred to as the host audit record (HAR). Next, a template-driven logic module analyzes the records for suspicious activity. At the lowest level, the agent scans for notable events that are of interest independent of any past events. Examples include failed file accesses, accessing system files, and changing a file's access control. At the next higher level,

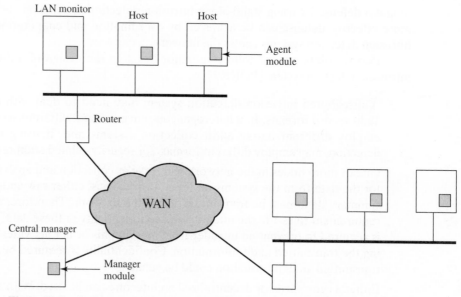

Figure 11.2   Architecture for Distributed Intrusion Detection

the agent looks for sequences of events, such as known attack patterns (signatures). Finally, the agent looks for anomalous behavior of an individual user based on a historical profile of that user, such as number of programs executed, number of files accessed, and the like.

When suspicious activity is detected, an alert is sent to the central manager. The central manager includes an expert system that can draw inferences from received data. The manager may also query individual systems for copies of HARs to correlate with those from other agents.

The LAN monitor agent also supplies information to the central manager. The LAN monitor agent audits host-host connections, services used, and volume of traffic. It searches for significant events, such as sudden changes in network load, the use of security-related services, and network activities such as *rlogin*.

The architecture depicted in Figures 11.2 and 11.3 is quite general and flexible. It offers a foundation for a machine-independent approach that can expand from stand-alone intrusion detection to a system that is able to correlate activity from a number of sites and networks to detect suspicious activity that would otherwise remain undetected.

Honeypots

A relatively recent innovation in intrusion detection technology is the honeypot. Honeypots are decoy systems that are designed to lure a potential attacker away from critical systems. Honeypots are designed to

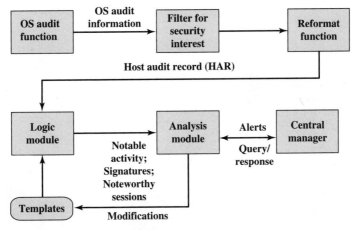

Figure 11.3 Agent Architecture

- divert an attacker from accessing critical systems
- collect information about the attacker's activity
- encourage the attacker to stay on the system long enough for administrators to respond

These systems are filled with fabricated information designed to appear valuable but that a legitimate user of the system wouldn't access. Thus, any access to the honeypot is suspect. The system is instrumented with sensitive monitors and event loggers that detect these accesses and collect information about the attacker's activities. Because any attack against the honeypot is made to seem successful, administrators have time to mobilize and log and track the attacker without ever exposing productive systems.

The honeypot is a resource that has no production value. There is no legitimate reason for anyone outside the network to interact with a honeypot. Thus, any attempt to communicate with the system is most likely a probe, scan, or attack. Conversely, if a honeypot initiates outbound communication, the system has probably been compromised.

Initial efforts involved a single honeypot computer with IP addresses designed to attract hackers. More recent research has focused on building entire honeypot networks that emulate an enterprise, possibly with actual or simulated traffic and data. Once hackers are within the network, administrators can observe their behavior in detail and figure out defenses.

Honeypots can be deployed in a variety of locations. Figure 11.4 illustrates some possibilities. The location depends on a number of factors, such as the type of information the organization is interested in gathering and the level of risk that organizations can tolerate to obtain the maximum amount of data.

A honeypot outside the external firewall (**location 1**) is useful for tracking attempts to connect to unused IP addresses within the scope of the network.

Figure 11.4 Example of Honeypot Deployment

A honeypot at this location does not increase the risk for the internal network. The danger of having a compromised system behind the firewall is avoided. Further, because the honeypot attracts many potential attacks, it reduces the alerts issued by the firewall and by internal IDS sensors, easing the management burden. The disadvantage of an external honeypot is that it has little or no ability to trap internal attackers, especially if the external firewall filters traffic in both directions.

The network of externally available services, such as Web and mail, often called the DMZ (demilitarized zone), is another candidate for locating a honeypot (**location 2**). The security administrator must assure that the other systems in the DMZ are secure against any activity generated by the honeypot. A disadvantage of this location is that a typical DMZ is not fully accessible, and the firewall typically blocks traffic to the DMZ that attempts to access unneeded services. Thus, the firewall either has to open up the traffic beyond what is permissible, which is risky, or limit the effectiveness of the honeypot.

A fully internal honeypot (**location 3**) has several advantages. Its most important advantage is that it can catch internal attacks. A honeypot at this location can also detect a misconfigured firewall that forwards impermissible traffic from the Internet to the internal network. There are several disadvantages. The most serious of these is if the honeypot is compromised so that it can attack other internal systems. Any further traffic from the Internet to the attacker is not blocked by the firewall because it is regarded as traffic to the honeypot only. Another difficulty for this honeypot location is that, as with location 2, the firewall must adjust its filtering to allow traffic to the honeypot, thus complicating firewall configuration and potentially compromising the internal network.

Intrusion Detection Exchange Format

To facilitate the development of distributed intrusion detection systems that can function across a wide range of platforms and environments, standards are needed to support interoperability. Such standards are the focus of the IETF Intrusion Detection Working Group. The purpose of the working group is to define data formats and exchange procedures for sharing information of interest to intrusion detection and response systems and to management systems that may need to interact with them.

The working group issued the following RFCs in 2007:

- **Intrusion Detection Message Exchange Requirements (RFC 4766):** This document defines requirements for the Intrusion Detection Message Exchange Format (IDMEF). The document also specifies requirements for a communication protocol for communicating IDMEF.

- **The Intrusion Detection Message Exchange Format (RFC 4765):** This document describes a data model to represent information exported by intrusion detection systems and explains the rationale for using this model. An implementation of the data model in the Extensible Markup Language (XML) is presented, an XML Document Type Definition is developed, and examples are provided.

- **The Intrusion Detection Exchange Protocol (RFC 4767):** This document describes the Intrusion Detection Exchange Protocol (IDXP), an application-level protocol for exchanging data between intrusion detection entities. IDXP supports mutual authentication, integrity, and confidentiality over a connection-oriented protocol.

Figure 11.5 illustrates the key elements of the model on which the intrusion detection message exchange approach is based. This model does not correspond to any particular product or implementation, but its functional components are the key elements of any IDS. The functional components are as follows:

- **Data source:** The raw data that an IDS uses to detect unauthorized or undesired activity. Common data sources include network packets, operating system audit logs, application audit logs, and system-generated checksum data.

- **Sensor:** Collects data from the data source. The sensor forwards events to the analyzer.

Figure 11.5 Model for Intrusion Detection Message Exchange

- **Analyzer:** The ID component or process that analyzes the data collected by the sensor for signs of unauthorized or undesired activity or for events that might be of interest to the security administrator. In many existing IDSs, the sensor and the analyzer are part of the same component.

- **Administrator:** The human with overall responsibility for setting the security policy of the organization, and, thus, for decisions about deploying and configuring the IDS. This may or may not be the same person as the operator of the IDS. In some organizations, the administrator is associated with the network or systems administration groups. In other organizations, it's an independent position.

- **Manager:** The ID component or process from which the operator manages the various components of the ID system. Management functions typically include sensor configuration, analyzer configuration, event notification management, data consolidation, and reporting.

- **Operator:** The human that is the primary user of the IDS manager. The operator often monitors the output of the IDS and initiates or recommends further action.

In this model, intrusion detection proceeds in the following manner. The sensor monitors data sources looking for suspicious **activity**, such as network sessions showing unexpected telnet activity, operating system log file entries showing a user attempting to access files to which he or she is not authorized to have access, and application log files showing persistent login failures. The sensor communicates suspicious activity to the analyzer as an **event**, which characterizes an activity within a given period of time. If the analyzer determines that the event is of interest, it sends an **alert** to the manager component that contains information about the unusual activity that was detected, as well as the specifics of the occurrence. The manager component issues a **notification** to the human operator. A **response** can be initiated automatically by the manager component or by the human operator. Examples of responses include logging the activity; recording the raw data (from the data source) that characterized the event; terminating a network, user, or application session; or altering network or system access controls. The **security policy** is the predefined, formally documented statement that defines what activities are allowed to take place on an organization's network or on particular hosts to support the organization's requirements. This includes, but is not limited to, which hosts are to be denied external network access.

The specification defines formats for event and alert messages, message types, and exchange protocols for communication of intrusion detection information.

11.3 PASSWORD MANAGEMENT

The front line of defense against intruders is the password system. Virtually all multiuser systems require that a user provide not only a name or identifier (ID) but also a password. The password serves to authenticate the ID of the individual logging on to the system. In turn, the ID provides security in the following ways:

- The ID determines whether the user is authorized to gain access to a system. In some systems, only those who already have an ID filed on the system are allowed to gain access.
- The ID determines the privileges accorded to the user. A few users may have supervisory or "superuser" status that enables them to read files and perform functions that are especially protected by the operating system. Some systems have guest or anonymous accounts, and users of these accounts have more limited privileges than others.
- The ID is used in what is referred to as discretionary access control. For example, by listing the IDs of the other users, a user may grant permission to them to read files owned by that user.

The Vulnerability of Passwords

In this subsection, we outline the main forms of attack against password-based authentication and briefly outline a countermeasure strategy. The remainder of Section 11.3 goes into more detail on the key countermeasures.

Typically, a system that uses password-based authentication maintains a password file indexed by user ID. One technique that is typically used is to store not the user's password but a one-way hash function of the password, as described subsequently.

We can identify the following attack strategies and countermeasures:

- **Offline dictionary attack:** Typically, strong access controls are used to protect the system's password file. However, experience shows that determined hackers can frequently bypass such controls and gain access to the file. The attacker obtains the system password file and compares the password hashes against hashes of commonly used passwords. If a match is found, the attacker can gain access by that ID/password combination. Countermeasures include controls to prevent unauthorized access to the password file, intrusion detection measures to identify a compromise, and rapid reissuance of passwords should the password file be compromised.

- **Specific account attack:** The attacker targets a specific account and submits password guesses until the correct password is discovered. The standard countermeasure is an account lockout mechanism, which locks out access to the account after a number of failed login attempts. Typical practice is no more than five access attempts.

- **Popular password attack:** A variation of the preceding attack is to use a popular password and try it against a wide range of user IDs. A user's tendency is to choose a password that is easily remembered; this unfortunately makes the password easy to guess. Countermeasures include policies to inhibit the selection by users of common passwords and scanning the IP addresses of authentication requests and client cookies for submission patterns.

- **Password guessing against single user:** The attacker attempts to gain knowledge about the account holder and system password policies and uses that knowledge to guess the password. Countermeasures include training in and enforcement of password policies that make passwords difficult to guess. Such policies address the secrecy, minimum length of the password, character set, prohibition against using well-known user identifiers, and length of time before the password must be changed.

- **Workstation hijacking:** The attacker waits until a logged-in workstation is unattended. The standard countermeasure is automatically logging the workstation out after a period of inactivity. Intrusion detection schemes can be used to detect changes in user behavior.

- **Exploiting user mistakes:** If the system assigns a password, then the user is more likely to write it down because it is difficult to remember. This situation creates the potential for an adversary to read the written password. A user may intentionally share a password, to enable a colleague to share files, for example. Also, attackers are frequently successful in obtaining passwords by using social engineering tactics that trick the user or an account manager into revealing a password. Many computer systems are shipped with preconfigured passwords for system administrators. Unless these preconfigured passwords are changed, they are easily guessed. Countermeasures include user training, intrusion detection, and simpler passwords combined with another authentication mechanism.

- **Exploiting multiple password use:** Attacks can also become much more effective or damaging if different network devices share the same or a similar password for a given user. Countermeasures include a policy that forbids the same or similar password on particular network devices.

- **Electronic monitoring:** If a password is communicated across a network to log on to a remote system, it is vulnerable to eavesdropping. Simple encryption will not fix this problem, because the encrypted password is, in effect, the password and can be observed and reused by an adversary.

The Use of Hashed Passwords

A widely used password security technique is the use of hashed passwords and a salt value. This scheme is found on virtually all UNIX variants as well as on a number of other operating systems. The following procedure is employed (Figure 11.6a). To load a new password into the system, the user selects or is assigned a password. This password is combined with a fixed-length **salt value** [MORR79]. In older implementations, this value is related to the time at which the password is assigned to the user. Newer implementations use a pseudorandom or random number. The password and salt serve as inputs to a hashing algorithm to produce a fixed-length hash code. The hash algorithm is designed to be slow to execute to thwart attacks. The hashed password is then stored, together with a plaintext copy of the salt, in the password file for the corresponding user ID. The hashed-password method has been shown to be secure against a variety of cryptanalytic attacks [WAGN00].

When a user attempts to log on to a UNIX system, the user provides an ID and a password (Figure 11.6b). The operating system uses the ID to index into the password file and retrieve the plaintext salt and the encrypted password. The salt and user-supplied password are used as input to the encryption routine. If the result matches the stored value, the password is accepted.

The salt serves three purposes:

- It prevents duplicate passwords from being visible in the password file. Even if two users choose the same password, those passwords will be assigned different salt values. Hence, the hashed passwords of the two users will differ.

- It greatly increases the difficulty of offline dictionary attacks. For a salt of length b bits, the number of possible passwords is increased by a factor of 2^b, increasing the difficulty of guessing a password in a dictionary attack.

- It becomes nearly impossible to find out whether a person with passwords on two or more systems has used the same password on all of them.

To see the second point, consider the way that an offline dictionary attack would work. The attacker obtains a copy of the password file. Suppose first that the salt is not used. The attacker's goal is to guess a single password. To that end, the

(a) Loading a new password

(b) Verifying a password

Figure 11.6   UNIX Password Scheme

attacker submits a large number of likely passwords to the hashing function. If any of the guesses matches one of the hashes in the file, then the attacker has found a password that is in the file. But faced with the UNIX scheme, the attacker must take each guess and submit it to the hash function once for each salt value in the dictionary file, multiplying the number of guesses that must be checked.

There are two threats to the UNIX password scheme. First, a user can gain access on a machine using a guest account or by some other means and then run a password guessing program, called a password cracker, on that machine. The attacker should be able to check many thousands of possible passwords with little resource consumption. In addition, if an opponent is able to obtain a copy of the password file, then a cracker program can be run on another machine at leisure. This enables the opponent to run through millions of possible passwords in a reasonable period.

UNIX IMPLEMENTATIONS Since the original development of UNIX, most implementations have relied on the following password scheme. Each user selects a password of up to eight printable characters in length. This is converted into a 56-bit value (using 7-bit ASCII) that serves as the key input to an encryption routine. The hash routine, known as crypt(3), is based on DES. A 12-bit salt value is used. The modified DES algorithm is executed with a data input consisting of a 64-bit block of zeros. The output of the algorithm then serves as input for a second encryption. This process is repeated for a total of 25 encryptions. The resulting 64-bit output is then translated into an 11-character sequence. The modification of the DES algorithm converts it into a one-way hash function. The crypt(3) routine is designed to discourage guessing attacks. Software implementations of DES are slow compared to hardware versions, and the use of 25 iterations multiplies the time required by 25.

This particular implementation is now considered woefully inadequate. For example, [PERR03] reports the results of a dictionary attack using a supercomputer. The attack was able to process over 50 million password guesses in about 80 minutes. Further, the results showed that for about $10,000 anyone should be able to do the same in a few months using one uniprocessor machine. Despite its known weaknesses, this UNIX scheme is still often required for compatibility with existing account management software or in multivendor environments.

There are other, much stronger, hash/salt schemes available for UNIX. The recommended hash function for many UNIX systems, including Linux, Solaris, and FreeBSD (a widely used open source UNIX implementation), is based on the MD5 secure hash algorithm (which is similar to, but not as secure as SHA-1). The MD5 crypt routine uses a salt of up to 48 bits and effectively has no limitations on password length. It produces a 128-bit hash value. It is also far slower than crypt(3). To achieve the slowdown, MD5 crypt uses an inner loop with 1000 iterations.

Probably the most secure version of the UNIX hash/salt scheme was developed for OpenBSD, another widely used open source UNIX. This scheme, reported in [PROV99], uses a hash function based on the Blowfish symmetric block cipher. The hash function, called Bcrypt, is quite slow to execute. Bcrypt allows passwords of up to 55 characters in length and requires a random salt value of 128 bits, to produce a 192-bit hash value. Bcrypt also includes a cost variable; an increase in the cost variable causes a corresponding increase in the time required to perform a Bcyrpt hash. The cost assigned to a new password is configurable, so that administrators can assign a higher cost to privileged users.

PASSWORD CRACKING APPROACHES The traditional approach to password guessing, or password cracking as it is called, is to develop a large dictionary of possible passwords and to try each of these against the password file. This means that each password must be hashed using each available salt value and then compared to stored hash values. If no match is found, then the cracking program tries variations on all the words in its dictionary of likely passwords. Such variations include backwards spelling of words, additional numbers or special characters, or sequence of characters,

An alternative is to trade off space for time by precomputing potential hash values. In this approach the attacker generates a large dictionary of possible passwords. For each password, the attacker generates the hash values associated with each possible salt value. The result is a mammoth table of hash values known as a **rainbow table**. For example, [OECH03] showed that using 1.4 GB of data, he could crack 99.9% of all alphanumeric Windows password hashes in 13.8 seconds. This approach can be countered by using a sufficiently large salt value and a sufficiently large hash length. Both the FreeBSD and OpenBSD approaches should be secure from this attack for the foreseeable future.

User Password Choices

Even the stupendous guessing rates referenced in the preceding section do not yet make it feasible for an attacker to use a dumb brute-force technique of trying all possible combinations of characters to discover a password. Instead, password crackers rely on the fact that some people choose easily guessable passwords.

Some users, when permitted to choose their own password, pick one that is absurdly short. The results of one study at Purdue University are shown in Table 11.3. The study observed password change choices on 54 machines, representing approximately 7000 user accounts. Almost 3% of the passwords were three characters or fewer in length. An attacker could begin the attack by exhaustively testing all possible passwords of length 3 or fewer. A simple remedy is for the system to reject any password choice of fewer than, say, six characters or even to require that all passwords be exactly eight characters in length. Most users would not complain about such a restriction.

Password length is only part of the problem. Many people, when permitted to choose their own password, pick a password that is guessable, such as their own name, their street name, a common dictionary word, and so forth. This makes

Table 11.3   Observed Password Lengths [SPAF92a]

Length	Number	Fraction of Total
1	55	.004
2	87	.006
3	212	.02
4	449	.03
5	1260	.09
6	3035	.22
7	2917	.21
8	5772	.42
Total	13787	1.0

the job of password cracking straightforward. The cracker simply has to test the password file against lists of likely passwords. Because many people use guessable passwords, such a strategy should succeed on virtually all systems.

One demonstration of the effectiveness of guessing is reported in [KLEI90]. From a variety of sources, the author collected UNIX password files, containing nearly 14,000 encrypted passwords. The result, which the author rightly characterizes as frightening, is shown in Table 11.4. In all, nearly one-fourth of the passwords were guessed. The following strategy was used:

1. Try the user's name, initials, account name, and other relevant personal information. In all, 130 different permutations for each user were tried.

2. Try words from various dictionaries. The author compiled a dictionary of over 60,000 words, including the online dictionary on the system itself, and various other lists as shown.

3. Try various permutations on the words from step 2. This included making the first letter uppercase or a control character, making the entire word uppercase, reversing the word, changing the letter "o" to the digit "zero," and so on. These permutations added another 1 million words to the list.

4. Try various capitalization permutations on the words from step 2 that were not considered in step 3. This added almost 2 million additional words to the list.

Thus, the test involved in the neighborhood of 3 million words. Using the fastest Thinking Machines implementation listed earlier, the time to encrypt all these words for all possible salt values is under an hour. Keep in mind that such a thorough search could produce a success rate of about 25%, whereas even a single hit may be enough to gain a wide range of privileges on a system.

ACCESS CONTROL One way to thwart a password attack is to deny the opponent access to the password file. If the encrypted password portion of the file is accessible only by a privileged user, then the opponent cannot read it without already knowing the password of a privileged user. [SPAF92a] points out several flaws in this strategy:

- Many systems, including most UNIX systems, are susceptible to unanticipated break-ins. Once an attacker has gained access by some means, he or she may wish to obtain a collection of passwords in order to use different accounts for different logon sessions to decrease the risk of detection. Or a user with an account may desire another user's account to access privileged data or to sabotage the system.

- An accident of protection might render the password file readable, thus compromising all the accounts.

- Some of the users have accounts on other machines in other protection domains, and they use the same password. Thus, if the passwords could be read by anyone on one machine, a machine in another location might be compromised.

Thus, a more effective strategy would be to force users to select passwords that are difficult to guess.

Table 11.4 Passwords Cracked from a Sample Set of 13,797 Accounts [KLEI90]

Type of Password	Search Size	Number of Matches	Percentage of Passwords Matched	Cost/Benefit Ratio[a]
User/account name	130	368	2.7%	2.830
Character sequences	866	22	0.2%	0.025
Numbers	427	9	0.1%	0.021
Chinese	392	56	0.4%	0.143
Place names	628	82	0.6%	0.131
Common names	2239	548	4.0%	0.245
Female names	4280	161	1.2%	0.038
Male names	2866	140	1.0%	0.049
Uncommon names	4955	130	0.9%	0.026
Myths & legends	1246	66	0.5%	0.053
Shakespearean	473	11	0.1%	0.023
Sports terms	238	32	0.2%	0.134
Science fiction	691	59	0.4%	0.085
Movies and actors	99	12	0.1%	0.121
Cartoons	92	9	0.1%	0.098
Famous people	290	55	0.4%	0.190
Phrases and patterns	933	253	1.8%	0.271
Surnames	33	9	0.1%	0.273
Biology	58	1	0.0%	0.017
System dictionary	19683	1027	7.4%	0.052
Machine names	9018	132	1.0%	0.015
Mnemonics	14	2	0.0%	0.143
King James bible	7525	83	0.6%	0.011
Miscellaneous words	3212	54	0.4%	0.017
Yiddish words	56	0	0.0%	0.000
Asteroids	2407	19	0.1%	0.007
Total	62727	3340	24.2%	0.053

[a]Computed as the number of matches divided by the search size. The more words that needed to be tested for a match, the lower the cost/benefit ratio.

Password Selection Strategies

The lesson from the two experiments just described (Tables 11.3 and 11.4) is that, left to their own devices, many users choose a password that is too short or too easy to guess. At the other extreme, if users are assigned passwords consisting of eight randomly selected printable characters, password cracking is effectively impossible. But it would be almost as impossible for most users to remember their passwords. Fortunately, even if we limit the password universe to strings of characters that are reasonably memorable, the size of the universe is still too large to permit practical cracking. Our goal, then, is to eliminate guessable passwords while allowing the user to select a password that is memorable. Four basic techniques are in use:

- User education
- Computer-generated passwords
- Reactive password checking
- Proactive password checking

Users can be told the importance of using hard-to-guess passwords and can be provided with guidelines for selecting strong passwords. This **user education** strategy is unlikely to succeed at most installations, particularly where there is a large user population or a lot of turnover. Many users will simply ignore the guidelines. Others may not be good judges of what is a strong password. For example, many users (mistakenly) believe that reversing a word or capitalizing the last letter makes a password unguessable.

Computer-generated passwords also have problems. If the passwords are quite random in nature, users will not be able to remember them. Even if the password is pronounceable, the user may have difficulty remembering it and so be tempted to write it down. In general, computer-generated password schemes have a history of poor acceptance by users. FIPS PUB 181 defines one of the best-designed automated password generators. The standard includes not only a description of the approach but also a complete listing of the C source code of the algorithm. The algorithm generates words by forming pronounceable syllables and concatenating them to form a word. A random number generator produces a random stream of characters used to construct the syllables and words.

A **reactive password checking** strategy is one in which the system periodically runs its own password cracker to find guessable passwords. The system cancels any passwords that are guessed and notifies the user. This tactic has a number of drawbacks. First, it is resource intensive if the job is done right. Because a determined opponent who is able to steal a password file can devote full CPU time to the task for hours or even days, an effective reactive password checker is at a distinct disadvantage. Furthermore, any existing passwords remain vulnerable until the reactive password checker finds them.

The most promising approach to improved password security is a **proactive password checker**. In this scheme, a user is allowed to select his or her own password. However, at the time of selection, the system checks to see if the password is allowable and, if not, rejects it. Such checkers are based on the philosophy that, with sufficient guidance from the system, users can select memorable passwords from a fairly large password space that are not likely to be guessed in a dictionary attack.

The trick with a proactive password checker is to strike a balance between user acceptability and strength. If the system rejects too many passwords, users will complain that it is too hard to select a password. If the system uses some simple algorithm to define what is acceptable, this provides guidance to password crackers to refine their guessing technique. In the remainder of this subsection, we look at possible approaches to proactive password checking.

The first approach is a simple system for rule enforcement. For example, the following rules could be enforced:

- All passwords must be at least eight characters long.
- In the first eight characters, the passwords must include at least one each of uppercase, lowercase, numeric digits, and punctuation marks.

These rules could be coupled with advice to the user. Although this approach is superior to simply educating users, it may not be sufficient to thwart password crackers. This scheme alerts crackers as to which passwords *not* to try but may still make it possible to do password cracking.

Another possible procedure is simply to compile a large dictionary of possible "bad" passwords. When a user selects a password, the system checks to make sure that it is not on the disapproved list. There are two problems with this approach:

- **Space:** The dictionary must be very large to be effective. For example, the dictionary used in the Purdue study [SPAF92a] occupies more than 30 megabytes of storage.
- **Time:** The time required to search a large dictionary may itself be large. In addition, to check for likely permutations of dictionary words, either those words most be included in the dictionary, making it truly huge, or each search must also involve considerable processing.

Bloom Filter

A technique [SPAF92a, SPAF92b] for developing an effective and efficient proactive password checker that is based on rejecting words on a list has been implemented on a number of systems, including Linux. It is based on the use of a Bloom filter [BLOO70]. To begin, we explain the operation of the Bloom filter. A Bloom filter of order k consists of a set of k independent hash functions $H_1(x), H_2(x), \ldots, H_k(x)$, where each function maps a password into a hash value in the range 0 to $N - 1$. That is,

$$H_i(X_j) = y \qquad 1 \leq i \leq k; \qquad 1 \leq j \leq D; \qquad 0 \leq y \leq N - 1$$

where

$X_j =$ jth word in password dictionary

$D =$ number of words in password dictionary

The following procedure is then applied to the dictionary:

1. A hash table of N bits is defined, with all bits initially set to 0.
2. For each password, its k hash values are calculated, and the corresponding bits in the hash table are set to 1. Thus, if $H_i(X_j) = 67$ for some (i, j), then the sixty-seventh bit of the hash table is set to 1; if the bit already has the value 1, it remains at 1.

When a new password is presented to the checker, its k hash values are calculated. If all the corresponding bits of the hash table are equal to 1, then the password is rejected. All passwords in the dictionary will be rejected. But there will also be some "false positives" (i.e., passwords that are not in the dictionary but that produce a match in the hash table). To see this, consider a scheme with two hash functions. Suppose that the passwords *undertaker* and *hulkhogan* are in the dictionary, but *xG%#jj98* is not. Further suppose that

$$H_1(\text{undertaker}) = 25 \quad H_1(\text{hulkhogan}) = 83 \quad H_1(\text{xG\%\#jj98}) = 665$$

$$H_2(\text{undertaker}) = 998 \quad H_2(\text{hulkhogan}) = 665 \quad H_2(\text{xG\%\#jj98}) = 998$$

If the password xG%#jj98 is presented to the system, it will be rejected even though it is not in the dictionary. If there are too many such false positives, it will be difficult for users to select passwords. Therefore, we would like to design the hash scheme to minimize false positives. It can be shown that the probability of a false positive can be approximated by:

$$P \approx \left(1 - e^{kD/N}\right)^k = \left(1 - e^{k/R}\right)^k$$

or, equivalently,

$$R \approx \frac{-k}{\ln(1 - P^{1/k})}$$

where

$k =$ number of hash functions

$N =$ number of bits in hash table

$D =$ number of words in dictionary

$R = N/D$, ratio of hash table size (bits) to dictionary size (words)

Figure 11.7 plots P as a function of R for various values of k. Suppose we have a dictionary of 1 million words and we wish to have a 0.01 probability of rejecting a password not in the dictionary. If we choose six hash functions, the required ratio is $R = 9.6$. Therefore, we need a hash table of 9.6×10^6 bits or about 1.2 MBytes of storage. In contrast, storage of the entire dictionary would require on the order of 8 MBytes. Thus, we achieve a compression of almost a factor of 7. Furthermore, password checking involves the straightforward calculation of six hash functions and is independent of the size of the dictionary, whereas with the use of the full dictionary, there is substantial searching.[1]

---

[1]The Bloom filter involves the use of probabilistic techniques. There is a small probability that some passwords not in the dictionary will be rejected. It is often the case in designing algorithms that the use of probabilistic techniques results in a less time-consuming or less complex solution, or both.

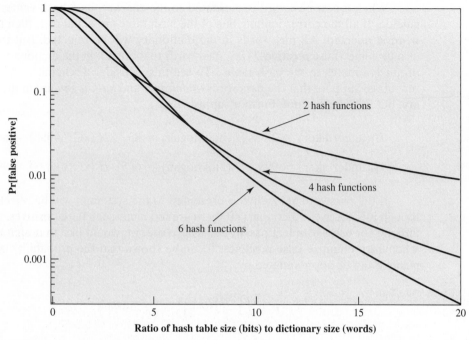

Figure 11.7 Performance of Bloom Filter

11.4 RECOMMENDED READING

[SCAR07] is a worthwhile treatment of intrusion detection. Two short but useful survey articles on the subject are [KENT00] and [MCHU00]. [PRED08] gives examples of insider attacks. [NING04] surveys recent advances in intrusion detection techniques. [CHAN09] is a thorough survey of anomaly detection techniques. [HONE01] is the definitive account on honeypots and provides a detailed analysis of the tools and methods of hackers.

[YAN04] provides an instructive analysis of password selection strategies. [ALEX04] is a useful introduction to password protection strategies in operating systems. [SCAR09a] is a comprehensive look at many issues related to password selection and management.

ALEX04 Alexander, S. "Password Protection for Modern Operating Systems." *;login*, June 2004.

CHAN09 Chandola, V.; Banerjee, A.; and Kumar, V. "Anomaly Detection: A Survey." *ACM Computing Surveys*, July 2009.

HONE01 The Honeynet Project. *Know Your Enemy: Revealing the Security Tools, Tactics, and Motives of the Blackhat Community.* Reading, MA: Addison-Wesley, 2001.

KENT00 Kent, S. "On the Trail of Intrusions into Information Systems." *IEEE Spectrum*, December 2000.

MCHU00 McHugh, J.; Christie, A.; and Allen, J. "The Role of Intrusion Detection Systems." *IEEE Software*, September/October 2000.

NING04 Ning, P., et al. "Techniques and Tools for Analyzing Intrusion Alerts." *ACM Transactions on Information and System Security*, May 2004.

PRED08 Predd, J., et al. "Insiders Behaving Badly." *IEEE Security & Privacy*, July/August 2008.

SCAR07 Scarfone, K., and Mell, P. *Guide to Intrusion Detection and Prevention Systems.* NIST Special Publication SP 800-94, February 2007.

SCAR09a Scarfone, K., and Souppaya, M. *Guide to Enterprise Password Management (Draft).* NIST Special Publication SP 800-118 (Draft), April 2009.

YAN04 Yan, J. et al. "Password Memorability and Security: Empirical Results." *IEEE Security & Privacy*, September/October 2004.

11.5 KEY TERMS, REVIEW QUESTIONS, AND PROBLEMS

Key Terms

audit record	intruder	rainbow table
base-rate fallacy	intrusion detection	rule-based intrusion detection
bloom filter	intrusion detection exchange	salt value
distributed intrusion detection	format	signature detection
honeypot	password	statistical anomaly detection

Review Questions

11.1 List and briefly define three classes of intruders.

11.2 What are two common techniques used to protect a password file?

11.3 What are three benefits that can be provided by an intrusion detection system?

11.4 What is the difference between statistical anomaly detection and rule-based intrusion detection?

11.5 What metrics are useful for profile-based intrusion detection?

11.6 What is the difference between rule-based anomaly detection and rule-based penetration identification?

11.7 What is a honeypot?

11.8 What is a salt in the context of UNIX password management?

11.9 List and briefly define four techniques used to avoid guessable passwords.

Problems

11.1 In the context of an IDS, we define a false positive to be an alarm generated by an IDS in which the IDS alerts to a condition that is actually benign. A false negative occurs when an IDS fails to generate an alarm when an alert-worthy condition is in effect. Using the following diagram, depict two curves that roughly indicate false positives and false negatives, respectively.

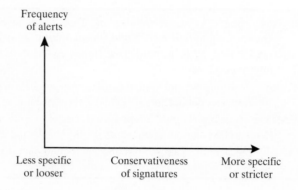

11.2   The overlapping area of the two probability density functions of Figure 11.1 represents the region in which there is the potential for false positives and false negatives. Further, Figure 11.1 is an idealized and not necessarily representative depiction of the relative shapes of the two density functions. Suppose there is 1 actual intrusion for every 1000 authorized users, and the overlapping area covers 1% of the authorized users and 50% of the intruders.

    a. Sketch such a set of density functions and argue that this is not an unreasonable depiction.

    b. What is the probability that an event that occurs in this region is that of an authorized user? Keep in mind that 50% of all intrusions fall in this region.

11.3   An example of a host-based intrusion detection tool is the tripwire program. This is a file integrity checking tool that scans files and directories on the system on a regular basis and notifies the administrator of any changes. It uses a protected database of cryptographic checksums for each file checked and compares this value with that recomputed on each file as it is scanned. It must be configured with a list of files and directories to check, and what changes, if any, are permissible to each. It can allow, for example, log files to have new entries appended, but not for existing entries to be changed. What are the advantages and disadvantages of using such a tool? Consider the problem of determining which files should only change rarely, which files may change more often and how, and which change frequently and hence cannot be checked. Hence consider the amount of work in both the configuration of the program and on the system administrator monitoring the responses generated.

11.4   A taxicab was involved in a fatal hit-and-run accident at night. Two cab companies, the Green and the Blue, operate in the city. You are told that:

    •   85% of the cabs in the city are Green and 15% are Blue.

    •   A witness identified the cab as Blue.

    The court tested the reliability of the witness under the same circumstances that existed on the night of the accident and concluded that the witness was correct in identifying the color of the cab 80% of the time. What is the probability that the cab involved in the incident was Blue rather than Green?

11.5   Explain the suitability or unsuitability of the following passwords:

    a. YK 334

    b. mfmitm (for "my favorite movie is tender mercies)

    c. Natalie1

    d. Washington

    e. Aristotle

    f. tv9stove

    g. 12345678

    h. dribgib

11.6   An early attempt to force users to use less predictable passwords involved computer-supplied passwords. The passwords were eight characters long and were taken from the character set consisting of lowercase letters and digits. They were generated by a pseudorandom number generator with 2^{15} possible starting values. Using the technology of the time, the time required to search through all character strings of length 8 from a 36-character alphabet was 112 years. Unfortunately, this is not a true reflection of the actual security of the system. Explain the problem.

11.7   Assume that passwords are selected from four-character combinations of 26 alphabetic characters. Assume that an adversary is able to attempt passwords at a rate of one per second.
   a.   Assuming no feedback to the adversary until each attempt has been completed, what is the expected time to discover the correct password?
   b.   Assuming feedback to the adversary flagging an error as each incorrect character is entered, what is the expected time to discover the correct password?

11.8   Assume that source elements of length k are mapped in some uniform fashion into a target elements of length p. If each digit can take on one of r values, then the number of source elements is r^k and the number of target elements is the smaller number r^p. A particular source element x_i is mapped to a particular target element y_j.
   a.   What is the probability that the correct source element can be selected by an adversary on one try?
   b.   What is the probability that a different source element $x_k (x_i \neq x_k)$ that results in the same target element, y_j, could be produced by an adversary?
   c.   What is the probability that the correct target element can be produced by an adversary on one try?

11.9   A phonetic password generator picks two segments randomly for each six-letter password. The form of each segment is CVC (consonant, vowel, consonant), where $V = \,<$a, e, i, o, u$>$ and $C = \overline{V}$.
   a.   What is the total password population?
   b.   What is the probability of an adversary guessing a password correctly?

11.10   Assume that passwords are limited to the use of the 95 printable ASCII characters and that all passwords are 10 characters in length. Assume a password cracker with an encryption rate of 6.4 million encryptions per second. How long will it take to test exhaustively all possible passwords on a UNIX system?

11.11   Because of the known risks of the UNIX password system, the SunOS-4.0 documentation recommends that the password file be removed and replaced with a publicly readable file called /etc/publickey. An entry in the file for user A consists of a user's identifier ID_A, the user's public key, PU_a, and the corresponding private key PR_a. This private key is encrypted using DES with a key derived from the user's login password P_a. When A logs in, the system decrypts $E(P_a, PR_a)$ to obtain PR_a.
   a.   The system then verifies that P_a was correctly supplied. How?
   b.   How can an opponent attack this system?

11.12   The encryption scheme used for UNIX passwords is one way; it is not possible to reverse it. Therefore, would it be accurate to say that this is, in fact, a hash code rather than an encryption of the password?

11.13   It was stated that the inclusion of the salt in the UNIX password scheme increases the difficulty of guessing by a factor of 4096. But the salt is stored in plaintext in the same entry as the corresponding ciphertext password. Therefore, those two characters are known to the attacker and need not be guessed. Why is it asserted that the salt increases security?

11.14   Assuming that you have successfully answered the preceding problem and understand the significance of the salt, here is another question. Wouldn't it be possible to thwart completely all password crackers by dramatically increasing the salt size to, say, 24 or 48 bits?

11.15 Consider the Bloom filter discussed in Section 11.3. Define k = number of hash functions; N = number of bits in hash table; and D = number of words in dictionary.

a. Show that the expected number of bits in the hash table that are equal to zero is expressed as

$$\phi = \left(1 - \frac{k}{N}\right)^{D}$$

b. Show that the probability that an input word, not in the dictionary, will be falsely accepted as being in the dictionary is

$$P = (1 - \phi)^k$$

c. Show that the preceding expression can be approximated as

$$P \approx \left(1 - e^{-kD/N}\right)^{k}$$

11.16 Design a file access system to allow certain users read and write access to a file, depending on authorization set up by the system. The instructions should be of the format:

READ (F, User A):   attempt by User A to read file F
READ (F, User A):   attempt by User A to store a possibly modified copy of F

Each file has a *header record,* which contains authorization privileges; that is, a list of users who can read and write. The file is to be encrypted by a key that is not shared by the users but known only to the system.

CHAPTER 12

FIREWALLS

12.1 The Need for Firewalls

12.2 Firewall Characteristics

12.3 Types of Firewalls

Packet Filtering Firewall
Stateful Inspection Firewalls
Application-Level Gateway
Circuit-Level Gateway

12.4 Firewall Basing

Bastion Host
Host-Based Firewalls
Personal Firewall

12.5 Firewall Location and Configurations

DMZ Networks
Virtual Private Networks
Distributed Firewalls
Summary of Firewall Locations and Topologies

12.6 Recommended Reading

12.7 Key Terms, Review Questions, and Problems

The function of a strong position is to make the forces holding it practically unassailable.

— *On War*, Carl Von Clausewitz

On the day that you take up your command, block the frontier passes, destroy the official tallies, and stop the passage of all emissaries.

— *The Art of War*, Sun Tzu

LEARNING OBJECTIVES

After studying this chapter, you should be able to:

◆ Explain the role of firewalls as part of a computer and network security strategy.

◆ List the key characteristics of firewalls.

◆ Discuss the various basing options for firewalls.

◆ Understand the relative merits of various choices for firewall location and configurations.

Firewalls can be an effective means of protecting a local system or network of systems from network-based security threats while at the same time affording access to the outside world via wide area networks and the Internet.

12.1 THE NEED FOR FIREWALLS

Information systems in corporations, government agencies, and other organizations have undergone a steady evolution. The following are notable developments:

- Centralized data processing system, with a central mainframe supporting a number of directly connected terminals

- Local area networks (LANs) interconnecting PCs and terminals to each other and the mainframe

- Premises network, consisting of a number of LANs, interconnecting PCs, servers, and perhaps a mainframe or two

- Enterprise-wide network, consisting of multiple, geographically distributed premises networks interconnected by a private wide area network (WAN)

- Internet connectivity, in which the various premises networks all hook into the Internet and may or may not also be connected by a private WAN

Internet connectivity is no longer optional for organizations. The information and services available are essential to the organization. Moreover, individual users within the organization want and need Internet access, and if this is not provided via their LAN, they will use dial-up capability from their PC to an Internet service provider (ISP). However, while Internet access provides benefits to the organization, it enables the outside world to reach and interact with local network assets. This creates a threat to the organization. While it is possible to equip each workstation and server on the premises network with strong security features, such as intrusion protection, this may not be sufficient and in some cases is not cost-effective. Consider a network with hundreds or even thousands of systems, running various operating systems, such as different versions of UNIX and Windows. When a security flaw is discovered, each potentially affected system must be upgraded to fix that flaw. This requires scaleable configuration management and aggressive patching to function effectively. While difficult, this is possible and is necessary if only host-based security is used. A widely accepted alternative or at least complement to host-based security services is the firewall. The firewall is inserted between the premises network and the Internet to establish a controlled link and to erect an outer security wall or perimeter. The aim of this perimeter is to protect the premises network from Internet-based attacks and to provide a single choke point where security and auditing can be imposed. The firewall may be a single computer system or a set of two or more systems that cooperate to perform the firewall function.

The firewall, then, provides an additional layer of defense, insulating the internal systems from external networks. This follows the classic military doctrine of "defense in depth," which is just as applicable to IT security.

12.2 FIREWALL CHARACTERISTICS

[BELL94] lists the following design goals for a firewall:

1. All traffic from inside to outside, and vice versa, must pass through the firewall. This is achieved by physically blocking all access to the local network except via the firewall. Various configurations are possible, as explained later in this chapter.

2. Only authorized traffic, as defined by the local security policy, will be allowed to pass. Various types of firewalls are used, which implement various types of security policies, as explained later in this chapter.

3. The firewall itself is immune to penetration. This implies the use of a hardened system with a secured operating system. Trusted computer systems are suitable for hosting a firewall and often required in government applications.

[SMIT97] lists four general techniques that firewalls use to control access and enforce the site's security policy. Originally, firewalls focused primarily on service control, but they have since evolved to provide all four:

- **Service control:** Determines the types of Internet services that can be accessed, inbound or outbound. The firewall may filter traffic on the basis of IP address, protocol, or port number; may provide proxy software that receives and interprets each service request before passing it on; or may host the server software itself, such as a Web or mail service.

- **Direction control:** Determines the direction in which particular service requests may be initiated and allowed to flow through the firewall.
- **User control:** Controls access to a service according to which user is attempting to access it. This feature is typically applied to users inside the firewall perimeter (local users). It may also be applied to incoming traffic from external users; the latter requires some form of secure authentication technology, such as is provided in IPsec (Chapter 9).
- **Behavior control:** Controls how particular services are used. For example, the firewall may filter e-mail to eliminate spam, or it may enable external access to only a portion of the information on a local Web server.

Before proceeding to the details of firewall types and configurations, it is best to summarize what one can expect from a firewall. The following capabilities are within the scope of a firewall:

1. A firewall defines a single choke point that keeps unauthorized users out of the protected network, prohibits potentially vulnerable services from entering or leaving the network, and provides protection from various kinds of IP spoofing and routing attacks. The use of a single choke point simplifies security management because security capabilities are consolidated on a single system or set of systems.

2. A firewall provides a location for monitoring security-related events. Audits and alarms can be implemented on the firewall system.

3. A firewall is a convenient platform for several Internet functions that are not security related. These include a network address translator, which maps local addresses to Internet addresses, and a network management function that audits or logs Internet usage.

4. A firewall can serve as the platform for IPsec. Using the tunnel mode capability described in Chapter 9, the firewall can be used to implement virtual private networks.

Firewalls have their limitations, including the following:

1. The firewall cannot protect against attacks that bypass the firewall. Internal systems may have dial-out capability to connect to an ISP. An internal LAN may support a modem pool that provides dial-in capability for traveling employees and telecommuters.

2. The firewall may not protect fully against internal threats, such as a disgruntled employee or an employee who unwittingly cooperates with an external attacker.

3. An improperly secured wireless LAN may be accessed from outside the organization. An internal firewall that separates portions of an enterprise network cannot guard against wireless communications between local systems on different sides of the internal firewall.

4. A laptop, PDA, or portable storage device may be used and infected outside the corporate network, and then attached and used internally.

12.3 TYPES OF FIREWALLS

A firewall may act as a packet filter. It can operate as a positive filter, allowing to pass only packets that meet specific criteria, or as a negative filter, rejecting any packet that meets certain criteria. Depending on the type of firewall, it may examine one or more protocol headers in each packet, the payload of each packet, or the pattern generated by a sequence of packets. In this section, we look at the principal types of firewalls.

Packet Filtering Firewall

A packet filtering firewall applies a set of rules to each incoming and outgoing IP packet and then forwards or discards the packet (Figure 12.1b). The firewall is typically configured to filter packets going in both directions (from and to the internal network). Filtering rules are based on information contained in a network packet:

- **Source IP address:** The IP address of the system that originated the IP packet (e.g., 192.178.1.1)
- **Destination IP address:** The IP address of the system the IP packet is trying to reach (e.g., 192.168.1.2)
- **Source and destination transport-level address:** The transport-level (e.g., TCP or UDP) port number, which defines applications such as SNMP or TELNET
- **IP protocol field:** Defines the transport protocol
- **Interface:** For a firewall with three or more ports, which interface of the firewall the packet came from or which interface of the firewall the packet is destined for

The packet filter is typically set up as a list of rules based on matches to fields in the IP or TCP header. If there is a match to one of the rules, that rule is invoked to determine whether to forward or discard the packet. If there is no match to any rule, then a default action is taken. Two default policies are possible:

- **Default = discard:** That which is not expressly permitted is prohibited.
- **Default = forward:** That which is not expressly prohibited is permitted.

The default discard policy is more conservative. Initially, everything is blocked, and services must be added on a case-by-case basis. This policy is more visible to users, who are more likely to see the firewall as a hindrance. However, this is the policy likely to be preferred by businesses and government organizations. Further, visibility to users diminishes as rules are created. The default forward policy increases ease of use for end users but provides reduced security; the security administrator must, in essence, react to each new security threat as it becomes known. This policy may be used by generally more open organizations, such as universities.

Table 12.1 is a simplified example of a ruleset for SMTP traffic. The goal is to allow inbound and outbound e-mail traffic but to block all other traffic. The rules are applied top to bottom to each packet.

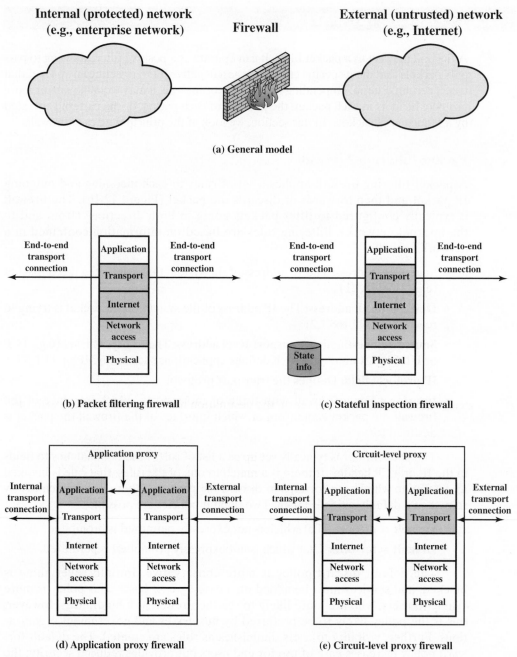

Figure 12.1 Types of Firewalls

A. Inbound mail from an external source is allowed (port 25 is for SMTP incoming).

B. This rule is intended to allow a response to an inbound SMTP connection.

C. Outbound mail to an external source is allowed.

Table 12.1 Packet-Filtering Example

Rule	Direction	Source Address	Destination Address	Protocol	Destination Port	Action
A	In	External	Internal	TCP	25	Permit
B	Out	Internal	External	TCP	> 1023	Permit
C	Out	Internal	External	TCP	25	Permit
D	In	External	Internal	TCP	> 1023	Permit
E	Either	Any	Any	Any	Any	Deny

D. This rule is intended to allow a response to an inbound SMTP connection.

E. This is an explicit statement of the default policy. All rulesets include this rule implicitly as the last rule.

There are several problems with this ruleset. Rule D allows external traffic to any destination port above 1023. As an example of an exploit of this rule, an external attacker can open a connection from the attacker's port 5150 to an internal Web proxy server on port 8080. This is supposed to be forbidden and could allow an attack on the server. To counter this attack, the firewall ruleset can be configured with a source port field for each row. For rules B and D, the source port is set to 25; for rules A and C, the source port is set to > 1023.

But a vulnerability remains. Rules C and D are intended to specify that any inside host can send mail to the outside. A TCP packet with a destination port of 25 is routed to the SMTP server on the destination machine. The problem with this rule is that the use of port 25 for SMTP receipt is only a default; an outside machine could be configured to have some other application linked to port 25. As the revised rule D is written, an attacker could gain access to internal machines by sending packets with a TCP source port number of 25. To counter this threat, we can add an ACK flag field to each row. For rule D, the field would indicate that the ACK flag must be set on the incoming packet. Rule D would now look like this:

Rule	Direction	Source Address	Source Port	Dest Address	Protocol	Dest Port	Flag	Action
D	In	External	25	Internal	TCP	> 1023	ACK	Permit

The rule takes advantage of a feature of TCP connections. Once a connection is set up, the ACK flag of a TCP segment is set to acknowledge segments sent from the other side. Thus, this rule allows incoming packets with a source port number of 25 that include the ACK flag in the TCP segment.

One advantage of a packet filtering firewall is its simplicity. Also, packet filters typically are transparent to users and are very fast. [SCAR09b] lists the following weaknesses of packet filter firewalls:

- Because packet filter firewalls do not examine upper-layer data, they cannot prevent attacks that employ application-specific vulnerabilities or functions. For example, a packet filter firewall cannot block specific application commands; if a packet filter firewall allows a given application, all functions available within that application will be permitted.

- Because of the limited information available to the firewall, the logging functionality present in packet filter firewalls is limited. Packet filter logs normally contain the same information used to make access control decisions (source address, destination address, and traffic type).

- Most packet filter firewalls do not support advanced user authentication schemes. Once again, this limitation is mostly due to the lack of upper-layer functionality by the firewall.

- Packet filter firewalls are generally vulnerable to attacks and exploits that take advantage of problems within the TCP/IP specification and protocol stack, such as *network layer address spoofing*. Many packet filter firewalls cannot detect a network packet in which the OSI Layer 3 addressing information has been altered. Spoofing attacks are generally employed by intruders to bypass the security controls implemented in a firewall platform.

- Finally, due to the small number of variables used in access control decisions, packet filter firewalls are susceptible to security breaches caused by improper configurations. In other words, it is easy to accidentally configure a packet filter firewall to allow traffic types, sources, and destinations that should be denied based on an organization's information security policy.

Some of the attacks that can be made on packet filtering firewalls and the appropriate countermeasures are the following:

- **IP address spoofing:** The intruder transmits packets from the outside with a source IP address field containing an address of an internal host. The attacker hopes that the use of a spoofed address will allow penetration of systems that employ simple source address security, in which packets from specific trusted internal hosts are accepted. The countermeasure is to discard packets with an inside source address if the packet arrives on an external interface. In fact, this countermeasure is often implemented at the router external to the firewall.

- **Source routing attacks:** The source station specifies the route that a packet should take as it crosses the Internet, in the hopes that this will bypass security measures that do not analyze the source routing information. The countermeasure is to discard all packets that use this option.

- **Tiny fragment attacks:** The intruder uses the IP fragmentation option to create extremely small fragments and force the TCP header information into a separate packet fragment. This attack is designed to circumvent filtering rules that depend on TCP header information. Typically, a packet filter will make a filtering decision on the first fragment of a packet. All subsequent fragments of that packet are filtered out solely on the basis that they are part of the packet whose first fragment was rejected. The attacker hopes that the filtering firewall examines only the first fragment and that the remaining fragments are passed through. A tiny fragment attack can be defeated by enforcing a rule that the first fragment of a packet must contain a predefined minimum amount of the transport header. If the first fragment is rejected, the filter can remember the packet and discard all subsequent fragments.

Stateful Inspection Firewalls

A traditional packet filter makes filtering decisions on an individual packet basis and does not take into consideration any higher-layer context. To understand what is meant by *context* and why a traditional packet filter is limited with regard to context, a little background is needed. Most standardized applications that run on top of TCP follow a client/server model. For example, for the Simple Mail Transfer Protocol (SMTP), e-mail is transmitted from a client system to a server system. The client system generates new e-mail messages, typically from user input. The server system accepts incoming e-mail messages and places them in the appropriate user mailboxes. SMTP operates by setting up a TCP connection between client and server, in which the TCP server port number, which identifies the SMTP server application, is 25. The TCP port number for the SMTP client is a number between 1024 and 65535 that is generated by the SMTP client.

In general, when an application that uses TCP creates a session with a remote host, it creates a TCP connection in which the TCP port number for the remote (server) application is a number less than 1024 and the TCP port number for the local (client) application is a number between 1024 and 65535. The numbers less than 1024 are the "well-known" port numbers and are assigned permanently to particular applications (e.g., 25 for server SMTP). The numbers between 1024 and 65535 are generated dynamically and have temporary significance only for the lifetime of a TCP connection.

A simple packet filtering firewall must permit inbound network traffic on all these high-numbered ports for TCP-based traffic to occur. This creates a vulnerability that can be exploited by unauthorized users.

A stateful inspection packet firewall tightens up the rules for TCP traffic by creating a directory of outbound TCP connections, as shown in Table 12.2. There is an entry for each currently established connection. The packet filter will now allow incoming traffic to high-numbered ports only for those packets that fit the profile of one of the entries in this directory.

Table 12.2   Example Stateful Firewall Connection State Table [SCAR09b]

Source Address	Source Port	Destination Address	Destination Port	Connection State
192.168.1.100	1030	210.22.88.29	80	Established
192.168.1.102	1031	216.32.42.123	80	Established
192.168.1.101	1033	173.66.32.122	25	Established
192.168.1.106	1035	177.231.32.12	79	Established
223.43.21.231	1990	192.168.1.6	80	Established
2122.22.123.32	2112	192.168.1.6	80	Established
210.922.212.18	3321	192.168.1.6	80	Established
24.102.32.23	1025	192.168.1.6	80	Established
223.21.22.12	1046	192.168.1.6	80	Established

A stateful packet inspection firewall reviews the same packet information as a packet filtering firewall, but also records information about TCP connections (Figure 12.1c). Some stateful firewalls also keep track of TCP sequence numbers to prevent attacks that depend on the sequence number, such as session hijacking. Some even inspect limited amounts of application data for some well-known protocols like FTP, IM and SIPS commands, in order to identify and track related connections.

Application-Level Gateway

An application-level gateway, also called an **application proxy**, acts as a relay of application-level traffic (Figure 12.1d). The user contacts the gateway using a TCP/IP application, such as Telnet or FTP, and the gateway asks the user for the name of the remote host to be accessed. When the user responds and provides a valid user ID and authentication information, the gateway contacts the application on the remote host and relays TCP segments containing the application data between the two endpoints. If the gateway does not implement the proxy code for a specific application, the service is not supported and cannot be forwarded across the firewall. Further, the gateway can be configured to support only specific features of an application that the network administrator considers acceptable while denying all other features.

Application-level gateways tend to be more secure than packet filters. Rather than trying to deal with the numerous possible combinations that are to be allowed and forbidden at the TCP and IP level, the application-level gateway need only scrutinize a few allowable applications. In addition, it is easy to log and audit all incoming traffic at the application level.

A prime disadvantage of this type of gateway is the additional processing overhead on each connection. In effect, there are two spliced connections between the end users, with the gateway at the splice point, and the gateway must examine and forward all traffic in both directions.

Circuit-Level Gateway

A fourth type of firewall is the circuit-level gateway or **circuit-level proxy** (Figure 12.1e). This can be a stand-alone system or it can be a specialized function performed by an application-level gateway for certain applications. As with an application gateway, a circuit-level gateway does not permit an end-to-end TCP connection; rather, the gateway sets up two TCP connections, one between itself and a TCP user on an inner host and one between itself and a TCP user on an outside host. Once the two connections are established, the gateway typically relays TCP segments from one connection to the other without examining the contents. The security function consists of determining which connections will be allowed.

A typical use of circuit-level gateways is a situation in which the system administrator trusts the internal users. The gateway can be configured to support application-level or proxy service on inbound connections and circuit-level functions for outbound connections. In this configuration, the gateway can incur the processing overhead of examining incoming application data for forbidden functions but does not incur that overhead on outgoing data.

An example of a circuit-level gateway implementation is the SOCKS package [KOBL92]; version 5 of SOCKS is specified in RFC 1928. The RFC defines SOCKS in the following fashion:

> The protocol described here is designed to provide a framework for client-server applications in both the TCP and UDP domains to conveniently and securely use the services of a network firewall. The protocol is conceptually a "shim-layer" between the application layer and the transport layer, and as such does not provide network-layer gateway services, such as forwarding of ICMP messages.

SOCKS consists of the following components:

- The SOCKS server, which often runs on a UNIX-based firewall. SOCKS is also implemented on Windows systems.
- The SOCKS client library, which runs on internal hosts protected by the firewall.
- SOCKS-ified versions of several standard client programs such as FTP and TELNET. The implementation of the SOCKS protocol typically involves either the recompilation or relinking of TCP-based client applications or the use of alternate dynamically loaded libraries, to use the appropriate encapsulation routines in the SOCKS library.

When a TCP-based client wishes to establish a connection to an object that is reachable only via a firewall (such determination is left up to the implementation), it must open a TCP connection to the appropriate SOCKS port on the SOCKS server system. The SOCKS service is located on TCP port 1080. If the connection request succeeds, the client enters a negotiation for the authentication method to be used, authenticates with the chosen method, and then sends a relay request. The SOCKS server evaluates the request and either establishes the appropriate connection or denies it. UDP exchanges are handled in a similar fashion. In essence, a TCP connection is opened to authenticate a user to send and receive UDP segments, and the UDP segments are forwarded as long as the TCP connection is open.

12.4 FIREWALL BASING

It is common to base a firewall on a stand-alone machine running a common operating system, such as UNIX or Linux. Firewall functionality can also be implemented as a software module in a router or LAN switch. In this section, we look at some additional firewall basing considerations.

Bastion Host

A bastion host is a system identified by the firewall administrator as a critical strong point in the network's security. Typically, the bastion host serves as a platform for an application-level or circuit-level gateway. Common characteristics of a bastion host are as follows:

- The bastion host hardware platform executes a secure version of its operating system, making it a hardened system.

- Only the services that the network administrator considers essential are installed on the bastion host. These could include proxy applications for DNS, FTP, HTTP, and SMTP.
- The bastion host may require additional authentication before a user is allowed access to the proxy services. In addition, each proxy service may require its own authentication before granting user access.
- Each proxy is configured to support only a subset of the standard application's command set.
- Each proxy is configured to allow access only to specific host systems. This means that the limited command/feature set may be applied only to a subset of systems on the protected network.
- Each proxy maintains detailed audit information by logging all traffic, each connection, and the duration of each connection. The audit log is an essential tool for discovering and terminating intruder attacks.
- Each proxy module is a very small software package specifically designed for network security. Because of its relative simplicity, it is easier to check such modules for security flaws. For example, a typical UNIX mail application may contain over 20,000 lines of code, while a mail proxy may contain fewer than 1000.
- Each proxy is independent of other proxies on the bastion host. If there is a problem with the operation of any proxy, or if a future vulnerability is discovered, it can be uninstalled without affecting the operation of the other proxy applications. Also, if the user population requires support for a new service, the network administrator can easily install the required proxy on the bastion host.
- A proxy generally performs no disk access other than to read its initial configuration file. Hence, the portions of the file system containing executable code can be made read only. This makes it difficult for an intruder to install Trojan horse sniffers or other dangerous files on the bastion host.
- Each proxy runs as a nonprivileged user in a private and secured directory on the bastion host.

Host–Based Firewalls

A host-based firewall is a software module used to secure an individual host. Such modules are available in many operating systems or can be provided as an add-on package. Like conventional stand-alone firewalls, host-resident firewalls filter and restrict the flow of packets. A common location for such firewalls is a server. There are several advantages to the use of a server-based or workstation-based firewall:

- Filtering rules can be tailored to the host environment. Specific corporate security policies for servers can be implemented, with different filters for servers used for different application.
- Protection is provided independent of topology. Thus both internal and external attacks must pass through the firewall.
- Used in conjunction with stand-alone firewalls, the host-based firewall provides an additional layer of protection. A new type of server can be added to the network, with its own firewall, without the necessity of altering the network firewall configuration.

Personal Firewall

A personal firewall controls the traffic between a personal computer or workstation on one side and the Internet or enterprise network on the other side. Personal firewall functionality can be used in the home environment and on corporate intranets. Typically, the personal firewall is a software module on the personal computer. In a home environment with multiple computers connected to the Internet, firewall functionality can also be housed in a router that connects all of the home computers to a DSL, cable modem, or other Internet interface.

Personal firewalls are typically much less complex than either server-based firewalls or stand-alone firewalls. The primary role of the personal firewall is to deny unauthorized remote access to the computer. The firewall can also monitor outgoing activity in an attempt to detect and block worms and other malware.

An example of a personal firewall is the capability built in to the Mac OS X operating system. This relatively simple utility can be turned on or off. If it is turned on, any applications, programs, and services unauthorized by the system won't be allowed to automatically accept incoming network traffic. Any active sharing services, such as file or printer sharing, are unaffected. In addition, there are three options available to the user, as shown in Figure 12.2. "Block all incoming connections" blocks all sharing services while allowing basic Internet connections. If this option is unchecked, then the window below that option lists individual programs and

Figure 12.2   Example Personal Firewall Interface

services. Above the horizontal line in the window, features of OS X itself are listed. These are features selected by the user in another window. The user can add applications to a list displayed below the line and designate each as blocked or unblocked.

The firewall also allows the user to enable a feature that allows software signed by a valid certificate authority to provide services accessed from the network. Stealth mode hides the Mac on the Internet by dropping unsolicited communication packets, making it appear as though no Mac is present.

12.5 FIREWALL LOCATION AND CONFIGURATIONS

As Figure 12.1a indicates, a firewall is positioned to provide a protective barrier between an external, potentially untrusted source of traffic and an internal network. With that general principle in mind, a security administrator must decide on the location and on the number of firewalls needed. In this section, we look at some common options.

DMZ Networks

Figure 12.3 suggests the most common distinction, that between an internal and an external firewall. An external firewall is placed at the edge of a local or enterprise network, just inside the boundary router that connects to the Internet or some wide area network (WAN). One or more internal firewalls protect the bulk of the enterprise network. Between these two types of firewalls are one or more networked devices in a region referred to as a DMZ (demilitarized zone) network. Systems that are externally accessible but need some protections are usually located on DMZ networks. Typically, the systems in the DMZ require or foster external connectivity, such as a corporate Web site, an e-mail server, or a DNS (domain name system) server.

The external firewall provides a measure of access control and protection for the DMZ systems consistent with their need for external connectivity. The external firewall also provides a basic level of protection for the remainder of the enterprise network. In this type of configuration, internal firewalls serve three purposes:

1. The internal firewall adds more stringent filtering capability, compared to the external firewall, in order to protect enterprise servers and workstations from external attack.

2. The internal firewall provides two-way protection with respect to the DMZ. First, the internal firewall protects the remainder of the network from attacks launched from DMZ systems. Such attacks might originate from worms, rootkits, bots, or other malware lodged in a DMZ system. Second, an internal firewall can protect the DMZ systems from attack from the internal protected network.

3. Multiple internal firewalls can be used to protect portions of the internal network from each other. For example, firewalls can be configured so that internal servers are protected from internal workstations and vice versa. A common practice is to place the DMZ on a different network interface on the external firewall from that used to access the internal networks.

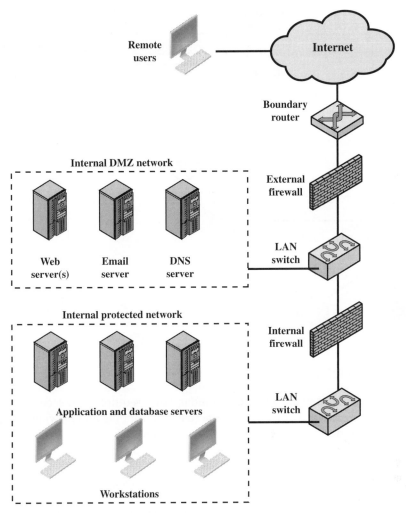

Figure 12.3 Example Firewall Configuration

Virtual Private Networks

In today's distributed computing environment, the **virtual private network** (VPN) offers an attractive solution to network managers. In essence, a VPN consists of a set of computers that interconnect by means of a relatively unsecure network and that make use of encryption and special protocols to provide security. At each corporate site, workstations, servers, and databases are linked by one or more local area networks (LANs). The Internet or some other public network can be used to interconnect sites, providing a cost savings over the use of a private network and offloading the wide area network management task to the public network provider. That same public network provides an access path for telecommuters and other mobile employees to log on to corporate systems from remote sites.

Figure 12.4 A VPN Security Scenario

But the manager faces a fundamental requirement: security. Use of a public network exposes corporate traffic to eavesdropping and provides an entry point for unauthorized users. To counter this problem, a VPN is needed. In essence, a VPN uses encryption and authentication in the lower protocol layers to provide a secure connection through an otherwise insecure network, typically the Internet. VPNs are generally cheaper than real private networks using private lines but rely on having the same encryption and authentication system at both ends. The encryption may be performed by firewall software or possibly by routers. The most common protocol mechanism used for this purpose is at the IP level and is known as IPsec.

Figure 12.4 (Compare Figure 9.1) is a typical scenario of IPSec usage.[1] An organization maintains LANs at dispersed locations. Nonsecure IP traffic is conducted on each LAN. For traffic off site, through some sort of private or public WAN, IPSec protocols are used. These protocols operate in networking devices, such as a router or firewall, that connect each LAN to the outside world. The IPSec networking device will typically encrypt and compress all traffic going into the WAN and decrypt and uncompress traffic coming from the WAN; authentication may also be provided. These operations are transparent to workstations and servers on the LAN. Secure transmission is also possible with individual users who dial into the WAN. Such user workstations must implement the IPSec protocols to provide security. They must also implement high levels of host security, as they are directly

---

[1]Details of IPSec are provided in Chapter 9. For this discussion, all that we need to know is that IPSec adds one or more additional headers to the IP packet to support encryption and authentication functions.

connected to the wider Internet. This makes them an attractive target for attackers attempting to access the corporate network.

A logical means of implementing an IPSec is in a firewall, as shown in Figure 12.4. If IPSec is implemented in a separate box behind (internal to) the firewall, then VPN traffic passing through the firewall in both directions is encrypted. In this case, the firewall is unable to perform its filtering function or other security functions, such as access control, logging, or scanning for viruses. IPSec could be implemented in the boundary router, outside the firewall. However, this device is likely to be less secure than the firewall and thus less desirable as an IPSec platform.

Distributed Firewalls

A distributed firewall configuration involves stand-alone firewall devices plus host-based firewalls working together under a central administrative control. Figure 12.5 suggests a distributed firewall configuration. Administrators can configure host-resident firewalls on hundreds of servers and workstations as well as configure personal firewalls on local and remote user systems. Tools let the network administrator set policies and monitor security across the entire network. These firewalls protect against internal attacks and provide protection tailored to specific machines and applications. Stand-alone firewalls provide global protection, including internal firewalls and an external firewall, as discussed previously.

With distributed firewalls, it may make sense to establish both an internal and an external DMZ. Web servers that need less protection because they have less critical information on them could be placed in an external DMZ, outside the external firewall. What protection is needed is provided by host-based firewalls on these servers.

An important aspect of a distributed firewall configuration is security monitoring. Such monitoring typically includes log aggregation and analysis, firewall statistics, and fine-grained remote monitoring of individual hosts if needed.

Summary of Firewall Locations and Topologies

We can now summarize the discussion from Sections 12.4 and 12.5 to define a spectrum of firewall locations and topologies. The following alternatives can be identified:

- **Host-resident firewall:** This category includes personal firewall software and firewall software on servers. Such firewalls can be used alone or as part of an in-depth firewall deployment.
- **Screening router:** A single router between internal and external networks with stateless or full packet filtering. This arrangement is typical for small office/home office (SOHO) applications.
- **Single bastion inline:** A single firewall device between an internal and external router (e.g., Figure 12.1a). The firewall may implement stateful filters and/or application proxies. This is the typical firewall appliance configuration for small- to medium-sized organizations.
- **Single bastion T:** Similar to single bastion inline but has a third network interface on bastion to a DMZ where externally visible servers are placed. Again, this is a common appliance configuration for medium to large organizations.

Figure 12.5 Example Distributed Firewall Configuration

- **Double bastion inline:** Figure 12.3 illustrates this configuration, where the DMZ is sandwiched between bastion firewalls. This configuration is common for large businesses and government organizations.

- **Double bastion T:** The DMZ is on a separate network interface on the bastion firewall. This configuration is also common for large businesses and government organizations and may be required. For example, this configuration is required for Australian government use (Australian Government Information Technology Security Manual—ACSI33).

- **Distributed firewall configuration:** Illustrated in Figure 12.5. This configuration is used by some large businesses and government organizations.

12.6 RECOMMENDED READING

A classic treatment of firewalls is [CHES03]. [LODI98], [OPPL97], and [BELL94b] are good overview articles on the subject. [SCAR09b] is an excellent overview of firewall technology and firewall policies. [AUDI04] and [WILS05] provide useful discussions of firewalls.

AUDI04   Audin, G. "Next-Gen Firewalls: What to Expect." *Business Communications Review*, June 2004.

BELL94b   Bellovin, S., and Cheswick, W. "Network Firewalls." *IEEE Communications Magazine*, September 1994.

CHAP00   Chapman, D., and Zwicky, E. *Building Internet Firewalls.* Sebastopol, CA: O'Reilly, 2000.

CHES03   Cheswick, W., and Bellovin, S. *Firewalls and Internet Security: Repelling the Wily Hacker.* Reading, MA: Addison-Wesley, 2003.

LODI98   Lodin, S., and Schuba, C. "Firewalls Fend Off Invasions from the Net." *IEEE Spectrum*, February 1998.

OPPL97   Oppliger, R. "Internet Security: Firewalls and Beyond." *Communications of the ACM*, May 1997.

SCAR09b   Scarfone, K., and Hoffman, P. *Guidelines on Firewalls and Firewall Policy.* NIST Special Publication SP 800-41-1, September 2009.

WILS05   Wilson, J. "The Future of the Firewall." *Business Communications Review*, May 2005.

12.7 KEY TERMS, REVIEW QUESTIONS, AND PROBLEMS

Key Terms

application-level gateway	firewall	personal firewall
bastion host	host-based firewall	proxy
circuit-level gateway	IP address spoofing	stateful inspection firewall
distributed firewalls	IP security (IPsec)	tiny fragment attack
DMZ	packet filtering firewall	virtual private network (VPN)

Review Questions

12.1   List three design goals for a firewall.

12.2   List four techniques used by firewalls to control access and enforce a security policy.

12.3   What information is used by a typical packet filtering firewall?

12.4   What are some weaknesses of a packet filtering firewall?

12.5   What is the difference between a packet filtering firewall and a stateful inspection firewall?

12.6   What is an application-level gateway?

12.7 What is a circuit-level gateway?

12.8 What are the differences among the firewalls of Figure 12.1?

12.9 What are the common characteristics of a bastion host?

12.10 Why is it useful to have host-based firewalls?

12.11 What is a DMZ network and what types of systems would you expect to find on such networks?

12.12 What is the difference between an internal and an external firewall?

Problems

12.1 As was mentioned in Section 12.3, one approach to defeating the tiny fragment attack is to enforce a minimum length of the transport header that must be contained in the first fragment of an IP packet. If the first fragment is rejected, all subsequent fragments can be rejected. However, the nature of IP is such that fragments may arrive out of order. Thus, an intermediate fragment may pass through the filter before the initial fragment is rejected. How can this situation be handled?

12.2 In an IPv4 packet, the size of the payload in the first fragment, in octets, is equal to Total Length − (4 × IHL). If this value is less than the required minimum (8 octets for TCP), then this fragment and the entire packet are rejected. Suggest an alternative method of achieving the same result using only the Fragment Offset field.

12.3 RFC 791, the IPv4 protocol specification, describes a reassembly algorithm that results in new fragments overwriting any overlapped portions of previously received fragments. Given such a reassembly implementation, an attacker could construct a series of packets in which the lowest (zero-offset) fragment would contain innocuous data (and thereby be passed by administrative packet filters), and in which some subsequent packet having a non-zero offset would overlap TCP header information (destination port, for instance) and cause it to be modified. The second packet would be passed through most filter implementations because it does not have a zero fragment offset. Suggest a method that could be used by a packet filter to counter this attack.

12.4 Table 12.3 shows a sample of a packet filter firewall ruleset for an imaginary network of IP address that range from 192.168.1.0 to 192.168.1.254. Describe the effect of each rule.

12.5 SMTP (Simple Mail Transfer Protocol) is the standard protocol for transferring mail between hosts over TCP. A TCP connection is set up between a user agent and a server program. The server listens on TCP port 25 for incoming connection requests. The user end of the connection is on a TCP port number above 1023. Suppose you wish to build

Table 12.3 Sample Packet Filter Firewall Ruleset

	Source Address	**Source Port**	**Dest Address**	**Dest Port**	**Action**
1	Any	Any	192.168.1.0	> 1023	Allow
2	192.168.1.1	Any	Any	Any	Deny
3	Any	Any	192.168.1.1	Any	Deny
4	192.168.1.0	Any	Any	Any	Allow
5	Any	Any	192.168.1.2	SMTP	Allow
6	Any	Any	192.168.1.3	HTTP	Allow
7	Any	Any	Any	Any	Deny

a packet filter ruleset allowing inbound and outbound SMTP traffic. You generate the
following ruleset:

Rule	Direction	Src Addr	Dest Addr	Protocol	Dest Port	Action
A	In	External	Internal	TCP	25	Permit
B	Out	Internal	External	TCP	>1023	Permit
C	Out	Internal	External	TCP	25	Permit
D	In	External	Internal	TCP	>1023	Permit
E	Either	Any	Any	Any	Any	Deny

a. Describe the effect of each rule.
b. Your host in this example has IP address 172.16.1.1. Someone tries to send
   e-mail from a remote host with IP address 192.168.3.4. If successful, this generates
   an SMTP dialogue between the remote user and the SMTP server on your host
   consisting of SMTP commands and mail. Additionally, assume that a user on your
   host tries to send e-mail to the SMTP server on the remote system. Four typical
   packets for this scenario are as shown:

Packet	Direction	Src Addr	Dest Addr	Protocol	Dest Port	Action
1	In	192.168.3.4	172.16.1.1	TCP	25	?
2	Out	172.16.1.1	192.168.3.4	TCP	1234	?
3	Out	172.16.1.1	192.168.3.4	TCP	25	?
4	In	192.168.3.4	172.16.1.1	TCP	1357	?

Indicate which packets are permitted or denied and which rule is used in each case.
c. Someone from the outside world (10.1.2.3) attempts to open a connection from
   port 5150 on a remote host to the Web proxy server on port 8080 on one of your
   local hosts (172.16.3.4), in order to carry out an attack. Typical packets are as
   follows:

Packet	Direction	Src Addr	Dest Addr	Protocol	Dest Port	Action
5	In	10.1.2.3	172.16.3.4	TCP	8080	?
6	Out	172.16.3.4	10.1.2.3	TCP	5150	?

Will the attack succeed? Give details.

12.6 To provide more protection, the ruleset from the preceding problem is modified as
      follows:

Rule	Direction	Src Addr	Dest Addr	Protocol	Src Port	Dest Port	Action
A	In	External	Internal	TCP	>1023	25	Permit
B	Out	Internal	External	TCP	25	>1023	Permit
C	Out	Internal	External	TCP	>1023	25	Permit
D	In	External	Internal	TCP	25	>1023	Permit
E	Either	Any	Any	Any	Any	Any	Deny

a. Describe the change.
b. Apply this new ruleset to the same six packets of the preceding problem. Indicate
   which packets are permitted or denied and which rule is used in each case.

12.7 A hacker uses port 25 as the client port on his or her end to attempt to open a connection to your Web proxy server.

a. The following packets might be generated:

Packet	Direction	Src Addr	Dest Addr	Protocol	Src Port	Dest Port	Action
7	In	10.1.2.3	172.16.3.4	TCP	25	8080	?
8	Out	172.16.3.4	10.1.2.3	TCP	8080	25	?

Explain why this attack will succeed, using the ruleset of the preceding problem.

b. When a TCP connection is initiated, the ACK bit in the TCP header is not set. Subsequently, all TCP headers sent over the TCP connection have the ACK bit set. Use this information to modify the ruleset of the preceding problem to prevent the attack just described.

12.8 A common management requirement is that "all external Web traffic must flow via the organization's Web proxy." However, that requirement is easier stated than implemented. Discuss the various problems and issues, possible solutions, and limitations with supporting this requirement. In particular consider issues such as identifying exactly what constitutes "Web traffic" and how it may be monitored, given the large range of ports and various protocols used by Web browsers and servers.

12.9 Consider the threat of "theft/breach of proprietary or confidential information held in key data files on the system." One method by which such a breach might occur is the accidental/deliberate e-mailing of information to a user outside of the organization. A possible countermeasure to this is to require all external e-mail to be given a sensitivity tag (classification if you like) in its subject and for external e-mail to have the lowest sensitivity tag. Discuss how this measure could be implemented in a firewall and what components and architecture would be needed to do this.

12.10 You are given the following "informal firewall policy" details to be implemented using a firewall like that in Figure 12.3:

1. E-mail may be sent using SMTP in both directions through the firewall, but it must be relayed via the DMZ mail gateway that provides header sanitization and content filtering. External e-mail must be destined for the DMZ mail server.
2. Users inside may retrieve their e-mail from the DMZ mail gateway, using either POP3 or POP3S, and authenticate themselves.
3. Users outside may retrieve their e-mail from the DMZ mail gateway, but only if they use the secure POP3 protocol, and authenticate themselves.
4. Web requests (both insecure and secure) are allowed from any internal user out through the firewall but must be relayed via the DMZ Web proxy, which provides content filtering (noting this is not possible for secure requests), and users must authenticate with the proxy for logging.
5. Web requests (both insecure and secure) are allowed from anywhere on the Internet to the DMZ Web server.
6. DNS lookup requests by internal users allowed via the DMZ DNS server, which queries to the Internet.
7. External DNS requests are provided by the DMZ DNS server.
8. Management and update of information on the DMZ servers is allowed using secure shell connections from relevant authorized internal users (may have different sets of users on each system as appropriate).
9. SNMP management requests are permitted from the internal management hosts to the firewalls, with the firewalls also allowed to send management traps (i.e., notification of some event occurring) to the management hosts.

Design suitable packet filter rulesets (similar to those shown in Table 12.1) to be implemented on the "External Firewall" and the "Internal Firewall" to satisfy the aforementioned policy requirements.

APPENDIX A

SOME ASPECTS OF NUMBER THEORY

A.1 Prime and Relatively Prime Numbers

Divisors
Prime Numbers
Relatively Prime Numbers

A.2 Modular Arithmetic

The Devil said to Daniel Webster: "Set me a task I can't carry out, and I'll give you anything in the world you ask for."

Daniel Webster: "Fair enough. Prove that for n greater than 2, the equation $a^n + b^n = c^n$ has no non-trivial solution in the integers."

They agreed on a three-day period for the labor, and the Devil disappeared.

At the end of three days, the Devil presented himself, haggard, jumpy, biting his lip. Daniel Webster said to him, "Well, how did you do at my task? Did you prove the theorem?"

"Eh? No . . . no, I haven't proved it."

"Then I can have whatever I ask for? Money? The Presidency?"

"What? Oh, that—of course. But listen! If we could just prove the following two lemmas—"

— *The Mathematical Magpie,* **Clifton Fadiman**

In this appendix, we provide some background on two concepts referenced in this book: prime numbers and modular arithmetic.

A.1 PRIME AND RELATIVELY PRIME NUMBERS

In this section, unless otherwise noted, we deal only with nonnegative integers. The use of negative integers would introduce no essential differences.

Divisors

We say that $b \neq 0$ divides a if $a = mb$ for some m, where a, b, and m are integers. That is, b divides a if there is no remainder on division. The notation $b|a$ is commonly used to mean b divides a. Also, if $b|a$, we say that b is a *divisor* of a. For example, the positive divisors of 24 are 1, 2, 3, 4, 6, 8, 12, and 24.

The following relations hold:

- If $a|1$, then $a = \pm1$.
- If $a|b$ and $b|a$, then $a = \pm b$.
- Any $b \neq 0$ divides 0.
- If $b|g$ and $b|h$, then $b|(mg + nh)$ for arbitrary integers m and n.

To see this last point, note that

If $b|g$, then g is of the form $g = b \times g_1$ for some integer g_1.

If $b|h$, then h is of the form $h = b \times h_1$ for some integer h_1.

So

$$mg + nh = mbg_1 + nbh_1 = b \times (mg_1 + nh_1)$$

and therefore b divides $mg + nh$.

Prime Numbers

An integer $p > 1$ is a prime number if its only divisors are ±1 and $\pm p$. Prime numbers play a critical role in number theory and in the techniques discussed in Chapter 3.

Any integer $a > 1$ can be factored in a unique way as

$$a = p_1^{a_1} \times p_2^{a_2} \times \ldots \times p_t^{a_t}$$

where $p_1 < p_2 < \ldots < p_t$ are prime numbers and where each a_i is a positive integer. For example, $91 = 7 \times 13$ and $11011 = 7 \times 11^2 \times 13$.

It is useful to cast this another way. If P is the set of all prime numbers, then any positive integer can be written uniquely in the following form:

$$a = \prod_{p \in P} p^{a_p} \quad \text{where each } a_p \geq 0$$

The right-hand side is the product over all possible prime numbers p; for any particular value of a, most of the exponents a_p will be 0.

The value of any given positive integer can be specified by simply listing all the nonzero exponents in the foregoing formulation. Thus, the integer 12 is represented by $\{a_2 = 2, a_3 = 1\}$, and the integer 18 is represented by $\{a_2 = 1, a_3 = 2\}$. Multiplication of two numbers is equivalent to adding the corresponding exponents:

$$k = mn \quad \rightarrow \quad k_p = m_p + n_p \quad \text{for all } p$$

What does it mean, in terms of these prime factors, to say that $a \mid b$? Any integer of the form p^k can be divided only by an integer that is of a lesser or equal power of the same prime number, p^j with $j \leq k$. Thus, we can say

$$a \mid b \quad \rightarrow \quad a_p \leq b_p \quad \text{for all } p$$

Relatively Prime Numbers

We will use the notation gcd (a, b) to mean the **greatest common divisor** of a and b. The positive integer c is said to be the greatest common divisor of a and b if

1. c is a divisor of a and of b.
2. Any divisor of a and b is a divisor of c.

An equivalent definition is the following:

$$\gcd(a, b) = \max[k, \text{ such that } k \mid a \text{ and } k \mid b]$$

Because we require that the greatest common divisor be positive, $\gcd(a, b) = \gcd(a, -b) = \gcd(-a, b) = \gcd(-a, -b)$. In general, $\gcd(a, b) = \gcd(|a|, |b|)$. For example, $\gcd(60, 24) = \gcd(60, -24) = 12$. Also, because all nonzero integers divide 0, we have $\gcd(a, 0) = |a|$.

It is easy to determine the greatest common divisor of two positive integers if we express each integer as the product of primes. For example,

$$300 = 2^2 \times 3^1 \times 5^2$$
$$18 = 2^1 \times 3^2$$
$$\gcd(18, 300) = 2^1 \times 3^1 \times 5^0 = 6$$

In general,

$$k = \gcd(a, b) \quad \rightarrow \quad k_p = \min(a_p, b_p) \quad \text{for all } p$$

Determining the prime factors of a large number is no easy task, so the preceding relationship does not directly lead to a way of calculating the greatest common divisor.

The integers a and b are relatively prime if they have no prime factors in common, that is, if their only common factor is 1. This is equivalent to saying that a and b are relatively prime if $\gcd(a, b) = 1$. For example, 8 and 15 are relatively prime because the divisors of 8 are 1, 2, 4, and 8, and the divisors of 15 are 1, 3, 5, and 15, so 1 is the only number on both lists.

A.2 MODULAR ARITHMETIC

Given any positive integer n and any nonnegative integer a, if we divide a by n, we get an integer quotient q and an integer remainder r that obey the following relationship:

$$a = qn + r \qquad 0 \leq r < n; q = \lfloor a/n \rfloor$$

where $\lfloor x \rfloor$ is the largest integer less than or equal to x.

Figure A.1a demonstrates that, given a and positive n, it is always possible to find q and r that satisfy the preceding relationship. Represent the integers on the number line; a will fall somewhere on that line (positive a is shown, a similar demonstration can be made for negative a). Starting at 0, proceed to $n, 2n$, up to qn such that $qn \leq a$ and $(q + 1)n > a$. The distance from qn to a is r, and we have found the unique values of q and r. The remainder r is often referred to as a **residue**.

If a is an integer and n is a positive integer, we define a mod n to be the remainder when a is divided by n. Thus, for any integer a, we can always write:

$$a = \lfloor a/n \rfloor \times n + (a \bmod n)$$

(a) General relationship

(b) Example: 70 = (4×15) + 10

Figure A.1   The Relationship $a = qn + r; 0 \leq r < n$

Two integers a and b are said to be **congruent modulo n**, if $(a \bmod n) = (b \bmod n)$. This is written $a \equiv b \bmod n$. For example, $73 \equiv 4 \bmod 23$ and $21 \equiv -9 \bmod 10$. Note that if $a \equiv 0 \bmod n$, then $n \,|\, a$.

The modulo operator has the following properties:

1. $a \equiv b \bmod n$ if $n \,|\, (a - b)$.
2. $(a \bmod n) = (b \bmod n)$ implies $a \equiv b \bmod n$.
3. $a \equiv b \bmod n$ implies $b \equiv a \bmod n$.
4. $a \equiv b \bmod n$ and $b \equiv c \bmod n$ imply $a \equiv c \bmod n$.

To demonstrate the first point, if $n \,|\, (a - b)$, then $(a - b) = kn$ for some k. So we can write $a = b + kn$. Therefore, $(a \bmod n) =$ (remainder when $b + kn$ is divided by n) = (remainder when b is divided by n) = $(b \bmod n)$. The remaining points are as easily proved.

The $(\bmod\ n)$ operator maps all integers into the set of integers $\{0, 1, \ldots, (n - 1)\}$. This suggests the question: Can we perform arithmetic operations within the confines of this set? It turns out that we can; the technique is known as **modular arithmetic**.

Modular arithmetic exhibits the following properties:

1. $[(a \bmod n) + (b \bmod n)] \bmod n = (a + b) \bmod n$
2. $[(a \bmod n) - (b \bmod n)] \bmod n = (a - b) \bmod n$
3. $[(a \bmod n) \times (b \bmod n)] \bmod n = (a \times b) \bmod n$

We demonstrate the first property. Define $(a \bmod n) = r_a$ and $(b \bmod n) = r_b$. Then we can write $a = r_a + jn$ for some integer j and $b = r_b + kn$ for some integer k. Then

$$
\begin{aligned}
(a + b) \bmod n &= (r_a + jn + r_b + kn) \bmod n \\
&= (r_a + r_b + (k + j)n) \bmod n \\
&= (r_a + r_b) \bmod n \\
&= [(a \bmod n) + (b \bmod n)] \bmod n
\end{aligned}
$$

The remaining properties are as easily proved.

APPENDIX B

PROJECTS FOR TEACHING NETWORK SECURITY

B.1   Research Projects

B.2   Hacking Project

B.3   Programming Projects

B.4   Laboratory Exercises

B.5   Practical Security Assessments

B.6   Firewall Projects

B.7   Case Studies

B.8   Writing Assignments

B.9   Reading/Report Assignments

Analysis and observation, theory and experience must never disdain or exclude each other;
on the contrary, they support each other.

— *On War*, **Carl Von Clausewitz**

Many instructors believe that research or implementation projects are crucial to the clear understanding of network security. Without projects, it may be difficult for students to grasp some of the basic concepts and interactions among components. Projects reinforce the concepts introduced in the book, give the student a greater appreciation of how a cryptographic algorithm or protocol works, and can motivate students and give them confidence that they are capable of not only understanding but implementing the details of a security capability.

In this text, I have tried to present the concepts of network security as clearly as possible and have provided numerous homework problems to reinforce those concepts. However, many instructors will wish to supplement this material with projects. This appendix provides some guidance in that regard and describes support material available in the **Instructor's Resource Center (IRC)** for this book, accessible to instructors from Prentice Hall. The support material covers nine types of projects:

1. Research projects
2. Hacking project
3. Programming projects
4. Laboratory exercises
5. Practical security assessments
6. Firewall projects
7. Case studies
8. Writing assignments
9. Reading/report assignments

B.1 RESEARCH PROJECTS

An effective way of reinforcing basic concepts from the course and for teaching students research skills is to assign a research project. Such a project could involve a literature search as well as an Internet search of vendor products, research lab activities, and standardization efforts. Projects could be assigned to teams or, for smaller projects, to individuals. In any case, it is best to require some sort of project proposal early in the term, giving the instructor time to evaluate the proposal for appropriate topic and appropriate level of effort. Student handouts for research projects should include the following:

- A format for the proposal
- A format for the final report
- A schedule with intermediate and final deadlines
- A list of possible project topics

The students can select one of the topics listed in the instructor's manual or devise their own comparable project. The IRC includes a suggested format for the proposal and final report as well as a list of fifteen possible research topics.

B.2 HACKING PROJECT

The aim of this project is to hack into a corporation's network through a series of steps. The Corporation is named Extreme In Security Corporation. As the name indicates, the corporation has some security holes in it, and a clever hacker is able to access critical information by hacking into its network. The IRC includes what is needed to set up the Web site. The student's goal is to capture the secret information about the price on the quote the corporation is placing next week to obtain a contract for a governmental project.

The student should start at the Web site and find his or her way into the network. At each step, if the student succeeds, there are indications as to how to proceed on to the next step as well as the grade until that point.

The project can be attempted in three ways:

1. Without seeking any sort of help
2. Using some provided hints
3. Using exact directions

The IRC includes the files needed for this project:

1. Web Security project
2. Web Hacking exercises (XSS and Script-attacks) covering client-side and server-side vulnerability exploitations, respectively
3. Documentation for installation and use for the above
4. A PowerPoint file describing Web hacking. This file is crucial to understanding how to use the exercises since it clearly explains the operation using screen shots.

This project was designed and implemented by Professor Sreekanth Malladi of Dakota State University.

B.3 PROGRAMMING PROJECTS

The programming project is a useful pedagogical tool. There are several attractive features of stand-alone programming projects that are not part of an existing security facility.

1. The instructor can choose from a wide variety of cryptography and network security concepts to assign projects.
2. The projects can be programmed by the students on any available computer and in any appropriate language; they are platform and language independent.
3. The instructor need not download, install, and configure any particular infrastructure for stand-alone projects.

There is also flexibility in the size of projects. Larger projects give students more sense of achievement, but students with less ability or fewer organizational skills can be left behind. Larger projects usually elicit more overall effort from the best students. Smaller projects can have a higher concepts-to-code ratio, and because more of them can be assigned, the opportunity exists to address a variety of different areas.

Again, as with research projects, the students should first submit a proposal. The student handout should include the same elements listed in Section B.1. The IRC includes a set of twelve possible programming projects.

The following individuals have supplied the research and programming projects suggested in the instructor's manual: Henning Schulzrinne of Columbia University; Cetin Kaya Koc of Oregon State University; and David M. Balenson of Trusted Information Systems and George Washington University.

B.4 LABORATORY EXERCISES

Professor Sanjay Rao and Ruben Torres of Purdue University have prepared a set of laboratory exercises that are part of the IRC. These are implementation projects designed to be programmed on Linux but could be adapted for any Unix environment. These laboratory exercises provide realistic experience in implementing security functions and applications.

B.5 PRACTICAL SECURITY ASSESSMENTS

Examining the current infrastructure and practices of an existing organization is one of the best ways of developing skills in assessing its security posture. The IRC contains a list of such activities. Students, working either individually or in small groups, select a suitable small-to-medium-sized organization. They then interview some key personnel in that organization in order to conduct a suitable selection of security risk assessment and review tasks as it relates to the organization's IT infrastructure and practices. As a result, they can then recommend suitable changes, which can improve the organization's IT security. These activities help students develop an appreciation of current security practices and the skills needed to review these and recommend changes.

Lawrie Brown of the Australian Defence Force Academy developed these projects.

B.6 FIREWALL PROJECTS

The implementation of network firewalls can be a difficult concept for students to grasp initially. The IRC includes a Network Firewall Visualization tool to convey and teach network security and firewall configuration. This tool is intended to teach and reinforce key concepts including the use and purpose of a perimeter firewall, the use of separated subnets, the purposes behind packet filtering, and the shortcomings of a simple packet filter firewall.

The IRC includes a .jar file that is fully portable and a series of exercises. The tool and exercises were developed at U.S. Air Force Academy.

B.7 CASE STUDIES

Teaching with case studies engages students in active learning. The IRC includes case studies in the following areas:

- Disaster recovery
- Firewalls
- Incidence response
- Physical security
- Risk
- Security policy
- Virtualization

Each case study includes learning objectives, case description, and a series of case discussion questions. Each case study is based on real-world situations and includes papers or reports describing the case.

The case studies were developed at North Carolina A&T State University.

B.8 WRITING ASSIGNMENTS

Writing assignments can have a powerful multiplier effect in the learning process in a technical discipline such as cryptography and network security. Adherents of the Writing Across the Curriculum (WAC) movement (http://wac.colostate.edu/) report substantial benefits of writing assignments in facilitating learning. Writing assignments lead to more detailed and complete thinking about a particular topic. In addition, writing assignments help to overcome the tendency of students to pursue a subject with a minimum of personal engagement—just learning facts and problem-solving techniques without obtaining a deep understanding of the subject matter.

The IRC contains a number of suggested writing assignments, organized by chapter. Instructors may ultimately find that this is an important part of their approach to teaching the material. I would greatly appreciate any feedback on this area and any suggestions for additional writing assignments.

B.9 READING/REPORT ASSIGNMENTS

Another excellent way to reinforce concepts from the course and to give students research experience is to assign papers from the literature to be read and analyzed. The IRC includes a suggested list of papers, one or two per chapter, to be assigned. The IRC provides a PDF copy of each of the papers. The IRC also includes a suggested assignment wording.

REFERENCES

In matters of this kind everyone feels he is justified in writing and publishing the first thing that comes into his head when he picks up a pen, and thinks his own idea as axiomatic as the fact that two and two make four. If critics would go to the trouble of thinking about the subject for years on end and testing each conclusion against the actual history of war, as I have done, they would undoubtedly be more careful of what they wrote.

—*On War,* Carl von Clausewitz

ABBREVIATIONS

ACM   Association for Computing Machinery
IBM   International Business Machines Corporation
IEEE   Institute of Electrical and Electronics Engineers
NIST   National Institute of Standards and Technology

ALEX04   Alexander, S. "Password Protection for Modern Operating Systems." *;login*, June 2004.

ALVA90   Alvare, A. "How Crackers Crack Passwords or What Passwords to Avoid." *Proceedings, UNIX Security Workshop II*, August 1990.

ANDE80   Anderson, J. *Computer Security Threat Monitoring and Surveillance.* Fort Washington, PA: James P. Anderson Co., April 1980.

ANDE95   Anderson, D., et al. *Detecting Unusual Program Behavior Using the Statistical Component of the Next-generation Intrusion Detection Expert System (NIDES).* Technical Report SRI-CSL-95-06, SRI Computer Science Laboratory, May 1995. www.csl.sri.com/programs/intrusion

ANDR04   Andrews, M., and Whittaker, J. "Computer Security." *IEEE Security and Privacy*, September/October 2004.

ANTE06   Ante, S., and Grow, B. "Meet the Hackers." *Business Week*, May 29, 2006.

ANTH10   Anthes, G. "Security in the Cloud." *Communications of the ACM*, November 2010.

AROR12   Arora, M. "How Secure Is AES Against Brute-Force Attack?" *EE Times*, May 7, 2012.

AUDI04   Audin, G. "Next-Gen Firewalls: What to Expect." *Business Communications Review*, June 2004.

AXEL00   Axelsson, S. "The Base-Rate Fallacy and the Difficulty of Intrusion Detection." *ACM Transactions and Information and System Security*, August 2000.

AYCO06   Aycock, J. *Computer Viruses and Malware.* New York: Springer, 2006.

BALA09   Balachandra, R.; Ramakrishna, P.; and Rakshit, A. "Cloud Security Issues." *Proceedings, 2009 IEEE International Conference on Services Computing*, 2009.

BALA98   Balasubramaniyan, J., et al. "An Architecture for Intrusion Detection Using Autonomous Agents." *Proceedings, 14th Annual Computer Security Applications Conference*, 1998.

BARK05   Barker, E., et al. *Recommendation for Key Management—Part 2: Best Practices for Key Management Organization.* NIST SP800-57, August 2005.

BARK09   Barker, E., et al. *Recommendation for Key Management—Part 3: Specific Key Management Guidance.* NIST SP800-57, December 2009.

BARK12   Barker, E., et al. *Recommendation for Key Management—Part 1: General.* NIST SP800-57, June 2012.

BARR05   Barrett, D.; Silverman, R.; and Byrnes, R. *SSH The Secure Shell: The Definitive Guide.* Sebastopol, CA: O'Reilly, 2005.

BASU12   Basu, A. *Intel AES-NI Performance Testing over Full Disk Encryption.* Intel Corp., May 2012.

BAUE88   Bauer, D., and Koblentz, M. "NIDX—An Expert System for Real-Time Network Intrusion Detection." *Proceedings, Computer Networking Symposium*, April 1988.

BECH11   Becher, M., et al. "Mobile Security Catching Up? Revealing the Nuts and Bolts of the Security of Mobile Devices." *IEEE Symposium on Security and Privacy*, 2011.

BELL90   Bellovin, S., and Merritt, M. "Limitations of the Kerberos Authentication System." *Computer Communications Review*, October 1990.

BELL94   Bellovin, S., and Cheswick, W. "Network Firewalls." *IEEE Communications Magazine*, September 1994.

BELL96a   Bellare, M.; Canetti, R.; and Krawczyk, H. "Keying Hash Functions for Message Authentication." *Proceedings, CRYPTO '96*, August 1996; published by Springer-Verlag. An expanded version is available at http://www-cse.ucsd.edu/users/mihir.

BELL96b   Bellare, M.; Canetti, R.; and Krawczyk, H. "The HMAC Construction." *CryptoBytes*, Spring 1996.

BHAT07   Bhatti, R.; Bertino, E.; and Ghafoor, A. "An Integrated Approach to Federated Identity and Privilege Management in Open Systems." *Communications of the ACM*, February 2007.

BINS10   Binsalleeh, H., et al. "On the Analysis of the Zeus Botnet Crimeware Toolkit." *Proceedings of the 8th Annual International Conference on Privacy, Security and Trust*, IEEE, September 2010.

BLOO70   Bloom, B. "Space/time Trade-offs in Hash Coding with Allowable Errors." *Communications of the ACM*, July 1970.

BROW72   Browne, P. "Computer Security — A Survey." *ACM SIGMIS Database*, Fall 1972.

BRYA88   Bryant, W. *Designing an Authentication System: A Dialogue in Four Scenes.* Project Athena document, February 1988. Available at http://web.mit.edu/kerberos/www/dialogue.html.

CASS01   Cass, S. "Anatomy of Malice." *IEEE Spectrum*, November 2001.

CERT01   CERT Coordination Center. "Denial of Service Attacks." June 2001. http://www.cert.org/tech_tips/denial_of_service.html.

CHAN02   Chang, R. "Defending Against Flooding-Based Distributed Denial-of-Service Attacks: A Tutorial." *IEEE Communications Magazine*, October 2002.

CHAN09   Chandola, V.; Banerjee, A.; and Kumar, V. "Anomaly Detection: A Survey." *ACM Computing Surveys*, July 2009.

CHAP00   Chapman, D., and Zwicky, E. *Building Internet Firewalls.* Sebastopol, CA: O'Reilly, 2000.

CHEN98   Cheng, P., et al. "A Security Architecture for the Internet Protocol." *IBM Systems Journal*, Number 1, 1998.

CHEN04   Chen, S., and Tang, T. "Slowing Down Internet Worms." *Proceedings of the 24th International Conference on Distributed Computing Systems*, 2004.

CHEN05a   Chen, J.; Jiang, M.; and Liu, Y. "Wireless LAN Security and IEEE 802.i." *IEEE Wireless Communications*, February 2005.

CHEN05b   Chen, J., and Wang, Y. "Extensible Authentication Protocol (EAP) and IEEE 802.1x: Tutorial and Empirical Experience." *IEEE Radio Communications*, December 2005.

CHES03   Cheswick, W., and Bellovin, S. *Firewalls and Internet Security: Repelling the Wily Hacker.* Reading, MA: Addison-Wesley, 2003.

CHEN11   Chen, T. M., and Abu-Nimeh, S. "Lessons from Stuxnet" *IEEE Computer*, 44(4), pp. 91–93, April 2011.

CHIN05   Chinchani, R., and Berg, E. "A Fast Static Analysis Approach to Detect Exploit Code Inside Network Flows." *Recent Advances in Intrusion Detection, 8th International Symposium*, 2005.

CHOI08   Choi, M., et al. "Wireless Network Security: Vulnerabilities, Threats and Countermeasures." *International Journal of Multimedia and Ubiquitous Engineering*, July 2008.

COHE94   Cohen, F. *A Short Course on Computer Viruses.* New York: Wiley, 1994.

COMP06   Computer Associates International. *The Business Value of Identity Federation.* White Paper, January 2006.

CONR02   Conry-Murray, A. "Behavior-Blocking Stops Unknown Malicious Code." *Network Magazine*, June 2002.

COST05   Costa, M., et al. "Vigilante: End-to-end Containment of Internet Worms." *ACM Symposium on Operating Systems Principles*, 2005.

CSA10   Cloud Security Alliance. *Top Threats to Cloud Computing V1.0.* CSA Report, March 2010.

CSA11a   Cloud Security Alliance. *Security Guidance for Critical Areas of Focus in Cloud Computing V3.0.* CSA Report, 2011.

CSA11b   Cloud Security Alliance. *Security as a Service (SecaaS).* CSA Report, 2011.

DAMI03   Damiani, E., et al. " Balancing Confidentiality and Efficiency in Untrusted Relational Databases." *Proceedings, Tenth ACM Conference on Computer and Communications Security,* 2003.

DAMI05   Damiani, E., et al. "Key Management for Multi-User Encrypted Databases." *Proceedings, 2005 ACM Workshop on Storage Security and Survivability,* 2005.

DAVI89   Davies, D., and Price, W. *Security for Computer Networks.* New York: Wiley, 1989.

DAWS96   Dawson, E., and Nielsen, L. "Automated Cryptoanalysis of XOR Plaintext Strings." *Cryptologia,* April 1996.

DENN87   Denning, D. "An Intrusion-Detection Model." *IEEE Transactions on Software Engineering,* February 1987.

DIFF76   Diffie, W., and Hellman, M. "Multiuser Cryptographic Techniques." *IEEE Transactions on Information Theory,* November 1976.

DIFF79   Diffie, W., and Hellman, M. "Privacy and Authentication: An Introduction to Cryptography." *Proceedings of the IEEE,* March 1979.

DIFF88   Diffie, W. "The First Ten Years of Public-Key Cryptography." *Proceedings of the IEEE,* May 1988.

EFF98   Electronic Frontier Foundation. *Cracking DES: Secrets of Encryption Research, Wiretap Politics, and Chip Design.* Sebastopol, CA: O'Reilly, 1998.

EMBL08   Embleton, S.; Sparks, S.; and Zou, C. "SMM Rootkits: a New Breed of OS-Independent Malware." *Proceedings of the 4th International Conference on Security and Privacy in Communication Networks,* ACM, September 2008.

ENIS09   European Network and Information Security Agency. *Cloud Computing: Benefits, Risks and Recommendations for Information Security.* ENISA Report, November 2009.

FEIS73   Feistel, H. "Cryptography and Computer Privacy." *Scientific American,* May 1973.

FLUH00   Fluhrer, S., and McGrew, D. "Statistical Analysis of the Alleged RC4 Key Stream Generator." *Proceedings, Fast Software Encryption 2000,* 2000.

FLUH01   Fluhrer, S.; Mantin, I.; and Shamir, A. "Weakness in the Key Scheduling Algorithm of RC4." *Proceedings, Workshop in Selected Areas of Cryptography,* 2001.

FORD95   Ford, W. "Advances in Public-Key Certificate Standards." *ACM SIGSAC Review,* July 1995.

FOSS10   Fossi, M., et al. "Symantec Report on Attack Kits and Malicious Websites." *Symantec,* 2010.

FRAN05   Frankel, S., et al. *Guide to IPsec VPNs.* NIST SP 800-77, 2005.

FRAN07   Frankel, S.; Eydt, B.; Owens, L.; and Scarfone, K. *Establishing Wireless Robust Security Networks: A Guide to IEEE 802.11i.* NIST Special Publication SP 800-97, February 2007.

FRAS97   Fraser, B. *Site Security Handbook.* RFC 2196, September 1997.

FUMY93   Fumy, S., and Landrock, P. "Principles of Key Management." *IEEE Journal on Selected Areas in Communications,* June 1993.

GARD77   Gardner, M. "A New Kind of Cipher That Would Take Millions of Years to Break." *Scientific American,* August 1977.

GEER06   Geer, D. "Hackers Get to the Root of the Problem." *Computer,* May 2006.

GEER10   Geer, D. "Whatever Happened to Network-Access-Control Technology?" *Computer,* September 2010.

GOLD10   Gold, S. " Social Engineering Today: Psychology, Strategies and Tricks." *Network Security,* November 2010.

GRAN04   Grance, T.; Kent, K.; and Kim, B. *Computer Security Incident Handling Guide.* NIST Special Publication SP 800-61, January 2004.

GUTM02   Gutmann, P. "PKI: It's Not Dead, Just Resting." *Computer,* August 2002.

HACI02   Hacigumus, H., et al. "Executing SQL over Encrypted Data in the Database-Service-Provider Model." *Proceedings, 2002 ACM SIGMOD International Conference on Management of Data,* 2002.

HAMM91 Hamming, R. *The Art of Probability for Scientists and Engineers.* Reading, MA: Addison-Wesley, 1991.

HASS10 Hassan, T.; Joshi, J.; and Ahn, G. "Security and Privacy Challenges in Cloud Computing Environments." *IEEE Security & Privacy*, November/December 2010.

HEBE92 Heberlein, L.; Mukherjee, B.; and Levitt, K. "Internetwork Security Monitor: An Intrusion-Detection System for Large-Scale Networks." *Proceedings, 15th National Computer Security Conference,* October 1992.

HEGL06 Hegland, A., et al. "A Survey of Key Management in Ad Hoc Networks." *IEEE Communications Surveys & Tutorials.* 3rd Quarter 2006.

HELD96 Held, G. *Data and Image Compression: Tools and Techniques.* New York: Wiley, 1996.

HOEP09 Hoeper, K., and Chen, L. *Recommendation for EAP Methods Used in Wireless Network Access Authentication.* NIST Special Publication 800-120, September 2009.

HOLZ05 Holz, T. "A Short Visit to the Bot Zoo." *IEEE Security and Privacy*, May–June 2005.

HONE01 The Honeynet Project. *Know Your Enemy: Revealing the Security Tools, Tactics, and Motives of the Blackhat Community.* Reading, MA: Addison-Wesley, 2001.

HONE05 The Honeynet Project. *Knowing Your Enemy: Tracking Botnets. Honeynet White Paper*, March 2005. http://honeynet.org/papers/bots.

HUIT98 Huitema, C. *IPv6: The New Internet Protocol.* Upper Saddle River, NJ: Prentice Hall, 1998.

IANS90 I'Anson, C., and Mitchell, C. "Security Defects in CCITT Recommendation X.509—The Directory Authentication Framework." *Computer Communications Review*, April 1990.

ILGU95 Ilgun, K.; Kemmerer, R.; and Porras, P. "State Transition Analysis: A Rule-Based Intrusion Detection Approach." *IEEE Transaction on Software Engineering,* March 1995.

JANS08 Jansen, W. *Guidelines on Active Content and Mobile Code.* NIST Special Publication SP 800-28, 2008.

JANS11 Jansen, W., and Grance, T. *Guidelines on Security and Privacy in Public Cloud Computing.* NIST Special Publication 800-144, January 2011.

JAVI91 Javitz, H., and Valdes, A. "The SRI IDES Statistical Anomaly Detector." *Proceedings, 1991 IEEE Computer Society Symposium on Research in Security and Privacy*, May 1991.

JHI07 Jhi, Y., and Liu, P. "PWC: A Proactive Worm Containment Solution for Enterprise Networks." *Third International Conference on Security and Privacy in Communications Networks*, 2007.

JUEN85 Jueneman, R.; Matyas, S.; and Meyer, C. "Message Authentication." *IEEE Communications Magazine*, September 1988.

JUNG04 Jung, J.; et al. "Fast Portscan Detection Using Sequential Hypothesis Testing." *Proceedings, IEEE Symposium on Security and Privacy*, 2004.

KENT00 Kent, S. "On the Trail of Intrusions into Information Systems." *IEEE Spectrum*, December 2000.

KEPH97 Kephart, J.; Sorkin, G.; Chess, D.; and White, S. "Fighting Computer Viruses." *Scientific American*, November 1997.

KLEI90 Klein, D. "Foiling the Cracker: A Survey of, and Improvements to, Password Security." *Proceedings, UNIX Security Workshop II*, August 1990.

KNUD98 Knudsen, L., et al. "Analysis Method for Alleged RC4." *Proceedings, ASIACRYPT '98*, 1998.

KOBL92 Koblas, D., and Koblas, M. "SOCKS." *Proceedings, UNIX Security Symposium III*, September 1992.

KOHL89 Kohl, J. "The Use of Encryption in Kerberos for Network Authentication." *Proceedings, Crypto '89*, 1989; published by Springer-Verlag.

KOHL94 Kohl, J.; Neuman, B.; and Ts'o, T. "The Evolution of the Kerberos Authentication Service." In Brazier, F., and Johansen, D., editors. *Distributed Open Systems.* Los Alamitos, CA: IEEE Computer Society Press, 1994.

KREI09 Kreibich, C., et al. "Spamcraft: An Inside Look At Spam Campaign Orchestration." *Proceedings of the Second USENIX Workshop on Large-Scale Exploits and Emergent Threats (LEET'09)*, April 2009.

KUMA97 Kumar, I. *Cryptology.* Laguna Hills, CA: Aegean Park Press, 1997.

LAMP04   Lampson, B. "Computer Security in the Real World." *Computer*, June 2004.

LATT09   Lattin, B. "Upgrade to Suite B Security Algorithms." *Network World*, June 1, 2009.

LEIB07   Leiba, B., and Fenton, J. "DomainKeys Identified Mail (DKIM): Using Digital Signatures for Domain Verification." *Proceedings of Fourth Conference on E-mail and Anti-Spam (CEAS 07)*, 2007.

LEUT94   Leutwyler, K. "Superhack." *Scientific American*, July 1994.

LEVI04   Levine, J.; Grizzard, J.; and Owen, H. "A Methodology to Detect and Characterize Kernel Level Rootkit Exploits Involving Redirection of the System Call Table." *Proceedings, Second IEEE International Information Assurance Workshop*, 2004.

LEVI06   Levine, J.; Grizzard, J.; and Owen, H. "Detecting and Categorizing Kernel-Level Rootkits to Aid Future Detection." *IEEE Security and Privacy*, January–February 2006.

LINN06   Linn, J. "Identity Management." In Bidgoli, H., editor. *Handbook of Information Security*. New York: Wiley, 2006.

LIPM00   Lipmaa, H.; Rogaway, P.; and Wagner, D. "CTR Mode Encryption." *NIST First Modes of Operation Workshop*, October 2000. http://csrc.nist.gov/encryption/modes.

LODI98   Lodin, S., and Schuba, C. "Firewalls Fend Off Invasions from the Net." *IEEE Spectrum*, February 1998.

MA10   Ma, D., and Tsudik, G. "Security and Privacy in Emerging Wireless Networks." *IEEE Wireless Communications*, October 2010.

MANT01   Mantin, I., and Shamir, A. "A Practical Attack on Broadcast RC4." *Proceedings, Fast Software Encryption*, 2001.

MCHU00   McHugh, J.; Christie, A.; and Allen, J. "The Role of Intrusion Detection Systems." *IEEE Software*, September/October 2000.

MCLA04   McLaughlin, L. "Bot Software Spreads, Causes New Worries." *IEEE Distributed Systems Online*, June 2004.

MENE97   Menezes, A.; van Oorschot, P.; and Vanstone, S. *Handbook of Applied Cryptography*. Boca Raton, FL: CRC Press, 1997.

MILL88   Miller, S.; Neuman, B.; Schiller, J.; and Saltzer, J. "Kerberos Authentication and Authorization System." *Section E.2.1, Project Athena Technical Plan*, M.I.T. Project Athena, Cambridge, MA, 27 October 1988.

MIRK04   Mirkovic, J., and Relher, P. "A Taxonomy of DDoS Attack and DDoS Defense Mechanisms." *ACM SIGCOMM Computer Communications Review*, April 2004.

MITC90   Mitchell, C.; Walker, M.; and Rush, D. "CCITT/ISO Standards for Secure Message Handling." *IEEE Journal on Selected Areas in Communications*, May 1989.

MORR79   Morris, R., and Thompson, K. "Password Security: A Case History." *Communications of the ACM*, November 1979.

NACH97   Nachenberg, C. "Computer Virus-Antivirus Coevolution." *Communications of the ACM*, January 1997.

NACH02   Nachenberg, C. "Behavior Blocking: The Next Step in Anti-Virus Protection." *White Paper*, SecurityFocus.com, March 2002.

NERC11   North American Electric Reliability Corp. *Guidance for Secure Interactive Remote Access*. July 2011. www.nerc.com

NEUM99   Neumann, P., and Porras, P. "Experience with EMERALD to Date." *Proceedings, 1st USENIX Workshop on Intrusion Detection and Network Monitoring*, April 1999.

NEWS05   Newsome, J.; Karp, B.; and Song, D. "Polygraph: Automatically Generating Signatures for Polymorphic Worms." *IEEE Symposium on Security and Privacy*, 2005.

NING04   Ning, P., et al. "Techniques and Tools for Analyzing Intrusion Alerts." *ACM Transactions on Information and System Security*, May 2004.

NIST95   National Institute of Standards and Technology. *An Introduction to Computer Security: The NIST Handbook*. Special Publication 800-12, October 1995.

NRC91   National Research Council. *Computers at Risk: Safe Computing in the Information Age*. Washington, D.C.: National Academy Press, 1991.

OECH03   Oechslin, P. "Making a Faster Cryptanalytic Time-Memory Trade-Off." *Proceedings, Crypto 03*, 2003.

OPPL97   Oppliger, R. "Internet Security: Firewalls and Beyond." *Communications of the ACM*, May 1997.

ORMA03   Orman, H. "The Morris Worm: A Fifteen-Year Perspective." *IEEE Security and Privacy*, September/October 2003.

PARZ06   Parziale, L., et al. *TCP/IP Tutorial and Technical Overview.* ibm.com/redbooks, 2006.

PATE06   Paterson, K. "A Cryptographic Tour of the IPsec Standards." *Cryptology ePrint Archive: Report 2006/097*, April 2006.

PELT07   Peltier, J. "Identity Management." *SC Magazine*, February 2007.

PERL99   Perlman, R. "An Overview of PKI Trust Models." *IEEE Network*, November/December 1999.

PERR03   Perrine, T. "The End of crypt() Passwords … Please?" *;login*, December 2003.

PORR92   Porras, P. *STAT: A State Transition Analysis Tool for Intrusion Detection.* Master's Thesis, University of California at Santa Barbara, July 1992.

PRED08   Predd, J., et al. "Insiders Behaving Badly." *IEEE Security & Privacy*, July/August 2008.

PROV99   Provos, N., and Mazieres, D. "A Future-Adaptable Password Scheme." *Proceedings of the 1999 USENIX Annual Technical Conference*, 1999.

RADC04   Radcliff, D. "What Are They Thinking?" *Network World*, March 1, 2004.

RESC01   Rescorla, E. *SSL and TLS: Designing and Building Secure Systems.* Reading, MA: Addison-Wesley, 2001.

RIVE78   Rivest, R.; Shamir, A.; and Adleman, L. "A Method for Obtaining Digital Signatures and Public Key Cryptosystems." *Communications of the ACM*, February 1978.

ROBS95a   Robshaw, M. *Stream Ciphers.* RSA Laboratories Technical Report TR-701, July 1995.

ROBS95b   Robshaw, M. *Block Ciphers.* RSA Laboratories Technical Report TR-601, August 1995.

ROS06   Ros, S. "Boosting the SOA with XML Networking." *The Internet Protocol Journal*, December 2006, cisco.com/ipj.

SALT75   Saltzer, J., and Schroeder, M. "The Protection of Information in Computer Systems." *Proceedings of the IEEE*, September 1975.

SCAR07   Scarfone, K., and Mell, P. *Guide to Intrusion Detection and Prevention Systems.* NIST Special Publication SP 800-94, February 2007.

SCAR09a   Scarfone, K., and Souppaya, M. *Guide to Enterprise Password Management (Draft).* NIST Special Publication SP 800-118 (Draft), April 2009.

SCAR09b   Scarfone, K., and Hoffman, P. *Guidelines on Firewalls and Firewall Policy.* NIST Special Publication SP 800-41-1, September 2009.

SCHN96   Schneier, B. *Applied Cryptography.* New York: Wiley, 1996.

SCHN00   Schneier, B. *Secrets and Lies: Digital Security in a Networked World.* New York: Wiley, 2000.

SEAG08   Seagate Technology. *128-Bit Versus 256-Bit AES Encryption.* Seagate Technology Paper, 2008.

SHAN77   Shanker, K. "The Total Computer Security Problem: An Overview." *Computer*, June 1977.

SHIM05   Shim, S.; Bhalla, G.; and Pendyala, V. "Federated Identity Management." *Computer*, December 2005.

SIDI05   Sidiroglou, S., and Keromytis, A. "Countering Network Worms Through Automatic Patch Generation." *IEEE Security and Privacy*, November–December 2005.

SING99   Singh, S. *The Code Book: The Science of Secrecy from Ancient Egypt to Quantum Cryptography.* New York: Anchor Books, 1999.

SMIT97   Smith, R. *Internet Cryptography.* Reading, MA: Addison-Wesley, 1997.

SNAP91   Snapp, S., et al. "A System for Distributed Intrusion Detection." *Proceedings, COMPCON Spring '91*, 1991.

SOUP12   Soup, M., and Scar, K. *Guide to Malware Incident Prevention and Handling for Desktops and Laptops*, NIST Special Publication 800-83 (Draft), July 2012.

SOUP12   Souppaya, M., and Scarfone, K. *Guidelines for Managing and Securing Mobile Devices in the Enterprise.* NIST Special Publication SP 800-124, July 2012.

SPAF92a   Spafford, E. "Observing Reusable Password Choices." *Proceedings, UNIX Security Symposium III*, September 1992.

SPAF92b   Spafford, E. "OPUS: Preventing Weak Password Choices." *Computers and Security*, No. 3, 1992.

SPAF00   Spafford, E., and Zamboni, D. "Intrusion Detection Using Autonomous Agents." *Computer Networks*, October 2000.

STAL11   Stallings, W. *Data and Computer Communications,* Ninth Edition. Upper Saddle River, NJ: Prentice Hall, 2011.

STAL12   Stallings, W., and Brown, L. *Computer Security,* Second Edition. Upper Saddle River, NJ: Prentice Hall, 2012.

STAL13   Stallings, W. *Cryptography and Network Security: Principles and Practice,* Sixth Edition. Upper Saddle River, NJ: Prentice Hall, 2013.

STEI88   Steiner, J.; Neuman, C.; and Schiller, J. "Kerberos: An Authentication Service for Open Networked Systems." *Proceedings of the Winter 1988 USENIX Conference*, February 1988.

STEP93   Stephenson, P. "Preventive Medicine." *LAN Magazine*, November 1993.

STEV11   Stevens, D. "Malicious PDF Documents Explained." *IEEE Security & Privacy*, January/February 2011.

STIN06   Stinson, D. *Cryptography: Theory and Practice.* Boca Raton, FL: Chapman & Hall/CRC Press, 2006.

SUMM84   Summers, R. "An Overview of Computer Security." *IBM Systems Journal*, Vol. 23, No. 4, 1984.

SYMA11   Symantec. "Internet Security Threat Report, Vol. 16." April 2011.

SZOR05   Szor, P. *The Art of Computer Virus Research and Defense.* Reading, MA: Addison-Wesley, 2005.

TSUD92   Tsudik, G. "Message Authentication with One-Way Hash Functions." *Proceedings, INFOCOM '92,* May 1992.

VACC89   Vaccaro, H., and Liepins, G. "Detection of Anomalous Computer Session Activity." *Proceedings of the IEEE Symposium on Research in Security and Privacy,* May 1989.

VANO94   van Oorschot, P., and Wiener, M. "Parallel Collision Search with Application to Hash Functions and Discrete Logarithms." *Proceedings, Second ACM Conference on Computer and Communications Security,* 1994.

VIGN02   Vigna, G.; Cassell, B.; and Fayram, D. "An Intrusion Detection System for Aglets." *Proceedings of the International Conference on Mobile Agents,* October 2002.

WANG05   Wang, X.; Yin, Y.; and Yu, H. "Finding Collisions in the Full SHA-1." *Proceedings, Crypto '05,* 2005; published by Springer-Verlag.

WAGN00   Wagner, D., and Goldberg, I. "Proofs of Security for the UNIX Password Hashing Algorithm." *Proceedings, ASIACRYPT '00,* 2000.

WARE79   Ware, W., ed. *Security Controls for Computer Systems.* RAND Report 609-1. October 1979.

WEAV03   Weaver, N., et al. "A Taxonomy of Computer Worms." *The First ACM Workshop on Rapid Malcode (WORM)*, 2003

WILS05   Wilson, J. "The Future of the Firewall." *Business Communications Review*, May 2005.

WOOD10   Wood, T., et al. "Disaster Recovery as a Cloud Service Economic Benefits & Deployment Challenges." *Proceedings, USENIX HotCloud '10,* 2010.

XU10   Xu, L. *Securing the Enterprise with Intel AES-NI.* Intel White Paper, September 2010.

YAN04   Yan, J. et al. "Password Memorability and Security: Empirical Results." *IEEE Security and Privacy*, September/October 2004.

YLON96   Ylonen, T. "SSH—Secure Login Connections over the Internet." *Proceedings, Sixth USENIX Security Symposium,* July 1996.

ZOU05   Zou, C., et al. "The Monitoring and Early Detection of Internet Worms." *IEEE/ACM Transactions on Networking,* October 2005.

CREDITS

Page 11: Sir Arthur Conan Doyle, The Case-Book of Sherlock Holmes; "The Adventure of the Lion's Mane," The Project Gutenberg Literary Archive Foundation.

Page 20: von Clausewitz, C. On War, Lake City, Utah. The Project Gutenberg Literary Archive Foundation, 2006.

Page 20: The Art of War, Sun Tzu, translated by Lionel Giles, The Project Gutenberg Literary Archive Foundation, May 1994.

Page 22: Guttman, B. and Roback, E.: National Institute of Standards and Technology. An Introduction to Computer Security: The NIST Handbook 1995.

Page 22: Shirey, R. "Internet Security Glossary, Version 2", Internet Engineering Task Force, Fremont, CA: August 2007.

Page 23: Standards for Security Categorization of Federal Information and Information Systems (FIPS PUB 199), NIST, Feb 2004.

Page 27: Shirey, R. "Internet Security Glossary, Version 2", Internet Engineering Task Force, Fremont, CA: August 2007.

Page 29: Shirey, R. "Internet Security Glossary, Version 2", Internet Engineering Task Force, Fremont, CA: August 2007.

Page 30: "Recommendation X.800 - Data Communication Networks: Open Systems Interconnection (OSI); Security, Structure and Applications" International Telecommunication Union (ITU): Geneve, Switzerland, 1991.

Page 42: Edgar Allen Poe, "The Gold Bug"; The Short-story by Atkinson, Harte, Hawthorne, Irving, Kipling, Poe, and Stevenson, The Project Gutenberg Literary Archive Foundation.

Page 42: Frazer, Sir James George, The Golden Bough, The Project Gutenberg Literary Archive Foundation, 2003.

Page 47: Feistel, H. "Cryptography and Computer Privacy." Scientific American, Vol. 228, No. 5, pp. 15–23, May 1973.

Page 52: Federal Information Processing Standards Publication 197.

Page 60: Kumar, I. Cryptology. Laguna Hills, CA: Aegean Park Press, 1997.

Page 64: Dworkin, M: Recommendation for Block 2001 Edition Cipher Modes of Operation Methods and Techniques, NIST (SP 800-38A), 2001.

Page 68: Lipmaa, H.; Rogaway, P.; and Wagner, D. "CTR Mode Encryption." NIST First Modes of Operation Workshop, October 2000.

Page 76: Frazer, Sir James George, The Golden Bough, The Project Gutenberg Literary Archive Foundation, 2003.

Page 78: Davies, D., and Price, W. Security for Computer Networks. New York: Wiley, 1989.

Page 79: Standard on Computer Data Authentication (FIPS PUB 113), NIST 1985.

Page 80: Tsudik, G. "Message Authentication with One-Way Hash Functions." Proceedings IEEE INFOCOM '92, The Conference on Computer Communications, Eleventh Annual Joint Conference of the IEEE Computer and Communications Societies, One World through Communications, May 4–8, 1992, Florence, Italy. IEEE, 1992, Volume 3.

Page 84: Jueneman, R.; Matyas, S.; and Meyer, C. "Message Authentication." IEEE Communications Magazine, September 1988.

Page 85: FIPS PUB 180-3, Secure Hash Standard (SHS), NIST, 2008.

Page 89: Krawczyk, H., Bellare, M., Canetti, R., HMAC: Keyed-Hashing for Message Authentication, RFC 2104, Fremont, CA, Internet Engineering Task Force, 1997.

Page 100: Diffie, W., and Hellman, M. "Multiuser Cryptographic Techniques." IEEE Transactions on Information Theory, November 1976.

Page 114: Frazer, Sir James George, The Golden Bough, The Project Gutenberg Literary Archive Foundation, 2003.

Page 126: Kohl, J.; Neuman, B.; and Ts'o, T. "The Evolution of the Kerberos Authentication Service." in Brazier, F., and Johansen, D. Distributed Open Systems. Los Alamitos, CA: IEEE Computer Society Press, 1994. Available at http://web.mit.edu/kerberos/www/papers.html.

Page 127: Bellovin, S., and Merritt, M. "Limitations of the Kerberos Authentication System." Computer Communications Review, October 1990.

Page 136: SERIES X: DATA NETWORKS, OPEN SYSTEM COMMUNICATIONS AND SECURITY X.509 - INTERNATIONAL STANDARD ISO/IEC 9594-8, Permission provided by International Telecommunication Union.

Page 137: Ford, W. "Advances in Public-Key Certificate Standards." ACM SIGSAC Review, July 1995.

Page 139: Shirley, R: Internet Security Glossary, Version 2 RFC 4949; Internet Engineering Task Force, 2007.

Page 154: Doyle, Sir Arthur Conan, The adventure of the Bruce-Partington Plans: The Project Gutenberg Literary Archive Foundation, 2000.

Page 158: Simon, D. Aboba, B. Hurst, R, RFC 5216 - The EAP-TLS Authentication Protocol, Fremont, Internet Engineering Task Force, 2008.

Page 159: Aboba, B., Blunk, L., Vollbrecht, J., & Carlson, J., Editor H. Levkowetz - RFC 3748 - Extensible Authentication Protocol (EAP), The Internet Society, Reston, VA, June 2004.

Page 164: Mell, P., Grance, T: SP-800-145 (The NIST Definition of Cloud Computing), NIST.

Page 168: Liu, F., Tong, J., Mao, J., Bohn, R., Messina, J., Badger, L. and Leaf, D.: SP-500-292 NIST Cloud Computing Reference Architecture, NIST.

Page 170: Cloud Security Alliance. Top Threats to Cloud Computing V1.0. CSA Report, March 2010.

Page 172: Swanson, M. & Guttman, B.: NIST 800-14 Generally Accepted Principles and Practices for Securing Information Technology Systems, NIST.

Page 175: Cloud Security Alliance. Security Guidance for Critical Areas of Focus in Cloud Computing V3.0. CSA Report, 2011.

Page 181: Lyric by Porter, Cole: From the song, "I've Got You Under My Skin".

Page 204: Ylonen, T., Lonvick, C.: The Secure Shell (SSH) Protocol Architecture, The Internet Society.

Page 209: Ylonen, T., Lonvick, C.: The Secure Shell (SSH) Protocol Architecture, The Internet Society.

Page 209: RFC 4254, The Secure Shell (SSH) Connection Protocol,, The Internet Society.

Page 217: Ma, D., and Tsudik, G. "Security and Privacy in Emerging Wireless Networks." IEEE Wireless Communications, October 2010.

Page 217: From THE HUMAN NATURE OF BIRDS (C) 1993 by Theodore Barber. Reprinted by permission of St. Martin's Press. All rights reserved.

Page 218: Choi, M., et. al. "Wireless Network Security: Vulnerabilities, Threats and Countermeasures." International Journal of Multimedia and Ubiquitous Engineering, July 2008.

Page 221: Souppaya, M. and Scarfone, K.: SP 800-124 (Guidelines for Managing and Securing Mobile Devices in the Enterprise) NIST.

Page 221: Soup, M., and Scarfone, K. Guide to Malware Incident Prevention and Handling for Desktops and Laptops, NIST Special Publication 800-83 (Draft), July 2012.

Page 225: IEEE 802.11™ WIRELESS LOCAL AREA NETWORKS The Working Group for WLAN Standards, IEEE.

Page 229: IEEE 802.11™ WIRELESS LOCAL AREA NETWORKS The Working Group for WLAN Standards, IEEE.

Page 231: Establishing Wireless Robust Security Networks: A Guide to IEEE 802.11i, NIST.

Page 237: Frankel, S.; Eydt, B.; Owens, L.; and Scarfone, K. Establishing Wireless Robust Security Networks: A Guide to IEEE 802.11i. NIST Special Publication SP 800-97, February 2007.

Page 240: Frankel, S.; Eydt, B.; Owens, L.; and Scarfone, K. Establishing Wireless Robust Security Networks: A Guide to IEEE 802.11i. NIST Special Publication SP 800-97, February 2007.

Page 242: Frankel, S.; Eydt, B.; Owens, L.; and Scarfone, K. Establishing Wireless Robust Security Networks: A Guide to IEEE 802.11i. NIST Special Publication SP 800-97, February 2007.

Page 249: The Tower Commission Report to President Reagan on the Iran-Contra Affair, 1987.

Page 255: Held, G. Data and Image Compression: Tools and Techniques. New York: Wiley, 1996.

Page 257: Resnick, P Ed: RFC 5322 - Internet Message Format, Internet Engineering Task Force.

Page 258: These materials have been reproduced by Pearson Education, Inc. with the permission of International Business Machines Corporation from IBM Redbooks® publication GG24-3376: TCP/IP Tutorial and Technical Overview (http://www.redbooks.ibm.com/abstracts/gg243376.html?Open"). COPYRIGHT © 2006 International Business Machines Corporation. ALL RIGHTS RESERVED.

Page 259: Freed, N. and Borenstein, N: RFC 2046: Multipurpose Internet Mail Extensions - (MIME) Part Two: Media Types, Internet Society.

Page 260: Freed, N. and Borenstein, N: RFC 2046: Multipurpose Internet Mail Extensions - (MIME) Part Two: Media Types, Internet Society.

Page 265: Bradner: RFC 2119 (Key Words for use in RFCs to Indicate Requirement Levels), The Internet Society.

Page 275: Fenton, J: RFC 4686: (Analysis of Threats Motivating DomainKeys Identified Mail), The internet Society, 2006.

Page 283: The Art of War, Sun Tzu, translated by Lionel Giles, The Project Gutenberg Literary Archive Foundation, May 1994.

Page 286: Huitema, C. IPv6: The New Internet Protocol. Upper Saddle River, NJ: Prentice Hall, 1998.

Page 287: Kent, S. and Seo, K: RFC 4301: Security Architecture for the Internet Protocol, The Internet Society, 2005.

Page 306: Huitema, Christian, IPv6: The New Internet Protocol, 2nd Ed., ©1998. Reprinted and Electronically reproduced by permission of Pearson Education, Inc., Upper Saddle River, NJ.

Page 320: von Clausewitz, C. On War, Lake City, Utah. The Project Gutenberg Literary Archive Foundation, 2006.

Page 322: Fossi M., et. al, "Symantec Report on Attack Kits and Malicious Websites." Symantec, 2010.

Page 329: Symantec, "Internet Security Threat Report, Vol. 16." April 2011.

Page 330: Mirkovic, J., and Relher, P. "A Taxonomy of DDoS Attack and DDoS Defense Mechanisms." ACM SIGCOMM Computer Communications Review, April 2004.

Page 333: Jansen, W.; Winograd, T.; Scarfone, K., Guidelines on Active Content and Mobile Code. NIST Special Publication SP 800-28, 2008 National Institute of Standards and Technology.

Page 333: Stevens, D. "Malicious PDF Documents Explained", IEEE Security & Privacy, January/February 2011.

Page 334: Kreibich, C. et al. "Spamcraft: An Inside Look At Spam Campaign Orchestration." Proceedings of the Second USENIX Workshop on Large-Scale Exploits and Emergent Threats (LEET'09), April 2009.

Page 335: Symantec, "Internet Security Threat Report, Vol. 16." April 2011.

Page 336: Chen, T.M.; and Abu-Nimeh, S. "Lessons from Stuxnet" IEEE Computer, 44(4), pp. 91–93, April 2011.

Page 336: Bacher, P., et. al: Knowing Your Enemy: Tracking Botnets. Honeynet White Paper, March 2005. http://honeynet.org/papers/bots

Page 339: Gold, S. " Social engineering today: psychology, strategies and tricks." Network Security, November 2010.

Page 339: Symantec, "Internet Security Threat Report, Vol. 16." April 2011.

Page 339: Chen, T.M.; and Abu-Nimeh, S. "Lessons from Stuxnet" IEEE Computer, 44(4), pp. 91–93, April 2011.

Page 341: Souppaya, M., and Scarfone, K. Guide to Malware Incident Prevention and Handling for Desktops and Laptops, NIST Special Publication 800-83 (Draft), July 2012.

Page 342: Stephenson, P. "Preventive Medicine." LAN Magazine, November 1993.

Page 345: Jhi, Y., and Liu, P., et. al: "PWC: A Proactive Worm Containment Solution for Enterprise Networks." Third International Conference on Security and Privacy in Communications Networks, 2007.

Page 346: Sidiroglou, S., and Keromytis, A. "Countering Network Worms Through Automatic Patch Generation." IEEE Security and Privacy, November–December 2005.

Page 351: Chang, R. "Defending Against Flooding-Based Distributed Denial-of-Service Attacks: A Tutorial." IEEE Communications Magazine, October 2002.

Page 355: The Treasure of Sierra Madre (film), written and directed by John Houston based on the novel by B. Traven, Warner Brothers Pictures, 1948.

Page 356: Cichonski, P., et. al: Computer Security Incident Handling Guide. NIST Special Publication SP 800-61, January 2004.

Page 358: Anderson, J. Computer Security Threat Monitoring and Surveillance. Fort Washington, PA: James P. Anderson Co., April 1980. NIST.

Page 359: Radcliff, D. "What Are They Thinking?" Network World, March 1, 2004.

Page 360: Ante, S., and Grow, B. "Meet the Hackers." Business Week, May 29, 2006.

Page 361: De Alvare, A. "How Crackers Crack Passwords or What Passwords to Avoid." Proceedings, UNIX Security Workshop II, August 1990.

Page 363: Anderson, J. Computer Security Threat Monitoring and Surveillance. Fort Washington, PA: James P. Anderson Co., April 1980. NIST.

Page 364: Porras, P. STAT: A State Transition Analysis Tool for Intrusion Detection. Master's Thesis, University of California at Santa Barbara, July 1992.

Page 365: Denning, D. "An Intrusion-Detection Model." IEEE Transactions on Software Engineering, February 1987.

Page 367: Denning, D. "An Intrusion-Detection Model." IEEE Transactions on Software Engineering, February 1987.

Page 371: Porras, P. STAT: A State Transition Analysis Tool for Intrusion Detection. Master's Thesis, University of California at Santa Barbara, July 1992.

Page 382: Klein, D. V., "Foiling the Cracker": A Survey of, and Improvements to, Password Security.

Page 382: Spafford, E. "Observing Reusable Password Choices." Proceedings, UNIX Security Symposium III, September 1992.

Page 383: Spafford, Eugene. "Observing Reusable Password Choices." Proceedings, UNIX Security Symposium III. September 1992. Accessed at http://docs.lib.purdue.edu/cgi/viewcontent.cgi?article=1969&context=cstech

Page 384: Klein, D.V., "Foiling the Cracker": A Survey of, and Improvements to, Password Security.

Page 392: Smith, R. Internet Cryptography. Reading, MA: Addison-Wesley, 1997.

Page 392: The Art of War, Sun Tzu, translated by Lionel Giles, The Project Gutenberg Literary Archive Foundation, May 1994.

Page 394: The Art of War, Sun Tzu, translated by Lionel Giles, The Project Gutenberg Literary Archive Foundation, May 1994.

Page 394: von Clausewitz, C. On War, Lake City, Utah. The Project Gutenberg Literary Archive Foundation, 2006.

Page 395: Bellovin, S., and Cheswick, W. "Network Firewalls." IEEE Communications Magazine, September 1994.

Page 395: Smith, R. Internet Cryptography. Reading, MA: Addison-Wesley, 1997.

Page 399: Bellovin, S., and Cheswick, W. "Network Firewalls." IEEE Communications Magazine, September 1994.

Page 399: Scarfone, K., and Souppaya, M. Guide to Enterprise Password Management (Draft). NIST Special Publication SP 800-118 (Draft), April 2009.

Page 403: Koblas, D., and Koblas, M. "SOCKS." Proceedings, UNIX Security Symposium III, September 1992.

Page 414: Lohwater, A. J., "The Devil a Mathematician Would Be, from Fadiman, Clifton Ed. The Mathematical Magpie, Springer; 2nd edition (April 4, 1997).

Page 419: von Clausewitz, C. On War, Lake City, Utah. The Project Gutenberg Literary Archive Foundation, 2006.

Page 423: von Clausewitz, C. On War, Lake City, Utah. The Project Gutenberg Literary Archive Foundation, 2006.

INDEX

A

Access, 32, 36
  control, 31
  threats, 36
Access control, 30
  defined, 31
Accessibility, 218
Access point (AP), IEEE 802.11, 227, 232
Access requestor (AR), 154
  supplicants, 154
Accidental association, 218
Account or service hijacking, 171
Active attacks, security, 27–29
Add Round Key, AES, 54
Ad hoc networks, 218
Alert codes, TLS, 199
Algorithms, 43, 48–54, 58–59, 97–105, 265–266, 296
  cryptographic, 265–266
  ESP, 296
  HMAC, 89–91
  S/MIME, 265–266
Advanced Encryption Standard (AES), 48, 51–54
Add Round Key, 54
  algorithm, 52–54
  Data Encryption Algorithm (DEA), 49
  Data Encryption Standard (DES), 49–51
  decryption, defined, 43, 95
  Diffie-Hellman key exchange, 100–103
  Digital Signature Algorithm (DSA), 104
  elliptic curve cryptography (ECC), 104–105
  encryption, 43, 94
  mix columns, 54
  public-key cryptography, 94–105
  RSA public-key encryption, 98–100
  shift rows, 654
  state array, 52
  structure, 52
  subkey generation, 48
  substitution bytes, 53
  symmetric block encryption, 48–54
  triple Data Encryption Standard (3DES), 50–51
Anti-replay service, ESP, 296–297
Architecture, 26–27
  open systems interconnection (OSI), 26–27
Attack(s), 27–29, 106, 130. *See also* Security attacks;
    Threats; Cryptanalysis
  active, 29
  chosen plaintext, 46
  ciphertext only, 45
  denial-of-service (DoS), 32
  kits, 320

known plaintext, 45–46
  man-in-the-middle, 103–104
  messages, types of for, 46
  passive, 27
  password, 127
  security, 27–29
  sources, 320–321
Attacking IRC chat networks, 335
Authentication, 31, 77–81, 158, 209, 181, 185–186. *See also* Message authentication; Message authentication codes (MAC)
  applications, 113–148
  client/server exchange, 129
  data origin, 31, 34
  dialogues, 117–123, 127–129
  forwarding, 126
  IEEE 802.11i phase, 232–234, 241
  IKE key determination, 307–308
  Internet Protocol (IP), 303
  interrealm, 127
  Kerberos, 116–129
  key exchange client and server, SSL, 193–194
  message, 75–106
  methods, 158
  peer entity, 31
  pretty good privacy (PGP), 249–255, 251
  public-key infrastructure (PKI), 139–141
  recommended reading and Web sites, 147–148
  server (AS), 117, 159
  service exchange, 128
  X.509 service, 131–139
Authority key identifier, 138

B

Backdoor (trapdoor), 337
Barcode readers, 218
Barrier security, 224
Basic service set (BSS), IEEE 802.11, 227, 228
Behavior-blocking software, 341
Block ciphers, 44, 48, 59, 59–61
  cipher block chaining (CBC) mode, 64–66
  cipher feedback (CFB) mode, 66–67
  defined, 44
  design of, 48
  electronic codebook (ECB), 64
  modes of operation, 64
  plaintext processing, cryptography, 44
Bogus reconfiguration commands. *See* Network injection
Boot sector infector, 325

Bots, uses of, 334–335
   attacking IRC chat networks, 335
   DDoS attacks, 334
   installing advertisement add-ons and BHOs, 335
   keylogging, 335
   manipulating online polls/games, 335
   sniffing traffic, 334
   spamming, 334
   spreading new malware, 335
Bring-your-own-device (BYOD) policy, 223
Broad network access, 164–165
Browser helper objects (BHOs), 335
Business continuity and disaster recovery, 178

C

Canonical form, MIME and S/MIME, 264
Certificates, 132–137, 141, 193–194, 200, 270
   certification authority (CA), 132, 139, 271
   enhanced security services, 272–273
   extensions, 133
   forward, 135
   issuer, 132, 133, 138–139
   key information, 133
   path constraints, 139
   period of validity, 133
   policy information, 138
   policy mappings, 138
   public-key, 129–130, 131
   reverse, 135
   revocation list (CRL), 137, 270
   revocation of, 136–137
   serial number, 132
   signature, 133
   signature algorithm identifier, 133
   S/MIME, 270
   subject, 133, 139
   TLS client types, 202
   unique identifiers, 133
   user, 270
   user's, obtaining, 134–136
   VeriSign, 271–272
   version, 132
   X.509, 131–139
Certificates-only message, S/MIME, 270
Certification authority (CA), 130, 139, 139
   key distribution, 130
   public-key infrastructure (PKI), 139–141
   VeriSign certificates, 271–272
   X.509 certificates, 132–134
Change Cipher Spec Protocol, 184, 188, 189, 195
Channels, 209–210, 217
Cipher block chaining (CBC) mode, 64–66
Cipher feedback (CFB) mode, 66–67
Cipher suites, TLS, 200
Ciphertext, 43, 94

Clear signing, S/MIME, 269–270
Client/server authentication exchange, 129
Client-side vulnerabilities, 331
   drive-by-download, 331
Cloud auditor, 169
Cloud-based applications, 221
Cloud broker, 169
   service aggregation, 169
   service arbitrage, 169
   service intermediation, 169
Cloud carrier, 169
Cloud computing
   abuse and nefarious use of, 170
   deployment models
      community cloud, 166
      hybrid cloud, 167
      private cloud, 166
      public cloud, 166
   elements, 164–167
   measured service, 165
   on-demand self-service, 165
   rapid elasticity, 165
   reference architecture, 168–170
   resource pooling, 165–166
   service models, 166
      Infrastructure as a service (IaaS), 166
      Platform as a service (PaaS), 166
      Software as a service (SaaS), 166
Cloud consumer, 168–169
Cloud provider, 168
Cloud security
   risks and countermeasures
      abuse/nefarious use of cloud computing, 170
      account or service hijacking, 171
      data loss or leakage, 171
      insecure interfaces and APIs, 170
      malicious insiders, 170
      shared technology issues, 171
      unknown risk profile, 171
   as a service
      business continuity and disaster
         recovery, 178
      data loss prevention (DLP), 177
      elements, 177
      e-mail security, 177
      encryption, 177–178
      identity and access management
         (IAM), 176
      intrusion management, 177
      network security, 178
      security as a service (SecaaS), 175
      security assessments, 177
      security information and event management
         (SIEM), 177
      web security, 177
   recommended reading, 178

Code, 197
  message authentication (MAC), 197, 205
Codebook, 64
  defined, 64
  electronic (ECB), 64
Community cloud, 166
Compression, 254–255
  PGP, 254–255
  SSL, 185, 191–192
Computer security, defined, 22
Confidentiality, 22, 23, 24, 231, 41–69, 254, 296, 300. *See also* Encryption
  data, 22, 30, 31, 242, 243
  Internet Protocol (IP), 302
  messages, 41–69
  pretty good privacy (PGP), 253–254
  traffic flow (TFC), 295
Connection, SSL, 184
Connection Protocol, SSH, 203, 209–213
Cookie exchange, 307
Countermeasures
  distributed intelligence gathering approaches, 344–345
  host-based behavior-blocking software, 341
  host-based scanners, 340–342
    first-generation scanner, 340
    second-generation scanner, 340
    third-generation scanner, 341
    fourth-generation scanner, 341
  malware countermeasure approaches
    detection, 339
    generality, 339
    global and local coverage, 340
    identification, 339
    minimal denial-of-service costs, 339
    removal, 339
    resiliency, 339
    timeliness, 339
    transparency, 339, 340
  perimeter scanning approaches, 342–343
    egress monitors, 343
    ingress monitors, 343
  perimeter worm countermeasures
    filter-based worm containment, 343
    payload-classification-based worm containment, 344
    rate halting, 344
    rate limiting, 344
    signature-based worm scan filtering, 343
    TRW scan detection, 344
  rootkit countermeasures, 342
  spyware detection and removal, 342
CRL issuer, PKI, 140
Credential theft, 336, 337
Cross-certification, PKI, 141
Cryptanalysis, 44–46

Cryptography, 44, 96–97, 100–103. *See also* Public-key cryptography
  algorithms, 101–102
  classification of systems, 44
  cryptosystems, applications for, 96–97
  encryption structure, 94–96
  public-key, 94–105
  requirements for, 96
Cryptographic computations, 195–196, 200–201

D

Data, 30, 31
  confidentiality, 30, 31
  integrity, 32
  origin authentication, 31
Data Encryption Standard (DES), 49–51
  algorithm (DES), description of, 49
  strength of, 49–50
  triple (3DES), 50–51
Data loss prevention (DLP), 171, 177
Data protection, cloud computing
  attributes, 174
  encryption scheme, 174
  multi-instance model, 173
  multi-tenant model, 173
  NIST guidelines on security and privacy, 172–173
  primary key, 174
  relation, 174
  tuples, 174
Decryption algorithm, 43, 95
Denial-of-service (DoS) attack, 32
  defined, 219
De-perimeterization, 221
Device security, 223–224
Diffie-Hellman key exchange, 100–101, 193, 196, 219
  anonymous, 193
  algorithm, 101–102
  ephemeral, 193
  fixed, 192
  introduction to, 100–101
  man-in-the-middle attack, 103
  protocols, 102–103
  SSL Handshake Protocol, 193, 196
Digital Signature Algorithm (DSA), 104
Digital Signature Standard (DSS), 104
Digital signatures, 104
Discovery phase, IEEE 802.11i, 234–236
Distributed denial-of-service (DDoS) attacks, 334, 345–350
  attack description
    direct, 347
    flooding-based, 348
    internal resource, 346
    reflector, 347

constructing attack network,
348–349
hit list, 349
local subnet, 349
random, 349
topological, 349
countermeasures, 349–350
detection and filtering, 349
prevention and preemption, 349
source traceback and identification, 350
Distributed intelligence gathering approaches, 344–345
Distribution system (DS), IEEE 802.11, 227
DomainKeys Identified Mail (DKIM), 273–280
e-mail threats, 275–276
functional flow, 278–280
Internet mail architecture, 273–275
strategy, 276–277
Double encryption, 127
Dynamic Host Configuration Protocol
(DHCP), 157

E

EAP-GPSK (EAP Generalized
Pre-Shared Key), 158
EAP-IKEv2, 158
EAP-TLS (EAP Transport Layer Security), 158
EAP-TTLS (EAP Tunneled TLS), 158
Eavesdropping. *See* Man-in-the middle attacks
Egress monitors, 343
Electronic codebook (ECB), 64
Electronic data interchange (EDI), 138
Electronic mail security, 248–280
DomainKeys Identified Mail (DKIM), 273–280
or instant messenger facility, 327
pretty good privacy (PGP), 249–256
radix-64 conversion, 255
Secure/Multipurpose Internet Mail Extension (S/
MIME), 257–273
Elliptic curve cryptography (ECC), 104–105
E-mail security, 177
Encapsulating security payload (ESP), 294–300
algorithms, 295
anti-replay service, 296–297
format, 294–295
padding, 296
transport mode, 297–300
tunnel mode, 300
Encrypted virus, 325
Encryption, 41–69, 78–79, 96–97, 100–103,
128, 129, 177–178, 219. *See also* Block
ciphers; Public-key cryptography;
Stream ciphers
Advanced Encryption Standard (AES), 48, 51–54
algorithms, 43, 48–54, 58–59, 97–105
block ciphers, 44, 48, 59, 59–61

ciphertext, 94
cryptanalysis, 44–46
cryptography, 44
Data Encryption Standard (DES), 49–51
decryption algorithms, 95
digital signatures, 104
double, 127
end-to-end, 115
Feistel cipher structure, 46–48
introduction to, 42–43
key distribution, 114–116, 129–131
message authentication and, 75–106
National Institute of Standards and Technology
(NIST), 37, 49, 85, 104
plaintext, 44, 45–46, 94
propagating cipher block chaining
(PCBC), 127
public-key, 94–105
RC4 algorithm, 61–64
recommended reading and Web sites, 69
RSA algorithm, 98–100
stream cipher, 44, 59–61, 66
symmetric, 43–48
symmetric block algorithms, 48–54
system dependence, 126
triple Data Encryption Standard (3DES), 50–51
End entity, PKI, 139
End-to-end encryption, 115
EnvelopedData, S/MIME, 267–268
Exchanges, 128–129. *See also* Key exchange
authentication service, 128
client/server authentication, 129
Kerberos, 126–129
ticket-granting service, 128–129
Extended service set (ESS), IEEE 802.11, 228
Extensible Authentication Protocol (EAP), 157
authentication methods, 158
EAP-GPSK (EAP Generalized Pre-Shared Key),
158
EAP-IKEv2, 158
EAP-TLS (EAP Transport Layer Security), 158
EAP-TTLS (EAP Tunneled TLS), 158
exchanges, 158–161
authentication server, 159
EAP authenticator, 159
EAP passthrough mode, 159
EAP peer, 159
RADIUS, 159
layered context, 157
messages
code, 160
data, 160
flow in pass-through mode, 160
identifier, 160
length, 160
External business requirements, 221

F

Feistel cipher structure, 46–48
File infector, 325
File sharing, 327
Filter-based worm containment, 343
Firewall, 124, 157
First-generation scanner, 340
Fortezza key exchange, 192, 193–194
Forward certificate, 135
Fourth-generation scanner, 341
Fragmentation, SSL, 186

G

GPS capability on mobile devices, 222
Group master key (PMK), IEEE 802.11i, 239–240

H

Handheld PDAs, 218
Handshake Protocol, 158, 190–193
Hash functions, 79–88
  HMAC, 88–91
  one-way, 79–81
  requirements, 81–82
  secure, 81–83
  Secure Hash Algorithm (SHA), 84
  SHA-1 secure functions, 84–88
  simple, 83–84
  strong collision resistance, 82
  weak collision resistance, 82
HMAC, 88–91
  algorithm, 89–91
  design objectives, 89
Host-based scanners, 340–342
Host keys, SSH, 203–208
HTTPS, 181, 201–202
Hybrid cloud, 167

I

Identity and access management (IAM), 176
Identity theft (MAC spoofing), 219, 337
IEEE 802.11 LAN, 224–230
  association-related services, 230
  message distribution, 229
  network components, 227–228
  protocol architecture, 225–227
IEEE 802.11i LAN, 230–244
  authentication phase, 233, 236–238
  characteristics of, 230–231
  connection termination, 234
  discovery phase, 233, 234–236
  key management phase, 234, 238–242
  phases of operation, 232–234
  protected data transfer phase, 234, 242–243
  pseudorandom function (PRF), 243–244
  Robust Security Network (RSN), 231–232
  services, 231

IEEE 802.1X port-based network access control, 156,
    161–163
  EAP-Key, 162
  EAP-Logoff, 162
  EAPOL-EAP, 162
  EAPOL-Start, 162
  packet body, 163
    length, 163
  packet type, 162
  protocol version, 162
  terminology related to IEEE 802.1X, 162
  802.1X access control, 163
Independent basic service set (IBSS), IEEE 802.11, 228
Information, 20, 36
  access threats, 36
  security, 20
Infrastructure as a service (IaaS), 166
Ingress monitors, 343
Initialization, 185
  PKI, 140–141
Insecure interfaces and APIs, 170
International Telecommunication
      Union (ITU), 26
Internet Architecture Board (IAB), 284
Internet Engineering Task Force (IETF), 37
  standards from, 37
Internet key exchange (IKE), 305–313
  cookies, 307
  header and payload formats, 309–313
  IKEv5 message exchange, 308–309
  key determination protocol, 306
Internet Protocol (IP), 126, 284–288. *See also* Internet
      Protocol security (IPSec)
  authentication plus confidentiality, 302
  combining security associations (SA), 301–305
  cryptographic suites, 313–315
  dependence, 126
  encapsulating security payload (ESP), 294–300
  Internet key exchange (IKE), 305–313
  security (IPsec), 288–294
  security association database (SAD), 289–290
  security policy database (SPD), 289, 290–292
  traffic processing, 292–294
Internet Protocol security (IPsec), 284–292
  documents, 286–287
  packets, 292–294
  policy, 288–292
  routing, 286
  transport mode, 287
  tunnel mode, 287–288
Internet security, 248–280
  defined, 21
  electronic mail, 248–280
  Internet protocol (IP), 157, 282–315
  Transport Layer Security (TLS), 158,
      197–201
  transport-level, 180–213

Internet Security Association and Key Management Protocol (ISAKMP), 305
Internet standards, 37
  Internet Architecture Board (IAB), 37
  Internet Engineering Task Force (IETF), 37
  RFCs, 37
Interrealm authentication, 127
Intrusion management, 177
ITU-T Recommendation X.800. *See* X.800 standard recommendations

K

Kerberos, 116–129
  authentication dialogues, 117–123, 127–129
  authentication forwarding, 126
  authentication server (AS), 117
  authentication service exchange, 128
  client/server authentication exchange, 129
  differences between versions 4 and 5, 126–127
  double encryption, 127
  encryption system dependence, 126
  environmental shortcomings, 126–27
  Internet protocol dependence, 126
  interrealm authentication, 127
  introduction to, 116
  message byte ordering, 126
  nonce, 128
  options, 128
  password attacks, 127
  principal, 125
  propagating cipher block chaining (PCBC) encryption, 127
  realms, 123–126, 128
  session keys, 127
  technical deficiencies of, 127
  ticket-granting server (TGS), 118–119
  ticket-granting service exchange, 128–129
  ticket lifetime, 126
  times, 128
  version 4, 116–126
  version 5, 126–129
Key distribution, 117–118, 132–134, 236, 240–242. *See also* Exchanges; Private keys; Public keys
  center (KDC), 115
  certificate authority (CA), 130
  hierarchy, 239
  IEEE 802.11i management phase, 234, 238–242
  permanent key, 115
  pretty good privacy (PGP), 249–255
  private key, 250–251
  public-key certificates, 129–130
  public-key distribution of secret keys, 130–131
  session key, 115
  wireless network security, 238–242

Keyed hash function. *See* Message authentication codes (MAC)
Key exchange, 100–104, 192–193, 207, 305–313
  certificate messages for, 193–194
  client authentication and, 194–195
  Diffie-Hellman, 100–104, 192
  Fortezza, 192–193
  Internet (IKE) key determination protocol, 306–313
  Internet, 305–313
  protocols, 103
  RSA, 192
  server authentication and, 193–194
  SSH Transport Layer Protocol, 204–205
  SSL Handshake Protocol, 192–193
Key generation, 197, 207–208, 270
  AP, 234
  S/MIME, 270
Keylogger, 336
Keylogging, 335
Key management. *See* Key distribution
Key pair recovery, PKI, 141
Key pair update, PKI, 141
Keystream, defined, 59

L

Link encryption, 115
Logical link control (LLC) layer, IEEE 800, 227
Logic bomb, 334

M

MAC protocol data unit (MPDU), IEEE 800, 226–227, 229, 235–236, 237
Macro viruses, 325, 326
MAC service data unit (MSDU), IEEE 800, 226–227, 229
Malicious association, 218
Malicious insiders, 170
Malicious software or malware, 318
  attack kits, 320
    crimeware, 320
  attack sources, 320–321
  classification of, 319–320
    blended attack, 320
  recommended reading, 350
  terminology, 319
  types, 318–321
Malware countermeasure approaches
  detection, 339
  generality, 339
  global and local coverage, 340
  identification, 339
  minimal denial-of-service costs, 339
  removal, 339
  resiliency, 339
  timeliness, 339
  transparency, 339, 340

Man-in-the-middle attack, 103–104, 219
Manipulating online polls/games, 335
Master secret creation, 196
Master session key (MSK), IEEE 802.11i, 238
Masquerade, 29
Measured service, 165
Media access control (MAC) layer, IEEE 800, 226–227
Media gateway, 155
Memory sticks, 221
Message authentication, 75–106
  approaches to, 77–81
  code (MAC), 78–79, 91–93
  digital signatures, 105
  encryption, and, 77–78
  hash functions, 79–81, 81–88
  introduction to, 77
  key distribution, 129–131
  one-way hash functions, 79–81
  public-key cryptography, 94–105
  recommended reading and Web sites, 106
  secure hash functions, 81–88
  SSL, 185–188
  technique, 91–93
  TLS, 197
Messages, 28, 29, 32, 41–69, 77–81, 128, 269–270, 311–312. *See also* Encryption; Public-key cryptography
  attacks on, types of, 45
  authentication, 75–106
  byte ordering, 126
  confidentiality of, 41–69
  modification of, 32
  pretty good privacy (PGP), 249–256
  release of contents, 27, 28
  Secure/Multipurpose Internet Mail Extension (S/MIME), 266–270
  SSH exchange, 208–209
Metamorphic virus, 325
Mix columns, AES, 53
Mobile code, 331
Mobile device security, 220–224
  cloud-based applications, 221
  de-perimeterization, 221
  elements, 223
  external business requirements, 221
  growing use of new devices, 220
  strategy, 222–224
    barrier security, 224
    device security, 223–224
    traffic security, 224
    VPNs, 224
  threats, 221–222
    applications by unknown parties, 222
    interaction with systems, 222
    location services, 222
    physical security controls, 221–222
    untrusted mobile devices, 222
    untrusted networks, 222
Mobility, 218
Model for network security, 34–36
Modification of messages, 29, 32
Morris worm, 329–330
Multipartite virus, 325
Multipurpose Internet Mail Extensions (MIME), 258–264
  canonical form, 264
  content types, 259–262
  transfer encodings, 262–264
Mutation engine, 325

N

National Institute of Standards and Technology (NIST), 37, 49, 85, 104
Network access control (NAC)
  access requestor (AR), 154
    supplicants, 154
  context, 155
  enforcement methods
    DHCP management, 157
    firewall, 157
    IEEE 802.1X, 156
    VLANs, 156
  NAS, 155
    media gateway, 155
    policy server, 155
    RAS, 155
  policy server, 155
  recommended reading, 178
Network access server (NAS), 155
Network injection, 219
Network security, 19–39, 113–148, 178, 216–245
  applications, 130
  authentication, 113–148
  computer security, 20
  defined, 20
  HTTPS, 181, 201–202
  information security, 20
  International Telecommunication Union (ITU), 26
  Internet and Web resources, 38–39
  Internet Engineering Task Force (IETF), 37
  internet security, 21
  Internet standards, 37
  introduction to, 19–39
  mechanisms, 25–26, 33–34
  model for, 34–36
  open systems interconnection (OSI) architecture, 26–27
  outline for study of, 37
  recommended reading, 38
  Secure Sockets Layer (SSL), 183–196
  Secure Shell (SSH), 202–213

services, 27, 31–34
threats, 40, 159
transport-level, 180–213
violations of, 21
wireless, 216–245
X.800 standard recommendations, 26, 29–30, 33–34
Nonce, 92, 308, 312
Kerberos, 128
Nonrepudiation, 30, 32
Nonsecret encryption. *See* Public-key cryptography
Nontraditional networks, 218

O

Oakley Key Determination Protocol, 305
On-demand self-service, 165
One-way function, 79–81
authentication, 79–81
hash functions, 79–81
Open systems interconnection (OSI), 26–27
Options, Kerberos, 128

P

Packet exchange, SSH, 204–207
Packets, IPsec, 292–294
Padding, 201, 294
Pairwise master key (PMK), IEEE 802.11i, 238–239
Pairwise transient key (PTK), IEEE 802.11i, 238–239
Passive attacks, security, 27–29
Password attacks, Kerberos, 127
Payload(s), 318
attack agent
remote control facility, 335
uses of bots, *see* Bots, uses of
Zombie, 334–335
classification-based worm containment, 344
information theft
credential theft, 336, 337
identity theft, 337
keylogger, 336
phishing and identity theft, 337
reconnaissance and espionage, 337
spyware, 336
stealthing
backdoor (trapdoor), 337
rootkit, 338
system corruption, 333–334
logic bomb, 334
ransomware, 333
real-world damage, 333–334
Stuxnet worm, 334
Peer entity authentication, 31
Peer-to-peer networks, 218
Perimeter scanning approaches, 342–343
Permanent key, defined, 115
Personal network Bluetooth devices, 218

Phishing and identity theft
phishing attack, 337
spear-phishing attack, 337
Physical layer, IEEE 800, 226
Physical security controls, lack of, 221–222
Plaintext, 44, 45–46, 94
chosen, attack, 46
defined, 44
known, attack, 45–46
processing, cryptography, 44
public-key encryption, 93
Platform as a service (PaaS), 166
Policy server, 155
Polymorphic virus, 325
Port forwarding, SSH, 211–213
Pre-shared key (PSK), IEEE 802.11i, 238
Pretty good privacy (PGP), 249–256
authentication, 251–253
compression, 254–255
confidentiality, 253–254
e-mail compatibility, 255
key distribution, 249–255
notation for, 250–251
Private cloud, 166
Private keys, 138, 250–251
pretty good privacy (PGP), 250–251
public-key cryptography and, 96–97
ring, 250–251
usage, X.509 authentication service, 138
Propagating cipher block chaining (PCBC)
encryption, 127
Protected data transfer phase, IEEE 802.11i, 234, 242–243
Protocol, 105. *See also* Internet Protocol (IP)
Diffie-Hellman, 100–101
key exchange, 100–101
PKIX management, 140–141
Pseudorandom function (PRF), 58, 197–199, 243–244
IEEE 802.11i, 243–244
IKEv2, 314, 315
TLS, 197–199
Propagation
infected content
macro viruses, 326
nature of viruses, 321–324
scripting viruses, 326
viruses classification, 324–325
social engineering, 332–333
spam (unsolicited bulk) e-mail, 332
Trojan horses, 332–333
vulnerability exploit, 327–331
client-side vulnerabilities, 331
drive-by-download**s**, 331
electronic mail or instant messenger
facility, 327
file sharing, 327

Propagation (*Continued*)
    mobile code, 331
    Morris worm, 329–330
    remote execution capability, 327
    remote file access or transfer
      capability, 327
    remote login capability, 327
    state of worm technology, 330
    target discovery, 327–328
    worm propagation model, 328–329
Public-key cryptography, 94–105
  algorithms, 94–105
  applications for, 96–97
  ciphertext, 94
  cryptography, 94–105
  decryption algorithm, 95
  Diffie-Hellman key exchange, 100–103
  Digital Signature Standard (DSS), 104
  elliptic curve (ECC), 104–105
  encryption algorithm, 101–103
  encryption structure, 94–96
  plaintext, 94
  private keys, 94, 96
  public keys, 94, 96
  requirements for, 96
  RSA public-key encryption, 98–100
  secret keys, 96
Public-key encryption, 94–105
  algorithm, 43
  digital signatures, 104
  structure, 94–105
Public-key infrastructure (PKI), 139–141
  certification authority (CA), 139
  CRL issuer, 140
  end entity, 139
  key pairs, 141
  PKIX management functions, 140–141
  PKIX management protocols, 141
  PKIX model, 139–141
  registration authority (RA), 140
  repository, 140
Public keys, 96–97, 132, 138
  authority key identifier, 138
  certificates, 129–130, 138
  cryptography, 94, 96
  defined, 96
  distribution, 129–130
  revoking, 139
  secret keys, distribution of using, 130–131
  subject key identifier, 138
  usage, X.509 authentication service, 138
Public cloud, 166

Q

Quick Response (QR) code, 222
Quoted-printable transfer encoding, 262

R

Radix-64 conversion, 255
Rapid elasticity, 165
Ransomware, 333
Rate halting, 344
Rate limiting, 344
RC4 algorithm, 61–64, 62
  generation, 62
  initialization of S, 61–62
  logic, 62
  strength of, 62–64
Realm, 116–129
  concept of, 123
  Kerberos version 4, 116–126
  Kerberos version 5, 126–129
Real-world damage, 333–334
Reconnaissance and espionage, 337
  credential theft, 337
  identity theft, 337
Record Protocol, 184, 185–189
Registration, PKI, 140
Registration authority (RA), PKI, 140
Release of message contents, 27, 28
Remote access server (RAS), 155
Remote Authentication Dial-In User Service
    (RADIUS), 159
Remote control facility, 335
Remote execution capability, 327
Remote file access or transfer capability, 327
Remote login capability, 327
Replay, 29
Replay attacks, 118
Repository, PKI, 142
Resource pooling, 165–166
Resources, 218
Request for Comment (RFC) standards, 27,
    257–258, 275–276
  RFC 4686, e-mail threats, 275–276
  RFC 5322, S/MIME, 257–258
  security recommendations, 26
Reverse certificate, 135
Revocation, 136–137, 141
  certificates, X.509 authentication service, 136–137
  request, PKI, 141
RFC. *See* Request for Comment (RFC) standards
Rivest-Shamir-Adleman (RSA) algorithm, 192, 196
  key exchange, 192, 196
  SSL Handshake Protocol, 185, 190
Rootkit, 338
  countermeasures, 342
  external mode, 338
  kernel mode, 338
  memory based, 338
  persistent, 338
  user mode, 338
  virtual machine based, 338

Round, 46, 48, 54
  Add Round Key, 54
  AES encryption, 54
  function, Feistel cipher, 46, 48
Routing, IPsec, 286
RSA, 98–100
  public-key encryption, 98–100
RSA algorithm. *See* Rivest-Shamir-Adleman
    (RSA) algorithm

S

Scripting viruses, 326
Second-generation scanner, 340
Secret keys, 43, 96, 130–131
  encryption using, 43
  key management, 130–131
  public-key cryptography, 96, 130–131
  public-key distribution of, 130–131
Secure Hash Algorithm (SHA), 84
Secure hash functions. *See* Hash functions
Secure/Multipurpose Internet Mail Extension
    (S/MIME), 265–266
  certificate processing, 270–272
  clear signing, 269–270
  cryptographic algorithms, 265–266
  functionality, 264–266
  messages, 266–270
  Multipurpose Internet Mail Extensions (MIME),
    258–264
Secure Shell (SSH), 202–213
  channels, 210
  Connection Protocol, 203, 209–213
  host keys, 203–204
  key exchange and generation, 207
  message exchange, 208–209
  packet exchange, 204–207
  port forwarding, 211–213
  Transport Layer Protocol, 203–208
  User Authentication Protocol, 203, 208–209
Secure Sockets Layer (SSL), 183–196
  Alert Protocol, 184, 188–189
  architecture, 184–185
  Change Cipher Spec Protocol, 184, 188
  cryptographic computations, 195–196
  Handshake Protocol, 185, 190–195
  Hypertext Transfer Protocol (HTTP), 184
  master secret, 185
  message authentication code (MAC), 185–186
  Record Protocol, 184, 185–188
  session, 185
Securing wireless transmissions, 219–220
Security as a service (SecaaS), 175
Security assessments, 177
Security association (SA), IP, 289–290, 301–305
Security association database (SAD), 289–290
Security attacks, 27–29

active, 29
defined, 27
denial of service, 29
masquerade, 29
modification of messages, 29, 32
passive, 27–29
release of message contents, 27–28
replay, 29
traffic analysis, 28
Security information and event management
    (SIEM), 177
Security mechanisms, 25–26, 33–34
  services and, relationship of, 34
  X.800 recommendations, 33
Security policy database (SPD), 289, 290–292
Security services, 25, 29–32
  access control, 31
  authentication, 31
  availability, 32
  data confidentiality, 31
  data integrity, 30, 32
  defined, 27, 32
  nonrepudiation, 32
Sequence number, 129
  Kerberos, 129
Service models, 166
Service request, SSH, 205
Service set identifier (SSID) broadcasting, 219
Service threats, defined, 36
Session keys, 56, 115, 127
  defined, 56, 115
  Kerberos, 127
Session, SSL, 184
Shared technology issues, 171
Shift rows, AES, 53
Signal-hiding techniques, 219
Signature-based worm scan filtering, 343
SignedData, S/MIME, 268–269
Smartphones, 221
Sniffing traffic, 334
Software as a service (SaaS), 166
Spamming, 334
Spam (unsolicited bulk) e-mail, 332
Spear-phishing attack, 337
Spyware, 336
  detection and removal, 342
State array, AES, 52
Stealth virus, 325
Stream ciphers, 59–64
  defined, 44
  design considerations, 60
  keystream, 59
  plaintext processing, cryptography, 44
  RC4 algorithm, 61–64
  structure of, 59–61
Stuxnet worm, 334

Subject field, 137, 139
Subkey, Kerberos, 129
Substitution bytes, AES, 53
Symmetric encryption, 43–48
  block cipher, design of, 48
  block size, 48
  ciphertext, 43
  computationally secure, 46
  cryptanalysis, 44–46
  cryptography, 44
  decryption algorithm, 43
  encryption algorithm, 43
  Feistel cipher structure, 46–48
  key size, 48
  plaintext, 43, 45–46
  principles of, 43–48
  requirements of, 43–44
  round function, 47, 48
  rounds, number of, 47
  secret key, 43
  subkey generation algorithm, 48

T

Tablets, 221
Target discovery, 327
  hit list, 328
  local subnet, 328
  random, 328
  scanning or fingerprinting, 328
  topological, 328
Threats, 28–30, 37, 118–120, 278–280. *See also* Attacks
  active attacks, 29
  denial-of-service (DoS) attack, 32
  masquerade, 29
  modification of information, 29
  network security, 116
  passive attack, 27–29
  release of contents, 27
  replay, 29
  service, 36
  traffic analysis, 28
Threshold random walk (TRW) scan detection, 344
Third-generation scanner, 341
Ticket-granting server (TGS), 118
Ticket-granting service exchange, 128–129
Ticket lifetime, 126
Times, Kerberos, 128
Timestamp authentication, 119, 128–129
Traffic analysis, 28
Traffic flow confidentiality (TFC), 295
Traffic processing, IP, 292–294
Traffic security, 224
Transport Layer Protocol, SSH, 203–206
Transport Layer Security (TLS), 61, 88, 158, 183,
    197–201

alert codes, 199
certificate types (client), 200
cipher suites, 200
cryptographic computations, 200–201
message authentication code (MAC), 197
padding, 201
pseudorandom function (PRF), 197–199
Transport-level security, 180–213
  HTTPS, 181, 201–202
  Secure Shell (SSH), 181, 202–213
  Secure Socket Layer (SSL), 181, 183–196
  Transport Layer Security (TLS), 181, 183, 197–201
  Web considerations, 181–183
Transport mode, IP, 287, 297–300
Triple Data Encryption Standard (3DES),
    50–51
Trojan horses, 332–333
Tunnel, SSH, 209, 212–213
Tunnel mode, IP, 287–288, 300

U

User Authentication Protocol, SSH, 203,
    208–209
Unknown risk profile, 171

V

VeriSign certificates, S/MIME, 271–272
Version number, TLS, 197
Virtual local area networks (VLANs), 156
Virtual private networks (VPNs), 224
Viruses
  concealment strategy, 325
    encrypted virus, 325
    metamorphic virus, 325
    mutation engine, 325
    polymorphic virus, 325
    stealth virus, 325
  nature of
    dormant phase, 322
    execution phase, 322
    infection mechanism, 322
    payload, 322
    propagation phase, 322
    triggering phase, 322
    trigger, logic bomb, 322
  structure, 322–324
    compression virus, 323, 324
    simple virus, 323
    traditional machine-executable
      virus code, 322
  target, classification by, 325
    boot sector infector, 325
    file infector, 325
    macro virus, 325
    multipartite virus, 325

W

Web security, 177–178, 181–183. *See also* Internet
    security
Web sites, 39, 69, 181, 182, 420
Wi-Fi hotspots, 218
Wi-Fi Protected Access (WPA), 225, 231
Wireless Ethernet Compatibility Alliance
    (WECA), 225
Wireless networking components, 218
Wireless network security, 216–245
  IEEE 802.11 LAN, 224–229
  IEEE 802.11i LAN, 230–244
  wireless security, 217–220
  Robust Security Network (RSN), 231
  recommended reading, 244–245
  Wi-Fi Protected Access (WPA), 231
  Wired Equivalent Privacy (WEP), 231
Wireless network threats, 218–219
  accidental association, 218
  ad hoc networks, 218
  denial of service (DoS), 219
  identity theft (MAC spoofing), 219
  malicious association, 218
  man-in-the middle attacks, 219
  network injection, 219
  nontraditional networks, 218
Wireless security, 217–220
  accessibility, 218
  access points, 220
  channel, 217
  measures, 219–220
  mobility, 218
  networks, 218, 220
  resources, 218
  threats, network, 218–219
  transmissions, 219–220
    encryption, 219
    signal-hiding techniques, 219
Worm propagation model, 328–329
Worm technology, state of
  metamorphic, 330
  multiexploit, 330
  multiplatform, 330
  polymorphic, 330
  transport vehicles, 330
  ultrafast spreading, 330
  zero-day exploit, 331

X

X.509 certificate, 131–139
  certificate revocation list (CRL), 137
  certificates, 132–134
  certification authority (CA), 139
  forward certificate, 135
  introduction to, 131
  issuer attributes, 138–139
  key information, 138
  path constraints, 139
  policy information, 138
  reverse certificate, 135
  revocation of certificates, 136–137
  subject attributes, 138–139
  user's certificate, obtaining, 134–136
  version 3, 137–138
X.800 standard recommendations, 26, 27, 29,
    31–32, 33–34

THE WILLIAM STALLINGS BOOKS ON COMPUTER

DATA AND COMPUTER COMMUNICATIONS, NINTH EDITION

A comprehensive survey that has become the standard in the field, covering (1) data communications, including transmission, media, signal encoding, link control, and multiplexing; (2) communication networks, including circuit- and packet-switching, frame relay, ATM, and LANs; (3) the TCP/IP protocol suite, including IPv6, TCP, MIME, and HTTP; as well as a detailed treatment of network security. **Received the 2007 Text and Academic Authors Association (TAA) award for the best Computer Science and Engineering Textbook of the year.** ISBN 978-0-13-139205-2

OPERATING SYSTEMS, SEVENTH EDITION

A state-of-the art survey of operating system principles. Covers fundamental technology as well as contemporary design issues, such as threads, microkernels, SMPs, real-time systems, multiprocessor scheduling, embedded OSs, distributed systems, clusters, security, and object-oriented design. **Third, fourth, and sixth editions received the TAA award for the best Computer Science and Engineering Textbook of the year.** ISBN 978-0-13-230998-1

BUSINESS DATA COMMUNICATIONS, SEVENTH EDITION
(with Tom Case)

A comprehensive presentation of data communications and telecommunications from a business perspective. Covers voice, data, image, and video communications and applications technology and includes a number of case studies. Topics covered include data communications, TCP/IP, cloud computing, Internet protocols and applications, LANs and WANs, network security, and network management. ISBN 978-0133023893

CRYPTOGRAPHY AND NETWORK SECURITY, SIXTH EDITION

A tutorial and survey on network security technology. Each of the basic building blocks of network security, including conventional and public-key cryptography, authentication, and digital signatures, are covered. Thorough mathematical background for such algorithms as AES and RSA. The book covers important network security tools and applications, including S/MIME, IP Security, Kerberos, SSL/TLS, SET, and X509v3. In addition, methods for countering hackers and viruses are explored. **Second edition received the TAA award for the best Computer Science and Engineering Textbook of 1999.**

COMPUTER SECURITY, SECOND EDITION (with Lawrie Brown)
A comprehensive treatment of computer security technology, including algorithms, protocols, and applications. Covers cryptography, authentication, access control, database security, intrusion detection and prevention, malicious software, denial of service, firewalls, software security, physical security, human factors, auditing, legal and ethical aspects, and trusted systems. **Received the 2008 Text and Academic Authors Association (TAA) award for the best Computer Science and Engineering Textbook of the year.** ISBN 978-0-13-277506-9

COMPUTER ORGANIZATION AND ARCHITECTURE,
NINTH EDITION
A unified view of this broad field. Covers fundamentals such as CPU, control unit, microprogramming, instruction set, I/O, and memory. Also covers advanced topics such as multicore, superscalar, and parallel organization. **Four-time winner of the TAA award for the best Computer Science and Engineering Textbook of the year.** ISBN 978-0-13-293633-0

WIRELESS COMMUNICATIONS AND NETWORKS,
SECOND EDITION
A comprehensive, state-of-the art survey. Covers fundamental wireless communications topics, including antennas and propagation, signal encoding techniques, spread spectrum, and error correction techniques. Examines satellite, cellular, wireless local loop networks and wireless LANs, including Bluetooth and 802.11. Covers Mobile IP and WAP. ISBN 0-13-191835-4

COMPUTER NETWORKS WITH INTERNET PROTOCOLS
AND TECHNOLOGY
An up-to-date survey of developments in the area of Internet-based protocols and algorithms. Using a top-down approach, this book covers applications, transport layer, Internet QoS, Internet routing, data link layer and computer networks, security, and network management. ISBN 0-13141098-9

HIGH-SPEED NETWORKS AND INTERNETS, SECOND EDITION
A state-of-the art survey of high-speed networks. Topics covered include TCP congestion control, ATM traffic management, Internet traffic management, differentiated and integrated services, Internet routing protocols and multicast routing protocols, resource reservation and RSVP, and lossless and lossy compression. Examines important topic of self-similar data traffic. ISBN 0-13-03221-0